NO WRONG TURNS

CHRIS POUNTNEY

ISBN-13: 978-1539023302
ISBN-10: 1539023303

Cover Design: © Chris Pountney
Interior Maps: © Chris Pountney

For more from the author, please visit:
www.differentpartsofeverywhere.com

To see photographs that accompany this book, please visit:
www.differentpartsofeverywhere.com/book/photos
or
www.flickr.com/photos/no-wrong-turns/albums

DEDICATION

This book is for my very special unicorn.

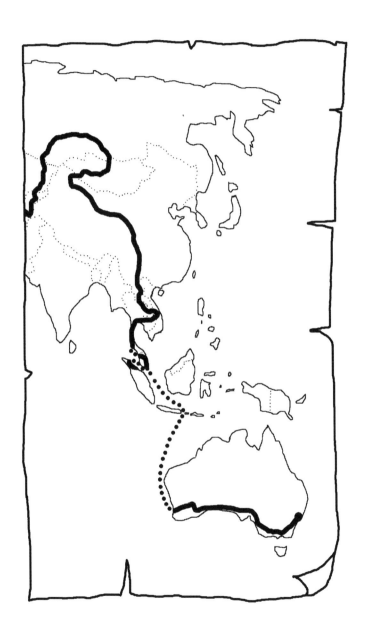

THERE ARE
NO WRONG TURNS
JUST
DIFFERENT PARTS
OF EVERYWHERE

This book is a true story.

A few names have been changed, because I couldn't
remember them, but it all really happened, honest.

Even the bit about the kangaroo.

Due to printing costs, this book is
sadly lacking in photographs.

If you would like to view the photographic
evidence that supports this book, please go to:

www.flickr.com/photos/no-wrong-turns/albums

I know that's quite a lot to type, but it's for
your viewing pleasure.

Now, on with the story...

PROLOGUE

There are times riding a bicycle when everything just feels right. The wind is at your back, the skies are clear, and the road is smooth and flat and disappearing easily beneath your wheels. In such moments the act of turning the pedals evolves into such a natural, rhythmical movement that it becomes practically effortless. You feel wonderful. You feel alive. You feel like the whole world is with you, as you glide along, smiling and waving at everyone. It is the very best of feelings. In those moments you truly understand what it means to be free.

Then, more often than not, you get a fly in your eye.

That's the problem with these moments of cycling nirvana. They don't happen very often, and they tend to be short lived. So I'm going to be starting my story with an altogether different scenario. A much more common kind of biking experience, actually. One when I was sweating and struggling and cursing my way up a steep hill under an inescapably hot sun.

And I'm afraid I've started my story with a lie, because I've just used the word 'inescapably' quite falsely. There were actually many locals who were doing a grand job of escaping the hot sun, lounging in the shade of their simple homes and keeping cool beneath corrugated roofs. Overweight men lay in hammocks, glancing casually at the crazy foreigner as I strained at the pedals to inch myself forward at an embarrassing wobble. Shadows of hard working women moved around inside these wood slat homes, and children peeked out from empty window frames, giggling and daring one another to be the first to shout "Gringo!"

My progress was reduced to a pitiful crawl as I fought against not only the gradient and the soaring temperatures but also a cruel headwind that bristled through nearby palm leaves. Sadly this wind did nothing to cool me down. It was no match for the sun, and merely slowed me further while giving me the unfortunate impression that I was cycling on into a fan-assisted oven.

I noticed a malnourished dog padding along the road, one of thousands of strays eking out a meagre existence feeding on whatever scraps they could find in this part of the world. Earning my misplaced envy, even this poor, diseased animal, with its rib cage pressing through its taut skin, was able to progress up the hill at greater speed than me. I watched the determined mutt as it disappeared up ahead, gaining ground on my companion, Karin. As my eyes looked up I was surprised to see that she had pulled off the road and was examining her own bike. It looked like she had a problem with it.

"I've got a flat tyre," she informed me, as I finally clawed my way up towards her.

"Good," I replied, collapsing into the shade of a café that by some small miracle happened to be right next to us. I'm not always a selfish man, but in my present condition I was extremely grateful for this excuse to get off the bike and have a rest, while she set to work fixing the problem.

After a little while I noticed another touring cyclist appear in the distance, and I sat and watched him as he made impressively steady progress up the hill. Within minutes he had arrived at the café and, perhaps seeing the damsel in distress with no sign of any gentleman offering her assistance, he rode over towards us.

He was a slightly red-faced and greying man of about forty, who laid down his bike and came to us, sweaty and out of breath. Proving my damsel in distress theory wrong immediately, he stepped straight past Karin into the café, sat down on one of the plastic chairs, and ordered a coke in perfect Spanish. I assumed it was perfect Spanish anyway, I don't know, I can't speak Spanish. Then he introduced himself to me, in his native English accent, as John. As befits any two cycle tourists meeting under such circumstances far from home, we then got down to the serious business of exchanging our travel stories.

I soon realised that mine were not going to compare with John's, as he proudly boasted of having been travelling for twenty-five years through more than a hundred countries. Not all by bicycle, mind you. He'd been a backpacker, and spent plenty of that time working as a language teacher in various parts of the world. Only recently had he discovered bicycle touring and begun to embrace the fun one could have cycling up steep hills in tropical furnaces.

I myself had caught the bug a couple of years earlier, when I'd seen a documentary about a Scottish guy named Mark Beaumont setting the world record for cycling around the world in the fastest time. Watching him jabbering to the video camera he held in his outstretched arm as he dashed around the planet in six months was probably the first moment when I realised that it was even possible to travel on a bicycle, though I'd always dreamed about travelling the world. As a young boy I used to sit for hours looking at the family atlas, tracing pretend lines across continents and allowing my imagination to run wild thinking about what it would be like to actually travel those finger strokes. As I grew up, graduated university, and entered into the difficult life phase of 'not knowing what the hell to do next', my ambition to make a big around-the-world journey was as strong as ever. Sadly the problem remained, exactly as it had when I'd been a child, that I had no money. So far as I could tell travel was prohibitively expensive. Then came the revelation that it was possible to travel by bicycle. After a little more research I began to find out that there were plenty of people out there who had made, or were making, long journeys on two wheels. I read about the exploits of people like Alastair Humphreys, who'd spent four years cycling around the world, and Heinz Stücke, who'd spent a whole lifetime. Suitably inspired, I decided to get involved and set off on a couple of six-week tours myself. I had a crap bike, no idea what I was doing, and spent far too much time walking because I could not fix punctures. Nevertheless, after these short trips I was hooked. I'd discovered that bicycle touring was not only the cheap mode of travel I'd always been looking for, but also a fantastic way to see places. I realised with some delight that it might be possible to fulfil my lifelong ambition, and see the whole world this way.

So in May 2010, with David Cameron just settling into 10 Downing Street, I decided it was the ideal time to get out of England for a while. I bought a Surly Long Haul Trucker, a proper touring bike that would certainly go on to live up to its name. I cycled it to Denmark, took a ferry to Iceland, cycled around some volcanoes, and then flew to the east coast of Canada. From there I'd intended to ride south to meet my German friend, Karin, in Central America, as we had made plans to cycle there together. Instead I made myself rather at home in Toronto and settled in for a Canadian winter. I'd met an attractive girl, Rachael, who distracted me because 1) she was an attractive girl and 2) I am easily distracted. After three months of being (admittedly quite happily) distracted by Rachael in Canada I awoke with a start one morning, looked at the snow piling up on the window frame, and cried out, "Oh bloody hell. I'm supposed to be meeting my friend in Central America." There was no longer enough time to cycle there, so I hopped on a plane and flew instead, arriving in Mexico just in time to meet with Karin and begin our cycle south together as planned.

John listened intently to my explanation as to how I had arrived here at this little café in the middle of Nicaragua. His coke bottle now sat empty on the table, and as I finished my story he turned to the bored waitress and ordered a Fanta.

"Gracias señorita," he said as it was delivered to him. Like I said, his Spanish was exceptional. Then his attention returned to me.

"The thing is," he said, "in my opinion if you're going to cycle around the world you should do it properly. Cycle the whole way. Not use any other transport."

This came across as a bit of a dig at me for having flown from Canada to Mexico instead of cycling. I felt like I needed to defend myself.

"She was very attractive, John. I was legitimately distracted."

"Fair enough," he laughed, "but you still can't say you cycled around the world, I think, if you miss bits out. If you take a bus, a train, a plane, whatever, then you haven't cycled the whole way have you? To do it properly you should cycle it all. And you should take boats across the water."

"Yeah, but everybody uses other transport sometimes."

And it was true. Ever since I had started researching the idea of bicycle touring I had read dozens of books and blogs of people who had 'cycled around the world' in some form or another. They had all resorted to using cars, buses or trains on occasions, or flown across the oceans. The idea of going *all* of the way around the world using *only* a bicycle and boats was crazy. It was simply too difficult, not only because of geographical obstacles like oceans and deserts, but also due to bureaucratic ones, like visa restrictions and war zones.

"Well, I think unless you do it all by bike and boat, then you haven't really cycled around the world," John repeated.

"But nobody has ever done that!"

Several hours later, as I was following Karin up yet another Nicaraguan hill, the conversation with John replayed in my head, as it would many more times in the weeks and months ahead.

'Silly man,' I thought. *Why should he think you have to travel entirely by bicycle and boats to qualify as having cycled around the world, when nobody has ever done that?'*

And then I thought about it a little more.

'Nobody has ever done that.'

I'd had an idea.

The Challenges

1. Circumnavigate the planet

Just to clarify, I mean Earth.

2. Do so using only my bicycle and boats

No planes, no buses, no trucks, no trains, and definitely no cars!

3. Pass through antipodal points

To ensure a true around-the-world journey.

4. Visit all of the inhabited continents

Not to rule out the uninhabited one, either.

5. Cycle at least 100,000 kilometres

Otherwise known as 62,137 and a bit miles.

6. Cycle in 100 countries

Might need a bigger passport.

7. Return with more money than I start with

Just to prove it's possible.

PART ONE

PARIS TO ISTANBUL

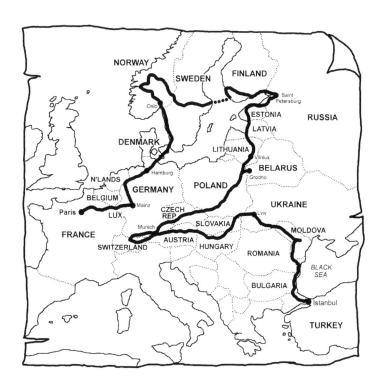

1

Paris, France
14th July 2013

It seemed as if France had got wind of my plans to start my
'around the world using only my bicycle and boats' journey from
the Eiffel Tower, because the night before my departure they
very generously put on a massive fireworks display to celebrate. I felt
truly honoured, especially as a crowd of 100,000 people had also
turned up for what I liked to think of as my leaving party. As the
pyrotechnic display lit up the sky in a dazzling array of colour behind
the iconic monument, I chose to ignore those naysayers around me
muttering things about it being Bastille Day and instead thought
about everything that I had ahead of me. Accompanying the fireworks was a playlist of music that seemed entirely appropriate to me
(and perhaps also, slightly, to the anniversary of the French Revolu-
tion) as most of the songs were concerned with the subject of freedom. As I stood there listening I felt absolutely free. I'd saved up
some money, enough for two years of travelling, and I was about to
set off around the world on my bike. Watching those fireworks I was
almost overwhelmed with the anticipation of all that was to come.

The next morning I was back at the Eiffel Tower to actually begin
the journey. I looked up at the wrought iron framework, the morning
sun glistening off it, and I was quite mesmerised. I'd chosen to start
from this great landmark as I had always seen it as such an iconic symbol of travel and adventure. When I was young it had seemed some-

where so very far away and exotic. Sitting in my bedroom looking at pictures of it I had hoped that one day I would be lucky enough to visit. Now I stood before it with my loaded bicycle and hoped that I would be lucky enough to make it back. My plan, in its simplest form, was to head east across Europe and Asia, then find a boat to Australia where I could stop and work. This was, coincidentally, also my plan in its most complex form. I was at the Eiffel Tower, and my goal was to ride my bicycle to the Sydney Opera House, it was as simple as that. Australia was only halfway around the world, of course, and I'd not yet given too much thought as to how I was going to get back home again, but I had two years to mull it over, and I was confident something would come to me.

I had written down a list of seven challenges, the idea being that these, while not being rules set in stone, would at least provide some structure to my journey. The first of these, the most important, was to:

1. Circumnavigate the planet.

Which was a fair old challenge in itself, although I decided to make it considerably more ambitious by adding:

2. Do so using only my bicycle (or perhaps bicycles) overland, and boats on water.

That's right. I'd decided that if I was going to do this, I may as well do it properly. There would be no skipping sections on a bus or a train, no lifts in cars or trucks, no flying between continents. I was going to have to be extremely disciplined to make this happen, by which I mean a lot less easily distracted by members of the opposite sex. In fact, after that thought-provoking meeting with John in Nicaragua two years earlier, Karin and I had cycled together only as far as Costa Rica, where we said goodbye and I had given in to the temptation of the aeroplane and flown back to Canada to see Rachael again. The flames of our earlier romance could not be rekindled, however, and I got back on my bike. But I was not able to get beyond North America before I returned home, both broke and brokenhearted. Looking back at the map of my route I saw a disjointed mess of bits of cycling interrupted by flights, with the whole thing spanning a mere two continents. This was not the continuous global journey I had dreamed of. Disappointed by this relative failure, here I was ready to start again, and with a determination to do things properly this time. The challenges were therefore of great importance, for they provided me with a framework that I hoped would ensure I stuck to the task.

Around midday on Monday the 15th of July 2013 I began cycling from beneath the Eiffel Tower. My now well-used bike was loaded down with the weight of four bright-yellow pannier bags, plus two extra backpacks that were strapped onto the top of the rear rack. I carried with me everything that I needed, with one rear pannier devoted to clothes, another to food. All of my camping gear (tent, sleeping bag, and roll mat) was in the backpacks on top. In one front bag I carried a couple of books and the things that I might need during the day, like a map and my camera. The other held a wide variety of tools and spare parts, as I knew that if I was going to make it all the way without ever taking a lift in a motor vehicle I was going to have to be as self-sufficient as possible. If I wasn't able to fix things myself at the side of the road then I was surely going to be in for some very long walks. With this in mind I even had a spare tyre slung over the top of everything, and altogether it made for quite a load.

Navigating the frenetic Parisian traffic on this heavy bike was my first problem, and I was almost taken out by one car that turned suddenly across my path. Having vowed not to use motor vehicles for an entire global circumnavigation, I would certainly have considered being carted off in the back of an ambulance after two kilometres to have been a major anticlimax. Fortunately I survived unscathed and found a bike path beside a canal that carried me safely out into the French countryside. I then spent the afternoon beneath a big blue sky, riding safely on quiet back roads through rolling hills of green and yellow crops, where the only sounds were pigeons cooing and bees buzzing. I felt so alive, and I took a big, satisfied inhalation of fresh country air to appreciate where I was. The overpowering smell of manure made me slightly regret that, but even so it could do little to dent the joy I felt now that my big trip was under way. It was a really special sort of happiness, something bordering on euphoria. It was a feeling brought on by the anticipation of what was to come, as I set forth on this journey that was sure to change my life forever. And it was all ahead. The deserts that needed to be crossed, the mountain ranges that would have to be conquered, the oceans to be sailed, the people to be met, the problems to be overcome. It was all out there. Everything was ahead of me. At no future point would I be able to say that. From here on, the anticipation would turn to experiences that all too soon would fade to memories. The way I felt now, at the very start of my adventure, was something to treasure, something that I would always remember. It was one of the best moments of my life.

After a while I was snapped back to reality when it suddenly occurred to me that I did not know where I was going. I had no phone or GPS, and my only map was of the whole of Europe at a scale of one to two and a half million. This, it turned out, was quite inadequate. However, I'd once read a book by Bear Grylls, and I was therefore confident enough to navigate using the sun. Using Bear's tried and trusted techniques I was able to maintain what I dearly hoped was an east-northeast course, no mean feat on the twisting, turning French roads.

Such an ability to navigate was going to be crucial if my journey was to be a success, and particularly if I was going to achieve the third of my targets:

3.   Pass through antipodal points.

In case you're sitting there scratching your head, I'll explain that antipodal points are locations that are geographically exactly opposite one another (Madrid in Spain and Wellington in New Zealand being an example). This seemed to me like a good way to ensure a 'true' circumnavigation, meaning that I could not simply remain high up in the northern hemisphere and take a short route around the planet. I did not, after all, want this to be easy.

And it certainly wasn't easy when I awoke the next morning, having enjoyed a first night wild camping on an abandoned railway line, to an entirely overcast sky. How on earth was I going to navigate now? I did my best to remain calm as I packed up my tent, and thought back to the Bear Grylls book. Surely there was some other advice in there that could help me. I remembered something about moss growing mostly on the north side of trees. Or was it the south side? I studied the trees around me closely. The moss was growing on the ground. What the hell does that mean, Bear? What the hell does that mean?

Fortunately the sun soon reappeared, allowing me to find my way again, and the weather remained fine as I made rapid progress across the rest of the country. My friend Steffen had invited me to a party in Germany and I wanted to be there, which meant I had to cover over 700 kilometres in the first five days. That was alright though, because in rural France there was precious little else to do besides cycle all day. The small roads were wonderfully peaceful, but so were the sleepy villages that I passed through every few kilometres, and it was rare that I should find anyone about to refill my water bottles. Each time that I did we had a similar conversation, with me whipping out my GCSE French to good effect:

Me: "Je voudrais de l'eau, s'il vous plaît." - *I want some the water, if you please.*

French Person: "Oui, oui." Followed by some impossible to understand French, spoken very fast.

Me: "Je ne parle pas français, je suis anglais." - *I don't speak French, I am English.*

French Person: More impossible to understand French, ever so slightly slower, while pointing at my bike.

Me, taking a guess at what they might be saying: "Tour du monde." - *Tour of world.*

French Person: "TOUR DU MONDE!" Followed by even more impossible to understand French, spoken twice as fast as anything that'd gone before.

Me: "Oui, oui. Merci. Au revoir." - *I wish we could talk longer, I really do, but I'm afraid I don't know what you're saying, and I've a party to get to.*

Clearly I was going to need to work on my communication skills, especially as I was planning to be travelling through a great many countries where they spoke languages that were not even remotely touched by the GCSE curriculum. Actually, I was going to need to practice an awful lot of different languages before I completed the fourth of my aims:

4.   Visit all of the inhabited continents.

And I should add that I was not entirely ruling out the uninhabited one either, but passing through Europe, Asia, Australia, North America, South America and Africa was enough to be getting on with. It didn't seem too much if you said it quickly, and I'd made a good start; within two and a half days I was already at the Belgian border and ready for my second country. France had been a nice, easy place to begin from, and I had covered 323 kilometres already. That did, however, slightly pale in comparison with my fifth challenge:

5.   Cycle at least 100,000 kilometres.

I'm not entirely sure what I was thinking when I came up with these challenges, to be honest with you. I decided not to worry about it at this early stage, and hurried quickly across a very small corner of Belgium until I was in Luxembourg. Now I've got nothing against Belgium, but I'd been there a couple of times before, and... yes, it is quite boring actually, isn't it? Luxembourg was better. It being one of the wealthiest countries in the world, I was struck by how thoroughly pleasant everything seemed as I made my way towards the capital (and only) city, also called Luxembourg. I'd been here before too and, though I was in a bit of a rush, I couldn't help but stop by again now to make a quick tour, as it was a place that I loved. The whole of the old town was once a great fortress sitting atop the cliffs of a giant valley. And what an imposing sight it must have been for an invading force, to look across at those fortifications blending almost imperceptibly into the steep valley sides. But these days several high bridges span the precipices, the bottom of the valley is a park filled with joggers and picnickers, and the old town a relaxed setting, where city workers and tourists mingle.

I continued out the other side of the city and across the rest of the tiny country until, a mere twenty-four hours after crossing the border from France to Belgium, I found myself crossing one from Luxembourg to Germany. The countries were coming thick and fast, and my sixth challenge,

6.   Cycle in 100 countries,

was starting to look like it was going to be the easiest. I was up to four now, and I had barely got warmed up. I had already begun a habit of commemorating each country by posing with the welcome sign at the border, and at the entrance to Germany I asked a fellow touring cyclist if he wouldn't mind taking the photo for me. He was an older German man with a white moustache and a bandana, who introduced himself to me as being burnt. Looking closely at his face, I saw that he did appear to have caught the sun a little. Perhaps he noticed me peering too intently at his reddened features, though, because he quickly clarified: "In English it is Bernard."

"Oh, Bernt! Your *name* is Bernt! Hi, Bernt."

Bernt was recently retired and explained to me as we cycled on together that he was making a gradual tour around the border of his home country, although he was having to do it in sections of a week or so at a time because his wife would not let him out for longer. I thought Bernt was a nice guy (if a little under the thumb), and I enjoyed cycling with him, but I am not sure that the feeling was mutual because he had an electric motor on his bike and he wasn't exactly waiting around for me. I did my best to keep up until we reached a camp ground where Bernt stopped and said he would spend the night. He suggested I stop too, but paying for accommodation was simply not in my budget. I was going to be camping out in the wild as much as possible. I already knew that doing that made cycling a very cheap way to travel, as day-to-day costs become limited primarily to food. I had a little under £6,000 in the bank, but I was confident that could last me for two years. Once I got to Australia I envisaged making more than enough money to continue for several more years. In fact I had so much confidence in these financial plans that the seventh challenge I had set myself was:

7.   Return with more money than I start with.

Aside from the obvious benefits, the reason that I had included this goal was to demonstrate something to others. I had not initially intended to make this trip alone, and during my months of preparation I had written to dozens of friends urging them to join me. I'd even imagined how great it would be if they all said yes; I had visions of a big band of us marching triumphantly together across the world. And there had been plenty of enthusiasm for the idea, at first. One by one, however, people dropped out, with by far the most common excuse being an inability to afford such a trip. Eventually there was just one left, a young Canadian named Daniel. That was alright though, as the two of us got on very well, and I thought Daniel would make an ideal sidekick. I saw him as a perfect Robin to my Batman, Tonto to my Lone Ranger, or Snowy to my Tintin. First of all he had a flair for languages that far exceeded my own, and secondly an ability to play the guitar sufficiently well that people would probably throw coins at him in the street, two things that I thought would make him an invaluable asset on such a trip. On the downside, I wasn't sure he'd ever ridden a bicycle before. But with just weeks to go until Paris he had written to tell me that he probably wouldn't be able to cycle with me to Australia, as his car had broken down.

"You don't need a car to cycle to Australia," I told him. "If anything it would just get in the way."

But he was adamant. His car was going to cost too much to fix. Then he lost his glasses. It was the final straw. He told me that there was no way he could afford to come with me.

So I was stuck doing this ride alone, but I thought it a terrible shame that anyone should ever miss out on cycling around the world again for such a silly reason as having no money. I hoped that my returning home with a profit would prove a point.

After five long days in the saddle, I arrived at the home of Steffen, my friend from Munich. Steffen is the kind of guy that, had he been born a generation earlier, would certainly have been a hippy. As it was he now lived in an old farmhouse in a village close to the city of Mainz and had just started working for a renewable energy company nearby. The party was in full swing by the time I arrived, exhausted from a 170 kilometre day, but I was pleased to make it and to see Steffen again, especially as he'd grown his hair into a big afro that made him look more than a little bit like a young, lanky, German Leo Sayer. Under normal circumstances I would never want to cycle such a long daily distance, but I was really determined to make it to this party. I saw it as a chance to unwind and relax, and also, perhaps, to meet girls. While I knew I was supposed to avoid being distracted by them this time, I was still quite aware of my own position in life as a twenty-eight-year-old, red-blooded male. I'd also been sensible enough to include one final challenge on my list:

Special Bonus Challenge: Find 'the one'.

I'd written a little footnote to this, that if I was lucky enough to stumble upon my special someone, the girl that I'd want to stop and settle down for, perhaps in outer Mongolia, then all of those other challenges could be forgotten. This was one part me being a hopeless romantic, and another part me wanting a get-out clause. I knew that if this around-the-world thing was a success I was likely to be at it for a good few years, and if I were to return home still single as I approached my mid-thirties, jobless, balding, and with an irritating number of travel stories, then there was every chance I was going to die alone surrounded by cats.

By a remarkable coincidence, Karin had also recently taken a job with the same company as Steffen, and she too was at the party. She greeted me with a warm hug and we sat down to chat. It was the first time we'd seen each other since we'd gone our separate ways in Costa Rica two years earlier and we had some catching up to do. The beer flowed and so did the stories. She asked me what had happened with Rachael, and I asked her about her old boyfriend. It turned out that we were both single now. In the past, one or the other of us had always been in a relationship and our time together had been entirely platonic. Now things were different. Was it my imagination or was she touching my arm an awful lot? I looked at her big brown eyes as she spoke and realised that they were actually really quite beautiful. Something was happening here. The topic came up as to where I was going to sleep.

"Don't worry, I brought my tent so that I can sleep in the garden," she said. "You can just share with me if you want."

A little later on the party died down, guests left, others went inside to sleep, and Karin and I were left alone in the garden. We climbed into the tent and lay down next to one another.

'Come on, make a move!' my brain (I think it was my brain) said. *'She wants you!'*

Karin shifted nervously, and looked towards me with those big eyes.

'Come on! Kiss her!'

I wasn't sure. We'd always just been friends. Was it worth the risk?

'Is it worth the risk to never know? Come on!'

I brushed her dark hair away from her forehead. Her lips curled in a smile.

'Kiss her! Come on! You're going to die alone surrounded by cats! Come on!'

I plucked up the courage, and moved my lips slowly towards hers.

2

Mainz, Germany
20ᵗʰ July 2013

What are you doing?!" Karin shrieked, pulling sharply away from me and leaving me kissing nothing but thin air. "We're just friends."

'Oh crap. Sorry. You probably shouldn't have done that,' said my brain, doing its best to fill in the awkward silence. Then it dawned on me that it hadn't actually filled in the awkward silence, which was getting quite long, and I had better try to say something out loud. Luckily for me I was well practised in dealing with this sort of situation.

"Sorry... I just thought... I mean... I like you... I'm sorry... We're just friends, it's fine."

Before this clumsy misstep of mine, the plan had been for me to spend a couple of days in Mainz hanging out with Karin, and I was pleased that the next morning all appeared to have been forgiven, and the plan was still on. If anything we seemed to be getting along even better with one another as we cycled the thirty kilometres from Steffen's village to her apartment in town, laughing and joking and having a good time riding together on the fantastic cycle paths. It was a beautiful day, sunny and warm, and typical of what was turning out to be a glorious summer. Along the way we met up with Steffen and his girlfriend, Eva, to spend some hours relaxing beside, and swimming in, a nice lake. I had probably rushed a bit too much through the first days of the trip, and it felt good to now have the chance to stop and relax with friends. For one thing lying in the sunshine gave me time to think about the important life choices I was now faced with, such as who would be cast to play our roles in the inevitable movie that I was sure would someday be made about my journey. I quickly decided that Karin would be played by Megan Fox and Eva by Heidi Klum, while for Steffen it was hard to look beyond Leo Sayer (although Sideshow Bob from *The Simpsons* was also a strong candidate). As for myself, there were quite a few options in contention for the lead role, but given my interest in finding 'the one' I finally decided that the ladies' favourite, Ryan Gosling, would be the ideal choice.

Karin and I had been getting on really well, and I was getting all the right signals from her that she had warmed to the idea of us being more than just friends, so the next afternoon, as we lay together in a park under the shade of a beech tree, my brain rallied me for another go. It took a little while for me to be convinced this time. I could no longer use naivety or drunkenness as an excuse should I fail, and I felt that I was at a greater-than-normal risk of being slapped. But my brain now believed that, at least on some level, I was Ryan Gosling, and it convinced me that it would be a good idea to move in for the kiss once more. This time, to the great astonishment of everyone involved, my advances were not rebuffed.

I spent the next week in Mainz enjoying the kind of whirlwind romance that would grace any movie script, as Karin and I discovered the fun that two friends can have when they decide to become more than just friends. We played games together, we went rock climbing together, we ate a huge ice cream together, and we spent a lot of time in bed, together. I was having a fantastic time, I really was. The one thing I wasn't doing, however, was cycling around the world. I had lost my focus. I had been distracted. I had done exactly the thing that I was not supposed to do. Reviewing my progress one day, I saw that in the eleven days since leaving Paris I had spent five days cycling and six days in bed with an attractive woman. This was alright, it wasn't a bad thing, I certainly wasn't complaining, but it wasn't the most efficient way to cycle around the world. Then Karin suggested a potential solution: "I've got the weekend off. Why don't I cycle with you from here to Cologne?"

It was the ideal compromise; we got to still be together, and I got to continue my journey. Appropriately, the route also took us along a section of the Rhine river known as the Romantic Rhine. It was a perfect setting; we soon found ourselves cycling on a flat path along the banks of the wide river, admiring the surrounding hillsides, where ancient castles were dotted sporadically in amongst a blend of vineyards and rocky outcrops. We laughed, we sang, we raced, we played. When we got too hot we jumped in the river and swam. When we got hungry we bought fruits from stalls beside the busy cycle path. I felt like things were exactly how they were supposed to be. All of my problems had been solved. Or at least they had until we arrived in Cologne after two days and Karin got on a train home.

After that I felt very alone as I continued north through Germany. Although I had made plans to see Karin again the following weekend in Hamburg there was still a sense that I had to prioritise the bike trip. It was somehow already the most important thing in my life and I knew that it was going to be a mostly solitary undertaking. Karin had just started a new career, and she was no more likely to be joining me permanently than Daniel or anybody else was, so I tried to get used to my own company again as I rode on the flat cycle paths of northern Germany. I briefly passed into the Netherlands for a few hours, primarily to get another country under my belt, but also to undertake the very fun activity of 'windmill spotting'. I was quite determined that I should see one, and I scoured the surrounding countryside as I pedalled amongst the Dutch cyclists – and it was a joy to see that everyone from school children to old grannies were out on their bikes in this most cycle-friendly of countries. After several hours my search finally met with success as I excitedly saw my first windmill. Later I came across one that was actually spinning around in the wind and I gasped with delight. I stopped to pose for selfies with it and even made a video. I was having such a fantastic time, I really was. Maybe I wasn't going to be such bad company for myself after all.

Even so, I was not averse to the idea of having a companion with me, and when I saw a blue parakeet digging at the grass next to a German cycle path I briefly considered taking it with me. I was confident that blue parakeets were not a native species of northern Germany and thought it might be of mutual benefit to have it come along with me. I had great visions of cycling the world with this parrot. It could fly alongside me, and when it got tired it would rest on my shoulder and just ride along with me. I'd call it Daniel, and I'd be able to forget all about the human Daniel who didn't want to come with me. The only trouble was that I didn't know how I was going to get the parakeet around to the idea without bribing it with food, and I did not want our friendship to be based on bribery any more than I wanted to waste food. I was also on my way north to Scandinavia, and I did not believe that Mr Parakeet would appreciate that too much when the first chilly nip of autumn hit us. Realising that it was not practical to take him with me I thought about what would be the most grown-up thing to do. I considered trying to call some sort of animal rescue agency, but I was hampered by not knowing the number, not being able to speak German, and not having a phone. In any case, I doubted very much that Mr Parakeet would have appreciated being sent back to a cage after he probably spent the last four years planning a daring escape from the last one. So I left him to his freedom with the sage advice to, "Fly south, Mr Parakeet. Fly south."

I entered Hamburg, arriving at the end of another 170 kilometre day, in Wilhelmsburg, a rough looking, graffiti-covered neighbourhood with shady looking characters everywhere. It seemed to me to be very much an ideal setting for a movie scene:

Gosling is cycling down by the docks of this shady neighbourhood. Suspicious characters are everywhere, half-hidden in the dusk shadows. But Gosling is all muscle and sweat and good looks, and is afraid of no one. A train rumbles by overhead, coming from across the water, where cranes and the spires of Hamburg are silhouetted against the final embers of the setting sun. As he rides through the twilight he spots an attractive woman sitting on the grass looking out at the water. He recognises her despite the darkness. "Karin!" he cries out, and the woman, Fox, stands and throws her arms around him, and they embrace in the night.

What probably won't be shown in the film is that I, tired from another long day on the bike, immediately suggested a safe and early night away from all the shady characters. But Karin, fresh from a five hour train ride from Mainz, had other ideas, and insisted on proving to me that this wasn't such a bad place after all. She used to live in Wilhelmsburg, and wanted me to meet some of her friends, so she walked me through the streets, holding my hand to comfort me, until we arrived at a backstreet concert in the middle of the night. It was being held in the unlikely setting of an empty room behind some old warehouses and Karin, recognising the music, told me excitedly that it was some of her friends performing. The lively music was great, but the room was hot and filled with sweaty Germans, so we quickly retreated back outside to sit on the floor and listen through the window instead. Here I met a collection of Karin's other friends. Most of them were German but there were also two Australians, one who had studied with Karin in Hamburg, as well as a friend from home who was visiting him. I was too tired to join in with much talking, so I laid back to rest on the cool concrete and look up at the stars, and I just listened. The Aussies dominated the conversation and their accents carried me away in visions of making it to the land down under. I tried to imagine what it would feel like to arrive at the Sydney Opera House, having made it there on two wheels. It seemed so impossibly far away. Was I really ever going to be able to ride my bicycle there?

Over the next couple of days, hanging out with Karin and her friends, I came to really enjoy it in Wilhelmsburg. The population was largely made up of foreign immigrants, most of them from Turkey and Eastern Europe, and we spent Saturday afternoon in a park where whole communities of different people mingled. Turkish families cooked barbecues as children ran around playing football and big fat men sat back contented with their bellies out. I looked around and thought *'Wow! This is amazing! What will Turkey be like?!'* As much as I was enjoying being with Karin, these little snippets of other cultures, intriguing insights into what I might find on the road ahead, confirmed that my trip was the most important thing in my heart. I knew deep down inside me that I had to keep it my number one priority this time, while at the same time being very careful with the hearts of others.

But the weekend with Karin and her friends was jam-packed with fun activities. On Saturday night we went to a big outdoor concert and watched a terribly foul-mouthed rapper. The next morning we were at the community allotments, where one of Karin's friends tried to convince me of the health benefits of drinking stinging nettle smoothies. Then in the afternoon we found ourselves on a solar-powered boat, of all things. Can you imagine? Another of Karin's friends belonged to a solar boat club, and he'd invited us for a trip around the waterways of Hamburg. The boat was a small white catamaran with a roof covered in solar panels. As it moved away from the docks it made not a sound, there was complete silence. I thought it the greatest boat I'd ever been on. People stopped and stared at us from the streets above as the sun shone down and powered us along. Karin, a big fan of renewable energy, had a grin from ear to ear. It was a simply brilliant way to see the mixture of old and new buildings of Hamburg, truly a memorable experience.

Come Sunday evening Karin and I said goodbye to everybody and the two of us went to a bar together for one more chance to experience some live music. This time it was a tiny little gig being performed by a long-haired guy who sang a mixture of English and German songs while strumming on his guitar. He was a very talented singer, and as I listened to his heartfelt vocals my mind drifted, as I thought back on my journey since Paris. From those first hot days under the French sun, the dash across Belgium and Luxembourg, all that had happened in Mainz, the Romantic Rhine, Dutch windmill selfies, a blue parakeet, and now a fantastic weekend in Hamburg. And it was only the beginning. I hadn't done anything yet, not really. There was an incomprehensible number of possible experiences awaiting me across Europe, Asia, and beyond. I had the memories from what had already gone, and I had so many hopes and dreams for the future, but I understood in that moment that the only thing that really existed was the present, and listening to those songs in the smoky bar with Karin's hand in mine, the present felt truly magnificent.

3

Hamburg, Germany
5th August 2013

I was starting to really quite dislike Mondays as Karin and I walked together into the crowded central station. As had been the case exactly one week earlier it was time for her to catch a train back home to Mainz. It was a sad moment, a real tear-jerking early scene for the film. This time it felt like the end. I was pushing my loaded bike with me, and the station was so packed with morning commuters that there was nowhere for me to lean it. I had to hold it as I hugged Karin goodbye. You can't really write symbolism like that. I had my girl in one hand, my bike in the other, and I could not choose both. I held her close, feeling her warm body against mine one last time as her train pulled up. We kissed and she slipped away, down the steps to the platform. Then with one final, fleeting glance back at me she disappeared onto her train. And there I was, still dumbly holding onto my bike. Karin was gone, and it felt like we would never see each other again. The present was no longer magnificent.

The train moved away and I was alone. I was surrounded by people rushing about in smart clothes on their way to work, but I was alone. I had no one besides my stupid bicycle. I pushed it back out into the sunshine and looked at it accusingly:

"Why do you always do this? Take me away from girls like this?"

"Hey, hang on a minute buddy. I'm not taking you away from anyone, that train took her away from us."

I didn't write much about my bike yet, but probably the most important thing for you to know would be that it could talk.

"And anyway, wasn't I the one who brought you to that girl in the first place? You never would have got together if it wasn't for me."

"Yes, I suppose you might be right."

"Damn right I'm right. Now get on me and start pedalling to Denmark. Doesn't Denmark sound fun?"

"Erm... I suppose so."

"That's the spirit. Lots of nice girls in Denmark. You'll be alright."

Despite having the company of an optimistic bicycle I felt quite alone as I continued north through the last of Germany. The unexpected romantic fling that had dominated the early days of my attempt to cycle around the world now only served to highlight how difficult and lonely it was going to be to spend the next few years primarily by myself. I did my best to settle back into my daily routine of cycling and camping, promising myself that things would get better. I knew that this trip was the best chance that I was ever going to get to live out my dreams, and I was determined not to allow myself to be distracted by a girl again. Well, at least not for a little while, anyway.

I continued to take advantage of the excellent network of cycle paths as I headed north toward Denmark. These segregated paths ran alongside the road, protecting me from the traffic and carrying me safely over gentle, rolling farmland, past fields of lettuce and cabbage, potatoes and turnips. Huge sprinklers watered these fields, tempting me to stop and escape the mid-summer heat by running beneath them. Tractors rumbled along the roads, flinging mud up behind them. Birds looked down at me from sporadic trees. Giant wind turbines loomed everywhere, watching over the land. The days were long and uneventful. The only real moment of excitement came one afternoon when I rounded a corner and was alarmed to see that blocking my way was a man who had fallen from his bicycle. He was sprawled across the path in front of me, with his legs still wrapped around his bike and blood pouring from a nasty wound on his finger.

He wasn't moving and appeared to be in quite a bad way. Alarmed, I leapt into action, leaning my bike on the ground and rushing to his side.

The stricken man looked up at me, and from that I was able to make a diagnosis. I was well qualified to do so, as, in order to save up money for this trip, I had worked as a rickshaw rider in Edinburgh. Having spent many a long night giving lifts at all hours to occupants of that fine city, I was very familiar with the glazed look that greeted me now. This gentleman, lying prone on the pavement before me, was as drunk as the proverbial skunk. If I'd only had my rickshaw with me I could have scooped him up and given him a lift home (charging him a fair price for my troubles), but I did not, and so I was unsure of what I could do for him. Cycling off seemed fair now, but he was blocking the whole path.

Then a woman on a bike came along. I explained the situation to her and she attempted to speak to the man in German, but received little more than a blank stare. An older gentleman on a bike arrived next, then two girls, and I retreated behind them all and watched. The growing crowd consulted, and someone suggested calling the emergency services. This statement had the effect of smelling salts on the drunkard, who quickly leapt to his feet and vaulted upon his bicycle. His balance was not quite the best, however, and he immediately toppled dramatically back to the ground. I had never seen anyone so drunk as this man in all my life, which is really saying something considering I used to live in Scotland. The older gentleman had seen enough now, and pulled out his phone to make the call to the emergency services. In response the drunk rose once more, shaking his hand in protest and inadvertently providing the number as he cried out, "Nein, nein, nein!"

It did not matter. There was no time for anyone to call anyone, as the intoxicated man cobbled together just enough in the way of coordination to get on his bike and pedal, swaying wildly from side to side, around the corner and out of sight. And even though I would have bet every penny of my savings that he had fallen down again within moments, we good Samaritans all shrugged our shoulders, and continued on our way.

I arrived in Copenhagen in drizzling rain, feeling uninspired by Denmark after a day of cycling on bike paths that ran alongside long, straight, boring roads. Luckily I had some friends to stay with in the city, an Irish/Danish couple named Conor and Malene. We'd met each other a couple of years earlier on the streets of Havana, when they had been looking a little lost and I'd pointed them the right way. We got to chatting, and before we knew it we were sipping mojitos and confronting criminals and having all sorts of crazy Cuban capers together. Malene had not joined Conor and myself with the mojitos, and now I got to meet the reason why as they introduced me to baby Sean. He was a little bundle of joy, and it was really nice to catch up with Conor and Malene again, but the differences in our lives were striking. Conor was about my age, and here he was living in a nice apartment (suspiciously situated directly above an Irish pub) overlooking the centre of Copenhagen, with a proper career and a family. It was almost like a vision of what my life might have been. It was certainly what I felt had been expected of me growing up.

I was brought up in a stable middle-class family, the younger of two children. My father always worked hard to provide my sister and me with the best possible start in life. My young eyes would snatch glimpses of him every morning as he'd come down the stairs in his suit and tie, place his briefcase in the back of his Ford Granada, and disappear off on the daily commute. Then each evening he'd arrive home late, pour himself a scotch, and sit down in front of the TV, tired from a long day of unknown business activities. The next day he would do the same. And the next day. And the next. This, so it seemed, was what life was all about. It felt like this was the path that I was inevitably to follow too. Do well in school, go to university, get a good job. That was it. That was success. That was life.

The only problem was that such a life never appealed to me. From as long back as I could remember I always wanted something else, something more, something different. Of course I wanted to be a footballer, first of all, but that dream faded with Peterborough United's fateful decision not to take on the thirteen-year-old me after my one and only trial. And if you look at the league tables and see where Peterborough United are now, you'll notice they made a mistake. But for me another fantasy soon took its place: I wanted to travel the world.

I wanted to see everything. I wanted to meet people. I wanted experiences. Most of all, I wanted to roam free. Watching TV and movies as a teenager I was always taken by the characters who drifted. The wanderers. The free spirits. I longed to be like them. I dreamed of travelling like that. Of hitching rides on freight trains, sleeping rough under the stars, being the mysterious stranger in town. The anonymity appealed. Every day a new place. Always another road to walk down. I was somehow drawn to this idea of existing on the fringes of society, free from its constraints.

The trouble was that "Drifter" was never an acceptable answer to the question "What do you want to be when you grow up?" It wasn't a serious option, not for a young British man of sensible upbringing, who had always done well in school. So I went to university, where I studied biology for no particularly good reason, and when that was done I got a job. In an office. Where I had to wear a suit. That was, after all, what I thought I was supposed to do.

Of course this arrangement brought me no happiness at all. It also didn't bring too much happiness to the company that had hired me to promote and sell their online media monitoring either, because I wasn't very good at it. My heart was not in it. I did not believe in the product. I did not believe that online media monitoring was something that really mattered. So I sat at my desk and spent my days staring out of the window. It was spring. Nature was in bloom. The trees were growing greener by the day. Daffodils sprung up as I watched. Birds frolicked. This was the real world. Right outside my window. It was where I wanted to be. It was more important than online media monitoring. I knew that I had to escape from this life that threatened to trap me like it trapped so many people. The computer screen, the suit, the tie, the weekly meeting in Costa Coffee. What was it all for?

What was the point? Why was I dialling the number for the CEO of some company to ask about their online media monitoring, when all I really wanted to do was go outside and roll around in the daffodils?

It was not easy to break free. The expectations that society places upon us can make it hard to deviate from the normal path. But I knew that I was not happy, and would never be happy until I could find the courage to go my own way. One Saturday morning I was swimming in my local pool when a man in my lane had a heart attack. I turned and saw him at the bottom of the pool. Instinctively I dived down and pulled him up, before the lifeguards took over, hauling him out of the water and performing CPR until the paramedics arrived. It was all in vain. The man died. For me the message was clear. Life was short. And I was done with wasting it.

I quit my job and set about trying to live the life I had always imagined. At first I made short trips, hitchhiking around Europe. Sticking my thumb out at the side of the road I was finally being true to myself and becoming who I wanted to be. I was adventuring and experiencing new things, beginning to see the world in a new light as I slept at the roadside or on park benches. Hitchhiking was cheap and interesting, but it was still an imperfect mode of travel. I wasn't completely free to go where I wanted, when I wanted, and I was too reliant on others. Then one day I discovered the concept of travelling by bicycle, and everything just fell into place.

When I told my mum that I was going to cycle around the world the first thing that she said was, "Don't be silly, you can't do that." This reaction, which would surely be the same for most mothers, only served to amplify my determination to do it. My parents thought this was all just 'a phase' I was going through, as if I were about to snap out of it at any moment, come to my senses, and become an accountant. I knew that this way of life was not what my parents or anyone else had expected of me. It was not what society requested from me. But it was what I wanted. It was all that I'd ever wanted, deep down inside of me. Taking the steps to quit everything, to go against everyone, was one of the hardest things of all. Everything that happened after that was simply carried by the momentum of those first decisions, a momentum that now promised to carry me ever onwards to bigger and better adventures, perhaps all the way around the world, just so long as I allowed it to.

4

Copenhagen, Denmark
8th August 2013

A very good thing happened during my time in Copenhagen. I spoke with Karin online and she told me that she had some holiday time coming up, and that she'd like to use it to come and cycle with me again, for a week or so this time. I immediately shifted my thinking, deciding that being distracted by a girl just a little bit more wouldn't be the end of the world. I imagined it'd probably be very good for my mood, actually. Looking at the rough plan I had for my itinerary, we agreed that the best place to meet would be in Finland in three weeks' time.

This gave my morale a tremendous boost. Now I had something to look forward to, something to aim for, and the world seemed a magnificent place the next morning as I awoke to see the sun shining brightly. Copenhagen, which had looked a dreary place the previous evening, was all of a sudden now a vibrant city, replete with colourful buildings lining harbours filled with sailing boats, and cycle paths everywhere overflowing with pretty blonde girls on bicycles. I rode out along the seafront past the famous statue of The Little Mermaid which, I was surprised to see, was not actually a mermaid. Through the throng of tourists I could clearly see that she had two legs, and was just wearing some slightly flipper-like boots. It didn't matter, it could not spoil my mood. Across the water I could already see Sweden, and I was itching to press on to my seventh nation.

My excitement grew as I boarded a ferry then watched as the small town of Helsingborg grew closer. Sweden was the first country of my journey that I had never previously travelled to, and consequently I did not know what I would find. All my mind could imagine was a land full of Ikea stores. This expectation was not realised upon my arrival in Helsingborg, an implausibly neat and tidy town of grand buildings and immaculate public spaces of modern art, where I saw no Ikea at all.

On my first couple of days in Sweden I cycled north along the west coast, and set about discovering what I could about the country. The first thing I realised, disappointingly, was that it was quite easy to get lost. Throughout Germany and Denmark I had found my way easily enough thanks to the world-class network of cycle routes, but these were nowhere to be found in Sweden. So I fell back on navigating by the sun, although this technique was hampered by the sudden rain clouds that frequently came along to soak me and block out my guiding light. Then I found out that the information centres that were in every town provided detailed regional maps for free, and my problems were solved. Now able to find my way, I was free to relax and enjoy the scenery, which was, sadly, quite monotonous. Sweden had a peculiar yellow and red colour scheme going on, with endless fields of golden wheat enlivened only by bright red barns. It looked as if every barn in the country was painted the exact same shade of red. I knew not why.

In the town of Varberg I needed to stop and refill my water bottles, and I found myself in the large, mostly empty, central square that every Swedish town seemed to be built around. As I looked about I noticed, across the square, a young black guy who was also on a bike tour. At least, he looked a bit like he might be on a bike tour. He was certainly on a bike, and he had a large rucksack on his back, and two things that might have been panniers strapped onto his rear rack. An oversized pair of headphones were slung around his neck and a blue cap was worn back to front on his head. I watched him as he went up to a pretty girl to ask for directions and I thought to myself, *'Now there goes a real bike tourist. Not one who plans and prepares, and gets all the right gear, one who just gets on a bike and goes.'*

I wanted to go and say hello to this interesting character, but he was some distance away, and I could see that the girl had already pointed him in the other direction. She was wearing a long, fashionable scarf, and as the young man went to cycle off this scarf got caught in his handlebars, and he almost dragged the poor girl off with him in an entirely comical manner. It was not unlike a scene from a sketch show. This guy appeared to be something of a cross between a gangsta rapper and Mr Bean.

I still needed water and I followed some signs for the information centre where I knew I would be able to get some. Arriving there I was delighted to see the mystery cyclist standing outside.

"Hello," he said with a big grin. "Nice to meet you. I'm Cherno."

"Cherno?"

"Yeah. You know, like Chernobyl, just without the byl."

As we spoke it became apparent that Cherno was a tremendous young guy, full of enthusiasm and positive energy. He explained that he was on a bike ride from his home in Germany to visit his brother in Oslo. He quickly suggested that we join forces and cycle together, and I was only too happy to accept. Ever since Daniel's decision to drop out of the running I had been on the lookout for a potential hapless sidekick, and Cherno seemed to be extremely well suited to the role.

Not five kilometres out of Varberg and I began to question my decision. Cherno's bike had already been making some suspicious creaking noises and things got worse as his back tyre soon deflated. Karin's decision to join me in Finland meant that I was once again on a tight schedule, and I did not have a huge amount of time to lose if I was going to be punctual for our reunion. Time was certainly being lost watching Cherno's hopeless attempts at patching up the puncture, so I stepped in and offered to do it for him, and we were soon on our way again. It had been a bit of a surprise that Cherno even had a puncture repair kit with him, as his whole set-up was delightfully amateur. In contrast to my expensive Ortlieb panniers, he'd bought his for eight euros from Aldi. They stuck out diagonally and awkwardly on either side of his rear wheel. The clips had apparently broken the first time that he'd used them, and they were now fixed on with a carabiner. He'd put his rucksack on the back of the bike by now, held down with bungee cords. Under these cords he'd strapped a variety of other items, and I soon learned that it was not wise to cycle too close behind Cherno, for these items were liable to come loose at any moment and shoot off behind him like missiles. Bread, water bottles, and bananas were among the projectiles that came flying towards me. But me cycling in front was little better, for Cherno soon came up to me and said, "I need to stop and buy more bananas, I seem to have lost mine somewhere."

Having the company of Cherno was extremely entertaining, and we got on very well as we cycled along chatting and telling stories. After a while the subject came up as to where we should spend the night, and he told me that he did not really enjoy sleeping in his cheap tent, and had been knocking on people's doors and asking to sleep in their homes instead. This seemed a bit forward to me, but Cherno insisted he had done it before, and it worked very well. In Varberg he'd apparently been staying with an African man who fed him chicken.

"But hasn't it ever got you in trouble?" I asked.

"Well, yeah," he said, starting on one of his great stories. "There was this one time when I asked someone in Germany, and he said I could stay, but he had to go somewhere first, so he told me to wait half an hour. Then he said 'watch out though man, there are lots of Nazis around here!'"

"Didn't that put you off?"

"No, not really. So I waited, and the guy came back and let me in. And it was like some kind of a crack house. I had to sleep on the floor, and people kept coming and taking drugs all night right next to me, and there was this strange trance music playing all the time."

"And you stayed?!"

"My tent is really crap, man."

"I can't believe it."

"Yeah, so I finally got to sleep. Then at about four in the morning there was this loud banging at the door, and the guys came over to me and told me to watch out because it was some Nazis outside, and if they got in they were going to kill me. But it was alright, they didn't get in."

This didn't sound like a really great way to organise sleeping arrangements to me. I was very happy camping out in the wild, and in a pinch I was alright with occasionally knocking on a door to request to camp in someone's garden, but asking a complete stranger to sleep *inside* their house? It sounded crazy, but Cherno wanted to do it all again in Gothenburg, and I decided I was going to have to go along with it, if only to see what would happen.

"Alright," I said, "But let's ask some beautiful blonde girls, okay?"

"Definitely!"

We arrived in Gothenburg just as it was getting dark, and Cherno asked some locals for directions to the student area, making a reasonable assumption that students might be more willing to host random strangers than the general population. I wanted to ask if there were any known crack houses in the student area, but Cherno had already raced off ahead up a big hill. I laboured after him and by the time I caught up he was standing in conversation with two Indian men.

"Yes, why not?" I heard one of them say to him.

So that was how easy it was to find a place to sleep in Gothenburg. The two Indian men were conveniently both called Nikhil, which I thought was great because I was tired and not in the mood for remembering more than one name. They lived in student halls and rather brilliantly both had a spare mattress in their rooms for us to sleep on. As well as a comfortable place to lay our heads we also got hot showers, delicious food, and the company of two friendly Indian men for the evening. In fact the generous hospitality of the two Nikhils was just enough to make up for not spending the night with two beautiful blonde girls as per our agreement, which I could only assume must have slipped Cherno's mind as he cycled up that hill.

The next morning we had a quick look around Gothenburg and then resumed our journey north. It started as a nice, sunny day, but the Swedish weather once again demonstrated its volatile nature and a hailstorm swept in unannounced. We hurried to seek shelter and fortunately enough soon came across a covered bus stop. From this location Cherno decided to call his mum to tell her that he was going to be cycling to Australia with me. My German is not perfect, but from what I understood of the conversation it went something like this:

"Mum, I am cycling to Australia."

"Cherno, you don't have your passport."

"Oh yeah, okay. Mum, I need you to send my passport to Oslo."

"Like hell I will."

I guess I wasn't going to be getting my hapless sidekick just yet, then.

The bad weather soon passed and we continued, and Cherno told me how it was to have a German mother and Gambian father, and about his large family in Africa. "You know, when I go there I am teased as being the white-boy. In Germany I have the opposite problem."

I later told Cherno about the movie that was going to be made about my trip, and how I was already casting characters. "I'm sure you remind me of someone famous. I just can't think who it is."

"You just think that because I'm black. People always think I look like black people but I don't, it's just because you think we all look the same." Then he paused as if in serious thought for some considerable time, before adding, with complete sincerity, "I think I'd like to be played by Denzel Washington."

I had to laugh. If there was one person Cherno did not look like, it was Denzel Washington.

With no decision made on the actor front we turned our attentions to playing some games. The most fun of these was the 'shouting at farm animals to get their attention' game. It was simple enough, we just took it in turns to shout very loudly at fields of animals, and scored a point for each one that looked up. Cherno was soon ahead after attracting the attention of a small flock of sheep and, although I had a couple of horses in the bag, I was lagging behind. Luckily it was my turn again when we came to a field with a huge herd of cows in it.

There were so many cows, it was going to be a massive score.

"Get ready to count, Cherno," I said confidently, before unleashing an almighty "OIIIIII!!!" Well, would you believe it, not one single cow lifted its head. I was devastated, and now my throat hurt so much I could barely speak.

We had been advised by the Nikhils that our best route option would be to pass through some islands just offshore and it was a fine choice. Agriculture made way to a superb, untouched landscape of big boulders, natural forest and idyllic watery inlets with only the occasional yacht or holiday home reminding us that we were still in the twenty-first century. Sadly for Cherno, this left us with few options for inviting ourselves into people's homes, and we had to put up our tents to sleep.

The next morning I waited until nine o'clock before trying to rouse Cherno. I was not greeted with much enthusiasm, and if the grunts and moans coming from his tent were anything to go by, he had not enjoyed his night in a field.

"I think I need to stay here and sleep a while longer," he said, "You go on alone. I can't do much today."

I was very disappointed to be leaving Cherno. We'd had such fun together and I would have loved to cycle more with him. Had I not been on such a tight schedule I would have done so, but as it was I was determined that I must both visit the Norwegian fjords and then make it to Finland to meet Karin, which required me to average a consistent 120 kilometres per day for the next couple of weeks. Once I was all packed up and ready to go, Cherno crawled out of his tent to say goodbye, before crawling immediately back in again. For all I know he may still be there to this day.

Secretly I was also a bit relieved. The wind was at my back and, with nothing to distract me, I made rapid progress on a long, straight road to the Norwegian border, the scenery becoming increasingly wild and untamed as I went. By the time I reached country number eight I was in the midst of a natural wilderness of thick forest and rocks, of waterfalls and lakes. It was my favourite kind of landscape, the sort where the trees seem to grow right out of the rocks and everything feels so wonderfully fresh and alive. Norway had certainly made a good first impression.

I left the forest and approached Oslo over the top of a big hill, which gave me a great view down over Norway's capital, and I was surprised to see something that looked more like it belonged in South America than Scandinavia. On my left side was the vast natural harbour of a bright blue fjord, spotted with green islands that stuck out of the water like giant bathing turtles. To the right a lot of white buildings formed the city centre, with tentacles of residential areas stretching up into the forested hillsides far beyond. Combined with the brightness of the sun I was reminded of Rio de Janeiro, a most unlikely comparison that I was sure would not hold true in winter.

Once I got down into the city there was much less uncertainty about where I was. The very clean and tidy streets, the mixture of old, but well-looked-after, wooden homes contrasting with ultra-modern new building designs, and the fashionable appearance of the people who strolled purposefully about the place was all stereotypically Scandinavian. Life here appeared to be extremely comfortable. I spent a few hours exploring the city, a highlight of which was walking on the famous sloping roof of the Opera House, before finding myself at the Frognerparken Sculpture Park. This park contains over 200 stone sculptures, and I believe I am right in saying that they are all of naked people. Many of these nudes were entwined in ways that looked almost sexual, yet weren't quite. I found it all a bit strange, and struggled to find the meaning. In amongst all the sculptures was one very famous statue, of an angry baby screaming madly, with his fists clenched, eyes scrunched up and mouth open in a pained wail. Surrounding him at all times was a crowd of Chinese tourists taking it in turns to pose for a photo with the stone child. I did not know where the angry baby's fame originated, and in a way I thought it a bit of a shame, particularly for the sculpture just a few feet away. That was of a baby girl who also looked distressed, but was not balling her eyes out and instead stood peacefully. No one stopped to take photos with her. She was being completely ignored. I thought the fame of the angry baby was sending out the wrong message, so I later posted an online request on my blog, asking that anyone visiting Oslo in the future please pose for a photo with this peaceful baby instead, in a campaign I titled 'All Hail Well-Behaved Baby!'

As well as hosting such silly and pointless ventures, my blog was a good way for me to share my experiences. I'd named it 'The Really Long Way Round' in a nod to the series in which the famous actor Ewan McGregor and the affable Charley Boorman rode motorcycles around the world. Years ago I'd been inspired watching them complete their own trip, although I have to say that one of the lines in the opening credits amused me. It was something about them having two support vehicles and a trained medical professional with them, but otherwise being on their own. My own tagline would start something more like 'I had a talking bicycle, and a box of paracetamol...'

I inserted the 'Really' into the title, not only to avoid being sued by Ewan McGregor, but also because I was not taking the most direct route towards my intended destination. In fact, from Oslo I turned north-west and started cycling in essentially the complete opposite direction from Australia. There was a reason for this. I wasn't aiming to get around the world as fast as possible. I didn't want to get it over with quickly. I wanted to see and experience as much of the world as I could. That was why I'd set myself the goals of cycling 100,000 kilometres through 100 countries on six continents. These challenges were not about ticking boxes, they were a way of ensuring I didn't just cycle around the world, but that I cycled around enough of the world to actually see it. And one of the things that I really wanted to see was the Norwegian fjords.

Up until this point I had enjoyed relatively flat terrain and easy cycling, but all of that soon changed as I began a new routine of slogging up and over steep mountain passes. Each day I would spend hour after agonising hour hard at work, putting all the energy I had into making painfully slow progress uphill. I would finally reach what I thought was the top, only to find that the road had other ideas and I was really only half way up, so I'd have to struggle on for a few more hours. Eventually the true summit would appear and, relieved, I'd launch myself down the other side at great speed. Usually it would start raining heavily at this point. Five minutes later I would be at the bottom, soaking wet, with the next huge mountain now standing in my way.

But all of this was worth it for the breathtaking views of the scenery that I discovered around the fjords. Great folds of grey and green mountains climbed majestically out of the calm waters, and spectacular waterfalls gushed down these cliffs as if God had, perhaps distracted by the beauty of his own creation, accidentally left all the taps running. The weather changed constantly, from being a beautiful sunny day one moment to pouring with rain the next, and so rainbows often added a colourful extra dimension, hanging over the water like a dazzling final touch. It was stunning. I was so glad I had made the effort to visit. This was what it was all about.

As I started to head back east from the fjords I travelled even higher into the mountains, and the road cut through a sparse, open landscape of moss and rocks. I was amongst the clouds, and at such altitude the air was a biting cold and snow lay in patches on the ground, making me glad that I did not have a parakeet to look after. There were hardly any passing cars, and I felt a delightfully long way from civilisation. So it came as a bit of a surprise when I saw a man come charging down the mountainside towards me. He was carrying an old bicycle on his shoulder and he clearly wanted me to stop as he bounded over the rocks. As he got closer to me I saw that he looked very wild and ragged, his face barely visible behind a fearsome amount of hair and his stocky body covered by a hundred layers of brown clothing. It appeared very much like I was being charged at by a Viking, so I stopped and prepared to surrender. Luckily, however, it turned out that all the man wanted from me was a bike pump, except he did not know how to say bike pump in English, and so he made the action of one, which could have been very disconcerting had I not already seen that he had a flat tyre.

My pump would not work, as his tubes had a different type of valve from mine. After I'd apologetically showed that to him, I tried asking him what he was doing up here. He mumbled something about a cabin, about having been up here for weeks. He had absolutely no interest at all in talking to me.

"Bye then," he said, gruffly. He was so wonderfully rude, this Viking-man of the mountains. I was in awe. I left him and cycled onwards, back towards Sweden, wondering to myself what on earth was going on with this strange, bearded man, all alone in the mountains with nothing but a bike and a few meagre possessions. The feeling, I'm sure, could have been mutual.

5

Turku, Finland
28th August 2013

I was so happy to see Karin's beaming face waiting for me as my ferry arrived in Finland, after an eleven hour voyage through a slalom course of little rocky islands from Stockholm. The long boat trip had at least given me a chance to recover slightly, as for several days I had been cycling like crazy down from the mountains and back across Sweden to make this boat. Rolling off the ferry and into Karin's warm embrace made all that effort seem entirely worthwhile. Now I could simply relax and enjoy myself as we had a whole nine days together to cover a relatively short distance between the west coast of the country and the capital of Helsinki.

Cycling with Karin again was just fantastic. With time on our side we began by making a detour north, visiting some of the little islands along the coast. Karin, so much more sensible than me, had bought a detailed map, so we were easily able to stick to the smaller, more enjoyable roads that were almost entirely traffic free. They took us through mile after mile of pristine coniferous forest, both on the islands and once we were back on the mainland. It seemed as if Finland was just one huge forest, interrupted only by mirror-like lakes that offered perfect reflections of the band of spruce and pine that encircled them. The weather remained consistently warm and sunny, and so we took advantage of the frequent lakes for swimming whenever we could. They also made excellent spots to camp next to, and we would often find ourselves at the end of the day with our arms around one another, happily looking out over the surface of the water as it was turned the colour of peaches by the reflection of the setting sun.

One morning I was packing up the tent at our lakeside campsite when I was suddenly startled by a large animal running at great speed. I recognised it as a deer as it shot past me, missing me by not more than a few feet. It had come down the hill from a road, clearly spooked by something, and in a blind panic it jumped straight into the lake. I had not been aware that deer could swim very well, but this one certainly could. I called Karin over, and we both watched, impressed, as it swam a good 200 metres, all the way across to the other side, where it climbed out again and went on its way.

With forest everywhere there was sadly no chance for Karin and I to compete in the 'shouting at farm animals to get their attention' game, but I was on the case, and soon came up with a much better idea for a game.

"Karin, I've come up with a much better idea for a game," I said.

"What is it?"

"It's called Pine Cone Wars!"

"I'm not sure I like the sound of that."

"No, it'll be really fun. We'll each get ten pine cones, and then we have to throw them at each other while we cycle. You'll score points depending on where you hit the other person. A head shot would be five points for example, and-"

"I don't think I want to play that game."

"Oh go on. It'll be fun!"

"No thanks."

Unfortunately Karin could not be swayed and, no matter what I said, simply refused to partake in Pine Cone Wars. So I invented a new game, Pine Cone Massacre, and just threw pine cones at her.

Aside from my occasional pine cone hurling, our days of cycling in Finland were peaceful and idyllic, and they were slipping by way too fast. It was easy cycling, in a safe and hospitable country, in the company of an attractive female. I could hardly ask for anything better.

But my mind would sometimes wander, and I'd fear what was going to happen when Karin left again, when I would be forced to go on into Russia – scary, inhospitable Russia – all alone.

"Are you sure you want to cycle around the world?" Karin asked me on one of our last days together. "Could you not settle for just cycling round and round Germany?"

Neither of us wanted to part, but sadly the ride with Karin could not last forever. Before we knew it, our time was up. We had arrived in Helsinki and she had to get on a ferry back to her life in Germany. This time I knew that it really was the end for us. I'd known it the moment she'd asked me that question. I couldn't settle. This time I had to succeed. My journey was simply too important to me, and the special bonus challenge only allowed me a get-out if I found 'the one'. I liked Karin a lot, I really did. But I'd come to the realisation now that she was never going to be 'the one'. She had just started a good job with a renewable energy company and her career was important to her. In contrast I had no interest in having a career. I had no desire to settle down. To stop now, to go back to Germany with Karin on a whim, would have been a big mistake.

I'd learnt a harsh, but important lesson from the experience of my first trip, in Canada. Then I'd given up the continuity of my journey to be with Rachael, and I'd ended up with a broken heart. Such wounds take time to heal and linger long in the memory. I'd been badly stung once, and I wasn't ready to make the same mistake again. I knew that this time I had to stay true to myself, to my dream of riding my bicycle right around the world, and I could not allow myself to give that up for a girl, no matter how attractive, unless somehow she were more important to me than the trip itself.

Karin understood. She knew. There had never been any insinuation that this would lead to anything more serious. It had been intense and amazing fun while it had lasted and we would part on the very best of terms. If only all relationships could be that way. Of course that didn't make it any easier to say goodbye, or to stop the warm tears rolling down my cheek as I held her for the final time.

I don't remember what the last thing that we said to each other was (most probably "Bye") but in the movie I'm sure Megan Fox will say something like "I have to go, the world needs wind turbines." Then Ryan Gosling will look deeply at her and reply, "I know, but I need the world."

And that was it. Karin slipped once more from my arms and cycled off through the gate to her ferry. I wiped my cheeks as I leaned against the chain link fence for one last glimpse of her, as she disappeared from my life for the final time.

I went off and explored Helsinki and it lifted my mood quite a bit. It was nice, in the slightly boring way of much of Scandinavia, but it had a bit of an edge to it, a bit of an atmosphere. Best of all it had a man walking a cat on a lead. I'm not sure what the cat thought of that, but I did enjoy watching it try to climb a tree against the wishes of its odd owner.

It wasn't until the next day that the fact that Karin was gone really hit me. I felt really rather empty and somehow like it was just pointless to be going on alone. I found the most wonderful of public swimming places at a lake, just like the ones we had been stopping at together, and it was so beautiful and clear and full of fish that all I could do was think about how Karin would have loved it. I felt more tears coming on.

I had to pull myself together. I reminded myself that I was trying to create the script for an action-adventure movie here, not a soppy romance. Ryan Gosling didn't cry. I tried to look for the positives. At least I could fart in the tent again now. And maybe it was good that Russia was fast approaching. Crossing the border was certain to take me into a completely different world, and right now it seemed like that was just exactly what I needed. Finland had been a clean, safe, secure country, modern and developed with excellent infrastructure, lovely nature and easy and enjoyable cycling. What awaited me on the other side of the border, I had no idea.

6

Russian border
9th September 2013

"Hoosedryver?" came the thick Russian drawl of the most depressed looking woman I had ever seen.

"I'm sorry. Do you speak English?" I replied.

"Hoosedryver?" She repeated, getting annoyed.

"What? I don't know what you're saying."

"WHO'S DRIVER?"

"Oh!" I said, finally understanding. "No, I'm not in a car. I'm on that bicycle over there."

The border official shook her head in annoyance and began tapping away at her computer. Around me was a scene of disorganised chaos. Everyone coming through the border had to leave their cars and come over to the woman's creaky old booth to have their passport checked. People were milling about everywhere, and it seemed impossible to keep track of what was happening. I guessed it didn't really matter much, there couldn't be too many people trying to sneak into Russia.

My passport was eventually stamped and I was waved through. Immediately I found myself in a completely different world. There was a big sign written in Cyrillic and I felt a rush of excitement to have travelled so far that I was now not only looking at things in a different language, but also in a different alphabet. Beyond the sign was a settlement made up of small apartment buildings of crumbling brick. I looked with curious eyes at everything. Washing was hanging from a line in the yard, and a few flowers made a desperate attempt to brighten the place up. A stray dog sauntered past a beat-up old car that sat alone in the street. An old woman, head wrapped in a scarf, fumbled with her keys on a doorstep. A lean man, dressed all in black, smoked a cigarette and stared at me, suspicious, unflinching. A shudder ran down my spine. Compared to Finland, life in Russia looked tough.

I began to cycle, taking the main highway, as it was a) relatively quiet and b) the only road. It was long and straight, and it passed through nothing besides thick forest for some considerable distance. Occasionally I would pass someone, more often than not an older woman, sitting at the side of the road with a bucket in front of them. These buckets contained blueberries or mushrooms, picked fresh from the forest. They were obviously on sale to passing motorists, but the lack of traffic clearly meant that the poor women couldn't be getting too much return on their efforts. I felt sorry for them and considered stopping to talk with them, just to see what they were like. But they all looked so sad and unfriendly, they had no smile for me, made no effort. So I never did pluck up the courage, and instead when I peeled off into the forest that night I found wild blueberries growing everywhere and picked them myself to enjoy at my campsite.

The next day I reached Vyborg and was fascinated to be in my first Russian city. Approaching from the north one of the first things that I came across was a mighty fortress dominated by an ivory white lookout tower with a green domed roof. It dated from the thirteenth century, when it was constructed by the Swedes as a defence against the Russians, which, it seemed, hadn't worked. The rest of the city was an interesting blend of a few nice buildings and a lot of things that were falling apart. There were plenty of Russian stereotypes – Ladas were the most common vehicle, tower blocks the dominant architectural feature, and the people walked around with dour faces and slumped shoulders. It was possibly the most depressed looking nation that I'd ever seen, and, yet again I remind you, I once lived in Scotland.

The road became much busier beyond Vyborg, and everyone was driving as if they did not care to live much longer, with overtaking apparently something of a national pastime. Nobody cycled here, and I felt a very long way from the lovely European cycle paths that I'd been on in Germany and Denmark. Now I was just extremely thankful that, at least most of the time, there was a strip of gravel next to the highway that I could cycle on to remain just out of harm's way.

I got a much better impression of Russia when I stopped in a smaller town called Sovetsky. A few kilometres from the highway, it was composed almost entirely of grey tower blocks but the streets were buzzing with life. Children ran around playing, teenagers rode skateboards, mothers pushed prams, old men sat on benches and old women stood around chatting. With all these people about, there was a real sense that this was a community, and it struck me that I had not seen this in Western Europe, where people were mostly inside, and just kept to themselves. The people here clearly did not have much, but they had each other.

I continued to follow the highway for several days around the Baltic coastline towards Saint Petersburg, a city I was looking forward to visiting and one of the main reasons for me coming to Russia. The gravel shoulder on the highway occasionally disappeared and when it did I was forced to cycle with the traffic, which was a harrowing experience. At one point a bus came hurtling towards me on the wrong side of the road, no doubt overtaking a Lada, and I dived out of the way just in time. It was extremely stressful, sharing the road with drivers that had no experience of cyclists, many of whom I felt sure would not have cared less had they knocked me down.

But the traffic was not my only concern. I also had to deal with a large number of stray dogs, many of which took great pleasure in chasing me. One afternoon I came across two particularly fearsome looking dogs that were at the side of the road ahead of me barking like mad at the cars going past. I was worried. If they barked like that at motor vehicles, I could only imagine what they might do to me, and so I came up with a cunning plan. The road was going slightly downhill and as I approached them I pedalled fast, building up a nice head of steam. Just at the point that they noticed me I stopped pedalling and made a loud, "Brrmmhh... brrmmhh, brrmmhh," noise which, if you can't tell, was me doing a very good impression of a motor scooter. I had thought that if these dogs chased bicycles, but only barked at motor vehicles, then all I had to do was glide past them like a motor vehicle. Unbelievably, this quite brilliant piece of logic didn't work, and I was soon forced to pedal like a lunatic to escape the enraged animals.

Given the state of Russian roads I had thought that cycling into Saint Petersburg was going to be an absolute nightmare, so you can imagine my unexpected joy at finding a segregated bicycle path that carried me safely into the outskirts of the city. From there I navigated the rest of the way through the vast jungle of bland tower block after bland tower block by cycling on pedestrian footpaths, something that is legal to do in Russia, presumably because very few people would ever survive cycling on city roads.

I had booked a couple of nights' stay at a hostel close to the centre, primarily in order to fulfil a bureaucratic requirement to be registered in the country. It was on the second floor of an apartment building, so I locked my bike up and went up the stairs, at the top of which I was greeted by a man who appeared to be from the seventies. I said hello to him and stepped inside to the reception desk, behind which, I was momentarily stunned to see, sat the most beautiful girl in the world. She had the most adorable baby face and long flowing blonde hair, and will be played by Anna Kournikova in the film, although I don't think even she could hope to do this girl justice. Bringing out the old Pountney charm I broke the ice with the classic line, "Hello, I've got a booking."

Even though I had been in Russia for several days now and the last thing that anybody had said to me in English was "Who's driver?" I had optimistically thought that the receptionist at a busy hostel might know a bit. Alas not, she looked utterly confused and lost, and her pretty blue eyes moved desperately to the older man for help. Victor was the owner and with his moustache and out-of-date haircut he had more than a passing resemblance to Ron Burgundy. He showed me around the dingy hostel, which was decorated with peeling brown and orange wallpaper and other such seventies décor, and had a very peculiar smell to it.

Victor checked me in and asked for the rather ominous payment of 666 roubles. Alarm bells began ringing in my head at the sight of this number. I was, after all, going to be staying in this creepy hostel on Friday the 13th. There seemed to be something very odd going on here. *'I've seen this movie before,'* I thought, getting annoyed because my action-adventure tale was in danger of turning into some sort of cheap horror flick. I was not going to ignore the warning signs and concluded, in my infinite wisdom, that the most beautiful girl in the world, still sitting innocently behind the desk, was almost certainly an alien, come to Earth disguised as the most beautiful girl in the world in order to try and kill me on this tacky seventies set. This explained very well why she could not speak. I checked her name badge. It said Юлия. This confirmed it.

In my dormitory I met two young guys, the first from Kazakhstan, the second from Dagestan, a troubled region of Russia next to Georgia and Chechnya which was firmly on the list of places my government recommended against travelling to. He was very keen to stress, "I am from Dagestan. Not Russia. Dagestan."

They were both really nice, but spoke little English, so our communication was via an elaborate combination of charades and Pictionary. The young Kazakh was delighted to find out that I was planning to visit his homeland, whilst the other looked dejected when I said I would not be visiting Dagestan. "My government says I will die," I mimed, quite brilliantly.

I went into the communal kitchen to make some pasta for dinner. Юлия, the most beautiful girl in the world, was sitting at a table, shyly stroking her hair and casting occasional glances in my direction. I was having trouble to get the ancient stove to work and she jumped up suddenly and came over to assist me, only she did not know what to say, and she just stuttered and stood there and eventually found the word "Help?" It was adorable. I could have died, she was just so cute. Falling in love with aliens was definitely not in the script.

I was only really staying at the hostel for the registration slip, and it was the first time I'd stayed at any hostel in four years. A sleepless night surrounded by snoring men reminded me why. I had positioned myself in the bunk closest to the balcony where my bike was, but this meant that I was also first in line for the mosquitoes that came in through the open door to bother me all night long. The young guy from Dagestan was confused by my complaints the next morning, as he had been in the bed furthest from the door. He then did an extremely funny charade of a mosquito going from bed to bed, getting fatter and fatter as it went, before exploding just before reaching his bed.

I was tired from my sleepless night but my spirits were lifted seeing that it was a beautiful day outside and I headed off to see Saint Petersburg. One of my first stops on my tour of the city was the vast Palace Square where an African man accosted me to ask if I was interested in going on a boat trip. I certainly was not interested in going on a boat trip, but I was so taken aback by somebody speaking good English to me that I immediately decided that I must make a friend of this man. His name was Franklin and he asked me to guess where he was from, and he was very impressed when I correctly picked Ghana. He told me that he was a student here, and that all of his classes were in Russian. Now it was my turn to be impressed. Studying in any foreign language is difficult, never mind one that considers 3 to be a letter. He was such a great guy, so happy and enthusiastic. I was sure he sold a lot of boat trips. I wished him well and continued on my way.

Saint Petersburg was an incredible place, one of the most extraordinary cities I had ever seen. The architectural wonders were so numerous that it was quite impossible to see all of them in one day, but I took in as many of the most famous that I could. A standout highlight was the ludicrously over the top Church of the Saviour on Blood, built on the site where Emperor Alexander II was fatally wounded, with its multiple elaborate domes resembling a collection of giant ice creams.

I spent all day walking, admiring the baroque architecture and soaking up as much as I could, before ending the day watching the sun setting behind the famous statue of Peter the Great. Then I could put it off no longer, and it was time to return to the hostel. I wandered back and opened the door, to find that Юлия was once again working on reception. And, was it just my imagination, or did she look really pleased to see me? *'Stay cool,'* I thought, *'don't forget it's Friday the 13th!'*

I hurried quickly past her to my dormitory. The two young guys from the night before were still there, but they had also been joined now by a man from Syria. He was able to speak a fair bit of broken English, and he told me that he was a beauty therapist and hairdresser, working for many years in Egypt, and now Moscow. What was interesting was that he was exactly like Sacha Baron Cohen's Borat character. The slightly camp mannerisms, the accent, the endearing smile, he was just exactly like Borat.

"In Western Europe," he said to me, "the hairdresser, he is a very important person in the community, isn't he? Everyone looks up to him. He is very respected, very important."

"Well," I said, "not really, no."

This was pretty much the end of our friendship.

No longer feeling welcome in the dormitory, I made my excuses and went out to the reception desk to check the weather. I did not, of course, have the slightest interest in checking the weather. Despite the inherent risk, what I was actually doing was giving in to the temptation to spend some time in the company of the most beautiful girl in the world. Юлия smiled and beckoned for me to come around to her side of the desk. I did not need to be asked twice. She typed something on her computer and used an internet translation tool to convert Russian/alien into English. I wrote back. In this way we communicated. She told me that she was from a town in Central Russia, and had only moved to the city a week ago to begin a six year medical degree. I remembered earlier Franklin had told me that the girls from Saint Petersburg were not generally very nice people, but those that arrived from other parts of the country usually were. So, Юлия was not only incredibly beautiful, she was smart, training to be a doctor, and, if a Ghanaian boat ride salesman was to be believed, also very nice. I liked her a lot, and from the way she kept touching my arm it appeared she liked me too. Holy heck in a handbasket, something was going on here.

We typed back and forth to each other all night. I helped her with her English homework. She taught me a little Russian. Before we knew what was happening it was four in the morning and I was completely in love with this girl. The whole universe seemed to have stopped, and was waiting for me to kiss her. But I did not. I did not, partly because it had only been a week since I'd said goodbye to Karin and, while I'll admit I did seem to be doing quite a good job of getting over her, I was not, contrary to popular opinion, a complete bastard. Mostly, though, it was because I had seen this movie too many times before, and I knew that it was always when going in for the kiss that the beautiful girl turns into her true alien self, and I did not want to open my eyes and find myself locking lips with a hideous monster. That had happened too many times in my student days.

So, instead of a night of passion with the most beautiful girl in the world, I went to bed and lay awake swatting mosquitoes and listening to a Kazakh man snore.

A few hours later it was daylight again and I got up and prepared to leave. Юлия was still on reception, looking sad that I was going.

"Don't worry," I promised her, "I'll see you in six years." It was absurd, but we had agreed that we would have to wait until after I'd cycled around the world and she had finished medical school before we could be together. She seemed to take it quite seriously.

"Yes," she said, then looked up a word on the computer, and added, "It is nec... ess... ary."

And then there was a final grand goodbye to me from everyone, with even Borat coming out to shake my hand and wish me well, and with Юлия looking even more sad I walked out the door thinking, *'Well, there goes the best looking girl I'll ever turn down.'*

I made my way out of Saint Petersburg in much the same way that I had arrived, bumping up and down the high kerbs of the footpaths, until I was once again back out in the wild, following a long straight road through the forest. I was now heading back west, towards Estonia and the European Union once more. My desire to experience a bit of Russia was sated, at least for the time being, and I was ready to return to a land of slightly more civilised driving standards. I did, however, get one more stereotypically Russian experience before leaving. Just before a town some seventy kilometres beyond Saint Petersburg I approached a road block where two guys in army camouflage uniforms were calling random cars to a stop. Most of the traffic was being waved through, so I did my best to cycle nonchalantly past, but they spotted me, and called me to a halt.

I told the man who had stopped me that I only spoke English, and he pointed me over to the other guy. I don't know why he bothered though, because the second man couldn't speak a word of English either. Nevertheless, it was obvious enough that he wanted to see my documents, so I handed him my passport, migration card, and registration slip from the hostel. I was confident that everything was in order and I was preparing my, "If you try to fine me I will have to phone my embassy. And I'll have to borrow your phone, because I don't have one," speech, as the guy looked at my registration card and shook his head.

"Saint Petersburg," he said. I was not entirely sure what he meant, but he soon clarified it for me.

"Saint Petersburg," he repeated, angrily, pointing at my registration card, then at me, then back down the road in a way that clearly indicated he thought I should go back to Saint Petersburg. I wanted to argue with him. The idea that I should have to cycle all the way back to Saint Petersburg, just because that was where I had registered, was patently absurd. How was I supposed to register in another town without being allowed to get there first?

Not really wanting to cycle seventy kilometres in the wrong direction I tried cycling around the booth when the soldiers were looking the other way, but one of them noticed, and advanced towards me, repeating once again, "Saint Petersburg," with his outstretched arm pointing me the way. All of this nonsense was no doubt just a ruse designed to have me offer them a bribe to be allowed to pass, but I was not going to give into such corrupt tactics. Besides, I only had about fifty pence worth of roubles left, and I wanted to use that to buy some bread. So I said, "Okay, Saint Petersburg," and I began cycling back in the direction from which I had come. Despite the nagging voice in my head which kept asking, *'But what if she wasn't an alien?'* I was obviously not actually going to go all the way back to Saint Petersburg. Instead, as soon as I was safely out of sight, I pushed my bike into the forest. Well hidden by the trees, I turned and detoured right around the roadblock to emerge, feeling triumphant at having outwitted the silly men, on the road well beyond them.

7

Narva, Estonia
15th September 2013

A cool breeze tickled my face as I walked between the two border posts, pushing my bike back to Europe across a bridge that spanned the River Narva. The riverbanks, covered in trees whose leaves were turning a brilliant yellow, rose sharply on either side of the water up to two giant fortresses that faced one another defiantly across the void. This was my introduction to Estonia, a relatively new country still finding its place in the world following the fall of the Soviet Union. Once through immigration I found information boards everywhere in the town that offered an insight into the region's troubled past. For example, I found a famous lion statue that had originally been built to commemorate the appalling number of Russians and Swedes that had died fighting here in the 1700 Battle of Narva. Presumably, it was intended as a reminder of the horrors of war in a 'let's never be so stupid again' kind of way. An ironic shame then, that the original statue had been destroyed during the Second World War, and a replica now stood in its place.

This kind of tainted history became a running theme throughout Estonia. This was a land that had been constantly fought over for centuries, and suffered terribly as first the retreating Red Army and then the retreating Germans laid waste to it during the Second World War. The Russians had proven to be dubious liberators and half a century of Soviet rule followed. Yet it seemed to me that, after little more than two decades of independence, Estonia was doing really rather alright for itself. A growing economy filtered down into benefits for me, with the best bicycle routes I'd seen since Denmark leading me safely across the country on a network of well-paved minor roads.

The scenery had changed abruptly at the border. After weeks of evergreen forests I was now back cycling primarily through open agriculture, the sudden change impressing on me just how dramatically mankind can shape our environment. The few trees I saw were now mostly deciduous, and the yellowing of their leaves came as a warning to me. Winter was on its way, and it was high time for me to turn my wheels south.

I discovered a long time ago that when you spend all day riding a bicycle it's important to stop and take frequent rest breaks. My habit was to ride about fifteen or twenty kilometres at a time, and then have a sit down with something to eat. For a rich/normal person that might mean stopping in restaurants and cafés, but I was neither of those things, and preferred to take my breaks in bus shelters. They were conveniently placed right next to the road and provided a perfectly adequate place to sit while protected from the rain or sun. And I'd found that I could tell a lot about a country from its bus shelters. For example, in Russia they had been huge corrugated iron constructions, half filled up with empty beer bottles and smelling strongly of urine. But in Estonia they had the most wonderful bus shelters I'd ever seen, often made of creative wooden designs. The most imaginative of them was shaped like the front end of a big wooden boat, with portholes for looking out for the bus. I would sit in these shelters and eat my cheap supermarket food. I made the most tremendous sandwiches, loaded up with beans, cream cheese, tomato, lettuce and cucumber. Biscuits, crisps, chocolate, and a variety of fruit made up my daily diet. It was high in calories, tasted good, and cost me no more than three or four pounds per day.

I greatly enjoyed my time in Estonia, but the same could not really be said of the next of the Baltic States, Latvia. The nice bicycle routes ended and I had to cycle on hectic main roads, and what made it worse was that it rained for my entire time in the country. But it was not a big country, so I got my head down and hurried across it in three miserable days. On the third day the rain reached its torrential peak. I was making slow progress, as I kept stopping to seek refuge in those ever-useful bus shelters. I would sit for a while dripping and getting gradually cold watching the relentless downpour, then I would man-up and convince myself to carry on cycling. I'd make it a few kilometres, but as soon as the next bus shelter would come into view I'd decide that I'd had quite enough of being a man and dive into it.

It was nearing the end of the day and I was hiding in one of these bus shelters and trying to work out how much of a man I would need to be to go out again, find somewhere for my tent, put up my tent in the rain, climb in soaking wet, and then try to sleep under such conditions. Then a miracle happened. A man walked up to me and asked me where I was going to sleep, and then told me that I could stay in his house across the street if I wanted to. Norman actually lived somewhere else, but owned the old wooden home that he planned to soon knock down and rebuild, so he showed me inside and left me to it. It was great to see inside one of these simple old houses, the likes of which I had been riding past throughout Estonia and Latvia. It was a not-very-big wood-panel building and it looked like a stiff breeze might blow it over, but it was ever so cosy inside, with a fine wood-burning stove that I huddled next to. I was kept toasty and warm as I threw on great logs of firewood and dried my wet clothes above it, reflecting on the kindness of strangers, and pleased that I had a good memory to take with me from Latvia.

Lithuania came next, and thankfully the weather was much improved. A good tailwind beneath clear skies carried me quickly on flat, straight roads to the capital, Vilnius.

I had arranged to stay with a host, Virginija, using the online hospitality network, 'couchsurfing'. I'd used couchsurfing many times before. It offers a means for travellers to search through a database of potential hosts, comprising people, generally travellers themselves, with a spare bed or couch they can offer up for the night. It's a great system, and it was providing me not only with free places to stay, but also with a fantastic way of connecting with people and getting an insight into their lives. Virginija was hosting me in her flat on the seventh floor of one of the old Soviet tower blocks that I had been seeing so much of recently. A bubbly woman with a mischievous glint in her eyes, Virginija was living here with her husband and one of her four grown-up children. Despite being in her fifties, Virginija was a frequent traveller herself, making several trips per year, using cheap airlines and staying with couchsurfing hosts to make it affordable. She told me that when she was younger she had wanted so much to see the world, but that it was impossible to travel beyond the borders of the USSR, and so she was making up for lost time now. I asked her more about those days, and she told me that if you wanted a car, you couldn't just buy one, you had to put your name on a list, and in two or three years you would get a car. It was like that with many things. If you wanted a sofa, it was the same, you had to wait years. In some ways life was more comfortable, but it was restricted.

"People had money," she said, "but we could not spend it. The shops were empty. Now the shops are full, but nobody has money."

She made other comparisons where she insisted that life was in some ways better in those days. "Everyone used to get together in their kitchens and talk with one another. Talk about hating the Soviets. Now everyone just stays in their own apartment watching TV, or looking at Facebook."

She went on to tell me about the period when Lithuania was finally able to reach out for its independence, of the final days of the Soviet occupation, when huge crowds protested in the city. Her husband went off to join the protests, and she did not know if he would return.

"We were all willing to die," she said, her eyes lighting up as she remembered. "Everyone went off to protest. We were all prepared to die for independence." She paused for a moment, lost in her thoughts, before adding, "I had to stay here and look after the children, of course."

Virginija and her family made me feel very welcome into their home and I was even given my own room with a computer in it. That was particularly useful as my main task while in Vilnius was to try to get myself a visa for the neighbouring country of Belarus. I did not know anything about Belarus, so I began by doing some research. I quickly discovered that it was home to the last remaining dictatorship in Europe, and its long-serving leader was doing a good job of holding onto its Soviet roots. In the past he'd apparently been good buddies with Saddam Hussein and Colonel Gaddafi, and the United States government had Belarus listed as the only remaining outpost of tyranny in Europe. All-in-all, it sounded like a nice place for a bike ride.

Getting a visa for Belarus was a tricky business as they did not seem to be terribly welcoming to foreign visitors, but I discovered that it was just about possible to organise one in Vilnius using a travel agency. The caveat was that I needed to book an expensive hotel for each night of my stay, and it was going to cost me over a hundred pounds for a single night. That was a lot of money for me, but for a day trip to a dictatorship I decided it was worth it.

I had to wait ten days for the visa and, deciding that staying that long with Virginija would probably be pushing the boundaries of acceptable guest behaviour, I left to spend a few days cycling around Lithuania. I looked at a tourist map of the area and there were a very large number of sights of interest marked on it, but on closer inspection they were mostly churches and hills. Lithuania was clearly trying very hard to encourage tourism, but seemed to be having a hard time balancing that with the fact that there was nothing of any real interest to see anywhere. I did go to one of the hills. It was a hill. It had an information board at the bottom that said it was a hill and steps going up to the top. I climbed up them. The view was blocked by trees. It was not a great attraction.

I discovered an interesting and problematic thing while I was cycling around, and that was when I saw a sign showing that the border that I had planned to use between Lithuania and Belarus was closed for repairs. Not being able to enter Belarus close to Vilnius was a big problem because I collected my visa, in Vilnius, on the 7th, and it was only valid for the 9th and 10th, meaning that I now had to cycle a really, really long way and divert through Poland on the 8th in order to get to a border that was open. To successfully do this I set myself the ambitious challenge of cycling over 200 kilometres in one day.

I began at three in the morning, cycling on completely empty roads in pitch darkness. There was no moon, no stars, just the beam from my one pound head torch to light the way. The roads were so long, flat and straight that keeping myself motivated and awake could have been difficult, but luckily I had recently heard the popular recording artist, Katy Perry's 'Eye of the Tiger' and it was stuck in my head. Awfully motivating, Katy Perry. Dawn came and soon after that I passed into my fourteenth country, Poland. I rode all day and on into the night once more, until I had my goal of 200 kilometres. But there was a chance for more, and I saw a unique opportunity to cycle 100 kilometres in two different countries in the same day, so I continued. My aching muscles protested greatly and begged for sleep, but my head just replied with *'I am a tiger, and you're going to hear me roar!'* I finally called it a night after 227 kilometres, 124 in Lithuania and 103 in Poland, and collapsed into a field.

So I was feeling rather tired as I approached the last great tyranny of Europe the next day, and I was also concerned because I'd read some information online that suggested that this border was only for use by motor vehicles. If I were not permitted to cross by bicycle I would have wasted a lot of time and money, because my self-imposed challenges meant that I would not get into a motor vehicle under any circumstances, not even to drive a hundred metres across a border.

Any concerns on this account were eased as I cycled past the long line of queueing cars and trucks and came across another man on a bicycle, himself also heading for Belarus. He was a chunky man dressed all in black, who looked rather like he belonged in The Sopranos. I thought it very likely he was up to no good, smuggling things across the border, but I didn't worry about that because he was very friendly to me. He took me under his wing and went through the checkpoints with me, insisting that I be allowed to push into the front of the queue, and I was sure his presence made the whole procedure run much more smoothly. Once we were safely through customs and into the country he pointed to my bags. "Marijuana?"

"Cocaine," I replied, patting my rear pannier.

I did not know what I was expecting from Belarus. It seemed such an isolated and secretive country that it was difficult to have any expectations, but I was quite surprised by how nice it looked on the twenty kilometre ride into Grodno. The road was in excellent condition. The bus stops that I saw, always a good indicator, looked nice and inviting too. The rural homes were relatively simple, but this was certainly not the poorest country in the world either. As I entered into Grodno I passed a great many tower blocks, but they looked freshly painted and in much better shape than those that I had seen in Russia and the Baltics. After spending a bit of time lost amongst them I eventually found my way to the city centre and my hotel. I was staying at the Hotel Semashko, which was sufficiently upmarket to have a doorman. He was rather taken aback at my ragged appearance, but was soon put in his place when I strolled past him to reception and said, "Good afternoon madam. I have a room booked. The name is Pountney. Thank you."

It turned out that I did not have a room booked at the hotel at all. Oh no, I had a whopping great suite booked at the hotel. It was huge. I had essentially been given a whole floor to myself. I had a big double bed, two showers, two televisions, three balconies. If I'm honest, as a man who was used to sleeping in a tent, this was more than I needed. I felt like a movie star, a feeling which increased even more when the phone in the room rang and there was a journalist on the other end of the line wanting to do an interview with me.

The journalist, a man named Aliaksei, had contacted me after I'd published something on the Grodno page of the couchsurfing website asking if anybody would like to meet, and so I soon found myself sitting in a café with him and his wife, who was also a journalist. With the newspapers in Belarus being state-owned and strictly controlled, my interviewers' work could only be published online on an internet news site. They were both friendly and keen to stress that there was more to Belarus than the crazy dictator president. When pushed on the issue they came up with the smuggling to Poland as an example of another point of interest. "Yeah," I said, "I met a nice man doing that. He was very helpful."

I found the interview quite hard work as I was so tired from the long ride of the previous day. I would have preferred to just talk naturally with them, but it was very much a question and answer session, although they did eventually manage to produce quite a flattering article from it. I was quite pleased when the interview was over, especially as it meant I could escape to meet with someone else that had replied to my online message. Hanna was a short and pretty girl with shoulder length blonde hair, and as well as that she also had the additional benefit of not being a journalist. As a result we were able to converse in a normal and enjoyable fashion as she walked me around the city. I'd love to be able to tell you more about what I saw and learnt of Grodno during this walk, I really would, but to be honest I was allowing myself to get a little distracted again, and I didn't pay a lot of attention to anything besides the girl that was walking next to me.

Hanna and I were getting on so well that we decided to continue on into the night at a Cuban bar. It was a great one too, with a lot of typical Cuban paraphernalia on the walls and a man playing traditional music (of Belarus, not Cuba) on an accordion. A very drunk man was entertaining everyone by dancing to this music, flailing his legs around in a quite ridiculous fashion. Inspired by what this intoxicated man was achieving, I decided that the only way to combat my extreme fatigue and not pass out in front of Hanna was, at this point, to drink lots of beer. This was not a problem because I had found my way into 120,000 roubles and I had to spend all of them before leaving Belarus the next day. Worth noting, however, that this rather large sounding amount of cash was based on a generous exchange rate of 12,000 roubles to the pound.

After the Cuban bar closed Hanna and I went on to another late-night watering hole to keep the night going. I was greatly enjoying her company as we chatted on, hour after hour. She was young, smart, ambitious. Exactly the type of girl I was not supposed to allow myself to be distracted by again. Still, I had to leave the country in a few hours, so there seemed little danger of my journey being disrupted too much. So, as we left the bar and wandered arm-in-arm through the empty, cobbled streets in the direction of my big double bed in my huge, fancy hotel suite (that was clearly much too big for just one person), it seemed to me, as a true gentleman, that it would be rude not to offer to share this luxurious residence.

8

Sokolka, Poland
11ᵗʰ October 2013

With a spring in my step I slipped out of Belarus and back into Poland. I began cycling on the main road towards Warsaw, but with absolutely no shoulder and a lot of traffic it was no place for a bicycle, so I stopped in the town of Sokolka and found the library. All over the world libraries proved useful for me, as public spaces where I could have a sit down and use the internet to do some research. In this instance I was able to plan a better route through Poland on smaller roads and make some print-outs of maps. This turned out to be a sensible course of action, as the small roads took me off through rural Poland and gave me a much better view of the country than I'd have got from the highway.

One evening I decided that I'd try to find a bar to watch the decisive football World Cup qualifier between England and Poland. The first challenge was to try and find a bar out in the Polish countryside, but after asking some locals I was able to establish that I should be able to find somewhere showing the match in a nearby small town. It was already dark by the time I reached the edge of this town, so I found a spot that was well hidden amongst some trees in a field, put up my tent, locked my bike, and headed off on foot. I felt a great sense of pride as I strolled purposefully into town. I was one of the very few English supporters to have bothered to make it out to Poland for this crucial match, although admittedly that was because the game was taking place at Wembley.

I realised that my presence as an Englishman in a Polish pub was not without its dangers, and I began to worry that I may get beaten up should England win. Luckily, as I walked I came up with another cunning plan. I rehearsed in my head how things might go:

Englishman walks into Polish bar ahead of crucial match between England and Poland. Thirty Polish skinheads turn to face Englishman.

"G'day guys! Strewth mate, what's that on the telly? Fair dinkum! I'll have a schooner of Foster's please, and throw another shrimp on the barbie, will ya mate?"

Polish skinheads relax and turn back to the TV, as the man who has entered is clearly Australian.

I was very happy with this plan, as my Australian accent was flawless. Then I had another worrying thought. What if the barman asked me for ID?

Barman looks at ID. Sees that Australian man has British passport.

"What is this? A British passport? Are you English?"

Polish skinheads turn towards bar. They stand up, patting crowbars menacingly.

"Och nae laddy, I dinnae think so. Arm from Scotland laddy. I dinnae care for the English... laddy."

"I thought you just said you were Australian?"

"Strewth mate, yes. Oh aye, dual nationality. Crikey, I'll have a whisky and a Foster's, and I dinnae think you need to worry about throwing the shrimp on the barbie."

Yep, it was foolproof alright.

I eventually arrived at a bar at the far end of town. I say it was a bar, it had the word bar outside. Inside it looked more like somebody's house. There were only four or five old men in there, none of them skinheads, all staring quietly at the TV with a complete indifference to me or my nationality. After a while I managed to figure out which one of the men owned the bar/house and I got myself a beer and sat at a table with a drunk Polish man who spoke to me a little as the game began. This conversation consisted almost entirely of footballers' names, although at one point it did extend to predicting the result of the match. I was relieved when he predicted a 2-1 victory for England – the expectations of these Polish fans appeared low. But I then made the mistake of predicting a 2-0 win for my homeland, and he seemed rather offended that I did not believe Poland would be good enough to score. An hour or so later the game ended in a 2-0 victory for England, and I slipped out quietly.

From Poland I next crossed into the Czech Republic. The only man that I ever knew from the Czech Republic was Jiří, the bike mechanic at my rickshaw company back in Edinburgh. He had told me that his country was fantastic for cycling in, something that I had dismissed at the time as the fantasies of a clearly deranged man. But, against all odds, I soon discovered him to be correct. Immediately after I crossed the border I came to a map-board showing a range of cycle routes on small roads. I followed one and was directed along lovely quiet roads through a colourful countryside that was bursting with the shades of the season. As a rule I would only ever wear bright colours when I was cycling – orange, red or yellow – as these were what made me most visible to motorists. Now, however, Mother Nature was replicating my style, and I was practically camouflaged against the autumnal backdrop. Thankfully, it didn't matter too much, as the cycle routes continued to be fantastic all the way across the country, and I rarely had to worry too much about traffic as I rode along merrily trying to catch leaves as they fell from the trees.

Such fantastic cycling conditions allowed me plenty of time to reflect on how much I was enjoying myself. I was on my great adventure now, living the way I had always wanted. And while it might seem like I was on a long and complex journey, the truth was that my day-to-day life was incredibly simple. I got up in the morning, rode my bike a bit, then went to sleep. I had few worries, no stress. I was free from the responsibilities and pressures of 'normal life'. There was no alarm clock, no boss, no bills, no one to answer to. When I woke up I had no idea what the day would bring. I didn't know who I would meet, what I would see. I had no clue where I would end up laying my head that night. All of my worldly possessions fitted into a few bags strapped to my bike. I had no junk, no excess clutter. Everything I owned had a purpose. I had no iPhone. I didn't need one. The real world was all the entertainment I needed. I felt so lucky to have found this way of life. Perhaps more than ever I felt free and I felt alive. People would sometimes ask me why it was that I was doing this, why I chose to live this way. The simplest and most honest answer I could ever give was, "Because it makes me happy."

My country count was now up to sixteen and everything appeared to be going surprisingly well, at least until I arrived at the next international border and I suddenly found myself back in Germany. In what could be described as almost going around in circles, I was three and a half months into the journey, and I was back in the country that I had first arrived at on day four. This was, I'm pleased to reveal, a deliberate move on my part. After the extraordinary number of beautiful girls I'd seen in Saint Petersburg I had decided that going back to Russia at some point later on might not be such a bad idea in my continued quest for 'the one', and in order to do that I needed to send my passport back to the UK to get a new Russian visa. I didn't really trust the mail systems of Eastern Europe, and so I decided to send it from Munich, where I also had some friends that I could hang out with while I awaited its return.

I arrived in Munich beside the Isar river, which carried me most of the way into the city before I even knew it was there. I had actually spent a couple of months living in Munich the previous year, so I had a place to stay and, not having had the chance to do so for a while, I arrived intent on painting the town red. The fact that bottles of beer were available in Germany for twenty-nine cents meant that I was soon well on my way, and it wasn't long before I was slightly inebriated and coming up with an unbelievably stupid idea. By an interesting twist of fate, Rachael, the Canadian girl who I'd been so enchanted by on my first trip, now lived and worked as an au pair just outside Munich. This was the Rachael that I had once cared so much about and, with enough alcohol in my system, I suddenly wanted desperately to see again. It was also the Rachael that had gone on to leave me heartbroken and abandoned in the Canadian woods, but by the sixth beer I had completely forgotten about that, so I left my friends and headed off on my bike to the nightclub that I knew Rachael was going to.

We had organised via the internet to meet outside of the club at a prearranged time, but, in a fairly typical Rachael move, she was nowhere to be seen. I decided to go in alone. It was Halloween, and everyone was dressed up in costumes, while I was just wearing my normal clothes. But that was alright; if anybody asked I could say I had come as a homeless guy. The club was a lot bigger inside than I had expected, and I walked around for a long time looking for Rachael amongst all the vampires and ghosts, but I did not see her anywhere, mostly because she was not there. I retreated to a position next to a bar, sent her a message to say where I was, and waited.

It turned out to be a mistake to sit by the bar because from that position I was able to see that the price of drinks was only fifty cents per shot, or one euro for a beer. At this point I decided that I not only had the budget to buy myself a few more drinks, but also to buy everyone around me drinks as well. I had a lot of new friends by the time Rachael finally arrived at the club and located me, slumped against the bar. What happened next I cannot accurately remember, but from the bits and pieces of information that I was later to gather together, it went something along the lines of: me declaring my forever undying love for Rachael, her telling me that she had a boyfriend, me getting somewhat rowdy at the disappointing news, then acting aloof towards some of her friends, insulting others, stealing the glasses of one, and getting mad when Rachael left in a taxi. I then attempted to cycle home, from which I have a vivid memory of crashing to the ground, before finally waking up on some steps in a part of the city that I did not recognise.

Or, to put it another way, I was never drinking again.

Even though I had a hangover, a really stinking hangover, I thought it might not be a bad idea to get out of Munich as quickly as possible the next day. My passport had been sent off to an agency in London and it would be a couple of weeks before it would return with a new Russian visa in it, so I thought I'd take the opportunity to cycle down to Switzerland. My friend from home had agreed to fly out to meet me in Zurich and cycle back to Munich with me, and there was also an opportunity to tick a few more countries off along the way.

In fact I soon managed to achieve the unique accomplishment of cycling in four different countries in a single day. I woke up in Germany, crossed diagonally through a corner of Austria, cycled across the entire nation of Liechtenstein in two and a half hours, and finally ended the day setting up camp in Switzerland. Liechtenstein, incidentally, was not only the smallest country I'd been to so far, and the hardest to spell, but also one of the best. I was riding once more on a fantastic paved cycle path beside the Rhine river, now in its upper reaches close to its source in the Swiss Alps. The path was flat, but the views I had were of jagged mountain ranges rising all around with the snow that was clinging to their slopes sparkling in the afternoon sun. The setting was spectacular, and I felt tremendous, safe in the knowledge that this was exactly where I wanted to be, and exactly what I wanted to be doing.

The same could not be said of Zurich. I had been to this city before, during one of my first hitchhiking trips several years earlier, and had quite enjoyed it. Perhaps that said something of how I myself had changed because now I saw it in quite a different light. I arrived late in the evening, locked up my bike, and took a walk around the narrow streets, which were filled with art galleries and fancy restaurants. The people were all well-dressed and seemed to be playing a part. From the street I looked through restaurant windows and saw business people in suits tucking into steaks, sipping fine wine and laughing insincerely at one another's jokes. Everything was clean and neat and perfect. It was too perfect. It had no charm, no character. It was the ultimate epitome of the consumer lifestyle. Materialism seemed to be all that mattered here. I walked those streets, ragged and dirty and out of place and I knew that I had reached that point I'd always fantasised about. I was there on the fringes of society. I was the outsider, looking in at what might have been. I was looking at a life I could have had, and I knew, really knew it in my heart and soul, that I was so much happier being who I now was.

I spent the night in a forest close to Zurich airport and woke up early to greet my friend, Dave, off his flight from London. To call him simply Dave, however, would be to do the man a great disservice after all the years of hard work he put in at medical school, so from now on I will refer to him with his full and proper title of Dr Dave. The two of us had gone to university together in England, and our friendship had been forged almost entirely on the fact that he would let me sit next to him in exams and copy his answers. To be absolutely honest, I probably owe my degree to Dr Dave. I was naturally keen to repay this favour, so as soon as he arrived I offered to carry his tent and sleeping bag on my bike for him. I kind of had to do this anyway, as he had an inexpensive road bike that provided no means for carrying luggage on it.

We set off cycling together, following excellent Swiss cycle routes on quiet back roads. After several days of cold and rain, Dr Dave's arrival had fortuitously coincided with a sudden heatwave, and we were blessed with blue skies and clear views back over green fields to the receding Alps. It was all very pleasant, although Dr Dave's lack of fitness was soon apparent, as he found himself walking up almost every single hill. In truth he was not really a cycling man, being over six feet tall and well built, in a way that some women might choose to describe as buff. Being also a man of considerable intellect he reminded me at times of Stephen Fry, and, being a doctor, at other times of George Clooney. That was surely going to leave casting with a choice to make, but there was one thing Dr Dave certainly was not, and that was a cyclist.

He had cycled with me once before though, joining me for three or four days on my first trip. He'd bought his bike especially for that excursion, and in the three years that had passed since, he'd ridden it a sum total of zero times. Consequently, I'd advised him to take it to a bike mechanic to check that it was still in good order before flying out to Zurich, but Dr Dave didn't seem to place too much stock in my advice, and he hadn't. So it wasn't too much of a surprise when he encountered problems. First his chain broke, but, being in Switzerland, we were close to a bike shop and we were able to get it fixed. Then, after a rather cold night camping, which Dr Dave really did not seem to enjoy very much, we crossed the border into Germany at Konstanz and his spokes started breaking. I resisted the temptation to say, "I told you so," which would not have been constructive, and instead said, "I'm hungry. I'm going to eat some crisps. You're going to miss your flight home you know."

But once again fortune favoured the good doctor, for Konstanz was a city of cyclists and finding another bike shop was easy. Dr Dave bought some new spokes and I fitted them for him, and tried to true the wheel. I made a right hash of it though, and the mechanic had to fix it. While he was doing that Dr Dave, who had been complaining a lot about his bottom, bought a new saddle. He must have really hated the one he had because he spent seventy euros on a new, ergonomically designed one, which was a lot considering we both knew that he was never going to cycle again after this trip was over. I'd noticed that there was quite a disparity between our spending habits these days.

We crossed Lake Constance by boat and spent the rest of the day cycling through quite hilly terrain. By which I mean, you know, one of us was cycling. With Dr Dave walking up the hills, plus all of the time that had been lost fixing his bike, we were behind schedule to make it to Munich, and as the day wore on we made the tough call that it was going to be necessary to utilise a train to get us there on time. Of course getting on that train went completely against the principles of my trip, so all I could do was stuff Dr Dave on it, and then cycle forty kilometres by myself in the dark.

The next morning I met my companion at our agreed rendezvous point. He'd spent the night in a comfortable hotel, and I was pleased to see he looked fresh and ready to go again. It was another nice day, spent cycling on peaceful roads, chatting about love, life and the universe. At some point in the afternoon I decided to spice things up a bit when we passed through a big pine forest and suggested we play Pine Cone Wars. Being a big, tough lad I thought Dr Dave would be up for it, but, as with Karin in Finland, he simply refused to see the fun in it.

"Come on, you'll love it," I pleaded. But Dr Dave stood firm, and picked up a rock and put it in his pocket as a warning to me not to play Pine Cone Massacre.

A little later I was some way ahead of the doctor, possibly because he was walking up a hill, and in a moment of inspiration I decided it would be a great idea to hide behind a tree and then spring out and hurl pine cones at him. I did just exactly that, and it was great fun, but for some reason it made Dr Dave quite mad. He pulled out his rock and threatened to throw it at me. Then a car came along the road behind him. I told him to get out of the way, but he did not believe me because it was a very quiet road.

"No, seriously Dave, there is a car coming."

He looked around, saw the car, and stepped out of the way. Then he looked back towards me. At precisely the moment that he did this, a pine cone landed squarely on his head. I don't remember exactly where it had come from, but I think it might have been my hand. Dr Dave got very, very angry. He jumped off his bike and ran towards me, knocked me to the ground and then kicked me in the ribs. I was shocked by this assault, and, feeling like he had gone too far, I got up and threw his tent and sleeping bag to the forest floor and told him he could carry his own stuff. We had had our first fight.

All of this had been very silly, of course, and we soon made up. We had to really, because Dr Dave couldn't carry his own stuff, nor did he know the way to Munich. That evening Dr Dave generously offered to buy me dinner and pay for us both to stay in a hotel by way of an apology, which was really very good of him considering that the whole thing had clearly been my fault. I think he also had a slight ulterior motive though, as one night of camping seemed to have been more than enough for him.

Our little fight and the obvious differences in our spending power made me wonder how my relationships with my old friends from home were changing as our lives took such different directions. I'd lost contact with a lot of them, as they followed the Zurich model of pursuing careers and possessions and financial security. One thing that I really appreciated about Dave was that he had held onto his adventurous spirit, and, despite being a very busy man, he'd made the time to come and spend a few days with me, living the way I did. As it turned out he hadn't exactly lived the way I did, he'd mostly slept in hotels, but he had at least tried.

The next day our luck with the weather broke, and we arrived into Munich in pouring rain. Somehow, after four days we were still friends, and we had made it all the way from Zurich to Munich, together, entirely by bicycle. Well, almost entirely by bicycle. Dr Dave had done a bit on a train, hadn't he?

9

Munich, Germany
24th November 2013

I spent another week back in Munich, during which time I got a bit bored. There was little for me to do besides apologise to Rachael and daydream about the road ahead, as I impatiently waited for my passport to return. Finally one day in late November it arrived, and I was pleased to see it came complete with a brand new Russian visa. The visa was date-specific and was only valid for thirty days, from the 1st to the 30th of August 2014. Now I had a time frame that was not negotiable, and, as I planned to use the visa to pass through Siberia from Kazakhstan to Mongolia, it was seriously time for me to start pushing east.

I left Munich in depressingly cold weather with light rain drizzling down from grey skies. Being caught up by winter was entirely my own fault, of course. After more than four months, I was only 687 kilometres from Paris as the crow flies, giving me a steady progress around the world of about 0.25 kilometres per hour. Or roughly half the speed of a typical garden snail. As this sobering comparison sank in I resolved to put a stop to my wayward meanderings and head once and for all eastwards, and my Siberian visa date was not the only motivation. I'd also heard from my Belarusian date, Hanna, and after our night together in Grodno she appeared surprisingly keen to meet again. This was promising. Hanna seemed a little more free than Karin. She wasn't tied to a career. Maybe there was a chance that she could be 'the one'. Of course, the logistics of dating at the same time as cycling around the world continued to prove an obstacle, but Hanna came up with an idea. She could easily travel by train from Belarus to Ukraine, so we could meet up there in a few weeks to spend Christmas together. I had been planning to spend Christmas alone in my tent, but Hanna sounded like much better company, and so I enthusiastically agreed.

But first I had to ride my bike to Ukraine, and after a couple of miserable, rainy days I finally left Germany behind for good and entered Austria. Here the weather improved as I followed a great cycle path alongside the Danube for many days, all the way across the country in fact. I had been told that this was the most popular cycling route in Europe, and I could see why, even though at this time of year I had it all to myself. The path ran right alongside the river, meandering with it through forested hills patterned with a patchwork of evergreens and bare, brown deciduous trees. The sun shone low in the cloudless sky throughout the day, as if afraid to drift too far from the horizon. Its low position reflected a mirror image of the hillsides onto the still water of the Danube with stunning clarity. It was simply beautiful. With nobody else around I would sometimes just stop and stare in awe at the great river. I'd pause beside it and just listen. There would be not a sound to disturb the clear winter air.

One morning I awoke and unzipped my tent to discover that the riverside patch of trees where I had made camp had been transformed overnight by a fine coating of white powder. I felt a surge of joy at the sight of this. Snow makes everything more beautiful, and it certainly added an extra sense of adventure to this day. As I was packing the last of my things up an Austrian woman who was out walking her dog saw me and asked if I had slept out here, and was I not cold? Actually I was now using two sleeping bags, including a thick winter one that I'd got at a flea market in Munich, so I had been quite toasty and warm.

"No, no," I said happily. "I think it's beautiful! I love it!"

And I did love it. I could think of few things I would rather be doing on such a crisp, fresh morning than riding my bike over the soft snow, admiring the raw beauty of nature as crystals of ice sparkled in the bare trees. Sure, cycling in winter did come with some drawbacks, such as numb fingers and toes, but it also had many benefits. For example, insects such as flies and mosquitoes, so irritating in the summer months, ceased entirely to exist. I also did not sweat nearly so much in the cold temperatures, which meant showers and laundry could be partaken with even less frequency than usual. And it got dark at four thirty in the afternoon, so I could stop early, and sleep for fourteen hours. What could be better than that?

I reached Vienna in high spirits and enjoyed a few days off in the city staying with a friend of mine. With Vienna being the home of classical music and opera I was worried that I would find it alienating in a similar way to Zurich, and it did seem to have plenty of aspects of upper class society about it, but it also had a bit of an edge to it too, provided by occasional graffiti, some quirky stores, and a large Turkish population.

No sooner had I got back on my bike and left Austria's capital than I arrived in Slovakia's. Vienna and Bratislava are the closest capital cities in Europe, and the latter is just a couple of kilometres over the border. I'd been to Bratislava before, quite by accident, when I was trying to hitchhike to Vienna. So I already knew that the things to look out for as I rode into it were the old castle on the hill overlooking the Danube, and the considerably more modern UFO Bridge crossing it, the main supportive pillar of which comes adorned, quite brilliantly, with a spaceship. One thing that I did not remember from my previous visit, probably because I'd come in July, was the cute little Christmas market in the town centre. Light snow began to fall again as I wandered through this market, at the end of which was an ice skating rink with the town's Christmas tree in the centre of it. It was, and I don't use this term lightly, a magical scene.

I crossed over the UFO Bridge and made my way out of Bratislava, reflecting on what a nice little capital it was. I'd really liked it on my first visit, and I liked it again now. But this was the last time, probably for years, that I would be going through a familiar place. I'd never been to Eastern Europe before, nor to Asia or Australia. From here on it was all going to be uncharted territory for me, a thought that sent shivers of excitement down my spine as I headed off towards the Hungarian border.

I was pleased to see that the good cycle paths I had been enjoying continued into Hungary, even though they veered away from the Danube. On my first night of camping I foolishly could not be bothered to peg out my tent properly and ended up having to get up and run around outside in the middle of the night, wearing nothing but my shorts and T-shirt, amidst a fierce blizzard to do so. This certainly made me appreciate my warm and cosy sleeping bags when I crawled back into their warm cosiness, with thunder and lightning crashing around outside.

Perhaps unsurprisingly, the next morning the world was once again covered by a delightful coating of snow. This made me very happy and I was also pleased to see a number of other tyre tracks in the powdered surface of the path. It was great to see so many other hardy cyclists out and about, even if most of them were looking a bit glum, smoking cigarettes with 'I wish I could afford a car' looks on their faces. I tried to smile and say hello to a few of these people, but they seemed cold, in more ways than one, and not too interested in me. But there were nice moments too, such as when I asked a woman tending the garden of a little school if she could fill up my water bottles. She was gone for quite a while and I admired the buildings around me in the village. The homes were mostly simple concrete buildings, but colourfully painted and well maintained. Hungary was clearly not as wealthy as many of the countries I had cycled through, but nor did it seem to be mired in poverty either. The woman came back with my water and, in a small but meaningful act of kindness, also passed me a handful of little sweets.

A couple of days later I was on my way towards Budapest when I did meet a friendly Hungarian cyclist. He was a young guy named Marcell, who told me about a bicycle tour that he had done in Iceland, and one that he was planning to do soon from Barcelona to Slovenia. Riding along together we fell easily into a long conversation about cycle touring, as cycle tourists tend to do. Marcell was a great guy, and as we entered Budapest, the spires of the city cast gloriously against a pink sky, he invited me to join him at an event that he was on his way to. It was a gathering of some sort of human rights group, and it did sound like fun, but I was supposed to be staying with someone, and I was already running a bit late.

"There will be free food," Marcell promised.

"Oh, alright then."

We arrived at the event to discover that there was indeed food being prepared in an outside area by some Afghan refugees. It looked and smelled great, but sadly was not near being ready. This was a shame because I had not stopped to eat for the last few hours as I normally would have. I'd been trying too hard to keep up with Marcell, and I now felt kind of dizzy and not too well. Then Marcell ushered me inside to a cabin, and within this cabin there was a long table that was completely covered in gingerbread pieces. Around the table were a dozen beautiful girls decorating the gingerbread with icing. At this point I assumed that I must have passed out from my low blood sugar levels, because this was definitely not the kind of fantasy that came true very often.

There was also a 3D printing machine at the far end of the cabin and for some reason Marcell wanted us to go and look at it, perhaps because he had somehow not noticed all the tasty food or beautiful girls. We came to a compromise of sitting at the end of the table closest to the 3D printer. I was terribly hungry, but rather annoyingly nobody else was actually eating any of the gingerbread, and because I'm British, and therefore terribly polite, I didn't either, even though I could have happily eaten all of the hundreds of pieces on the table. So instead I tried to talk with some of the girls, but I'm afraid I can't remember what they said, because the room was starting to spin. Marcell, finally noticing my deterioration, gave me two of the gingerbread pieces as a present, and forced me to eat them, which gave me just enough strength to walk back outside and find that the Afghans had finished preparing the real food. Once I'd devoured a bowlful of that I suddenly remembered that I was supposed to be at my hosts' house several hours ago, and so, very much against my own better judgement, I never went back into that magical gingerbread cabin.

My supposed hosts were the family of Bence, a Hungarian man I had lived with back in Edinburgh. He had warned me that they lived at the top of a big hill, though this proved to be quite the understatement. It just went up and up and up. It seemed like it would never end. Eventually I concluded that whoever had declared Mount Everest to be the highest point on Earth had made a mistake, and there would need to be a recount, because this hill on the edge of Budapest was clearly much higher. And then when I did finally get to the top, exhausted and confused, I knocked on the wrong gate, got chased away by an angry man, and had to sleep in my tent anyway.

Wild camping had become almost instinctive for me by now, and it was an aspect of cycle touring that I greatly enjoyed. There's nothing quite like waking up to a perfect sunrise, the sound of birdsong, or the smell of a damp forest. There was something primeval about it. It was exciting not knowing where I would sleep each night, and it was like a game trying to find somewhere. The first time that I'd ever tried wild camping had been during a hitchhiking adventure with Dr Dave during our student days (when he was just called Dave). We'd only made it as far as Calais on our first day, and, inexperienced as we were, inadvertently pitched our tent on a footpath used by many of the asylum seekers that resided in Calais. Being woken up in the middle of the night by five Iraqi men unzipping our tent had been an interesting introduction to the world of wild camping. We survived the experience unharmed of course, what with Dave being so buff. But I'd got a bit better at finding places since then. In fact, I had it down to a fine art. As dusk would approach I'd start to look out for an appropriate spot as I pedalled. Forests were preferred, though any patch of flat ground that was well-sheltered and in a location that people would be unlikely to go at night would be considered. Once a promising place was spotted I'd wait for a break in the traffic so that I could slip away unseen. Safely out of sight I could then lean my bike against a tree and assess the area on foot, before deciding on the best place for the tent.

It was rarely a problem to find somewhere, but on my last night in Hungary I simply could not find anything. Fences blocked access to farmed fields and I had no choice but to keep on cycling after dark. Eventually I came to a small forest. Relieved, I pushed my bike into the trees, set up my tent, and climbed inside. It seemed a pretty good place to be, snuggled up in my sleeping bags, hidden away in this forest. Or at least it did until I heard a car pull off the road, the ice crunching beneath its wheels as it came to a stop about twenty metres from my hiding place. I heard car doors opening and closing and men's voices drifting through the darkness. Scared, I held my breath and dared not move. What could these men be doing out here in the woods? Surely they were up to no good. We were a long way from any villages, close to the Hungary-Slovakia border, and the only reasonable conclusion my brain could envisage was that they were out here to bury a body. What other reason could there possibly be? I heard footsteps coming into the forest. They traipsed towards me, as if they knew I was there. Suddenly the light of a torch fell upon my tent, and a man began grunting in Hungarian. My cover had been blown.

"I haven't seen anything," I said. "You just carry on. No witnesses here."

The Hungarian babbling continued. Whoever it was, they were standing right outside the tent, and seemed very much to want me to step outside. *'If only Dave were with me,'* I thought. I looked frantically around for weapons, but the only thing to hand was my extremely blunt pocket knife. A better weapon might have been my heavy chain lock, which I was sure could knock a man out cold with one well-timed swing, though it wasn't of much use at the present time, being locked to both my bike and a tree.

I got up and unzipped the tent to see an absolute bear of a man, big, fat and mean. I gave up on the pocket knife. He continued to talk aggressively at me until I informed him that I could only speak English. At that he called over one of the other men, who looked a little friendlier as he told me, "Hunting, danger, hunting."

Oh! Realising now who these men were I felt quite silly. I had been having this terrible image of them as cruel and bloodthirsty men, who had come to the woods to do some terrible, senseless killing, when in fact they were just hunters. I tried to explain what I was doing myself, but nothing was understood, and so a phone was found and handed to me, with a woman who could speak English on the other end of the line. After she had translated my story to the men she left me with some sensible advice: "They are hunting here. You can stay, but you should remain in the tent. Don't get up and walk around, or they will shoot you."

I did as I was told.

I cycled back into Slovakia the next day, and as I made my way across the country the temperatures dropped below freezing, the snowfalls becoming heavier. Now I was really riding through a winter wonderland of paper white fields and glistening silver trees, of seeing my own breath in front of me replicating the smoke that poured from the chimney pots of little cottages. It was not always easy cycling and on one memorable occasion I hit a patch of ice and my bike slid out from beneath me, leaving me momentarily pedalling in mid-air. Gravity soon brought me down again, but I was quick enough to make sure I landed on my feet and my momentum carried me on down the road at a steady jog. For a second I considered just carrying on in this fashion and leaving the bike behind. It was just slowing me down, after all. But then I remembered it had my sandwiches, and I went back for it.

With the weather being what it was I was pleased to have a couch-surfing host organised in Košice. Gejza was a man in his fifties who welcomed me into his apartment with a warming mug of tea. He then told me that his wife did not like him hosting guests at home, and that the two of us would actually be going to spend the night at his cabin in the woods. Alarmed by how much this sounded like the plot of another horror movie, I checked the calendar. It was Friday the 13th again. *'Seriously? How often does this happen?'*

For a moment I was sure Gejza was planning to kill me. He didn't exactly seem the type, but then they never do, do they? Either way, I did not really want to spend a night in the woods, whether it would mean fighting for my life or not. I was sure for many of Gejza's guests spending the night in the woods would be an exciting novelty, but for me it was the novelty of a night in a centrally heated building that I had set my sights on. The final straw was when Gejza told me that this cabin in the woods was a very long way outside of town, and that we would be getting there in his car. I'd written on my couchsurfing profile and in my messages to him that I would not use motor vehicles under any circumstances, but he had clearly misunderstood.

"I can just bring you back in the morning," he said. But that wasn't the way I was doing things. For me, this had to be a continuous journey. There were to be no side-trips in cars, no out and back in again, no starting where I'd left off. No breaks in the line. I wanted it to be one, pure, continuous ride around the world, with me propelled at no point overland by anything other than my own pedalling.

"I'm sorry, I can't," I told him. "It would really go against the principles of my trip. I won't get in a car. I'll just find somewhere else to sleep."

To be fair, Gejza now understood my point of view, or at least pretended that he did, and insisted that I could stay in the apartment, and his wife would just have to lump it (not his exact words). He also didn't try to kill me. Which was awesome.

10

Ukrainian border
20th December 2013

This really was Eastern Europe now. The number of people staring at me had tripled, the faces hard and unsmiling. Chickens ran free at the side of the road, loosely affiliated with dilapidated wooden homes. A horse-drawn cart trundled out from the winter mist of the main highway, the lone horse struggling terribly to haul its cargo, which consisted of one guy at the reins and another sitting upon a massive pile of sand. I couldn't help but wonder just what those two planned to do with all that sand when the poor pony collapsed and died, as it was surely about to at any moment. The road was as crazy as any I'd seen, and I had to constantly pay attention to watch out for Ladas being overtaken by buses being overtaken by trucks, all of which were simultaneously weaving about the road in a game I would come to know as 'Pothole Slalom'. I had entered Ukraine.

I was keen to press on to get to Lviv, where I was going to spend Christmas with Hanna. But it was too far for me to reach Lviv on my first night in Ukraine, and instead I camped early in a big forest. After events in Hungary I was keeping a very keen eye out for hunters, and I even went so far as to put on my high-visibility vest before sitting on a fallen tree to eat my supper. Surely, I hoped, not even the most vodka infused of hunters could believe a deer would be sitting on a log wearing a high-visibility vest? Yet, as I sat there stabbing hopelessly at my frozen chocolate spread I heard a loud bang. It was a gun-shot for sure, and at very close range too. I froze in fear. It was a truly terrifying moment, the first shootout of the movie. *What would Ryan Gosling do?'* Bang! Another shot. *'He'd probably dive down behind the log and return fire wouldn't he?'* I didn't have a gun. I did have a bag of peanuts to hand though. *'I'm a pretty good throw, aren't I? Maybe I could-'* Bang! I was still sitting there in my high-vis-ibility vest like a lemon. *'Okay, Ryan Gosling definitely would have done something by now. He wouldn't just wait here like a sitting duck!'* I scoured the trees for the source of these gunshots, and it was then that I finally noticed the fireworks display that was taking place nearby. Bang!

As so often seemed to be the case of late I woke up feeling relieved to have survived the night, and pushed on towards Lviv. I was really looking forward to seeing Hanna again. Back in Belarus we had enjoyed that *Before Sunrise* night together, and I was looking forward to the sequel. Anyone who has seen *Before Sunset* will be aware that the sequel to that particular movie was a bit of a mistake that kind of ruined the first film, but I wasn't worried, because real life is not a movie, is it? Hanna, by the way, will be played by Kirsten Dunst.

On the edge of town I stopped at a shop and bumped into a young man who we shall call Andriy, for that was his name. He was ridicu-lously friendly, and so impressed by what I was doing that he insisted on paying for my potatoes. Not content with that he also bought me oranges and chocolate. I was running a little late, but he was so nice that I told him I would be in town for a few days and suggested we meet again.

I hurried on into the bustling town centre where I found Hanna sat waiting for me beside a fountain. It was so good to see her again. Because I'd only had a two-day visa for Belarus we had previously only spent fifteen hours with one another, so it seemed like the logical next step was to now move into an apartment together. We'd found one close to the centre that we could rent out for a few days and it was surprisingly spacious, modern and well-equipped. Looking at it for the first time I realised just how happy I was to have the opportunity to spend some time off the bike, away from the cold, unforgiving road, and to get to know this girl better in such comfortable surroundings.

Over the course of the next few days we did get to know each other better as we explored Lviv. It was a very picturesque and interesting old city that had not been affected by the protests that were taking place in the capital Kiev and elsewhere across the country. That was because Lviv was already very pro-Europe, and there probably wouldn't have been much point protesting to a city that already had the European Union flag flying over City Hall. At the time, the protests taking place in Kiev against President Yanukovych and his Russian ties were still entirely peaceful, and from the people that I spoke with about it there was little to suggest the carnage that was to ensue a few months later.

Even so, it seemed to me that the majority of young people in western Ukraine saw their future with Europe. I was made aware of this during a pleasant dinner conversation on Christmas Eve when Hanna and I welcomed a Ukrainian couple, Illia and Anna, who we had met whilst exploring the city, as well as Andriy and his girlfriend, also called Anna. Despite the complicated politics it was a lovely evening with great company that helped to soften the blow of homesickness that came with being away from my family at this time of year.

I awoke on Christmas morning and I couldn't wait to leap out of bed to see what Santa had brought me, which I eventually found the energy to do at around ten o'clock. Unfortunately all he had managed was a single woolly sock, which was not exactly what dreams are made of, but luckily there was a blonde girl sitting there, frantically knitting me a second, which kind of was.

Hanna's friend, Dasha, was also visiting us on Christmas Day, as she was on her way down from Belarus, where she lived, to Romania, where she would celebrate New Year's Eve. I say that she was visiting us on Christmas Day, but actually both Ukraine and Belarus are Orthodox countries that celebrate Christmas on the 6th of January, and exchange gifts at New Year, so it wasn't really Christmas Day for anyone except me. Even so, Dasha had kindly brought me a present, a children's alphabet book with large pictures that would finally give me a chance of decoding the difficult Cyrillic letters. I stashed it safely in my panniers, confident that it would come in useful, and we got on with having a tremendous Christmas together. The girls did their best to cook a traditional Christmas dinner, but with us all being vegetarian, and only one stove point and no oven to work with, it ended up being more of a vegetable hot pot. Very delicious it was too. Then we played games, and we ate too much chocolate, and we even watched the Queen's speech. It was a wonderful Christmas if ever there was one.

The trouble with all this loveliness, of course, was that it had to end. I had such a good time with Hanna and there was even talk of her maybe getting a bike and joining me cycling for a few days, but she had never done a bike tour before and Ukraine in the middle of winter just didn't seem like a good place to start. Instead, after four fun days together, it was time for her to take a train north back to Belarus and for me to turn my bike south, towards Moldova, Romania, Bulgaria, and the end of Europe. There was no way around it. This was it, the end of another little fling. The journey was more important. Better not to get distracted. I knew that, but as we said goodbye in a park surrounded by pigeons it did not feel that simple. Another girl was walking away, and there was nothing to do about it, except get back to the cold and lonely road. As Hanna disappeared from view I needed someone to blame. I looked at my bike.

"Why do you always do this? Take me away from girls like this?"

"Hey! No, no, no!" my talking bicycle replied, "We've been through this. And, by the way, I am an inanimate object, and you are the one pushing me along right now. I'm not doing anything."

"Yeah, but..."

"But nothing. And one more thing, this conversation is taking place entirely within the confines of your own head. I am, as I said, an inanimate object and you, you are completely insane."

"That's a little harsh. Can't you see I'm a bit upset at the moment?"

"I know what will cheer you up. A nice trip to Moldova. Doesn't that sound great?"

"Well... no... not really."

But I knew that my bike was right; the only way to get over it was to get back to pedalling. To get back to the simple motion of turning my wheels, propelling myself forward towards greater adventures. I only wished that cycling across Ukraine wasn't so utterly miserable. The snow had long stopped, but it was still bitterly cold and a heavy fog descended and remained for days. The roads were busy and chaotic, and I found that I enjoyed taking part in 'Pothole-Slalom' much less than I did most games.

After several days of uninspiring cycling I did not feel like spending New Year's Eve alone, and hoped that I would find an evening of partying and laughter in the southern town of Chernivtsi to lift my mood. Andriy had offered to organise a place for me to stay with a friend of a friend of a friend, and I knew nothing other than that my host was named Sergei, and I was to meet him at the university. I'd assumed that meant that he was a student, but when I arrived I was greeted by a man of about thirty, and I have absolutely no idea why we met at the university because we then walked halfway across the city to get to Sergei's apartment. He lived alone in a very simple place with just three rooms, one for him to sleep in, one for me, and a tiny little kitchen. It was all very sparsely decorated. Sergei fed me bread with margarine and I saw inside his fridge which was completely empty except for two eggs which he tried to give to me but I refused to take. We tried to talk, but he spoke almost no English, although the few words he knew offered me some hope that this New Year's perhaps wasn't going to be a complete write-off. "My friend. He speak good English. He come soon. Tonight, party. Small party."

At around half past ten the first guests arrived. I'm afraid I did not quite catch their names, but one of them had a goatee beard and the other was missing a front tooth, so I'll refer to them as Goatee and Toothy. Goatee was the one who could speak English and, although he was a long way from fluent, I was just happy to have someone I could communicate with. Toothy was a strange little man of a nervous disposition. At one point the other two went out of the room and, left alone with me, he suddenly burst out talking to me in Ukrainian and did not stop for five minutes, a continuous, animated monologue of which I understood not one word.

There was a bottle of vodka, obviously, and every so often we would all have to stand and drink a shot. The guests had also brought a frightening amount of chicken, and a large number of cigarettes, and we all crammed into the little kitchen so that they could cook and smoke. This was not, if I'm being completely honest, what I had in mind when I'd asked Andriy to find me a fun place to spend New Year's, and I made a mental note to tell him I prefer more girls and fewer bad smells at my parties. Still, I did my best to enjoy it, at least until my only English-speaking companion, Goatee, leaned over to me and said in an extremely depressed voice, "I cannot remember the last time I felt happy without alcohol."

I did my best to sympathise with him, but unfortunately he did not appear happy even *with* alcohol, which he was consuming at quite a pace. Far from being a happy drunk, he seemed to be quite an angry drunk. Which was bad luck for me because the other guys were his friends, and I soon became the sole target of his anger.

"You are from England," he said accusingly, "You are rich. You have money. You have no problems. You are rich."

'Rich enough to sleep in a tent and eat jam sandwiches for dinner,' I thought to myself, without quite being brave enough to say it out loud.

"You come to my country and you don't speak my language. Why are we speaking English? You should speak in Ukrainian."

'A good point, but I've only been here ten days, and it is quite difficult.'

"You must learn Ukrainian!"

'I don't know if it'll be worth it. I'm leaving tomorrow. If anything I should learn Moldovan.'

But the angry man was quite insistent, and set about teaching me some Ukrainian, which involved him writing down swear words and drawing grotesque little pictures to show me what they meant.

More vodka shots followed and now Goatee got even more angry with me for refusing to drink any more, but I thought it might be wise to keep my reflexes sharp, as this idiot was well on his way to picking a fight with me. The atmosphere was horrible. Sergei knew that his friend was being a пеніс, but there was nothing he could do about it other than apologise, as Goatee repeated swear words in my ear and told me that I was not welcome in his country.

I wanted to leave, of course, but I had nowhere to go, as it was late on New Year's Eve and I did not dare to risk cycling in the dark with the likelihood of drink drivers. Some more guests arrived and the situation at least defused slightly. Midnight came and went and we all survived Goatee popping a champagne cork across the room and waving sparklers around wildly. It was, without question, the worst New Year's party I could imagine, spent with a bunch of sour-faced men smoking, eating meat, and drinking heavily, and an ignoramus of a man making everyone, especially me, feel very uncomfortable. As another bottle of vodka appeared from somewhere I decided that it was time for me to take my leave, and go into my room to try and get some sleep.

As I left the kitchen and started down the hall another man arrived through the front door. He had a very round head on a very round body and he somehow seemed to have a smile that was bigger than his very round face. "Happy New Year!" he beamed, "Hello to you! Welcome to my country! Nice to meet you! Welcome! Welcome! Happy New Year!" He was the happiest man in the world.

Where the hell have you been all night?' I thought.

I went to bed, paranoid about Goatee. He was getting absurdly drunk and really did seem to hate me, so I was genuinely worried he might slip away from the party and come to get me. There was no lock on my door, which opened outwards, and I could not even find my blunt pocket knife. I was actually considering making a run for it out of the window when I heard someone approaching down the hallway. There was a rattle of my door handle. I held my breath in fear and pulled the bed covers up around me. I was really scared. Suddenly the door opened and a dark figure stood there. It was him. I was sure it was him. He advanced towards me. There was no time to react.

"Chris! I am so sorry! I am so sorry!" With great relief I saw that it was Mr Happy with the too-big-for-his-big-round-face smile. "He is a bad man, a very bad man! I am so sorry! Please, you are welcome in my country! We want to be Europe too! Please! We love you! I love you!"

And he wrapped his arms around me, and gave me a big hug.

11

Chernivtsi, Ukraine
1st January 2014

I awoke to the comforting sight of daylight seeping in through the blinds. Relieved to have made it through the night, I crept past the sleeping Sergei into the kitchen and saw with some relief that my evil tormentor had left, along with everyone else. Sergei awoke from the noise of me carrying my bike out and he got up to say goodbye, a considerable achievement on his part given how closely he resembled a corpse. It looked very much like the second bottle of vodka had been polished off, judging from the way he mumbled goodbye, squinting at me through pained, red eyes, before collapsing back onto his bed.

In contrast I felt so very good, just to be alive and to step outside into the refreshing air of a cold Ukrainian morning. It was the beginning of a brand new year and everything felt possible. I didn't really know where I was, but that was a small detail. I headed off on the empty early morning streets and found my way into the centre of town to try and regain my bearings. There, a group of youngsters around the age of twenty approached me, thankfully in a friendly manner. They told me that they had seen in the new year on a train from Kiev, and were only planning to spend a day in Chernivtsi before returning. I must admit I did not really understand why they did that, but they were smiling and happy and really interested in my bike and what I was doing. In fact they were so friendly that they immediately and wholeheartedly restored my faith in the Ukrainian people. The previous night had been my first bad experience with anyone on the whole trip, and it was beneficial to be so quickly reminded that the vast majority of people in the world were fundamentally good.

I continued cycling, everything still shrouded in fog as I headed on towards Moldova. I witnessed a strange sort of New Year's Day custom along the way. People were dressed up in all sorts of crazy costumes, from doctors to goblins to giant white bears, and stood in the road blocking cars' progress. They appeared to be requesting something, maybe money, maybe candy, before allowing the vehicles to pass. It looked to be something along the lines of Halloween trick-or-treating for adults, or legalised mugging, or illegal road tax enforcement, depending on your viewpoint. Perhaps understandably not everybody was getting into the spirit of things, and I've never seen a group of Santa Clauses scatter as fast as I did when a coupé accelerated towards them at full speed.

I entered Moldova with no great expectations for the country, which was good because for the first few days it certainly would have struggled to live up to them. I cycled south on the poorly maintained main highway, which was driving me mad by going continuously up and over one hill after another. It was almost like it was seeking out the hills, and to make matters worse I was riding into a headwind and constant fog that never lifted no matter how much I pleaded with it. I felt trapped, repetitively cycling through a world of grey, like a hamster on a wheel.

On the third day of this uninspiring cycling I decided that something had to be done, so I left the highway and headed off to find a village. I needed to buy some food, and I needed to see something different. Luckily the village proved to be quite interesting. The homes were just little wooden shacks or simple concrete structures as might be expected from the poorest country in Europe, with corrugated iron roofs and doors falling from their hinges. There were plenty of people around and I was pleased that one or two of them smiled and waved at me. I found the little village shop, which had everything on shelves behind the counter, so that it was necessary to ask the little woman owner to get each item for you. This was a time-consuming way of doing things, especially as I had to wait for the woman who was already in the shop to ask for and be given all of her items first, and then I had to wait for the old man who came in after me but pushed in to get all his things given to him, and then I had to wait for the mother with two kids who came in after him as well. Finally it was time for me to be served, which proved difficult because my Moldovan wasn't what it might have been, and jam is really hard to do in sign language. After half an hour I eventually left the shop with two loaves of bread, a stick of butter, and five chocolate eclairs.

Cycling into Moldova's capital of Chisinau (pronounced Kishinow) was predictable in its drabness, with row after row of grey concrete buildings maintaining the country's depressing colour scheme.

Desperate for a warm shower and a bit of comfort, I decided to book into paid accommodation for only the third time in six months, partly because of the lack of couchsurfing hosts in Moldova, and partly because of the relative success of my stays in the hostel in Saint Petersburg and the hotel in Belarus. And so you can imagine my delight when I arrived at this new hostel to discover that the receptionist was once again the most beautiful girl in the world. Not the exact same one, obviously, that would have been really weird. This one was, like so many girls in Eastern Europe, called Ana, and she had long dark hair and a face so sweet and angelic that it made me wish Moldova wasn't already so firmly entrenched on my list of countries that I wanted never to return to.

It was a small hostel and we were stood right next to the social area as Ana checked me in. Behind me other guests were sat chatting, and one loud voice held the floor. It belonged to an old man with a droopy white moustache, eyes sunk deep into a withered face above which a few white hairs boldly did their best to cover a mostly deserted pate. He spoke with a booming English accent and reminded me of an old Sergeant Major as I caught bits of the monologue. I heard him refer to, "Us in the east," which I thought odd as I was sure he was English.

"Eastern Europe is so much better than Western Europe," he added.

Ana handed my passport back to me and I turned to the table, with impeccable timing, for at that very moment the old fellow announced, "Now, show me an Englishman with a soul. I bet you can't!"

"Hello," I said. "I'm from England. Nice to meet you."

The old fellow introduced himself as Gerry and, without apologising, explained that he was Bulgarian, his accent a result of being educated in England. He was an extraordinary man, and he entertained everyone in the hostel with his stories all evening. He had apparently spent many years working for military intelligence, and later on had then somehow made a dramatic career shift to become tour manager for The Police, James Brown, and Alanis Morissette. There was another name on that list as well, though I can't remember who it was now, and it wouldn't be right for me to make things up. He'd lived in Canada for fifteen years, Venice for twelve, had been to 129 countries and could speak sixteen languages, including both French and French Canadian (I personally can speak both English and English Canadian, though I don't like to brag). He'd just finished writing an autobiography of his incredible life, that was going to be published by a Romanian publisher, although he also mentioned at another time that he hated Romania and never wanted to go there again, which I thought might prove a bit of a stumbling block. Finally the sixty-six-year-old Gerry confessed to me privately that he had a twenty-six-year-old girlfriend in Georgia. "So there's life in the old dog yet!"

All of Gerry's stories seemed somewhat dubious, coming as they did from an old man in a youth hostel in the back of beyond. Still, I would not be so bold as to suggest Gerry was lying. At least not about the music career. Him being best friends with Sting I could just about get on board with, but the twenty-six-year-old girlfriend? This I found questionable, particularly if she had ever spent the night with the dear old man. Because after midnight everyone retired to their beds, and Gerry was on the bunk below mine. I was lying awake waiting for the snoring to begin. But, to my surprise and relief, it seemed that Gerry was not a snorer. Perhaps a decent night of sleep in a hostel might actually be achieved. I dared to believe in the idea, at least for a few precious moments. Then the farting started. Big riproaring farts that made the whole room shake. Constantly. All night long. Dear Lord, no, Gerry, no! I was never going to stay in a hostel ever again, not for all the most beautiful women in the world. It just wasn't worth it.

It remained foggy for most of the rest of my time in Moldova, but thankfully as I approached Romania the sun finally reappeared for the first time since Lviv. To be honest, I had actually been quite fortunate with the weather, as normally this part of the world would be covered by a foot of snow in January, yet I had seen none at all since Slovakia. And as I cycled south down the Black Sea coast through Romania and Bulgaria it became unseasonably warm, with temperatures as high as sixteen or seventeen degrees. This was a fantastic way for me to end Europe, in countries that I found surprisingly welcoming. I had expected Romania to be similar to Moldova given their common ancestry, yet membership of the European Union meant there was a clear Western European influence, with German supermarkets and banks being all over the towns. Whether or not the benefits of that filtered down to the common man I was not sure, with horse-drawn carts still being a fairly frequent sight on the country roads. I did not mind at all, as I found these were fantastic to draft behind whenever the wind was blowing the wrong way.

I raced through Romania and Bulgaria in just a few days, as I was so keen to get on to the very exciting challenge of Turkey. On my last full day in Bulgaria it was another beautiful, sunny day. Up until this point the cycling in Bulgaria had varied between pleasant and terrifying, but on this day it moved firmly to the category of magnificent. By chance I found a nice, quiet road that took me through lovely countryside and then out to the coast one last time. The Black Sea was neither black, nor technically really a sea, but it was at times quite stunning to look out over, with sandy beaches and quaint little harbours. From there I had a long, long climb up towards the Turkish border on an almost empty road. It was a special moment to cycle on such a nice, peaceful road, with the setting sun turning the sky golden orange behind the bare trees of the forest, the whole of Europe behind me and the unknown mysteries of Turkey calling me onwards. Only one thing took the edge off the moment, and that was when I noticed a lot of play in my crank arms and realised that my bottom bracket was broken. It would soon need replacing, but for now the pedals were still going around and I knew I should be able to get to Istanbul on this one. It was, however, yet another problem, coming on top of my front rack being cracked, not to mention the fact that the only way for me to shift down gears was to give my front derailleur a swift kick with my heel. I was about to try to cycle across Asia from one side to the other, and my bike was quite literally falling apart beneath me.

But Bulgaria was not about to let me go too easily, and on that last night I discovered that I was camping in a forest that was populated with wolves. I knew this for a fact because I could hear them howling from my tent. By which I mean that I was in my tent, not the wolves. Could you imagine if the wolves were actually in my tent howling? That would have been TERRIFYING! No, they were out in the forest somewhere, and naturally I was concerned that they might come too close for comfort. At one point I thought that I heard an animal rustling around outside of the tent, and, convinced that it meant that the wolves were coming for me, I sat bolt upright, desperately gripping my blunt pocket knife. Now, when they make the movie of this trip, and I'm still sure that they will, what will likely happen is this:

A pack of wolves is seen circling the tent. The fearless Ryan Gosling unzips the tent and is suddenly face to face with one of these snarling beasts. Gosling leaps out and wrestles this wolf, just kicking it off in time to see another one leaping towards him. He swings his right arm and knocks this one down, then in the next half second does a spectacular back-flip out of the way of a third wolf, before scissor kicking a fourth in the air. Then when it seems like the final wolf is about to get him from behind, Lassie appears side left, and takes it out with a flying rugby tackle. And then Gosling retires to his tent, and Jessica Alba is in there somehow.

(This is not really important, but what actually happened was I opened the tent, gripping the blunt pocket knife and shaking nervously, and came face to face with some plants rustling in the wind.)

12

Turkish border
24th January 2014

I had high hopes for Turkey. My extended ride around Europe had been great, not to mention very good for my country count; I'd already chalked up twenty-five nations in just six months. This had given me a small insight into a large variety of cultures, but with Turkey being quite big I would now finally have the opportunity to spend more time in just one country, and really get to know it, really sink my teeth into it. And with me having been a vegetarian for the past few years, I hadn't sunk my teeth into turkey since Christmas 2009. Putting terrible jokes aside, I was genuinely very excited, as this country, the link between Europe and Asia, where West meets East, was surely where my journey was going to start to get really interesting.

On the Bulgarian side of the border the road was narrow and had so many potholes that it resembled the surface of the moon, but as I passed easily through border control and continued on the Turkish side it suddenly became four lanes wide with a big shoulder and immaculately smooth tarmac. It was a fantastic road, and many of the cars and trucks that passed me tooted their horns in support. This was something that had happened only very rarely in Europe (and I think it was usually intended more in a 'what-are-you-doing-cycling-about-in-the-fog, get-off-the-road kind' of way). Here it was every few minutes, and I was sure it was done with more encouraging intentions, as it was often accompanied by a friendly wave. I loved Turkey already.

I was feeling so excited on my way into the first town of Kırklareli to see what it was like, but before I had got anywhere into the town, practically from the first building that I passed, a man shouted out to me.

"Welcome!" He cried. "Welcome!"

He was frantically waving at me from the steps of a shop on the opposite side of the road. I cycled over to him, and he shook my hand enthusiastically with a warm smile. I explained that I had no money to buy anything from his shop as I had not yet been to an ATM to get my Turkish lira.

"No problem!" He said. "Come in! Drink tea? No money, no problem! Come in! Welcome!"

The man, Süleyman, was about forty, had greying hair and a big, round nose and was dressed in jeans and a warm sweater. For some reason he kept pouring boiling water from the kettle into a glass and then back into the kettle, constantly shaking and spilling water as he did so. The poor man was so excited it seemed a miracle nobody was scalded before the tea was eventually passed to me.

Süleyman sat me down and asked about my trip, but could not believe that I had been to so many countries. He made me name them all, and looked extremely sceptical about Liechtenstein. Then he found a map of Turkey and unfolded it onto a table in front of us. His finger fell on Istanbul, the city I was so looking forward to visiting that was now just a couple of days' ride away. Süleyman suddenly started to count on his fingers. "One, two, three, four, five." He switched to the other hand and continued, slowly and deliberately. "Six, seven, eight, nine, ten." Then back to the first hand, "Eleven, twelve, thirteen, fifteen." He'd missed out fourteen, but, perhaps realising his mistake he moved to his second hand again and held up the first finger. He paused, looking unsure.

"Sixteen," I helped him.

"Yes, sixteen," and then he held up the seventeenth finger and proudly declared, "Eighteen million people in Istanbul."

Ah, it was the greatest glass of tea that I ever had, and a most amazing introduction to the famed Turkish hospitality, but unfortunately I could not stay forever, and I was convinced that there was plenty more of it ahead. I said farewell to the still-grinning Süleyman and cycled off into town in a fabulous mood. I found an ATM and a supermarket, in the fruit section of which there was an old man working polishing apples. Just think of that. An old man, polishing apples. This really did seem like a wonderful place. I went outside and sat on a bench to eat and watch the people. All kinds of people there were too. Most of them wore Western clothes, the older women covered their heads, the younger women did not. That being said, there were not too many women about. It was about eighty percent men in the streets. Certainly not my preferred ratio, but at least the people looked happy. The miserable faces of Eastern Europe had been replaced by smiles that held so much promise for the road ahead.

Unfortunately for me, the road ahead had other ideas, and I was about to endure one of the most difficult days of the trip. It started overnight with a heavy rainfall, which was followed by the sudden onset of freezing temperatures in the hours before dawn. Disappointed to see that I had not yet left winter behind, I awoke to light snow and began the process of dismantling my tent. Unfortunately, the rainwater which had seeped into everything had now frozen solid. The poles were frozen together, the poles were frozen to the tent fabric, the pegs were frozen to the ground, the tent was frozen to the pegs, the pegs were frozen to my hand, and my hand was just frozen. It took me the best part of an hour of rubbing and breathing on everything to get it sufficiently thawed out to be able to disassemble it before I was ready to get on my way.

Except I still wasn't yet ready to get on my way because I now had to turn my attentions to my bike. My first concern was the brakes. The brake levers were frozen solid, the brake units themselves were frozen solid, and the cable was frozen solid within the housing that surrounded it. I once again set about the process of thawing everything, but I could not get the cables moving as it was proving very difficult to rub or breathe upon a cable encased in housing. I gave up and tried the gears, and found the same problem. Things got worse as I pulled hard on the gear cable to try and get it moving again and it snapped. "Oh, bother," I said politely and calmly, or something along those lines. I had a spare gear cable with me, but it was not of too much use, as I stupidly had no cable cutters and so I could not install it.

I decided the thing to do was to just start cycling and see how things would go. The road, which was at least a quiet one, went gently uphill for a while and I ground along noisily in one gear. But then I came to a downhill, and I had to get off and walk because I had no brakes. The situation was ridiculous. I got back to cycling slowly along on the next flat section but knew that I really needed to stop again and try to get things working better, so I pulled off into a lay-by to do so. Unfortunately, what I did not see until too late was the big puddle that was stretching across the width of this lay-by. I noticed it just the briefest of split seconds before I hit it, and, with no time to stop, I decided instinctively to just try and power straight through it. Sadly, this puddle was much deeper than it looked, and my bike ground to a halt halfway across. Not wanting to put my feet down into this murky water I jumped off with, I must say, outstanding agility and skill, and landed on a small mud island in the centre of the puddle. My feet were dry but any elation I may have felt at this small victory was cut short by the sight of my bicycle collapsing into the puddle. My front right pannier, the one with my passport, wallet, camera, diaries, books and important papers, broke off and became submerged in the dirty water, while the rear right pannier, that containing my laptop, took the weight of the fall as it landed in the puddle. I quickly grabbed the front pannier and hurled it onto the mud island, then reached down and hauled the bike into an upright position so that only the wheels were underwater now. With everything in relative safety I paused for a moment in this absurd position, bent over holding the bike up in a muddy puddle, no real idea as to how to extricate it, and wondering just what in the world I had done to deserve all of this.

With the kind of untapped superhuman strength that people are sometimes able to use to lift cars off of trapped victims in extreme situations, I managed to propel my bike out of the muddy waters. After leaning it down I then went through my bags to survey the damage. Luckily my laptop was unharmed, my decision to triple bag that proving to be one of my finer achievements. As for the front pannier, rather a lot of water had seeped in, although my passport was only a little damp and everything else was okay after being dried off. Nevertheless, going through each item in turn and drying it off with tissue paper wasted a lot of time, on top of all that had already been lost. Not that I had any idea what the time was, as I could not access the time function on my cycle computer – the button was frozen solid.

All of these delays were especially frustrating as I actually had a place to stay that evening, with a man named Özgür just outside of Istanbul, eighty kilometres from where I had started the day (and seventy-seven kilometres from where I now stood, four hours into the day). I so very much wanted to get there, to have a nice, warm place to dry myself, my clothes, my bike, my tent. It was tantalisingly close, and yet felt so impossibly far away.

I finally got my brakes working and carried on into the snowy wind. I hadn't eaten all day, and after twenty kilometres struggling on up the hills without being able to change gears, I thought I'd really better stop and refuel before I collapsed (even though collapsing felt like a *great* idea). I pulled into another lay-by and then, just when it looked like I might finally get the chance of a rest, a gang of wild dogs appeared from the nearby trees, barking at me angrily, and very persuasively encouraging me to get the hell out of their territory. Without further ado I turned my bike around and returned to the cold and lonely road.

Wondering just what was coming next to try and strike me down, I arrived in the town of Subaşı, where I found a brief reprieve from my woes in the form of a mechanic. He was a young man in his thirties who happily lent me a cable cutter, then rushed off to find me a glass of sweet tea. Tajuk was a friendly chap, dirty-faced and wearing a bobble hat and overalls, although he spoke no English, and I had no time. I drank my tea quickly and set to work. I had to chip more ice off the bike to thread the cable through, and in my frantic jabbing I managed to cut my hand quite badly. Tajuk soon came to my aid with a box of plasters, giving me one to cover the cut. Perhaps worried that he wasn't being hospitable enough, he gave me another to wrap over the top of the first and then, no doubt thinking that I was very unlikely to make it through the rest of the day without further injury, he insisted I take the whole box.

After this simple act of kindness I now had my full range of gears and a working set of brakes. As I climbed a hill out of Subaşı I heard the call to prayer ringing out from a mosque and could see a Turkish flag fluttering in the breeze, reminding me that, for better or worse, I was a long way from home and in the midst of a terrific adventure here. It seemed, just for a fleeting moment, like everything was going to be just fine.

It wasn't though. Next to join my day of horrors was another gang of wild dogs. The stray dogs in this part of Turkey were just plain mean and nasty, and very territorial. These ones were quite a long way from me in a field as I cycled into what they considered their land, but unfortunately I was going up a steep hill. They started barking at me and ran over towards the highway, looking worryingly vicious. There were six of them and they really looked like they meant business, so I stepped on the pedals and started going up the hill as fast as my tired legs could carry me. I looked back and saw them entering the roadway from the opposite side of the six-lane highway, which at this moment contained absolutely no traffic whatsoever. Why was it that there were no big trucks around, the one time I actually needed them?

Some of the dogs crossed over onto my side of the highway and they pursued me menacingly, now spread out behind me in a line. They basically had one lane each, sprinting as if they were in the Olympics. It was an absurd sight, six ferocious, snarling dogs spread out across what was essentially a traffic-free motorway, gaining ground on me as I pedalled furiously. They probably won't even include this scene in the film, as it would be considered too unrealistic. Finally I arrived at the top of the climb, heart racing, blood pumping, gasping for breath, but with just enough energy to turn back with my middle finger raised to coolly whisper, "So long, suckers," before zooming away from danger down the hill.

But do you believe this was the end of my trials? Not a chance. Next I passed some sort of quarry, and the road suddenly became insanely busy with yellow dumper trucks carrying materials for the construction of a new airport, and a new bridge, and new roads of all kinds for the ever expanding Istanbul. As these juggernauts passed me they sprayed a fine mist of water, mud, and filth from their back tyres that went all over me, even with me cycling on the shoulder. One after another, after another, they kept lumbering past, throwing this disgusting spray upon me.

Getting covered in an ever expanding layer of filth was just about tolerable because I at least had the shoulder to cycle in, but then the road inexplicably shrank to just one lane in each direction, and I had to share a lane with these yellow monsters. Of course most of the drivers had no patience and tried risky overtakes justified by the prior use of the 'nice to see you, welcome to my country, but I might be about to kill you' horn beep. On the worst occasion a passing truck, seeing something coming the other way, suddenly moved back in towards me. I dived out of the way into the dirt, just in time, but this near-death experience was the final straw. All of my pent-up happiness boiled over as I let out a joyous scream in the direction of the departing truck that I do not wish to repeat, but that I can reveal rhymed with "Duck flew!" This felt so good that I could hardly contain myself when the next truck driver blared his horn as he came storming past and I let out a second delighted chorus, this one rhyming with "Duck flew flew, flew ducking duck!"

Thankfully the shoulder soon returned and I composed myself, though I could not help but wonder what would be next. I still had a bit of a way to go to get to Özgür's, although I could no longer tell exactly how far as my cycle computer was now broken. Then I ripped my trousers on the chainring of my bike, which, honestly, seemed like one of the better experiences of my day. *What's next? What's next for me, oh cruel world?'* Just then a flock of birds flew over my head, and one of them saw this as a good opportunity to relieve himself. A splatter of white bird poop landed directly in front of me, in the road, literally a centimetre from my front wheel. If it had been half a millisecond later, it would have landed right on my head. *'Wow,'* I thought. *'It must be my lucky day.'*

The final challenge was a last, steep climb to Özgür's town on a narrow and twisting road, which was very busy with people driving home in the dark. I got chased by one more vicious dog on this road, though I could hardly raise the energy to care any more. A man driving his car actually saw this, and slowed down to beep his horn and swerve at the dog to get it to leave me alone. It was a small act of kindness that showed me that not everyone in a car was in such a rush as to not give a duck about a poor down-on-his-luck cyclist. I raised a hand in grateful salute.

At long, long last I arrived at Özgür's apartment. I should think that when he'd originally offered to host me, he did not exactly have in mind the battered and bedraggled figure that would finally crawl up to his door. I was quite literally covered in mud and filth from head to toe. I was exhausted, I had hardly eaten all day, I was dripping wet, I was probably bleeding again, I can't remember. I was on the verge of collapsing, I was practically on my knees. Özgür opened the door.

"Help... me..." I croaked.

13

Bahçeköy, Turkey
27th January 2014

Özgür, recovering well from the shock of seeing me in such a sorry mess, moved swiftly into action. With me and my bike standing on his doorstep competing to see which one of us could look the most filthy, he ran off to fetch a bucket of cold water. For a moment I feared he was going to pour it over me as he came running back, and I think in many ways he would have sorely liked to, but he kindly reserved it for the bike. After several trips back and forth with the bucket my bike was clean, relatively speaking, and it was my turn. I was ushered inside Özgür's apartment and directed towards the shower, where I spent the next few hours disinfecting myself and all of my belongings. Emerging from the bathroom I felt like a new man, and a delicious dinner soon followed courtesy of Özgür's lovely old mother. I was made to feel so very welcome into their home, and once again the incredible kindness of strangers had given me a lift when I needed it most.

Özgür was a soft-spoken man in this thirties, the kind of gentle, warm-hearted soul that you could not imagine ever hurting a fly. He lived alone with his mother, a short, white-haired woman who had the cheeky grin of a seven-year-old, in a little apartment overlooking the small town. It was a perfect place for me to recover for a couple of days, and yet, despite the relaxed atmosphere, I soon fell ill. What had made me sick I could not say. Sleeping out in the cold was one possibility, or perhaps inhaling the muddy road spray from a thousand passing trucks. Personally, I thought I might have drunk too much tea. That would explain why I failed to recover despite Özgür's mother forcing me to drink glass after glass of it. After a couple of days I was supposed to leave and cycle into Istanbul, where I had a place to stay, ironically enough, with a doctor. The trouble was that I just did not feel up to cycling, leaving me in this terrible catch-22 position of having a man who might be able to make me better, but not being able to get to him.

One thing that was not aiding my recovery was the fact that Özgür's apartment was directly opposite a mosque, which meant that five times a day, most annoyingly at sunrise, a very distinctive sound would wail out from the speakers on the minaret. Most of the time I loved to hear the call to prayer; it was the soundtrack to Turkey, a constant reminder that I was heading east, far away from the familiar. But hearing it at such close proximity, at five in the morning, with a headache, I must admit it began to lose its appeal.

After five days at Özgür's I still felt unwell, but I decided that I was probably never going to get better, and I still needed to cycle around the world, so I thought I'd just get on with it. Luckily for me, I had inadvertently stumbled upon the best way to cycle into Istanbul. It was notorious for being a very dangerous city to cycle into from the west, but I'd gone north of the city to visit Özgür, and I could now approach it heading south along the shoreline of the mighty Bosphorus. It was a much safer route, and a lot of the time I could cycle on the pavement and gaze out across the water to the far bank, where my eyes fell eagerly upon Asia for the first time.

My couchsurfing host was named Bekran. I was disappointed to find that he was not actually a doctor, only medical student, and he had little desire to diagnose my condition, nor even very much to offer in the way of sympathy. "You slept outside in this weather? Of course you have a headache." But he did give me some super strength painkillers, for which I was extremely grateful.

Because I'd been delayed in arriving, I could only stay one night with Bekran rather than the three originally planned, and so, with some reservation, I had to move to a hostel for a few days. This meant that for the first time I was heading into the historic centre – through the busy streets, across a bridge lined with hundreds of fishermen trying their luck in the Bosphorus, and on into the beating heart of central Istanbul. It was a beautiful, extraordinary place, with the architectural marvels of Hagia Sophia and the Blue Mosque facing one another across a public fountain in a park filled with excited people. I could see that this was really a special city, surely one of the world's greatest, alive with a vibrancy that attacked the senses from every angle.

My senses still weren't too keen on being attacked, however, and I was happy to get to the hostel to relax and continue my recovery. When I arrived I was extremely disappointed to find that the receptionist was not the most beautiful girl in the world. In fact, he wasn't even a girl. *'Well, this is a waste of eight pounds,'* I thought to myself as he showed me to my dormitory. Much to my continued dismay there weren't even any girls in there either, just an old Egyptian man of a quite astonishing appearance. The front of his dark head was bald, but at the back he had thick, grey dreadlocks that seemed to be hanging on for all they were worth. As if to balance it out, a long grey-white beard was also trussed into matching dreadlocks and descended all the way down his front to his groin. He introduced himself as Ibrahim.

"How do you like Istanbul?" I asked him.

"I don't like it," he snapped. "I don't like the touristy things. You've seen one church, you've seen them all. You've seen one mosque, you've seen them all."

"Oh," I was a little surprised by his negativity. "Well, why do you travel then? Do you like to meet people?"

"No. I hate people. They're all the same. Nothing interesting."

I was even more disappointed by this response. It was as if the old man had completely failed to notice that I was a person. A person that he was meeting, no less. We didn't talk much more after that. However, his snoring, farting and occasional random wailing certainly made my nights at the hostel once again memorable, for all the wrong reasons.

I needed to stay in Istanbul for a while to apply for visas to enter Iran and Tajikistan. The Iranian visa took several days to process and cost a lot of money. I'd decided that it was worth it, however, as I had heard and read so many interesting things about Iran from other cyclists, and I felt like I needed to go there and see it for myself. But I must say the enforced rest was certainly most welcome and gave me the chance to recover before continuing. It also gave my bike time to recover too, and I took the opportunity to replace the bottom bracket and to have my front rack welded back together by an old man in a tiny little workshop. I had to act as the old man's assistant, holding the rack up in tongs while he did the welding. In that moment I felt completely immersed amongst the life of the chaotic back streets, as all around me men hurried around carrying pipes and tyres to workshops, as others dodged through the crowds carrying trays of tea for the workers.

Fortunately, I managed to find new hosts for my last days in Istanbul, and on my way to their apartment I bumped into two other cycle tourists. They were a couple in their forties, a big, friendly man from New Zealand named Dino and his partner, Suzy, from the UK, who were also cycling across Europe and Asia to eventually visit Dino's family on the other side of the world. As we chatted in the street it became clear that they were planning to follow a similar route to me, and, although we had different immediate plans for Turkey, I felt confident that I was going to see them again somewhere along the road.

I was welcomed by my new host, a young American named Ross, who showed me quickly around the apartment he shared with his Turkish wife, Banu. He then had to leave for work, so he gave me a key, and just left me all alone to make myself at home. I found it really wonderful and amazing how trusting people could be. Once he was gone I quickly stripped the place of everything valuable, found a large amount of cash hidden in his room, stole his wife's jewellery, and made off with the telly. No, I didn't. Not really. Not at all. I was feeling better by now, so I went out, and I soaked up Istanbul all that

I could. It was such an amazing place to be, I just wanted to appreciate it while I had the chance.

On my last night in the city I sat and spoke with Chloe, another traveller who was also staying with Ross and Banu. She was a lovely girl, just visiting Istanbul for a week, and every day she went rushing out with a detailed itinerary, taking in all of the mosques and all of the museums. She asked me why it was that I did not do these tourist things. I thought for a moment, and then I told her that I preferred to just walk around and watch the people. From the shoe shiners who sat diligently waiting for custom and insisted that they could clean my muddy trainers up if only I'd give them the chance, to the men who sold me pomegranate juice from a stall, freshly squeezed from a great pile of the fruit stacked up head-high on the footpath, to the kids that I saw run into a sweet shop, then straight back out again with handfuls of stolen goodies, to the aproned man who ran after them, hopelessly brandishing a spatula, to the head-scarfed, shy women of the historic centre, to the confident, beautiful girls, walking down Istiklal with their hair flowing free, to the old men who sat and played chess in the park hour after hour, and to the young boys who jumped on the back of the tram and had a free ride, clinging on, giggling. In all of them was the beating heart of glorious Istanbul, before my very eyes. So tell me please: with all that to see, who wants to spend their afternoon in a flipping museum?

Progress Report
Istanbul, February 2014

1. Circumnavigate the planet

The Eiffel Tower is at a longitude of: 2.3° E.
Istanbul is at: 28.9° E.
So, 26.6° out of 360° around the planet.
(7.4 % of the way around.)

2. Do so using only my bicycle and boats

So far, so good.

3. Pass through antipodal points

Got one of them, I'm sure.

4. Visit all of the inhabited continents

One out of six, about as good as can be expected without leaving Europe.

5. Cycle at least 100,000 kilometres

13,233 kilometres completed. Just the 86,767 to go.

6. Cycle in 100 countries

Tweny-six down, seventy-four more needed.

7. Return with more money than I start with

Total spend: about £1,500 in six months.

PART TWO

ISTANBUL TO MORI

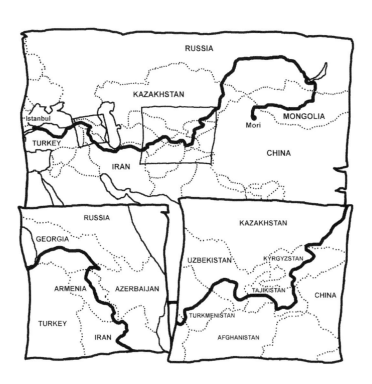

14

Istanbul, Turkey
8th February 2014

The ferry ride across the Bosphorus strait was not a long one – ten, maybe fifteen minutes of bumping across choppy, grey water. The mosques of the historic centre shrank behind the boat, as seagulls glided effortlessly alongside. It was in many ways quite an unremarkable little boat trip. Istanbul on the far side did not even look very much different from Istanbul on the near. Yet that ferry ride actually held great significance, for it took me – geographically, politically, officially – from Europe, the continent where I had spent most of my life, to Asia, a continent I had never been to before. As I wheeled my bike off the boat and through the melee of people at Kadıköy I had arrived at the start of a great unknown, of something that held the potential to be extraordinary. My mind, daydreaming about the adventures ahead, flitted briefly to my next planned transcontinental boat ride, which I imagined would most likely be from Singapore or Indonesia, to Australia, a year and a half or more in the future. It seemed ridiculous to imagine that I would be able to ride my bicycle all the way from Istanbul to Singapore, and yet I was also sure that it was possible. My tactic in Europe of not taking the most direct route, but weaving around, taking my time, cycling a distance four or five times greater than I needed to, had taught me patience. And in arriving in Istanbul I had learnt that I would always get where I was going eventually, so long as I just kept on moving. All

I had to do now was continue with this same basic outlook; take things one day at a time, immerse myself entirely within the journey, and the destination would surely someday appear.

Out of Istanbul I followed a fine bicycle path, the last that I would see for a very long time, and then headed off in the direction of Turkey's capital city, Ankara, 500 kilometres to the east. The road that took me there carried me through a variety of scenery as it rose up from fields of olive groves into mountains of pine forest, before plummeting down again towards a surreal landscape. Here I found great hills of bare rock that were coloured, by some freak quirk of nature, with horizontal stripes of light pink and yellow. It was an astonishing sight, like nothing I had ever seen before. I felt like I'd ridden so far that I'd made it to another planet.

One thing struck me during those early days in the Islamic world, and that was the extraordinary openness and warmth that the people showed towards me. Every single day, without fail, I would be invited to drink tea in one of the thousands of tea houses across Turkey. I would sit there, drinking the sweet tea, trying to communicate as best I could with the men (and it was always men) in the tea house, and not once was I ever allowed to pay. On one memorable occasion I was sat by the road taking a break, having just finished one chocolate spread sandwich and about to prepare another, when a man arrived on a tractor. The man, who was short and balding, with a black moustache and kind brown eyes, came over, shook my hand and insisted I follow him to a nearby tea house. He showed me inside the establishment, which I think he owned, and introduced me to his teenage son, who brought us tea. We sat and drank this in front of a TV that was showing music videos featuring surprisingly scantily clad women. I was able to establish that the man's name was Mehmet, but not a whole lot else, for, although he talked to me almost continuously, it was in a language that I did not understand. Neither was he the best at communicating by sign language, and I got little of what he meant, other than when he pointed at the girls on the TV and made an unmistakable body gesture to represent what he would like to do to them. His wife, by the way, was outside sweeping the driveway.

I thanked Mehmet for the tea and continued on my way, but a few kilometres later a tractor approached me from behind and beeped at me. It was a grinning Mehmet, back again, and he beckoned for me to go with him down a side road. Out of curiosity I went along, and followed the tractor as it led me to another tea house. Mehmet brought me inside, where we sat once again and drank tea, this time with some other men. It struck me as a little odd that a man who owned a tea house should be drinking tea elsewhere, but I could only guess that he had enjoyed sitting down to the first glass with me so much that he wanted to repeat the experience. I was a little concerned that he might go with me on his tractor all the way to Ankara, stopping to buy me tea at every opportunity, of which there would be many. This idea seemed even more plausible when we went back outside and Mehmet once again indicated that I should follow his tractor. This time he took us into a town, where we somehow lost one another without a proper goodbye. It was a little sad, but perhaps for the best. I really had drunk enough tea for the time being.

I arrived in Ankara to find a busy, modern, metropolitan city overrun with cars. It lacked the significant history of Istanbul and consequently felt more clinical and practical, with a lot less character about it. That was a shame because I had to spend close to two weeks in the city, its wealth of embassies and consulates making it a necessary pit stop for me to obtain more of the visas I needed for Central Asia. I spent many hours getting passport photos, filling in forms, photocopying things, and sitting in banks waiting to make payments, but eventually I was well on my way to gaining permission to enter Kazakhstan, Turkmenistan and Uzbekistan.

My long wait for visas was made worthwhile by the range of friendly hosts that I stayed with. They did their best to show me around the interesting parts of Ankara, which basically consisted of taking me to visit the mausoleum of Mustafa Kemal Atatürk. It would be difficult to overstate the impact of this man on Turkish history, or his place in the hearts of the nation. Without exception the impression I got from everyone in Turkey was that Atatürk was their hero. Following the fall of the Ottoman Empire, he had been the leader of the people during the Turkish War of Independence, ultimately leading them to victory and forming the new nation of Turkey. The name Atatürk literally means 'Father of the Turks' and was given to him in 1934, and forbidden to any other person.

There weren't too many other things to do in Ankara, and on one memorable morning I found myself alone at the main bus station, in what I'm sure will be another great movie scene:

> *Ryan Gosling is wandering aimlessly around Ankara's main bus station. The reason for this is not made clear to the viewer. He is looking devilishly handsome though. After several minutes of wandering aimlessly around, Gosling takes a seat on some steps. As he is waiting, looking all handsome and that, his eye is suddenly caught by a blonde girl, played by Kirsten Dunst, running towards him. It is Hanna, the girl he first met in Belarus, and with whom he spent Christmas in Ukraine. He is amazed that she has turned up here, completely out of the blue. He stands to meet her.*
>
> *"Hanna! What are you doing here?" he says, handsomely.*
>
> *"What do you mean? We agreed to meet here. I'm coming cycling with you, remember?"*
>
> *"Oh, how romantic. What a wonderful surprise!"*
>
> *"Surprise? What are you talking about? We arranged all of this. That's why we met here."*
>
> *"Yes, I'm flabbergasted. What a lovely surprise."*
>
> *"But we arranged all of this. I told you I was coming."*
>
> *"Shh, Hanna. That's not in the script. It's a romantic surprise, alright?"*

Okay, so our conversation didn't go exactly like that. Obviously I knew that Hanna was coming. But we had arranged everything not more than a few days earlier, when she had suddenly told me that she had a flight to Istanbul, and she wanted to track me down and join me cycling. I'd enjoyed my Christmas with her in Ukraine and, while I had my doubts that she was really the right girl for me, I welcomed this chance to spend a bit more time with her. The appeal of female company cycling alongside me was more than enough to override any doubts about our long term compatibility. The plan was that she would ride with me across the rest of Turkey and into Georgia and Armenia.

Unfortunately, things did not go exactly according to plan. For one thing, after two weeks of being stuck in Ankara with beautiful sunshine, it was inevitably raining on the day that we finally set off. That was the least of our worries, however, as the task of cycling out of Ankara, one of the least cycle-friendly cities I had ever seen, was made more difficult by Hanna feeling quite unwell. She fought through that first day, and we made it out of the city, but the next morning she really appeared to be struggling. And by 'appeared to be' I mean 'definitely was' and by 'struggling' I mean 'puking her guts up at the side of the road'. We made slow progress with lots of breaks, until eventually coming across a village where we went to look for a tea house so that she could get some rest. Like in tea houses all across Turkey we found a room full of content old men sitting in flat caps around a warm stove, a photo of Atatürk beaming down from the wall. The sight of a blonde-haired girl appearing in the room aside, this was a day just like any other for these men. The owner, Hasan, could speak a few words of English and welcomed us inside, pouring us each an extra-large glass and placing four sugar cubes on the side. I put all four in and should have quite liked to have added the one that Hanna had left too, but Hasan had kindly given us a packet of biscuits as well, so my sweet tooth was quite satisfied.

With Hanna feeling a bit better we decided to try and continue, and took a small road out of the village which was technically closed, but that I saw would connect to the highway further up. But before we got that far Hanna had to stop again. Her petite body looked fragile and weak, and the Turkish hills were too much. She was really very sick, and it was clear that she could not go on. It was only midday, but I suggested that we stop again to rest.

I scouted the area for a good place for the tent but there was nowhere suitable, so I went back to Hanna and laid out all of our sleeping bags in the road and told her to sleep. As the road was closed it clearly wasn't going to be used by anyone, and so I thought it might as well be used as a bed. Hanna went to sleep, snug as a bug in all those sleeping bags, and I did a little tinkering with my bike wheel, trying to think of a plan. After we'd been there for a couple of hours with nobody coming by I was starting to think that maybe we could just put up the tent right next to the road, which seemed like a pretty good plan, at least until I noticed the two policemen up on the highway shouting down at me.

Where we had been resting was just about within sight of the highway, but I hadn't thought that anybody would notice us as they zoomed past. Somebody clearly had, however, and they were probably quite shocked at the sight of two bicycles lying in the road, one with its wheel removed, a pale-faced woman lying in the road in what looked like some sort of body bag, and a man sat near her stuffing his face with pizza crackers.

"Get up Hanna!" I cried. "And act less dead please!"

I ran over to the policemen who, thankfully, were very friendly. Once they heard our story they were keen to help, and quickly organised a place for us to stay back in the village. We followed their car back down the hill, where they left us in the care of a shopkeeper. Kazim was a man in his fifties, a little overweight, with a neat moustache, flat cap, and spectacles that sat right on the end of his nose. He had a face that seemed to be friendly and angry all at the same time. After forcing us to drink another glass of tea, he then led us a little way from the shop to an old house where we would be staying. It appeared to be his former home and was now completely empty, but there was a sofa outside that he insisted we bring in. That took a considerable effort, with him and I struggling to squeeze the thing in through the door frame for a long time, twisting it, turning it, shouting at each other, and forcing it through, until eventually it was inside. Kazim left us to it, and I told Hanna to sit down while I brought the bikes and bags inside. When I came back, she was sitting on the cold, hard floor.

"What are you doing? Why aren't you sitting on the sofa?"

"It's soaking wet!"

I set up all of the warmest sleeping bags on the floor and let Hanna get some much needed rest, then went and sat out on the doorstep of our new home. We were on a little hill, and I looked out over the village of orange-tiled roofs, white minaret at the heart of it, and yellow, grassy hills all around. I listened for a while to sheep bleating and dogs barking, until they were interrupted by the call to prayer ringing out from the mosque, bouncing and echoing from the hills. I felt happy to be here, comforted once again by the kindness these people had shown us, and only hoping Hanna would be better soon.

The next day Hanna was not better, and we decided to spend a second night in the village. By the end of this rest day she had perked up a bit and begun to hold down some food, so the next day we had another go at cycling. This time we made quite good progress, but there was still something really not right about Hanna, and cycling through the hilly terrain we were in was not helping. We camped that night, and I laid awake for most of it wondering just what to do. Morning came and I felt Hanna's pulse. Her resting heart rate, first thing in the morning, when it should've been at its lowest, was over one hundred. Clearly this was not normal. I turned to her and prepared for a difficult discussion and with much regret said to her, "Hanna, I think you need to go home. You aren't well. You should be sleeping in a warm bed, you should be eating real food, you should be resting." There would be a time for cycling over mountains, for sleeping in a tent, for eating chocolate spread sandwiches, but that time was not now, not for her. She nodded sadly.

The road was mercifully quite flat to the next big town of Kırıkkale, and so we were able to cycle there together. Hanna booked a bus back to Istanbul for the following morning and, with just one last night together we decided to splash out on a hotel, before going out to eat an authentic Turkish dinner. As we walked the busy streets looking for a traditional food called kumpir, a sort of baked potato with an excessive number of fillings, a man approached us. We were obviously strangers in town, and probably looked a little lost, so he wanted to help us. He couldn't speak English, but was fluent in German, and I think I might have fooled him into thinking I was too with an extraordinarily well pronounced, "Was ist dein name?" It was so well pronounced, in fact, that I think he may even have believed I *was* German. He answered that his name was Osman, and he seemed determined to help find us a place to eat.

We walked up and down the streets of Kırıkkale, following Osman as he went in and out of places asking, without success, if they served kumpir. All the time he continued talking to us in German, and Hanna, so good with languages, nodded along and translated bits for me. He was a very nice man, well built with broad shoulders under a dark coat, with slightly grey, slightly curling hair. In the film he'll be played by David Hasselhoff. He walked with a limp, but in a forth-right fashion, and whenever we had to cross the road he would step right out into traffic with his arm raised to call it to a halt before waving us across. Finally, we ended up in a fast food restaurant, where they did not sell kumpir, but they did sell french fries in a wrap. It looked like an intriguing concept, and we were getting a bit tired of walking around, so we decided to stay and try some.

Hanna and I sat upstairs to eat our french fries wraps, which did not taste as good as they might sound, in plastic booths that looked just like in McDonald's. It was a long way from the romantic final meal together I had envisaged. The food was far too starch-heavy, especially as it came with a quite unnecessary extra helping of fries. If fries in a wrap with a side of fries was typical Turkish food, then Turkish cuisine was simply not what I had hoped it might be. Then there was the uncomfortable furniture and the headache-inducing bright lights. But I suppose the biggest mood killer of all was the fifty-year-old man with a passing resemblance to David Hasselhoff who had sat himself down at the table and continued to regale us with stories in German.

After our romantic meal for three, Osman next declared that he would like to take us for chai. We then walked halfway across town, past a great many suitable tea houses, until we arrived at one that he liked the look of. We sat outside and I noticed that they served some traditional Turkish food too.

"This would have been a nice place to eat," I said to Hanna.

"Shhh," she replied.

Osman ordered us all tea and was so into speaking German that he even accidentally said, "Danke," to the man who brought it out. This Turkish waiter, to his very great credit, replied, "Bitte."

For another hour or two Hanna listened patiently to more of Osman's German stories, while I just looked around and thought about how wonderful and alive the Turkish streets were by night.

Finally, we said "Gute nacht" to Osman, and Hanna and I escaped back to our hotel. We both collapsed onto the bed, exhausted.

After a while Hanna turned to me and said, "I've just realised... I don't know how to speak German."

15

Kırıkkale, Turkey
2nd March 2014

The next morning I said my goodbyes to Hanna and then watched as her bus pulled away and she disappeared from my life forever. It all seemed so awfully unfair. She had only just arrived, and now she was gone again. I knew it was for the best though. Her health, of course, was the most important thing, the only thing that really mattered. But it was still all so terribly sad as I rode on alone out of Kırıkkale. I looked down at my talking bicycle and opened my mouth to speak. "Don't start," it said.

My spirits were soon lifted back up again by men offering me tea, and then even more so as I reached Cappadocia, an extraordinary part of the world that I had dreamed of visiting for many years. Here whole towns had been carved from the most unbelievable of rock formations, a series of nooks and caves that resembled something out of a sci-fi movie. The orange-yellow rocks rose into pointed peaks above the caves like flickering flames. In nearby Love Valley other rock pinnacles stood erect, pointing skywards. An information board suggested the valley's name came from these 'slightly phallic' structures, although there was nothing the least bit subtle about them. *'At least this proves that if there is a God, he's got a sense of humour,'* I thought, as I looked out over the valley of giant stone penis towers.

Cappadocia was one of the most amazing places that I'd ever visited. People had even lived in the cave towns until as recently as 1952, when they were evacuated on safety grounds. It must have been a shame, really, to have been forced to move from what was probably the most stunning place to live that one could ever imagine. "But this is the most beautiful home in the world," they must have protested, "and our ancestors have lived here for thousands of years."

And those evacuating them must have looked at them and replied, "Yeah, I know, but health and safety and all that."

I wasn't so worried about such things, and, because I could not be bothered to put my tent up, even went so far as to spend a night sleeping in one of the caves myself. It was away from the main tourist area and up a little hill. The cave, maybe five metres wide and eight metres deep, was carved into a large cone-shaped rock that looked like a giant teepee. It even had little cubbyholes in the walls and a window at the back, and offered a spectacular view over the Cappadocia region. It was AMAZING! In sleeping here I was fulfilling a lifelong ambition that, if I'm honest, I never even knew that I'd had. I was spending the night in a cave in Cappadocia! It was undoubtedly the coolest thing that I, or anybody else, had ever done.

As I sat at the front of my cave that night, looking out at a beautiful orange sunset, I realised something important. I was alone, but I was happy. Hanna had gone, and clearly the two of us were never meant to be, just like Karin and I were never meant to be either. I was no nearer to finding 'the one' than I'd been when I'd set off from Paris. But it didn't really matter. Of course I wanted to find love, but finding love would also complicate matters, which was why I had looked upon finding 'the one' as my get-out-of-jail-free card. It was the only legitimate excuse I could think of that would allow me to stop and give up on going right around the world, or on visiting a hundred countries, or all the other crazy challenges I'd set myself. But right now, I didn't want a get-out-of-jail-free card. I didn't want to have a reason to quit. I was in love alright, but it wasn't with a girl, it was with the journey, with the world. I was living my dream, and I felt a real sense of contentment. In that moment, sitting there alone at the edge of my cave, watching the sunset over the most extraordinary of places, I felt like I had all I really wanted.

From Cappadocia I continued cycling east, covering a great distance across vast empty lands before turning north. I wanted to go to Georgia, which meant following the Black Sea, and to get there I had to cross a mighty range of mountains that separated me from the coastline. I awoke one morning at 700 metres above sea level, with my challenge being to ride up and over a high pass that peaked at 2,200 metres. Considering the size of the task I was in a poor state of mind for it, feeling quite fatigued as I started out, trundling along at six kilometres per hour. To make matters worse the road was not following a river, as most climbs did, but instead choosing its own path, rising steeply, then dropping back down, then rising again. This was a frustrating and exhausting way to climb a mountain, and only added more and more to the total amount of altitude that I would have to gain.

After forty kilometres of this I passed through a small village and a group of men stopped me. With charming inevitability they asked if I would like to stop for tea, but I had to decline as I realised that if I hoped to make it over the summit before dark I had little time to waste. Instead I just asked them how much further it was to the top, and one of them told me that it was just four kilometres. This was excellent news, and most unexpected; perhaps I would have time to stop for tea after all. Then, just to be sure, and with some considerable over-familiarity, the man put his finger on my thigh and traced out a number four. Disappointingly, he did not stop there, and moved his finger over slightly to draw a zero next to it. It seemed I still had forty kilometres to go. Marvellous.

A short while later I passed through a bigger town, Şebinkarahisar, and then the real climb began. Up until the town, I had been riding through relatively uninteresting scenery on a good road with a fair bit of traffic. Beyond it the road suddenly narrowed and the traffic thinned to almost nothing as I made my way up through a dramatic canyon. This was obviously not a frequently used road, and it wasn't too long before I found myself being stopped by a concerned police car. As ever there was a language barrier, and I stood there feeling frustrated as one of the officers blocked my path while the other played with his phone for ten minutes. Eventually, he got someone on the line who could speak English, and he passed it to me:

"Hello?" I said.

"Hello. This is the commander."

"Hello commander."

"The weather is very slowly."

"What?"

"The weather is very slowly."

"What?"

"The weather is very snowy."

"Oh! Okay."

"Okay?"

"Okay."

"Okay?"

"Okay."

"Okay."

"Okay!"

After this very helpful conversation, the officers that were with me, seeing that I was not put off by the idea of a little snow, drew me a diagram. It was pretty good, and showed me that we were now at an altitude of 1,600 metres, and that the summit, at 2,200 metres, was another eighteen kilometres away. It was three in the afternoon now, and I calculated that I had just enough time to get up to the top of the pass before it got dark at six. Whether I would have time to make it down the other side was another matter, but by now I had a serious case of summit fever, and nothing was going to stop my relentless crawl upwards.

I hurried through ten kilometres in the next hour, leaving me with just eight kilometres to go as the road then began to climb more steeply in a series of switchbacks. I reached the snow line and saw that the commander had known what he was talking about, with heavy snow at the roadside and more falling softly from the sky above. I was a little worried that the road ahead might be closed, as I had seen no traffic at all for half an hour, but then a big lorry came down the switchbacks towards me. The truck came to a halt beside me and the driver leaned out of the cab window. I couldn't understand what he said to me, but the implication was obvious enough, as his sign language was very good. I was particularly taken by his impression of a dead man. The message was clear – continue cycling up this mountain now and you will not live to see the other side.

I thought he was being a little pessimistic, so I carried right along. The road became ever more difficult, climbing steeper and steeper as I got higher and higher. The snow was now piled high at the roadside and a swirling wind was blowing it across the road where it formed ridges and froze. The cycling was now a kind of torture, with the biting cold wind and the hazardous road surface. But there was no turning back now. I'd come too far, it was all or nothing. Daylight was dwindling, my legs were aching, but I just kept pressing on through the pain, almost mechanically, up and up, edging towards my goal.

And then finally I saw the silhouette of a building through the whiteness. It marked the summit, I was sure. I turned the final switchback and headed towards it, stopping only to pose briefly with a photo next to a summit sign in the last of the day's light. I had made it, this was the top. The building was occupied by a team of snowplough drivers. They were hanging out of the windows to see me cycle up. One man ran over to me and insisted that I come inside. I could not have refused even if I'd wanted to, as he practically bundled me in out of the cold. The warmth of the building hit me like a very comforting sledgehammer. I was at the highest point of my journey so far, at the top of a windswept mountain pass, and of course there was a Turkish man handing me a glass of tea. Hamdy showed me around, and I was soon enjoying a warm shower, a warm meal, and a night in a warm bed. Turkish hospitality had extended to the most extraordinary of places.

I slept fitfully that night, constantly being disturbed by the noise of the blizzard that battered against the boarded up window beside my bed, and of the snowploughs boldly heading out to battle it. Come morning I ran upstairs to look out of the windows there, the only ones that were not boarded up, and was alarmed by what I saw. The snow was still falling, almost horizontally in the strong wind, and the road had almost disappeared under a blanket of white. I watched as a car that was bravely trying to persevere over the pass skidded and became stuck in a snowdrift. It looked as if I might be moving into the plough house on a more permanent basis.

Over a leisurely breakfast Hamdy kept repeating the words, "Problem, big problem," to me. The drivers clearly did not think I would be able to ride my bicycle down from this mountain, but when I went upstairs again I saw that the snow had stopped, the wind had died down, and the car was gone. If a car could do it, I sure could. It felt like now was my chance. There was, however, much opposition to my going back out into the cold. Hamdy tried to hold me back, repeating, "Problem, problem," and then telling me that a police car was on its way up the mountain to get me down. That was it, there was no way I could ruin the journey now by being forced into a police car. I had to get down and quickly. There were no happy goodbyes, just me forcing my way back out into the cold with frustrated and concerned men watching me from the doorway.

There was plenty of snow and ice on the road, but it was all downhill and very steep, so there was no need at all for me to pedal. In fact, the only real challenge was in keeping my speed down to a safe fifteen kilometres per hour. To do this I not only constantly held down my front and back brakes, but also skidded my feet along in the snow to slow me further. It was not easy, but the snow-covered mountain scenery was an achingly beautiful reminder that this, right here, was exactly the sort of adventure I'd signed up for.

After fourteen kilometres of skidding along I made it down to below the snow line and finally returned to a clear, tarmac road. At almost this exact point I was met by a police car driving up the mountain. Three officers got out and walked over to me, before the magic of a smartphone was called upon to act as our translator. 'Road conditions bad. We go down together,' one of them typed. I pointed at the road, and indicated that it was clearly fine for cycling now. 'We got news that you were in trouble.'

"Not from me, you didn't."

Happy that I was safe, the police officers left me to it, although I didn't like to think about what might have happened had I not left the summit when I did. My unbroken line of travel without using motor vehicles overland had almost been put in jeopardy, albeit by the best intentions of kind strangers. It did, however, highlight one of the reasons why I was so keen to do every single inch under my own power. It was not just because of what one man had said to me one afternoon in a Nicaraguan café. That had been the catalyst, and I certainly thought of the idea of a continuous, entirely uninterrupted journey around the world by bicycle and boats as a beautiful, romantic concept, but it also ran a little deeper than that. During my time cycling, on my first trip and this one, I had gradually grown to dislike motor vehicles more and more, until I began to look at them with something like hatred. Society has a certain automatic acceptance of cars, but from the perspective of a cyclist I had seen them in a different light. I realised that if you were to start from scratch, and try to design a transportation system that was as dangerous, inefficient, uneconomical, polluting, and anti-social as possible, you would probably design the personal motor vehicle. People buy cars because they believe it gives them freedom, and yet surely the opposite is true. Cars enslave people, forcing them to work all the time to pay for the car, to essentially fund oil corporations that destroy the planet. And that's before mentioning that 3,000 people also die every day because of motor vehicles, a death toll that is for some reason deemed as acceptable to most people. I would sometimes wonder how that could possibly be the case. If microwaves, for example, killed 3,000 people every day, would people still feel comfortable using them? Would people not say, "This is madness," and look for a safer method of cooking their food? With these thoughts constantly being reinforced every day that I shared the roads with reckless drivers I had, somewhere along the way, decided that I did not want to be a part of it. I just didn't want to use motor vehicles any more. Not at all. And I wanted to prove that bicycles could do anything that cars could, like getting over a snowy mountain pass, for example. I knew that having these extreme principles made me highly unusual, but I also hoped that if I could circumnavigate the entire planet without ever once getting in a motor vehicle, it might just inspire one or two people that they could perhaps do their shopping without one.

The road continued all the way down to the Black Sea, where I joined the shoulder of a major highway east towards the Georgian border. To my left, across the road, was the huge inland sea, and to my right, green hillsides covered in tea plantations. It was a nice place to be riding, but I was feeling exhausted from the exertions of coming over the mountain, and consequently had some reservations about an appointment that I'd made. I'd earlier been contacted online by a teacher, Ayşe, who'd asked me to stop by and help the kids at her school with their English. I'd been happy to agree, but began to regret it as I approached the town. Having to deal with a school of excited young kids wasn't high on my to-do list when I was in such a tired state.

I met with Ayşe and a couple of other teachers for lunch before going to the school, where it was revealed to me that I was not going to be talking with little kids, but was in fact on my way to a female-only boarding school, home to several hundred girls aged between fifteen and eighteen. For some reason this perked me up a little.

We walked to the school and entered through the gates together. Immediately girls started screaming. Some ran across the playground to me and asked questions, others were peering out of the windows of the buildings, still more giggled from on benches and behind trees. My arrival had caused quite a stir, and, perhaps for the first time on the whole journey, I actually began to feel like Ryan Gosling. I was quite unprepared for it. I'd certainly never had this much female attention before. *This is definitely not how I remember high school!* I thought.

As I locked up my bike and followed the teachers inside, one particularly bold girl came up and took my arm to walk me into class. I looked to Ayşe for help but the situation was beyond her control. It was all a bit much, although it was great to see young girls with so much confidence. All the way across rural Turkey I had only been seeing and meeting men, the women always pushed to the background. Here, at least, I saw the strong, confident females that suggested there was perhaps a chance of an equalling of the sexes in the future.

The classroom erupted with screaming and giggling when I walked in. I still had no real idea what was going on, other than that I now had a much better idea of what it must be like to be Justin Bieber. Ayşe introduced me and then the students fired questions at me in English. They were the usual questions that I got asked all the time, although they seemed somehow more fun to answer now. The novelty did start to wear a little thin after the fifth or sixth class that Ayşe dragged me to, however, and great credit must go to the one girl who stretched her vocabulary to ask me, "And what are your opinions of the Ottoman Empire?" I can only assume she was a little disappointed by my limited, uninspired, and some might say downright ignorant response.

My reward for all of this was to be offered a bed and given permission to spend the night at an all-girl boarding school. One might have considered that a little risky, but fortunately Ayşe saw the danger, and locked me in the medical building for the night. It was probably for the best.

16

Georgian border
19th March 2014

I felt sorry to be leaving Turkey after two wonderful months, but there was plenty more to look forward to as I moved on into the Caucasus. Crossing into Georgia did come as a bit of a culture shock though, as I abruptly exchanged the Islamic world for the Christian one. Mosques were replaced by monasteries, long dresses by short skirts, and, most striking of all, instead of men calling out for me to join them for a glass of chai, there were men calling out for me to join them for a glass of chacha. It didn't take long for me to discover that chacha was a homemade spirit similar to vodka, a sort of Georgian moonshine. I was told by the first group of men that invited me to join them at their broken picnic table beside the road that it was sixty-five percent alcohol, although I doubted that anybody really knew for sure. They encouraged me to down a shot with such merry enthusiasm that it was impossible to disappoint them. It tasted very much like paint thinner.

There were about seven or eight men around the table, of different ages but all dressed in the well-worn clothes of simple country folk. Introducing themselves to me, it seemed as if almost all of them were called George, and they were all very, very friendly. In fact, the George who sat beside me locked his arm through mine, while another put his hand on my thigh. I had heard that Georgian men were very comfortable with close physical contact, yet fiercely homophobic, and so I wasn't as alarmed by this attention as I might otherwise have been. I forgot all about cycling as the chacha flowed, and I was happy to accept when one of them invited me to stay with his family that night.

He was a short young guy of about twenty, with a closely cropped haircut and kind eyes, who helpfully distinguished himself from the rest of the Georges by shortening his name to Gio. I was led by Gio up a steep track to his simple stone house where I met with his mother and sister (his father was away working on a ship). Inside the house a small living room was centred around a wood-burning stove, with a sofa and lots of other chairs surrounding it, and a picture of Jesus looking down upon us from walls that were painted a garish pink. We sat around the stove and talked, as Gio and his sister were able to speak a little English, and during the course of the evening an awful lot of people came to visit. There must have been twenty or twenty-five people passing through at one time or another. They all seemed delighted by the novelty of meeting me, and the feeling was mutual – it was amazing for me to get a little insight into this humble Georgian way of life. Best of all was when a twelve-year-old named Luka showed up. He was a delightful, chubby boy, with a cheeky smile and a happy personality. I asked him what it was that he would like to do when he grew up, and he told me that he'd like to be a singer, so I asked him to sing. He responded by belting out a traditional Georgian song, and quite brilliantly too. *'Here's the real Georgian life,'* I thought, as I sat inside this genuine old stone house, listening to traditional music around the fire, with the men sat with arms draped affectionately over one another.

In the morning I awoke to a picture postcard view down the valley from the hillside home. The mountains were a vibrant green, the sky a brilliant blue, and the air felt warm and fresh. The family invited me to stay another day, and I could think of no good reason not to accept.

The neighbours next door were already out working hard in their fields, and I was invited over to see it by Luka, who had arrived to meet me with his beaming smile. I saw that they were planting potatoes, and it took an extraordinary team effort to do so. They had a small motorised plough, but it was clearly not the best, and it took four men working together, two pushing and two pulling, to get it to move through the field. Women followed along behind, spreading manure and fertiliser and finally planting the potatoes by hand. It was incredible to see this family working together, farming their land in the traditional way, just as they must have done for generations. I wanted to help, but these proud people strongly opposed the idea of their guest getting his hands dirty. All I could do was sit back and be grateful for the opportunity to see into the lives of a typical Georgian neighbourhood. The close-knit families, passionate religious beliefs and strong community values inspired me, the worryingly over-the-top homophobic statements and alcohol consumption less so.

I so very much appreciated the hospitality of these people, and there were sad goodbyes all round when it was finally time for me to move on. Gio's mother, who had not spoken one word of English the whole time, suddenly blurted out, "Stay!" But I couldn't, there was too much more out there waiting for me.

I took smaller roads east across Georgia, trying to avoid the main road as the standard of driving here was amongst the worst that I'd seen. The scenery was fantastic as I rode on through more green valleys, with the snowy peaks of mountain ranges away to either side of me, glistening like diamonds beneath the bright blue skies. Clear rivers and streams flowed down from the mountains, only adding to the idyllic landscape. I felt like I could have been back in Switzerland, or at least I did so long as I ignored the bad roads, litter that was strewn about everywhere, Ladas, shabby houses, and drunk men shouting at me.

In fact, it was the drunk men that sadly ended up ruining Georgia for me. Every day I would be stopped by them, and it was certainly one of my least favourite experiences to be shouted at by a very drunk man in a language that I did not understand, who would then get angry when I did not respond. On one memorable occasion I was requested to stop by two men on a bench and I did so before I realised just how drunk they really were. One of them, a red-faced, balding man, with a white beard that made him look a bit like a sunburnt Santa Claus, poured me a glass of wine as he walked over to me. Despite being remarkably intoxicated he did seem very friendly towards me. Too friendly, actually, as he leaned in for a kiss on the lips.

"Whoa! That ain't gonna happen, buddy!"

Disappointed, he offered me the glass, no doubt hoping that after a couple of drinks I might let my guard down. I looked at the wine. There was something dubious floating in it.

"No, that ain't gonna happen either, sorry."

But the drunks were not always so romantically inclined, and at other times I was asked for money or cigarettes, and one guy even slapped me in the face. He did it in a jovial way, but even so, he slapped me in the face. Eventually it got to the point that I decided not to stop and talk with anybody else who said hello at the side of the road for the rest of my time in Georgia. It was a real shame. I thought back to Turkey, where in two months I could not remember a single bad experience with anyone. In Georgia it happened a couple of times a day, and, whilst a lot of people were very nice, thanks to the alcohol problems I found myself longing to be back in the Islamic world and just enjoying a nice glass of tea.

I soon had the chance to do exactly that as I left Georgia behind and entered Azerbaijan. My plan was to cycle for just a couple of days here in a little loop, then return briefly back to Georgia before entering and going down through Armenia. This slightly confusing detour was the only way that I could visit all three of these countries, as the fierce hatred Azerbaijan and Armenia harbour for one another meant that the border between the two was firmly closed. I'd also read that I would not be able to enter Azerbaijan if I'd already been to Armenia, so visiting there first was my only option. When I got to the border between Georgia and Azerbaijan I was very careful not to mention my Armenia plan to the border control agents who, thinking I was on my way directly to Iran, allowed me in.

With just a couple of days in Azerbaijan I was determined to soak up all that I could of the country, and I was naturally delighted when I was almost immediately invited into a little café. Inside I sat and drank my tea, which here came with the terrific addition of a slice of lemon, as an old, head-scarfed woman smiled at me through gold teeth. Men who in Georgia might have been drunk, here sat around playing backgammon amicably, and I felt a twinge of happiness.

After this great welcome things only got better. In fact, it would be extremely difficult to convey just how fantastic my first hours of cycling in Azerbaijan really were. The sun was shining, the road was flat, the wind was at my back, and the people, the people were just awesome. Almost everyone waved and shouted greetings to me, and they seemed to sense my great mood and to share in it. I passed a couple of boys on bikes and fell into a really fun race with them which ultimately ended when I backed off and let one of the kids win. A short while after that I had another race, this time with a Lada that pulled out next to me. I was laughing and joking with the passengers as their old car struggled to pick up speed next to me, and this race ended much the same as the first. Everything here felt fun, everything felt safe. It would be no exaggeration to describe those first hours in Azerbaijan as the most fun cycling, with the most friendly people, that I could ever remember.

The next day I reached the town of Qazax, which was busy and alive with people. I sat on a bench and began to eat from my bag of dates. A boy of about eight or nine came along and started talking to me. He looked like a Victorian street urchin, with a dirty face and hands, and dark hair which splayed down over his forehead. I did not know what he was saying but I was suspicious, as back in Georgia, in a similar situation, a gypsy girl had grabbed a bunch of my bananas and made a run for it. Naturally enough, then, I guarded my dates carefully as he continued talking. Actually, we had rather a long conversation, goodness knows what about. I soon realised that he was a sweet kid as he nibbled his way through a packet of sesame seeds, spitting out the shells as he went. I wondered where he lived, what his story was. The dirt on his face and hands was not just day-to-day dirt, it was the kind of dirt that was always there. I guessed he must live on the streets. Then he offered me some sesame seeds. Embarrassed, I offered him the dates. He wouldn't take any, and I felt ashamed for having ever thought the worst of him. Before he left he forced me to open my hands, and then poured sesame seeds into them. My heart just melted.

I loved Azerbaijan and I would have enjoyed seeing more of the country, but the entry date of my Iranian visa meant that I soon had to head back. Fortunately, however, the small corner of Georgia that it was necessary for me to pass through to reach Armenia was populated almost entirely by Azeris, and consequently I got to enjoy a little more of their culture. On my one evening in this region I was called over to share yet another glass of tea with a group of men. It was wonderful to sit there with these Muslim men and think about just how far I had come from Paris. Behind me a man stood tending his cows beside my bike, around me a crowd of gold-toothed, leathery-skinned Azeris peered at me, and in front of me an old broken down car sat with its bonnet open as a horse and cart made its way along the road beyond. It was a fantastic scene, simply fantastic, and when the kindly man sitting next to me offered to let me sleep in his house that night, I happily accepted.

The man, named Ramis, had really quite a large belly, and with his greying moustache and hair I put him in his late fifties. To my astonishment he slammed down the bonnet of the beat up old car in front of us, and got in, instructing me to follow. I had to wait quite a while before I could follow anything, however, as it took a few goes for the old machine to kick into life. When it finally did there was then still the monumental task of completing a three point turn for it to undertake. The forward bit went okay, then Ramis rolled it back down the verge at the roadside, almost taking out the tea table and a cow or two along the way. It then took several attempts to get up enough power to drive back up onto the roadway, before finally we were on our way, with me following the trail of dark smoke coming from the exhaust pipe, which, incidentally, was tied on with a piece of string.

We trundled along to the wooden shack that Ramis called home, and I was encouraged to push my bike into the living room where it would be safe. Ramis then took me back outside and signalled that I should get in the car, as we were off to the shops. Oh dear. This was a bit awkward. Of course I would not be getting in any motor vehicle, least of all this one. Fortunately, as with almost all of the former Soviet states, people here spoke some Russian, and I had by now picked up a few words, just enough to be able to say, "Car, no. Bicycle, yes. Car, no." Ramis responded by saying the word for shop and making a cupping motion over his breasts, which I took to mean there was a big-chested woman working at the shop. This wasn't quite enough to swing it for me, however, and Ramis agreed to me staying in his house while he went to do the shopping.

But before he left I realised that it was important that he know I was a vegetarian, because if he brought home a steak it was going to be very rude and awkward for me not to eat it. The question was how to do it, as the Russian word for vegetarian was one of the many that I did not know. I tried making animal noises and saying, "No, no, no," but this only brought confused looks from the poor man. Then, in a moment of inspiration, I remembered the children's alphabet book that Dasha had given to me at Christmas. It had pictures of lots of different things in it, and I thought I could just point at all of the vegetables and say yes, and all of the animals and say no. It was a fine idea, a real success story for my brain. I ran off and fished it out of my panniers, and flicked through it in front of Ramis. The pictures were not as useful as I'd hoped. There weren't any vegetables, only one picture of some apples, which I pointed at and said, "Yes, yes." The only picture of an animal that one might associate with food was a pig, which I pointed at and said, "No, no," not realising until later the irony of this particular instruction to my Muslim host. Then, just to be sure, I flicked through the book and said no to a few other animals as well. Eventually I think Ramis had the message, and the message was, quite clearly, "Buy apples, don't buy pig, don't buy rabbit, don't buy fox, don't buy squirrel. Buy apples."

Ramis left to do the shopping, leaving me to relax for half an hour, before his car spluttered back up the driveway. He entered the house, as you may well have already guessed, carrying a huge bag of apples. I honestly thought we were going to be eating apples for dinner (which would have certainly been better than squirrel) but then Ramis found some potatoes and a jar of tomato sauce and made us a delicious meal. While we were enjoying this, and presumably to celebrate our new found friendship, he poured us each a large glass of cognac and proposed a toast. It was the strongest, most foul-tasting alcohol I had ever had the misfortune to taste. Ramis then interrupted the meal to take me into another room and show me a picture of Allah, indicating to me that he was a Muslim. The reason why he did this only became clear when he gave the next toast and I noticed that as he raised the glass to his lips he stopped short and didn't drink any. He pointed again towards Allah, and I twigged that he didn't drink because of his faith. Perhaps pleased for the opportunity to get rid of his alcohol he still egged me on to drink my shot, and so I gulped down the foul-tasting liquor once more, then looked at him with a rueful smile.

I arrived at the Armenian border on a cold, overcast morning and soon discovered that the 'Armenia won't care if you've been to Azerbaijan' theory was a load of baloney. The border guard, looking suspiciously Russian in his fur hat, paused his flicking through my passport as soon as he came upon the Azerbaijan visa, and went off to find an even more miserly official to interrogate me. I say interrogate, 'questioned' would probably be a more appropriate term, but interrogate just makes it sound more dramatic doesn't it? In the movie there will likely be some waterboarding. In reality I was standing outside talking to the man through the window of a booth.

"Why did you go to Azerbaijan?" he queried. "Why do you come to Armenia? Do you travel alone? Why do you travel alone? Do you have no friends? Why do you have no friends?" It went on and on. "Did you serve in the army? Why did you not serve in the army?" During the questioning another guard stepped out of the booth and the door handle fell off onto the floor. It was that kind of ramshackle setting. My interviewer was writing my answers down on nothing more than a piece of scrap paper. It was quite the dossier he was putting together. Eventually he was done with the questions and he handed me back my passport saying, "Welcome to Armenia," with a look that said, "We'll be watching you."

Well I was in Armenia and I felt like I had travelled back in time to the Soviet Union. Cold faces stared at me as I went to change money in a dilapidated building. Nobody spoke to me or said hello. People pushed into the queue in front of me. It was an unfriendly place. I walked outside, and it suddenly seemed freezing cold, the skies dark. A shiver ran down my spine. I started cycling on a narrow road, following a river up into a canyon, with imposing, grey mountains looming over me on both sides. It seemed a harsh and unforgiving place. The houses I saw looked miserable, matching the faces of the people. The contrast with Azerbaijan was almost unbelievable. All I wanted to do was to go back.

I was still feeling nervous following the difficulties at the border, and after twenty kilometres a white Lada pulled up just opposite me and a big man got out and walked towards me. He was wearing a uniform that looked like it belonged to an army general, although he told me, in a serious tone of voice, that he was police and that he needed to see my passport. It was ridiculous that a man like him – big, strong, intimidating – was driving around in such a silly little car, but there was no doubt I needed to take him seriously. I showed him my passport and he asked me a few more questions about what I was doing here, before, to my great relief, he nodded his head and left me to it. Even so it had been an unpleasant moment, and it occurred to me that nobody really knew that I was here in Armenia, and that it was a country that I knew almost nothing at all about. Paranoid visions of being taken away and genuinely interrogated, perhaps never to be seen again, crossed my mind as it began to rain and I continued on alone through the narrow canyon. I was honestly quite scared.

I carried on cycling and that night decided to seek out a guest house, as I wasn't too keen on wild camping in my present state of mind. This turned out to be a very good idea, as it gave me a chance to meet with some friendly Armenians, including the very kind woman running the guest house, and also to do a little research into the country online. This was enough to reassure me that I was actually in a safe enough place and that tourists, as a rule, generally did not go missing in Armenia.

Feeling more relaxed now I cycled south through the rest of the mountainous little nation. It was clearly a very poor place with grey, dilapidated towns and a population for whom it looked as if life was a terrible struggle. Life also became a struggle for me too, though for quite different reasons. It was the daily grind of cycling up and over extremely steep and high mountain passes covered in snow that took their toll on me. This, I knew, was not a fair comparison. I was aware of how self-inflicted my own troubles were. I chose to cycle over those mountains. I chose to sleep in a tent. I chose this life. Looking at the lives of people born to poverty with no prospects of escape from the way of life they were born to in little Armenian towns, I had no real right to complain. But by the morning of my last full day in Armenia, I felt like complaining anyway.

I had good reasons, though, beyond the fact that I had just spent a night in a bramble bush. I also had an awful toothache. It had been getting worse and worse for a few days, and I had by now realised that I needed to get to a dentist. Not an Armenian dentist, however, as given the rows of gold teeth that sparkled from every Armenian mouth, I would likely end up having a tooth removed and replaced with a piece of 24-carat. I needed to get to an Iranian dentist, and that meant getting to Iran, which was still one very high mountain pass away. As if the thought of slogging up yet another 2,000 metre ascent was not enough, I also had to do it into the face of a fearsome head-wind that was blowing at me down the valley. I was completely exhausted from days of similar climbs, my tooth was in agony, and I was really struggling. During my time in Armenia, almost for the first time in the whole trip, I had been finding the going really tough. I was starting to get really fed up of being alone all of the time, and of having been travelling for such a long time without having made very much actual progress towards Australia. I wished that I had some company. I wished that Daniel had come with me, my hapless sidekick who was so hapless that he forgot to show up for the ride. And what was more, going down to Iran had been his idea. I hadn't even wanted to go to Iran during the planning stage. I wouldn't even be slogging over these mountains if it wasn't for him. Yes, I remembered our conversation very well:

Daniel: "I want to go to Iran."

Me: "No, I think it's too dangerous. We might disappear or get beheaded or something."

Daniel: "No, no. It'll be fun. Let's go there."

Me: "Yeah, okay."

Of course, after Daniel had failed to join me I could have just changed my route, but his argument had been so damn persuasive. I'd also heard some positive things about Iran from other travellers, such as that they had proper dentists. I still had to get there, though, and I really did not feel like cycling up this mountain. I couldn't do it. I could not do it. So I gave up, and turned around to go back to the town I'd just passed through and find a hotel.

'No, no. I must not quit.' I was not a quitter. I turned back around again.

The wind hit me full in the face. *'Oh yeah, the wind.'* Then a car zoomed past, scaring me as it blasted its horn. *'Ah, I am so sick of those bloody horns! I've had enough!'* I turned around again, back toward the hotel.

'No. No. I can't quit.'

I realised that this farcical little episode was almost a metaphor for my whole journey. If I gave up on this day, just because the going was a little tough, what was to stop me quitting on the whole trip? I turned back around again, and started into the wind, with a renewed sense of determination. *'I can do this!'* I turned my frustration into aggression, and powered up the mountain. Very, very slowly.

After a few hours I reached a town higher up the valley, where some young guys called me over to a bar where they worked. They invited me inside and gave me food and water, and let me use the wifi, all for free. It was a nice gesture that lifted my spirits enormously.

Having learnt my lesson from arriving in Armenia unprepared, I made use of the internet here to do a little research into what I could expect from Iran, and checked out the British government website travel advice section:

'British travellers to Iran face greater risks than nationals of many other countries due to high levels of suspicion about the UK, and the UK government's limited ability to assist in any difficulty. There's a risk that British nationals could be arbitrarily detained in Iran despite their complete innocence. British nationals were arbitrarily detained in-'

Okay, I'd read enough of that. Nothing about dentists anyway.

But before I could be arbitrarily detained in Iran I still had to get up the rest of the mountain, and beyond the town the road climbed away from the valley in a series of steep switchbacks. These seemed to be never-ending as I crawled along, but I felt much better now, and I was determined to make it, no matter how long it took me. I climbed until I was once again above the snow line, with magnificent views of a sea of mountain ranges behind me. Up and up I went, until eventually, triumphantly, I reached the summit of the pass. I had made it. Armenia had proven by far my toughest challenge yet, but I had faced my demons and overcome them all. I felt, high up amongst those snowy peaks, like I was on top of the world. I felt like I could do anything now.

Which was lucky really, because ahead of me lay Iran.

17

Iranian border
9th April 2014

I was feeling both excited and nervous about the prospect of entering the Islamic Republic of Iran and crossing it by bicycle. I had heard such good things about the country from others that had been there, yet on the other hand I still couldn't entirely shake off the picture of Iran painted by the Western media and politicians as a dangerous, terrorist-ridden land. I also knew that, with no British embassy in the country, I was going to have to be very careful not to get myself into any trouble while I was there. With this in mind, on my last night in Armenia, with Iran just a few short kilometres away, I found a peaceful riverside camping spot and emptied out all of my possessions, going through all of them meticulously to ensure that I didn't have anything that the Iranians might not approve of. This might sound like an extreme thing to do, but considering that I was about to enter a country of strict Islamic laws that made owning playing cards illegal, I felt like I couldn't be too careful. I pulled out a copy of the FCO British Government Travel advice and read it through to help me:

'The FCO advise against all but essential travel to Iran.'

'Oh well,' I thought, 'Not much I can do about that now. Anyway, my travel is all but essential. I need to get to a dentist.'

I started with my clothes pannier.

'Men should wear long trousers and long-sleeve shirts.'

'Hmm... does that mean I should bin my shorts and short-sleeve shirts? Surely they can't be illegal, can they?'

I put them in the 'maybe' pile and moved on.

'Penalties for importing and possessing drugs are severe and enforced. Many individuals convicted of drug offences, including foreign nationals, have been executed.'

I threw my paracetamol away.

'Relationships between non-Muslim men and Muslim women are illegal. Sex outside of marriage is illegal under Iranian law and can carry the death penalty.'

'The death penalty! Holy moly!'

I looked at my condoms. Ever the optimist, I had quite a lot of them.

'These could definitely get me in trouble.'

As a non-Muslim man with a strong aversion to the death penalty, I probably wasn't going to be needing these condoms now, so I threw most of them on the rubbish pile. I decided it was worth keeping a few very well hidden ones though, on the off-chance that I might find 'the one', convert to Islam, and get married. I was only planning to be in the country a month, but stranger things had happened.

My moment of truth at the actual border arrived the next morning, at an obscure little outpost deep in a valley surrounded by imposing shark-teeth cliffs. With much more in the way of barbed wire than signs of life it seemed very much like the sort of place where solo travellers might disappear without a trace, and the apprehension I'd felt on entering Armenia returned once again as I prepared to move even further into the unknown. I passed anxiously through a couple of armed checkpoints, before going into a building to be questioned by a man whose own gun, tucked loosely into his belt, I noted was held together with Sellotape. He was particularly keen to know my father's name; I could only guess this was so that they'd know who to address the ransom note to, or the death certificate, perhaps. But I answered his questions sufficiently well as to be granted an entry stamp, and then it was only the burly man on customs who stood between me and Iranian soil. This was it. I wheeled my bike over to him, bracing myself for a thorough search of my bags and desperately hoping that he would not notice that I had my short shorts on under my long trousers. But then, instead of the expected intrusion into my privacy, the man simply nodded and waved me straight through. He didn't open a single bag, didn't ask me one question. Ruddy hell, I'd thrown away a whole box of johnnies for nothing!

My painless transition across the border was in sharp contrast to the pain that was coming, with ever increasing severity, from my tooth, as I took my first tentative pedal strokes in Iran. I was following the muddy brown river of the valley, Armenia still visible on the far bank, but it certainly felt like I had entered a completely different world. Sporadic dust-brown adobe houses seemed to rise straight out of the earth, and dark, Persian eyes peered out at me suspiciously from beneath covered heads. Throughout the trip my overloaded bicycle had identified me as an outsider, an anomaly, but now I felt monumentally out of place. I was like a lost boy, who had wandered too far, all alone in this far-flung, scary land. Feeling out of my depth, for the first hour in Iran I was cautious of everyone I saw. But then one kind, old gentleman came to my rescue and broke down the barriers, calling out to me and inviting me into his shop for a glass of tea.

Relieved to see a friendly face, I took a seat on a wooden stool in the middle of this man's shop which, I was delighted to see, stocked almost nothing other than biscuits. He poured me a hot glass of tea and gave it to me with a toothless grin that I thought quite consistent with a man who owns a shop stocking such items. I made a mental note not to bother asking him about a dentist, as I sipped on my tea and listened to the old fellow speak to me rapidly, with me doing my best to nod along in all the right places. But then the pain in my tooth, exacerbated by the hot liquid, suddenly went up a few notches. It was a screaming pain, absolute torture. As a rule I preferred to avoid taking painkillers, but right now there was no doubt that I needed some drugs, and I needed them fast. Such a shame I had thrown away my small stash of them in a blind panic the previous evening. I turned to the old man and, in a series of charades that blurred uncannily with reality, successfully conveyed to him that I was in agony. His reaction was to reach for a large cardboard box on a dusty back shelf and bring it down onto the desk before us. I looked inside and saw that it was filled to bursting with packets of pills and tablets, including several with the word Codeine on them. God bless you, sir!

But the drugs were not a long term solution, and I really did need to get to a dentist soon, a prospect that did not seem at all likely given that my riverside road continued to be very remote. I spent my first night wild camping in Iran struggling to sleep, because meeting a nice old man with a box of painkillers had unfortunately only had a marginal effect in terms of relieving both my anxiety about Iran, and the pain that throbbed in my right jaw.

The next morning I was outside of another village shop when I fell into conversation with a young English-speaking man, of whom I quickly noted two things. The first was that he had a large rifle slung across his back, which made me think I should be very nice to him. The second was that he had a lovely set of shiny white teeth, which made me think I should ask him about his dentist. I did both of these things.

"My dentist is in Tabriz," he said, citing the big city that was a few hundred kilometres away, and not exactly on my route. "The dentists in Tabriz are very good."

He then drew me a surprisingly good map of a shortcut to Tabriz through the mountains, and as he did so it was his dazzling pearly whites that had me convinced that Tabriz was where I needed to be.

The road through the mountains was a good one that took me up through a rocky grey landscape dotted with hardy shrubs, as the scenery continued to evolve from the forests of Armenia toward the deserts of the Middle East. I rode on through this pleasant scenery, occasionally being nice to men with guns and otherwise keeping my head down, until I arrived in a place called Ahar. This was my first experience of an Iranian town and it was a chaotic mess, heaving with cars and people, noises and smells. Horns beeped loudly everywhere as the streets clogged with traffic jams, macho men shouted and tossed live animals into trucks, women shuffled along covered head-to-toe in black burkas, others settled for just covering their hair, whilst a brave few skirted the legal requirement to cover their heads in public with scarves that hung back off the top of their hair. It occurred to me that this bustling town must be plenty big enough to have a dentist and, with my teeth in agony and Tabriz still a day's ride away, I stopped to make enquiries.

To my surprise the first locals that I asked directed me without hesitation towards a nondescript wooden door just a few feet away. After locking my bike up I cautiously went inside and climbed a flight of grimy stairs, at the top of which I found something that did look remarkably like a dentist's surgery, albeit a slightly primitive one. There was nobody there apart from the dentist himself, a middle-aged man who looked trustworthy enough, by which I mean he had a clean shirt on. I tried to explain my problem but he spoke no English, and just encouraged me over to the dental chair so that he could perform an examination. This procedure consisted of poking around in my mouth with a lolly stick, then stabbing rather violently at each and every one of my teeth with the blunt end of a pair of tweezers. After just a few minutes the inspection was complete (with more of my teeth in pain than when it had begun), and the dentist went over to his desk to write something down. I sat up to find that the previously empty room was now filled with the gawping faces of a dozen men. The dentist handed me a piece of paper on which he had written a bunch of squiggly lines, and I was encouraged to leave, my new entourage in tow. Back outside I tried to ask the men just what this coded message meant, and after looking at it they all rather worryingly pointed to their backsides and repeated a word that sounded an awful lot like 'poo'. Surely, I thought, this dentist could not really have examined my throbbing teeth and then written me a prescription to go away and take a good dump?

One of the men offered to walk me down the street, presumably to the nearest toilet, and, giving up control of my own destiny, I simply followed. But instead of the lavatory he led me to a small room where a head-scarfed young woman in a clinical white coat greeted me, looked at my piece of paper, and then ushered me behind a curtained off section at the back of the room. She then indicated to me that I should lie down on a bed and pull down my pants. This was the first interaction that I'd had with any woman in Iran, and I tell you what, I quite liked it, but warnings about the death penalty were still fresh in my mind, and I thought I'd better not get too excited. Besides, the massive syringe that the woman was pointing in my direction was a huge mood killer, as it dawned on me that the real reason I was here was to have an injection in my buttocks. Well, this seemed like a mightily unorthodox dental procedure to me, but I had to admit it was still more fun than having my teeth drilled. Even so, I wasn't convinced that Iran's Islamic laws wouldn't frown upon me for having something inserted into my butt by a woman I didn't know.

"Are you sure this is okay?" I asked, helplessly. "Shouldn't we get married first?"

She laughed, although I have to say I don't think it was at my joke, and stuck it in.

As I thanked the woman for her troubles and limped back outside it seemed that the injection had at least done its job. The pain in my teeth subsided quite quickly, although it may have been the case that the pain in my teeth only *appeared* to have subsided quickly, relative to the considerable pain that was now coursing through my left arse cheek. At least my toothache had not prevented me from cycling. Now resting my sore posterior on a bicycle saddle seemed an altogether unappealing prospect. Fortunately, a short, stocky man with a lazy eye and a determined monobrow clocked me hobbling past his computer shop and sympathetically invited me inside to take a seat, an invitation I was more than happy to accept when I saw the soft leather chair that was on offer. The man's name was Hossein, and he told me that I was welcome to sit and use the internet while he ran off to buy me a can of coke and a slice of cake. The heavily censored internet in Iran was so slow that Hossein had returned and I'd finished this most perfect of post-dentist snacks by the time my e-mails had loaded. When they finally did I saw that I'd received a message from Dino and Suzy, the couple that I'd met briefly in Istanbul who were themselves cycling from the UK to New Zealand. Knowing that we were all going the same way, naturally we had kept in touch, and this latest instalment revealed that they were in Tabriz, and were willing to wait for me there if I was nearby so that we could cycle on as a three. Well, I wasn't convinced that whatever had just been injected into my backside was going to provide a permanent fix for the problems in my mouth, and going to Tabriz to find a dentist equipped with more than a lolly stick and a pair of tweezers seemed a logical course of action anyway, but now I had a tremendous extra incentive. After all, what better way to banish the uneasiness I'd been feeling about being all alone in this foreign land than by teaming up with two fellow travellers, one of whom was quite big?

Hossein, evidently concerned that cake and coke wasn't a sufficient gift for a man that he didn't know, also bought me a pot of salad and some soup for lunch. He was such a lovely man, and it was the beginning of my introduction to the real and genuine kindness of the Iranian people. Shortly after thanking Hossein and hitting the road again (sitting a little lop-sided on my saddle), a car stopped next to me and I was invited to eat an omelette in a restaurant by two students. With my bottom still sore I accepted and enjoyed a delicious second lunch. Then a few kilometres further down the road another car stopped and an older man leapt out brandishing a big smile. *'Seriously?'* I thought. *'I really can't eat any more.'* But fortunately there weren't any restaurants nearby, and the man, Kamal, an English teacher with surprisingly bad English, only wanted to give me his phone number in case I should need any help while I was in his country.

I put this sudden popularity of mine down to a self-imposed nationality change that I had recently undergone. During my first couple of days in Iran people had been a little frosty with me, and it seemed that this detachment began at the moment when I revealed that I was from England, a perhaps understandable reaction given the relationship of the two countries. To counter this I had come up with another of my trademark cunning plans, and I'd started to tell people that I came from Scotland. This was not a lie, because Edinburgh had been my most recent home, so I had technically come from there.

And if the evidence of this day was anything to go by, people from Scotland were very much welcome in Iran. Either that, or the people of Iran had no idea where or what Scotland was.

I reached Tabriz early the next morning, and not before time either, as the beneficial effects I'd got from the injection had well and truly worn off overnight. The city turned out to be much bigger than I'd imagined, and the only map I had was a rather weather-beaten one that I'd scavenged from the side of the road. That didn't really matter though, because I didn't care where I was half as much as I cared where a dentist was in relation to me. To try to garner that information I stopped at some sort of office where I could see through the window a man sitting alone behind a big computer, and went inside to ask if he knew of anywhere that I might be able to use the internet. The man, Ali, was keen to help, and, once he had safely established that I was from Scotland, eagerly encouraged me to sit down and use his computer. Clearly trusting me to look after the office, he then ran off to buy me a packet of biscuits. This was certainly shaping up to be the sort of hospitable, biscuit-loving country that I'd been searching for all my life, but for once the sweet treats were not a welcome sight. The pain was now coursing through the entirety of my right jaw, and it seemed to be gaining in magnitude by the minute. It came in waves of excruciating torture, a pain the severity of which I had honestly never experienced before. The internet was again incredibly slow and finding the address of a dentist was frustratingly difficult, especially as every few minutes the pain would reach such an unbearable level that I had to go outside and scream like a madman.

Ali sensed my distress and, realising that the internet wasn't going to be fast enough to save me, he indicated that I should jump in the back of his car so that he could drive me quickly to get help. One could only imagine his confusion when, instead of gratefully accepting this kind offer of assistance, I, between screams, insisted that I really would rather ride my bicycle there.

All of this will probably make for a scene of high comedy in the movie, though in my agony I struggled to see the funny side as Ali drove his car randomly through the packed streets, with me following along behind on my bike. Every so often he would pull over and ask somebody for directions to a dentist, which, judging by the circles we kept going around in, didn't seem to be a very effective strategy. This farce went on for a frustratingly long time, until eventually an old man that he asked actually got in the car himself, and directed us personally. This was an extraordinary act of kindness for which I felt unbelievably grateful as we finally arrived at a dental surgery a few minutes later.

To my immense relief the experienced dentist here looked like he might actually know what he was doing, and if the certificates that plastered all the walls were anything to go by, he wasn't shy about advertising the fact. He took an x-ray and declared that he would need to anaesthetise my mouth and perform a root canal operation, for which I would have to pay ninety pounds. By this point I would have paid ninety pounds just for the anaesthetic, so I quickly coughed up the cash and Dr Meristagi, or Dr Merastagi, or Dr Miristagi, or Dr Merrastagi, depending on which certificate you looked at, went to work.

I'd never been so pleased to have someone stick a big needle in my gums. The terrible agony gave way to mere mild discomfort as my mouth turned numb and all was quite alright with the world again as I looked dreamily up at the white ceiling. Unfortunately, this moment of bliss was soon disturbed as the masked face of what I dearly hoped was the dentist appeared above me, wielding a Black & Decker cordless drill in a rather terrifying manner, and the operation began.

By some miracle it seemed like the dentist did know what he was doing, and after what felt like several hours he said that he was done, and declared my root canal operation to have been a complete success. At least I chose to believe that is what he declared, I couldn't really understand a word he said. But most importantly my own teeth were no longer torturing me, and the happiness that this engendered was multiplied by the sudden appearance at the dental surgery of Dino and Suzy. Back home in the UK Suzy worked as a detective, and it seemed she'd put some of her skills to good use to somehow track me down in this huge city.

We went together for a milkshake opposite the dental surgery, and as I sat there sucking my strawberry shake through a straw I felt a huge sense of relief. My tooth was finally better, and with any luck I'd never have to go through anything like that again, but I was also feeling very pleased that my early concerns about being in Iran had so quickly been erased by the cast of friendly characters that had led me to this point of salvation. Best of all I was now sitting with two friends, laughing and joking and enjoying a delicious dairy-based beverage, looking forward to all of the (hopefully less painful) adventures that we had ahead of us.

18

Tabriz, Iran
15th April 2014

I cycled with Dino and Suzy for nine days, from Tabriz to Iran's capital, Tehran. An immensely likeable couple in their forties, they hailed from England's south coast, but like me they had found that telling people their nationality didn't go down exceedingly well in Iran, and they had taken to saying that they were from New Zealand. In the case of Dino, at least, this was true, as he was born and grew up a Kiwi, his Maori heritage evidenced by his dark skin tone and flowing, curly, black hair. He was a fantastically laid-back man with a refreshingly carefree attitude to everything, while Suzy seemed to be the strong and sensible one holding everything together. The three of us immediately gelled well together as a team, and it was so nice, for the first time in months, to have company with me for an extended period. Our first night camping together we played an improvised game of boules using rocks. During the day we chatted about our journeys and raced each other. The next night I built a campfire and we sat around it talking into the night. I felt really lifted by these simple moments of comradeship that I missed out on when I was alone.

The road that we followed took us across a desert of dry, dusty rocks. Given its barren appearance this area was surprisingly populated, with towns and villages appearing frequently, and we had plenty of opportunities to embrace more of the incredible Iranian hospitality. People would constantly invite us to stop our pedalling and join them, offering us tea or food. For the locals, simply stopping their car, laying out a blanket, and having a picnic on the verge at the side of the road was common and normal behaviour, and we were often invited to join in with these picnics as we rode by. The people, in complete contrast to what we had been led to believe back home in the West, were some of the nicest, most friendly human beings on the planet.

An example of this came when we arrived one day upon the disorderly streets of a town called Mianeh. We'd only just pulled ourselves away from a group of workmen who had insisted that we sit down on the pavement with them and eat bread and cheese, when we were stopped by a well-dressed man who wanted to take a photograph with us. After obliging him, the man, Behrouz, then offered to take us all to a restaurant and buy us lunch. It had only been twenty minutes since we'd eaten breakfast, but he was so keen that it was quite simply impossible to say no. As we sat down and tucked into skewered kebabs, an old man also joined us at the table. Upon hearing of Dino and Suzy's nationality, he stated, in broken English but with great sincerity, "I want to go to New Zealand and live with the sheep."

We all paused for a moment to take in the gravity of this statement. I was frankly impressed by his knowledge of the country. But then he took things too far: "New Zealand is in Europe?"

After we had finished eating, Behrouz told us to follow him as he went outside and got on his moped. The three of us just shrugged our shoulders and decided that we'd better go along with it and see what would happen. We struggled to keep up with him as he weaved his bike through the gridlocked streets, almost getting taken out by a car at one point, until he made a sudden left turn down a little alleyway. The street was lined with stalls and carts of various goods and I only just caught sight of Behrouz making another turn and disappearing in amongst them. I followed him and was amazed to find myself in a typical Iranian bazaar, an indoor market of small shops crammed tightly together and selling an incredible variety of goods. A narrow passageway led in past clothes stalls and butchers, craft stores and greengrocers. The scent of great barrels of spices wafted towards my nostrils as I weaved my loaded bicycle in and out between women out shopping in their long black burkas. These poor women dived out of the way left and right, no doubt a little taken aback by the sight of a moped zipping through the narrow walkway of their bazaar, followed by three panting foreigners on bicycles. It was a completely insane moment, probably the most fantastic of the trip for me so far, with it crossing my mind just how very far from home I now was as I partook in this crazy scene. Eventually Behrouz came to a halt at a jewellery shop. He explained that he was the owner of this store, and had brought us here to show it to us. There were men sitting in the small shop, hand crafting pieces of fine jewellery behind a display cabinet of exquisite pieces. Behrouz, perhaps thinking that buying us all lunch wasn't quite kind enough, now gave Suzy a necklace as a further gift. It was one that she was reluctant to accept, but Behrouz insisted. At times the generosity of Iranians felt overwhelming, especially as we had little that we could offer in return, but their friendliness towards us was a heartwarming reminder that, whatever political differences might exist between countries, human beings are always capable of treating each other with kindness and respect. Even many of the women shopping in the bazaar came to us to speak and ask us about our lives in a friendly manner, which was especially good of them considering we had just almost run half of them over. Most of them were cloaked from head to toe in black, but even though the more extreme religious practices here appeared, at first glance, to repress the women greatly, in fact they were able to come up to speak to us and in other ways also seemed to have much more freedom than the women of rural Turkey had.

But I did wonder how it would be to live in a country of such strict Islamic laws. It was a question I would put to Benam and Amir, two young guys who we met in the next town of Zanjan. Benam was a friendly guy in his twenties who wanted one day to ride his own bicycle around the world. He had arranged for us to stay with his friend, Amir's, brother, Ali, while we were in Zanjan. Ali was older than Benam and met us in an ill-fitting suit. He was a very thin man, balding, and he comically ran in front of our bikes with his stick legs flailing to show us to his house. Inside we met with his wife and eight-month-old daughter. Amir arrived soon after; a young, muscular man with sunglasses on his slicked-back hair, he very much resembled a Bollywood star and looked nothing at all like his brother.

Benam and Amir walked with us around Zanjan, showing us through another lively bazaar and taking us to a grand mosque. As we walked the streets we passed a girl who smiled at me with a glint in her eye. She looked cute too, beneath her colourful headscarf, yet I knew that there was nothing I could do. Even if I were a local it would be technically illegal for me to socialise with a member of the opposite sex that I did not know. It seemed like this must make it terribly difficult to find romance. Certainly my quest for 'the one' was being stifled, even as Amir noticed the girl and nudged me encouragingly.

"I don't want to die," I told him. He just laughed, as if to confirm that I might. "But seriously, how is it for you? How do you meet girls here?"

"It's very difficult," he said. "I can't."

But perhaps he misunderstood my question, for a little later he and Benam consulted, and then started asking me if I wanted a girl, and offered to try and arrange it for me. It was impossible and illegal, and we might all end up in prison, but it seemed the Iranians really would do anything in the name of hospitality.

"No, it's okay, thank you."

That evening we ate dinner at Ali's home. As is traditional in Iran we ate very late, at around eleven, and sat on the floor around a large mat covered in bowls of delicious food. It came served with flat bread that we had seen before being made in large ovens, baked on stones over a fire so that the stones left imprints onto a final product that looked like inverted bubble wrap. As I scooped up a piece of fried egg with this stiff bread I listened as Ali, who worked so hard to provide for his family, spoke of his dream to emigrate to Australia for a better life. From the way he talked it seemed like he thought of Australia as a land of great promise, a much better opportunity for him and his family. Yet from what I had seen of Iran, it was a developed nation with such wonderfully good people, and I worried that Ali might ultimately find only disappointment in the Western way of life should his dream ever become reality.

Ever since Eastern Europe I had been encountering stray dogs wherever I went, and, with the exception of the small region of European Turkey where they had been nasty and territorial, I had been making friends with them. One would often come up to me when I was sitting taking a break at the side of the road, and I would feed it some scraps of food and give it an imaginative name. Occasionally they would try to follow me for a while, and in Turkey I even adopted a couple of dogs, named Willow and Cheeky, for an hour or so before they eventually got too tired of running behind me to keep up. The idea of keeping one of these dogs and travelling the world with it appealed to me, but I knew that it was impractical; the added complication of crossing international borders with a pet was prohibitive enough, even before considering the practicalities. But one day in Iran, with Dino and Suzy ahead of me, I noticed a stray puppy at the roadside. It looked terribly weak, with a small, emaciated body, and there was no sign of a mother. I threw down some pieces of bread for the poor little thing, which it ate heartily. Saddened by the puppy's plight but knowing there was nothing more that I could do, I began to cycle off. But the dog whimpered and yelped at me, almost pathetically, as I did so. I looked back to see it trotting after me. I stopped. It looked at me with desperate eyes. It was all skin and bones. If I did nothing it was surely going to die soon. I sighed, picked up the poor little thing, and put it on the back of my bike. Then, as I prepared to cycle again, the puppy fell to the floor in a sorry heap. "Let's never tell anyone about that, Puppy," I said, picking him up again, and this time placing him in my pannier and strapping him in.

A few kilometres later I caught up to Dino and Suzy and introduced them to the puppy, that I had decided to permanently name

Puppy. This was, I like to think, in an attempt to not get too attached, rather than because of any lack of imagination on my part. I went into a shop and bought some milk, then put Puppy on a wall and poured it into a bowl for him. He lapped it up in a way that made me think that I should have named him Kitten. His tail started wagging. Suzy said that it looked like a rat's tail, but it didn't. Despite laughing and going along with it, I wasn't sure that Dino and Suzy were hugely impressed by my decision to adopt a fourth team member, particularly as I had no real idea what I was going to do with Puppy long-term. We were only a day away from Tehran now, and we had some hosts organised in the city that I hoped might fall in love with him and want to keep him. It seemed unlikely, however, as Islam views dogs as unclean and they are generally not kept as pets in Muslim countries. For all I knew, I might well be breaking the law again by trying to help Puppy.

I put the poor animal back in my front pannier, ignoring Suzy's question about whether he was toilet trained, and we continued cycling. Unfortunately, it was a very hot day, and it probably wasn't ideal weather for being enclosed in a pannier, bumping along on a busy road. When we stopped for a break after another fifteen kilometres, Puppy seemed quite relieved to be free, and celebrated by running off into a bush and refusing to come out again. It appeared very much that he had lost faith in me as his saviour and new mother. I tried to coax him back out, but he wasn't interested, and eventually I had to concede that he was happier going it alone. The bush where he now resided was outside of a factory, and I consoled myself with visions of him surviving on leaves and insects, before one day growing up to be the factory guard dog.

Cycling into Tehran was awful. It was choked with traffic and probably the worst place that I'd ever been to for riding a bicycle. At times we had to cross several lanes of vehicles to make turns and it was a nerve-racking experience, to say the least. Iranian drivers were not the best, and we were probably an added distraction that only made things worse on the roads. This was certainly the case when one car came to a sudden halt only so that the driver could say hello to us, causing the car behind to bump into the back of him, and the car behind to go into the back of that one, and so on. Seemingly oblivious to the pile-up he had just caused, the driver still got out to shake our hands and wish us well.

Luckily our hosts lived in a suburb in the northwest of the city and the Turkmenistan embassy, which I needed to visit to collect the visa I'd applied for in Ankara, was in the northeast, so I could skirt around in the north to avoid the worst of the traffic mayhem. In order to get my visa I needed to provide a passport photo, which I had made at a photo studio. It was a most elaborate photo shoot, with a very serious photographer getting me from many angles. When I saw the result on his camera I was impressed but noticed that I had sweat on my forehead, a consequence of the intense heat that had engulfed us over the past week. "Don't worry," he said, "Photoshop." I should probably have told him not to do it, but at the time I didn't see any harm in him editing out the sweat. An hour later I returned to collect my six photos and was quite amazed by what I was given. Not only had the sweat gone, but so had every single blemish on my face as well as the stubble from my neck. My skin was so smooth I resembled a doll. It was ridiculous. At the embassy I handed in one of these photos and the man stared at it for a very, very long time, before eventually stapling it to my application and giving me my visa. I resolved to throw the other five away.

Our hosts were a recently married couple named Ali and Sarina. As ever they were extremely welcoming and it was nice to spend a couple of evenings relaxing with them in their apartment in what would also be my last nights with Dino and Suzy before we went our separate ways. Sitting around the dinner table we discussed what life was like living in Iran, and how Ali and Sarina, who were not themselves religious, found it to live under Islamic law. Sarina, now away from the public eye, had removed her head coverings, something that she was not legally supposed to do in front of us. She was also wearing a short skirt, which was definitely not allowed. But she said that she accepted having to dress moderately in public, as that was just how things were. There were so many things that they were not supposed to do, but often there was a way around it. I had just been using Facebook on Ali's computer, another activity that was technically outlawed but easily circumvented. In the apartment below us we could hear a party taking place.

"That party is breaking the law too," Ali said.

"You aren't allowed to have parties?" I asked.

"Yes, parties are allowed. But boys and girls have to sit separately, and there must be no music or dancing."

"Really? No music? It doesn't sound like much of a party without music."

"No. But clapping is allowed."

The experience with Ali and Sarina was in contrast to a night I spent with a devoutly Islamic family a few nights later. With Dino and Suzy wanting to do a side trip of a bus journey around the south of Iran and with my own visa running out, I'd been forced to press on alone once more. One evening, as I was eating an orange at the side of the road, a car stopped and a man got out and invited me to come and stay with him and his family. He lived just a few kilometres up the road and, after cycling there, I was welcomed in by the man, whose name was Mansour. He had a pointy grey beard and he was dressed in a long white robe, with a matching skull cap on his head, in contrast to the majority of Iranian men who wore relatively Western clothes. After removing my shoes I entered and took a seat on the carpeted floor with Mansour and his nephew, Joseph, who had been studying for a PhD in Portugal and could speak some English. As we sat and conversed over hot tea I felt a worrying twinge of pain from my teeth. It was hurting in much the same way as before, only now on the other side of my mouth. I could have cried.

It wasn't too long before more guests arrived, Mansour's brother-in-law with his wife and their three grown-up daughters. The three sisters came in looking stunning in brightly coloured, long flowing dresses that made me, at least temporarily, forget the pain. They spoke good English, especially the oldest, tallest, and most beautiful of all, Sara, who worked as an English teacher. I spoke a lot with her, and if ever I were going to convert, it would probably have been then, as she smiled at me, adjusting the head-covering that flowed imperceptibly into her yellow dress. But I got the impression that her father, also bearded and dressed in a white robe, might not approve of too much attention being paid to his daughters by an atheist, and so I behaved myself. At one point the call to prayer came, and he and Mansour rolled out two mats right there in the room and bent down to pray for several minutes.

Dinner was served on the floor and we all tucked in, although, in what was always an awkward situation, I'd had to have a special vegetarian meal prepared for me. I knew that sticking to my principles on this matter meant that I would sometimes miss out on tasting cultural foods, and I was aware that it was sometimes hard for people to even understand vegetarianism. But I thought that was also a good reason for sticking to it. As I saw it, my travels not only taught me about other ways of life, but also brought my way of life to other people, so that we might both learn something. To help people understand I would sometimes explain that not eating animals was something that I believed in, almost in a religious way.

"Our religion says that we are supposed to eat animals," Sara translated from her father. "God made animals for us to eat. Allah says that the animals want to be eaten."

I wasn't too sure about that. I was always under the impression that animals were against the idea of being eaten, on the whole, but I wasn't going to argue the point, and the conversation moved on. In fact it swayed constantly throughout the evening, one moment about politics, the next about football. "I think the British government lied about Iraq," would be met with, "Stamford Bridge is Chelsea's ground, yes?" At one point I was asked about my family, and I told them about my sister.

"She has two young children," I said.

"Then she is married?" Sara asked.

I hesitated for a moment.

"No," I said, knowing that this would not be acceptable here.

"No," Sara said sternly, "if this happened here she would be forgotten by the family, she would be disowned."

"Yeah, that's what I wanted to do," I joked, "but my parents said we had to keep her."

The next morning my tooth was hurting even more, and Mansour offered to drive me to his friend, who was a dentist. But he lived thirty kilometres in the wrong direction, and so I declined, saying that I would wait until I reached the city of Mashhad, still several days' ride away.

"You would rather have many days of pain than half an hour in a car?"

"Yes, yes I would," I replied, happy that I was continuing to spread the wisdom of my principles around the world, even if they were generally being taken, some might argue correctly, as the words of a madman.

I thanked Mansour for his kindness and continued eastwards, through a forested national park where I saw wild boars for the first time in my life, and then into another area of desert where dung beetles rolled their piles of poop along the hard shoulder. My tooth was getting more painful and I realised that I was very likely experiencing the exact same problem as I'd had on the other side of my mouth, with decay spreading into the root. I could not comprehend how I could be so terribly unfortunate to be going through this all over again. I was still several days from Mashhad in a big, empty desert when the pain reached excruciating levels. I had hoped that the pain I had experienced three weeks earlier in Tabriz would never be repeated, yet now it was being exceeded. It was completely unbearable misery. It was so bad that it was impossible to sleep and I spent my nights outside under the stars doing countless press-ups and star jumps like a fool, as the only way I had found to alleviate the pain slightly was to be physically active. I literally did thousands of press-ups those nights, mildly tripping out from the cocktail of drugs that I was self-medicating myself with. My front pannier looked like it belonged to Lance Armstrong, with all manner of pills rattling around in it, as I furiously pedalled 170 kilometre days to get to Mashhad as fast as I could, genuinely screaming like a lunatic and frothing at the mouth like a rabid dog as I went. Even the friendly Iranians were wise enough to keep their distance.

I finally arrived in Mashhad and by some small miracle one of the first buildings along the road was a hospital. I hurried inside and raced to find a doctor, indicating in no uncertain terms that I would really appreciate a painkilling injection in my buttocks as soon as possible. Thankfully this was soon delivered.

With the pain eased I went into town and found a dentist who, despite not being quite as professional as Dr Meristagi, performed a root canal operation that I deemed a complete success, if only because it made the pain go away. I had now been the recipient of two complex dental procedures in Iran, and I decided to celebrate by sitting in an internet café. No longer looking quite so rabid I here made friends with the owner, a young man named Reza, who invited me to stay with him for a couple of nights to recover. He asked me where I was from, and I told him Scotland. "I thought so, I can tell by the accent," he said.

I stayed with Reza in the apartment he shared with his brother, Amir, and sister, Marie. She was religious, the brothers not, and it was interesting to see a family living together with conflicting beliefs. Despite this they were all incredibly generous, and before I left they gave me a camping stove and a head torch, items that I had somehow managed to get this far without, as well as two T-shirts, a lot of food, and an awful lot of love. As I neared the border with Turkmenistan it was one final reminder of the remarkable generosity of this nation, and I thought back again on the apprehension I'd had about initially entering Iran. In less than a month my thoughts on the country had been completely turned around, and I would be leaving feeling bemused, and almost angry, about how a country filled with such incredibly good people could possibly warrant the reputation it has in the West.

19

Turkmen border
7th May 2014

On my way towards the border I was distracted, and rightly so, by the sight of one hundred camels. The humped animals plodded along, their massive herd stretching out all of the way to the horizon. Two men, dressed in baggy old clothes and carrying simple wooden staffs, were doing their best to shepherd the whole lot of them across the sand. It seemed that we were mutually intrigued by each other's undertakings in life, and I stopped to meet with these men. After a little while playing charades, one of them ran off towards a baby camel and, after several attempts at sneaking up on it, finally managed to get a hold of it by the neck. The other fellow then indicated that I should go and jump on the back of the bucking animal. Given the camel's obvious level of distress, and my inadequate level of insurance, I thought it wise not to do that, but this strange apparition of camels confirmed that I was moving once again into a different kind of landscape. This was the real desert now. Not the semi-desert of Iran, dry and rocky and populated, but the real deal, *Lawrence of Arabia* stuff. Huge swaths of empty and uninterrupted sand dunes loomed ahead and would provide the dramatic setting for almost all of the next country of Turkmenistan.

Having enjoyed Iran so much despite its reputation, I was doing my best not to worry too much about Turkmenistan, even though it came with the tagline of the 'North Korea of Central Asia'. A dictatorship with a terrible human rights record and complete lack of freedom of the press were the primary reasons for the catchy slogan, although for me the most pressing impact was the paranoid visa restrictions that meant I had only been granted five days to cross the entire country. As a result, the only border out of Turkmenistan that I could realistically get to was one into Uzbekistan, 500 kilometres of desert away. The challenge to make it on time, which other cyclists had already christened 'The Desert Dash', was a real potential threat to my hopes of cycling every last metre of my journey, especially as the wind reportedly had a nasty habit of blowing pretty consistently in the wrong direction. Looking at online blogs of those that had gone before me, The Desert Dash was something that around fifty percent failed to successfully achieve without resorting to other means of transport.

Just how difficult it was going to be became even more apparent after a large part of the first of my five allotted days was wasted just getting into Turkmenistan. In the crumbling brick border building my passport was taken from me, passed around, looked at by many curious eyes, it disappeared out of a door, it reappeared, it spent some time on a desk, it reappeared again. Eventually, an official woman came to me with it and demanded to know my intended route to Uzbekistan. I told her, but she wanted to see it on a map. I had to dig in my bags to find a print-out to show her. It was completely absurd – there was only one road.

Next all of my bags had to be thoroughly searched by a young man who eyed me nervously as I put each one up onto the desk for him. His task was a tough one, but he began with great gusto, flicking through some of the photos on my camera, inspecting carefully each finger of my gloves, sniffing my toothpaste. He showed admirable resolve to do his job properly, though I don't think even he really knew what it was that he was looking for. He was finally broken by my front left pannier, the one with all of my tools and similar items in it. I had not looked too much at it since I'd cleaned it out before entering Iran, and I did not think it could have got too messy in a month. I was wrong. Something had cracked and spilt – my hand soap perhaps, or maybe some insect repellent – and things were coming out sticky. This was merging with general dirt and filth and oil, and the man understandably began to look a little put out. He kept at it, popping open my puncture repair kit and sending patches flying everywhere, but his determination was waning with every sticky, dirty item brought out onto his previously clean desk. Eventually he declared "Enough!" and the last of my bags got nothing more than a poke. He never found the condoms.

Wasting so much time at the border was frustrating, and the beginning of my race across Turkmenistan was further hampered by a series of checkpoints that appeared every few kilometres manned by young army recruits. At one I was stopped by a teenage officer who, alone at his post and naturally inexperienced, nevertheless tried his luck and asked me for "Dollars?" That was all he said. "Dollars?" It seemed like he was asking for a bribe, and yet he had completely failed to come up with any kind of story or reason for me to give him anything.

I looked at him, and thought, *'Sorry, buddy, but you've got to try a bit harder than that. You haven't even got a gun, just a silly baton.'*

"I'm sorry, but I don't have any dollars," I said. He looked terribly glum, sighed, and waved me on. I got the impression that this happened to him a lot.

Once I was through with all of the formalities I was at least able to make good progress throughout the afternoon, whizzing freely across the flat desert, and I ended the first day with a respectable ninety kilometres in the bank. That still put me slightly behind schedule, however, and I decided to wake early the next morning to get as much distance done as possible. I was on my way by half past five, but the fierce headwind that greeted me did not make me feel at all happy to be on the bike at such an hour. It was blowing at me with fearsome strength, reducing my speed to a pathetic six kilometres per hour as I battled into it. I was never going to make it to Uzbekistan on time going at such a speed. And to make matters worse, the wind was blowing sand in my eyes and making them red raw and painful. And, even worse than that, I had a Backstreet Boys song stuck in my head.

This was *not* a good way to start a day.

Fortunately, after making it just twenty kilometres in three hours, the road made a sharp right turn out of the face of the wind, and I was free to pedal again. Relieved, I began to enjoy the feeling of being out in the desert, occasionally dodging stray camels, and otherwise just clocking up the distance towards my goal. Then I saw something quite unexpected, another touring cyclist taking a break at the roadside. I had assumed that I wouldn't meet any in Turkmenistan now, as I thought I would have surely seen any that were attempting The Desert Dash at the border. But Andreas, a middle-aged Austrian man cycling from Vienna to Siberia, had a relaxed attitude to things, and told me he'd crossed the border sometime in the afternoon. My immediate reaction to this was to wonder just how in hell he had managed to get here before me. "Yes," he explained, "I took the short-cut."

"Shortcut! Shortcut! You can't take shortcuts on The Desert Dash challenge!" I was outraged.

"Why not?"

"Well... I don't know..."

"It's not really cheating, is it?"

"No, I suppose not. No. Not really cheating. Quite clever really. Well done."

"I also took a lift in a car. The headwind this morning was really bad."

"Yes, now that really is cheating, I'm afraid."

Andreas was obviously not as strict about cycling the whole way as me. In fact he'd only left Vienna about six weeks earlier, and done much of the journey by bus. Dressed in white Lycra and sporty sunglasses, he was a nice, if slightly odd, man, who seemed blissfully ignorant of much of what was going on. For example, he told me that he had spent quite a long time at the border arguing about the twelve dollar entry fee, the one which everybody had to pay and that he had mistook for the demands of a corrupt border official. Furthermore, he had not bothered to change any money into the local currency, yet was planning to spend the night in a hotel that night in Mary. At least he was before I told him, "You do know that you can't get any money here, don't you? There are no ATMs." The look on his face suggested he did not know this.

"Oh. I suppose I won't be staying in a hotel then."

It was comforting to have the company of a fellow cyclist, but Andreas was faster than me, and so I told him that he was welcome to just go on ahead without me. He palmed off this suggestion. "No stress," came his friendly response. "We make it together."

Then he cycled off without me.

I felt very, very tired. The wind, now coming diagonally towards me, blew sand from the desert across the road, stinging me as it hit my exposed arms, legs, and face. Big trucks zoomed past, and each time that they did I would be blown about like a pedalling rag doll as the wind was momentarily blocked, creating a vacuum that was immediately replaced by more wind gusts in the truck's wake. My eyes were sore with sand, and I seemed to have some sort of an allergy to this desert, for my nose ran and ran, and I sneezed and sneezed, and felt like throwing up. I felt wretched, but I had to keep going, there was simply no time in the schedule for stopping, no matter how hard things got. But then I got a puncture, so I stopped.

I had not suffered too many flats on the trip so far, thanks to the thick, puncture-resistant nature of my Schwalbe Marathon Plus tyres, but I still had all the equipment that I needed to quickly repair the problem and get back on my way. I did have to stop again almost immediately, however, as a sandstorm whipped the desert up into a frenzy. With absolutely no shelter I was horribly exposed and had little option but to stand there covering my face until the worst of it passed by.

Fortunately, this did not take too long, but my troubles were not yet over, for next I ran out of water. Running out of water in the desert sucks, and I should know, for it had happened to me before, twice in fact. The first time, when I was cycling through California's Death Valley during my first trip, I had ended up having to stop a car to ask for water. But I hated to rely on a motor vehicle for help. It was almost like an admission of weakness in my chosen method of travel, and I was quite determined not to have to do that this time. The only trouble with my stubbornness was that I soon grew extremely thirsty in temperatures that were edging towards forty degrees, and the only town on my entire route, Mary, was still some distance away. I had to make it there though, otherwise I might die, and that thought spurred me on as I grew more and more dehydrated. I had no more water, but I did have an orange and a pear, which I stopped to eat. They were the juiciest, most succulent pieces of fruit I had ever had the good fortune to enjoy, but they provided only temporary relief. I kept going, seeing nothing but endless desert in all directions, and feeling like there was no way my situation could possibly get any worse. Then the Backstreet Boys song came back into my head. This was a terrible, terrible thing. I chased it away with another song by, believe it or not, One Direction. "Cause we danced all night, to the best song ever!" I sang to myself, and this had the remarkable effect of invigorating me and spurring me on. As you may be able to tell, I was in very, very dire mental straits by this point.

Finally I arrived at a village just before Mary and burst into a shop. I was exhausted and about ready to collapse, but I had just enough energy left to slam some money down on the desk, grab a bottle of water from the shelf, and pour the entire contents into my parched mouth. The old woman behind the counter looked at me with startled curiosity. "That was delicious, thank you," I said to her. "I'll take four more please."

On the morning of Day Three of The Desert Dash challenge I cycled into Mary, the halfway point of the crossing, and I was very surprised by what I found. In complete contrast to the bumpy desert highway, the streets of this town were in perfect condition, with clean footpaths and well-maintained gardens. The buildings around the centre were eye-catching and in pristine condition. It looked like a thoroughly modern and developed city. And in addition to this, I couldn't help but notice that the girls were some of the most beautiful in the world, looking elegant in long, brightly-coloured dresses, their hair tied up in plaits.

I wasn't sure if this was what the girls here always wore, or if it was just because of a parade of some sort that I noticed taking place in the city centre. People were flocking towards it, and I could see from a distance that there were giant flags and kids in sports uniforms and a marching band and rows and rows of those beautiful girls in those beautiful dresses. Naturally, I wanted to investigate further, so I locked up my bike and walked over towards it all. But then a security guard came over to me and ushered me away, leading me back to my bike and telling me to leave. By way of explanation he pointed to my cap, which was covered in dust, my shirt, which used to be red but was now faded to a dull pink/grey, my shorts, with their glue stain and burn mark, and my shoes, which were falling apart. He didn't point at my socks, which were in surprisingly good condition, if a little smelly. I looked around at the other spectators, all well dressed, and I realised what was going on. I wasn't smart enough for watching this parade. Not smart enough to even *watch* a parade. In *Turkmenistan*. This was surely a new low.

With another 200 kilometres of open desert to go to get to the border town of Türkmenabat I loaded up my bike with sixteen litres of water. This made it awfully heavy, but I was desperate not to run out of water in the desert again. Oh yes, I had learnt my lesson now alright, I wasn't stupid. Never let it be said that I make the same mistake four times.

I rolled on back out towards another long stretch of nothing, but before I got very far I was met by the sight of four touring cyclists coming the other way. I was surprised to discover that they were from Turkmenistan, and they had just ridden here from Türkmenabat. They invited me to go back to a café that I had just passed for a drink and, as I was now ahead of schedule, I agreed.

The men, each aged around fifty, had dark skin, tanned from long days out under the hot sun, but were remarkably sprightly considering they had just cycled across a desert. They explained, worryingly, that this was because the wind had been at their backs the whole way and they had barely needed to pedal. Trying not to think too much about what that would mean for me, I took a keen interest in what they were riding, which were cheap road bikes with innovative methods for attaching their luggage. My own system of racks and panniers, employing top-of-the-range German brands, looked unnecessarily cumbersome in comparison to their ingenious amateur use of inexpensive bags and string.

As I was admiring their set-ups I was further surprised to see Andreas roll up. It seemed he had stopped much earlier than me the previous evening, and I had passed him at some point during my delirious search for water. So the six of us all went inside to exchange our stories, as a feast of food was brought out for us to enjoy. The Turkmen guys generously insisted on paying, something that I didn't feel too bad about as it was mostly meat and I couldn't eat much of it anyway. Andreas was quite happy to eat for two. I told him that I was carrying sixteen litres of water, and asked him how much he had. "Three and a half," he said. "Do you think I need more?"

The café was the last place before the desert began, and Andreas and I cycled out into it together. He was still a faster cyclist than me, of course, and I again told him that he was welcome to go on ahead if he felt like it. "No stress. We make it together," he said once more.

The road now turned directly into a strong headwind. I considered drafting behind Andreas. It would surely help a lot, but would it not be cheating? Of course I was okay with drafting behind other cyclists normally, I mean I'd drafted behind horse-drawn carts in Romania, but until Andreas had arrived this had been a very special sort of challenge. It was me against the elements, me against the desert. Could I allow myself to draft behind him now? Would I still be able to consider The Desert Dash to have been a complete personal success? I looked up from my thoughts. He was gone, far off ahead, without me.

I was getting a strong sense of deja-vu as I went on alone, with sand blowing across the road and into my eyes, making me cry. It was tough going. I felt wretched, but I had to keep going, there was simply no time in the schedule for stopping. But then I got a puncture, so I stopped.

Feeling like my movie had turned into *Groundhog Day*, I stopped to fix the problem. It was an internal puncture this time, on the rear wheel, that I thought might have been caused by too much weight on the back. I resolved the issue by moving some of the many plastic bottles of water I had on the back, strapping them instead to the outside of my front panniers. This had the unexpected but utterly brilliant side effect of making it look like I had rocket launchers on my bike, and I spent all afternoon pretending to fire them on any trucks that beeped too loud or passed too close.

By the time I pitched my tent that evening in the shelter of a few robust desert shrubs, I had somehow managed to put in another good distance. A total of 350 kilometres had now been completed in three days, and things were looking good, even if the hardships of the desert had taken their toll on me. The heat was intolerable, the wind incessant, the sand, the flies, the punctures, all of it was annoying and exhausting. I felt sick and I felt tired from the pressure of having to ride all day long. But the hardest thing of all, the real worst of it, was the mildly irritating, middle-aged Austrian man who kept racing ahead of me looking like he wasn't even trying. I decided that, even though he didn't know it, Andreas and I were in a race to the border. Forget The Desert Dash, this was The Desert Duel. It was the classic case of the tortoise and the hare. He would race ahead of me, of course, but I had my chance if I could cycle a little later each evening, get up a little earlier. As if to confirm my character in the metaphor I had seen a few real tortoises crossing the road that evening, and had even taken the time to carry one or two of them across to safety. Considering the barrenness of the environment, it was surprisingly full of life. In setting up camp I saw some desert foxes, then a scorpion scampered away across the sand the next morning when I stepped back outside.

Being very careful where I stepped, I made my way back to the road to make another early start on Day Four, keen to build a good lead on my opponent. It was tough going, as the wind was again directly against me and very strong, but I plugged away like any good tortoise would. Then at about eleven o'clock, with forty kilometres under my belt, I saw a shiny white hare appear in my mirror. Andreas was back.

We greeted each other and spoke for a few minutes, and once again it seemed I'd overtaken him the night before, some time after he'd made camp. He was now looking fresh-faced and healthy, while I was no doubt looking, and certainly feeling, quite the opposite. I decided that he might not actually be human, and that in the movie he should be played by the evil robot man from *Terminator Two*. He reminded me of him quite a lot.

With the wind so fiercely against us Andreas suggested that we draft behind one another, taking turns at the front to make sure that we both made it to the border on time. I had to concede that it was a very sensible idea and gave in to the temptation, although I considered the fact that he had been the one to put forward the suggestion to be very much a moral victory.

Such was the force of the wind we swapped the leader every kilometre. I didn't want to slow Andreas down, so I worked hard to keep my speed up to his level when it was my turn at the front. Each kilometre with me in the lead was an agonising, lung-busting feat of endurance, each kilometre at the back a brief respite that seemed to last mere seconds. And so the afternoon went on in this fashion across an endless sea of desert.

After about forty kilometres of this we stumbled upon a café, randomly placed in the middle of nowhere. What it was doing out here I could not say, but Andreas decided it was a fine place to stop for a meal and a long rest. Here was my chance. I knew how this parable worked. This was my moment to press on ahead while the hare gorged himself, so I boldly declared that I would now go on alone, and left Andreas to his soup.

Without company the going became almost unbearably difficult. The wind was so powerful and unforgiving, like a cruel, invisible hand holding me back. I had been pushing my body too hard for too long. I felt weak, helpless. I forced myself to keep pedalling, but my progress was pitiful. After just a couple of kilometres I stopped to eat a snack and try to get my strength back. I only stopped for a second, but when I looked around there was Robocop coming over the horizon towards me. "Andreas," I cried, "I stopped to wait for you. Let's go on together."

Working as a team once more we battled on somehow into evening and eventually fought our way to the 100 kilometre mark for the day. Neither of us knew exactly how far we now had left to the border, but with more than 450 kilometres done after four days, The Desert Dash looked like it was surely in the bag now. We set up camp near to one another, although as we did so I began to feel really rather unwell, and flies were buzzing around me, irritating me the whole time. Andreas was merrily pitching his tent nearby, whistling as he did so.

"Are the flies even bothering you?" I asked.

"No," he replied, cheerfully.

"I didn't think so."

I decided to camp on the other side of a dune, as it provided a more sheltered spot, but it meant doing several trips carrying my bike and bags over it, which only tired me further. After dropping off a couple of bags I climbed back up the dune to see that Andreas had removed his shirt and was reaching down for his bicycle shorts. I looked away just in time. After waiting a couple of minutes to give him time to get dressed, I then squinted back in his direction through my fingers. The man was standing there butt naked next to his tent. I seriously did not need to see that.

As I lay down in my tent I felt very sick. My stomach lurched. I think the naked Austrian man had been the tipping point. I got out of my tent as fast as I could, crawled a few metres, and threw up. Yuck. You know how sometimes you feel better after vomiting, like it cleanses your system or something? That was not what happened here. I felt even worse. I puked some more. And some more. Soon I had nothing left in my stomach to throw up, but I kept on retching anyway. This was really not good. I felt absolutely awful. I couldn't get back in the tent. I just lay down on the sand, no longer having the energy to care if there was a scorpion there or not. I stared up at the stars spinning above me, my head swimming, and the night drifted by in a haze. Every so often my stomach muscles would convulse and force me to turn and retch and vomit nothing. I tried drinking water but this was immediately rejected back to the sand. My body ached and cramped all over. I had nothing left in my system, my body would not accept water, and I was in the middle of a desert. This was a very serious situation. If I still couldn't hold down water in the morning then I was certainly not going to be cycling anywhere, and with my visa expiring in fifteen hours the prospect that my continuous journey by bike was about to come to a dramatic, cruelly enforced end was suddenly an all too real one.

20

Turkmen desert
11th May 2014

I barely slept all night, but by daybreak I was able to hold down a little water, and with that I felt like there was still a glimmer of hope that I might somehow be able to cycle the rest of the way to the border. I was feeling incredibly weak though, and I knew I was going to need the help of Andreas. If I could cycle behind him out of the wind the whole way, with him riding a little slower than his usual pace, then maybe, just maybe, I could make it. Oh yes, this tortoise was going to make it alright, clinging on to the back of the hare's tail for dear life, all the way to the finish line.

It took all of my strength just to stand up. His tent was away from mine, over the top of the dune. It was such an extraordinary effort to walk up it now, with my feet sinking and slipping with every step. I finally staggered up to the top and looked down to where he had placed his tent. I saw nothing but sand. Andreas had gone without me.

I wondered how it was that sand could be so uncomfortable. I had tossed and turned all night long, never feeling one bit relaxed. I was back lying on it again, drifting in and out of consciousness. The sun had come up, but I couldn't move, couldn't find the energy to get up again. My hopes of making it around the world entirely by bicycle were fading away. I cursed my bad luck, to get sick like this on the last day of my visa, in a country that would not look kindly on me overstaying. I had given it everything, but I could not go on by bicycle alone now. It was too hard. Too impossibly hard. I couldn't move. I had no plan beyond continuing to lie there until the sun rose high in the sky and finished me off.

After a while I heard a voice calling out to me and saw a hazy white figure hovering over me. "Chris..." the voice said, eerily, in an otherworldly tone. "Chris... I heard you being sick. You are very weak. I think you should cycle behind me the whole way today. And don't worry, we make it together."

Good God, I had only been dreaming before. He hadn't left at all. My Austrian robotic bunny was still with me, and he was going to save me. An angel of a man really.

The wind seemed to be blowing even more strongly than the day before, but Andreas cycled into it with impressive vigour. This was annoying because I struggled to keep up with him, even while drafting behind. I did my best to concentrate on sticking as close as I could to his back wheel, but I was feeling so tired that I often fell back, desperately shouting out to Andreas as I did. Sometimes he would hear me, but sometimes my cries would be lost to the wind and he would disappear off ahead. To his great credit, every time this happened he stopped and waited for me to catch him up again.

We made slow progress, and every few kilometres I had to stop to take a rest. I was struggling to stomach anything, and all I had with me was dry food – bread and biscuits – which was completely unappetising. I knew that I needed to eat something, so I tried dipping bread in water, but could not manage more than a few bites. I was running on empty, but somehow I kept running.

We continued gradually onwards until eventually an archway welcoming us to the city of Türkmenabat appeared ahead of us out of the desert. Sick of the taste of warm water and bread I had been fantasising for hours about stopping at the first available place and drinking some cool fruit juice to replenish much needed fluids and energy. I was therefore slightly annoyed when the first café appeared and Andreas went on ahead and zoomed straight passed. Only slightly annoyed, mind you, because there was nothing in the world going to stop me from going in and getting a drink myself. Andreas was free to go on ahead now, it didn't matter. We had made it across the desert to Türkmenabat, and the border was just the other side of the city. It was over. I had done it. I staggered into the café and bought a litre of juice. I then laid down on one of the traditional rug-covered tables to recover, relieved to be out of the sun. That had been a close one. But the worst was over, success in The Desert Dash was a mere formality now.

I relaxed for about an hour and then decided to get up and get the rest of the day over with. Walking back outside was awful as it was by now one in the afternoon, the hottest part of the day. I assumed it would take me an hour or so to navigate through Türkmenabat, and then the border looked like it couldn't be more than ten kilometres out the other side. I had no worries about making it to the border before it closed at six. What I was annoyed about, however, was that I really needed to rest for a couple of nights in a hotel, and there would be plenty in Türkmenabat, none of which I could stop at because I needed to leave the country. On the Uzbekistan side of the border there would be nothing but desert again.

It took a lot longer than I had anticipated to get into Türkmenabat, and then I got a bit lost on the confusing streets. Starting to feel just a little concerned I stopped to ask some locals for directions to the border, and how far away it was. I knew by now that asking people these questions would always provide answers that should be taken with a pinch of salt, and on this occasion I received estimates ranging from three to 150 kilometres. Not really any the wiser, I eventually found a man who had a smartphone, so that I could borrow it and look at a map to see for myself just exactly what my situation was. I looked at it and froze in horror. The border was still really far. Really, really far. Oh, this was bad. This was very, very bad.

I started cycling as fast as I could. I was in a sudden state of panic. I had less than three hours now until the border would close, and I still had forty or fifty kilometres to ride. Up until this point I had been crawling along at six or seven kilometres per hour, and, in case you're not too hot at maths, let me tell you, you cannot cycle forty or fifty kilometres in three hours going at six or seven kilometres per hour.

Desperate, I found some inner strength and started moving faster through the streets of the city, pausing only to ask people the way, then following their pointing arms. The exhaustion of my sickness was temporarily forgotten as I realised that my whole trip was once again in jeopardy. If I didn't make it to the border on time I would have overstayed on my visa, and I would be in danger of being arrested, driven away, and thrown in a Turkmen jail forever. I couldn't let that awful fate befall me. There was simply no way I could go in a car.

I got beyond the city and, with two hours left on my visa, I asked another man how much further it was to the border. "It's twenty kilometres to Farap," he said, citing the border village, "but the border itself is actually another twenty kilometres after Farap."

'No, no, no. Forty kilometres! No, no. It can't be! I can't do it!'

I was frantic. I pedalled as hard as I could, but I was soon stopped by a police checkpoint, where I again asked how far it was, and was this time told that it was only twenty kilometres. That was okay, much better than forty, anyway. I could do twenty kilometres in two hours.

Ten kilometres of sprinting later I came to a fork in the road. There was another checkpoint, so I quickly cycled over and called out to the man, "Whith... wa... t... Uthb..." My mouth was so dry I couldn't speak.

"I'm sorry. Do you speak English?" he chuckled, pleased with himself. I took a sip of water. I'd hardly eaten or drunk anything all day. I had no idea how it was that I was even still standing.

"Which way to Uzbekistan?"

He pointed.

"And how far is it?"

"Twenty kilometres."

"Arghhh!"

I continued, pounding the pedals, sprinting with all that I had, finding reserves of energy that I had never known existed. This was so hard, so frustrating. Everyone was telling me different things and I had no real idea how much further I needed to cycle, but one thing was for sure; I was fast running out of time.

The road crossed a canal, but as I cycled up and over the bridge a man called out to me from a yard, and indicated that I should turn off here on a small road that ran alongside the canal. It was a tiny, nondescript, completely unsignposted road. It couldn't be the way to the border, surely? The man seemed certain, but I could not afford to go wrong here. There was yet another police checkpoint across the road, so I went over to them to ask. They looked at me like I was mad, and I probably did have a mark of insanity about me by this stage, as I rode up desperately asking the way to Uzbekistan. The officer paused, saying nothing.

"Dude, I totally respect your authority, but right now I do not have time for this. I need to get to Uzbekistan. Is that the road to Uzbekistan?"

He nodded.

"And how many kilometres is it?"

He held up ten fingers.

"Arghhh!"

The road took me directly into the face of a formidable headwind once again. What in the world had I done to deserve this? I only had forty minutes until the border closed, so if it was ten kilometres I wasn't going to make it. The wind was just too much. I could only go ten kilometres per hour at full effort. I was exhausted. I was going to collapse. I stopped for five seconds to drink some coke, hoping that the sugar and caffeine might spur me on to some final superhuman effort. But it was too little, too late. The clock was ticking around towards the deadline. I wasn't going to make it, I knew that, but I forced myself to keep going anyway. *'It's not over until it's six, and it's not six. Just keep going as hard as you can until six.'*

I kept on pushing. The wind kept on pushing back. It was so frustrating. Agony. Torture. My body hurt so much but it was the thought that my dream could be about to end that cut deepest. I wanted to cry. A car came the other way and stopped, the female driver handing me a bottle of orangeade which I gulped down eagerly. She was a money changer driving home from the border and she wanted to know if I needed to change money. There was no time for that, of course, but I asked her how far the border was and she told me five kilometres. She drove there every day, if anyone should know, she should, and I decided to trust her. The time was 5:40 p.m. I still had twenty minutes. All I had to do was average fifteen kilometres per hour for twenty minutes. It should have been easy, but the wind made it impossible. I was going eleven, twelve kilometres per hour. *'Come on! You have to find something extra! I don't care where it comes from, you have to find something more! Push harder! Work harder!'* Thirteen, fourteen kilometres per hour.

Ahead of me a row of trucks appeared, parked up at the side of the road, and at the same time a convoy of trucks came the other way very slowly, combining to block out some of the wind. Fifteen, sixteen, seventeen, eighteen kilometres per hour. *'Come on! You're doing it! Yes! Come on!'* Then all of a sudden I was beyond the last of the trucks and back out into the desert, and the wind hit me like a freight train. Eighteen, seventeen, sixteen, fifteen, fourteen, thirteen, twelve, eleven, ten kilometres per hour.

Just when it seemed like all hope was gone another row of trucks came into view and beyond them a fence and a building. It was the border. It was definitely the border. Finally. It was 5:55 p.m. and still more than a kilometre away, but nothing was going to stop me now. I stood up and slammed down on the pedals with everything that I had, every last drop of energy. My speed increased, but the clock kept ticking. 5:57... 5:58... 5:59... I got into the shelter of the trucks and my speed went up again, more than twenty kilometres per hour, as I cried out to a truck driver for directions to the border gates and he pointed the way as I zoomed past in a blur. I rounded the last row of trucks and at long, long last there it was, the border. The guards were just pulling the gate closed as I skidded up to them. They let me through and closed the gate behind me. It was 6:00 p.m. exactly.

21

Uzbek border
11th May 2014

I couldn't think straight. My heart was beating out of my chest. I was panting wildly for breath. I had never, ever, in all my life, pushed myself that hard before. Somehow I made it into the customs building, but I could do no more than lean my bike against a desk and then collapse into a chair. My belongings were evidently supposed to be searched again here, but I lacked the ability to lift them up onto the desk, and everyone was keen to get home, so I was spared. All I was required to do was stagger up to passport control, where two officers laughed at me, mostly because they had to encourage me a great deal to lift my head off their counter long enough for them to check I was the guy in my passport photo. As I didn't look like I was dying in my passport photo they may have struggled to make a positive identification, but I think they wanted to go home too, and they gave me the exit stamp anyway.

I pushed my bike through the building and out the far door, then collapsed outside on the concrete floor. I was still gasping for breath. I was a complete mess. Some guards came in a van, found me lying on the ground, and encouraged me to move on towards the Uzbekistan side of the border. Annoyingly, this was half a kilometre of road away. I walked a little way towards it, away from the van, then collapsed on the ground again. Lying down just felt too awesome. The van drove over, and the guard told me, more firmly this time, that I really must get up and go.

There followed the slowest half kilometre ever in the history of cycling. Three Uzbek officials, young men in army uniforms with machine guns, stood outside of a brick hut, watching as I made my extremely gradual approach. I finally made it to them, gave them my passport, then motioned that I would like to sit down on their step. Two of them agreed that I could, one thought that I should not. *'Sorry buddy, but you're outvoted.'* To be honest, I was going to sit down anyway, even if I'd had three machine guns pointed at me.

But the guys were generally being nice, and as they flicked through my passport admiring my visas I thought I'd ask them if I could just put my tent up next to their little hut, and we could worry about me entering their country in the morning. I really didn't feel capable of going further at the moment. Alas, they shook their heads, and pointed me to the main customs building, which appeared to be about a million kilometres down the road.

I really wasn't up to travelling that far. In fact I was quite impressed with myself that I even had the capability to crawl a few metres away from the hut before throwing up again. This display did, however, demonstrate the seriousness of my predicament to the young guards, and they started talking about ambulances and hospitals.

"No, no," I protested. "Please, I don't need an ambulance. I just need to sleep."

"Okay, a doctor will come here," one of them explained. That sounded like a much better idea than me standing up, so I gave a big thumbs up to signal my approval.

Some time later a truck arrived and a few men jumped out – more young border guards and a bigger, older, and much balder man, wearing a suit jacket over jeans. He was apparently a doctor, but there was no common language and making a diagnosis was difficult. Regardless, he gave me a little pink pill and I swallowed it. Then he indicated to me that I should get up and head for the customs building. Unfortunately his magic pill had not worked, and I still couldn't muster the strength, so I just sat there. Then he took my bike and started pushing it himself, walking off with the border guards that had arrived with him, and indicating that I should follow.

I usually hated it when other people pushed my bike, and it was an indication of what a dire condition I was in here that I failed to raise any objections. I did, however, manage to get off the ground and stumble along behind everyone. After the event I would feel a little bad about having let someone push my bike for me, but looking back at the challenges I'd set myself it seemed it was okay, I was still good. My goal was to personally circumnavigate the planet using nothing other than my bicycle and boats. As long as I didn't use anything else to power *me* I was okay, nothing to worry about. "Christopher you must get in the truck," the doctor said suddenly. "Get in the truck now!"

"No, no, no, no, no!" I responded. It was an extraordinary thing, but the order to get in a motor vehicle really did have the most reviving effect upon me, as I leapt forward and grabbed my bike from him.

"Then you must cycle," he told me. Realising the seriousness of the threat, I found more energy from somewhere and started to do just that. The doctor and his guards jumped in the truck and followed behind me, giving them front row seats for the least impressive, most wobbliest bike ride ever witnessed.

Finally I made it to the building, where I was joined by the doctor. Ironically, the first stage of the border procedure was a medical check, where I would either be declared fit and healthy to enter Uzbekistan, or... well, I wasn't really sure what the alternative was. Probably nobody had ever *not* been declared fit and healthy before. I was, however, a hell of a good candidate to be the first, especially when I responded to the first question by taking a seat on the floor.

The doctor, who was actually a nice and sympathetic man, seemed greatly concerned. He suggested that I needed an ambulance to take me to a hospital. I had to agree with him on one point. I probably *did* need to go to a hospital, but maybe not an Uzbek hospital, and certainly not in an ambulance. "No, no, no," I said, suddenly revived again. I explained via sign language and the Russian word for tent, that what I needed right now, more than anything, was to go to sleep. He went away, presumably to make enquiries on my behalf, then came back and told me that it was okay for me to put my tent up in no-man's land for the night. I was delighted.

It still took all of my willpower and strength to get my tent up, but eventually it was done and I could crawl inside and lie down. Oh, it was bliss. I took a big drink of orangeade to celebrate. Oh dear, my stomach didn't like that at all. I felt it coming straight back up. I reached for the tent zip. It was stuck. I yanked at it frantically. Too late. I puked in my tent. There was more coming. I got the zipper open a bit, stuck my head out, and threw up the rest. The doctor was standing nearby. "Normal," he said. "Christopher, everything normal?"

"Yes, this is surprisingly normal for me."

The next morning I awoke feeling much better and went to see a different doctor to see if he thought me okay to enter the country now. He took my temperature and showed the result to me, but didn't look at it himself, then declared me fit and healthy. His approval came as a great relief, particularly as the thermometer had read 35.2°C, which I'm pretty sure meant I had hypothermia.

The rest of the border process was also easy enough, with me having gained some sort of celebrity status among the guards. I think everyone was just pleased to see I'd made it through the night, to be honest. I was still very tired, but the worst was over. I was into Uzbekistan, and I could now cycle on to the city of Bukhara, less than a hundred kilometres away, where I could find a nice hotel to recover in. I was happy. I cycled away from the border in high spirits, and straight into the face of a hundred-mile-an-hour headwind. *'Arghhh! Seriously? I mean, seriously? Why?!'*

The wind was brutal, even worse than it had been in Turkmenistan, but there was nothing else for me to do – I had to cycle. I said at the start of my journey that I didn't want it to be easy. I didn't want it to be this hard either, I probably should have mentioned that, but I knew that I had to persevere. Surely things would get better

Chris Pountney

eventually. And at least I started to come across a few buildings, a bit more habitation than I'd been seeing, and the gradual conversion of desert to agricultural land. This gave me hope that I might be able to find a hotel to rest in before Bukhara, as I knew I wasn't going to make it there in one day with the wind so cruelly against me. So I was pleased when I reached a small town and my requests for a hotel were met with positive responses. I was pointed with some confidence towards the centre of town by one of a great number of men that were standing at the roadside ready to assist me. I was told it wasn't quite right. I was pointed back. I was pointed another way. Now I was on track. I was directed down the main street. A lot of people were staring at me. A lot of people were calling out to me. I was pointed on a bit further. Yes, just a bit further. Just down there. No, it's not here. Back there. Then a taxi driver stopped and told me that, as a foreigner, I was not allowed to stay in the hotel here, and I would have to go to Bukhara. That sounded like a ruse to me, so I ignored him and looked to the help of other men. I was pointed another way now. Down there. Around the corner. Back a bit. I was getting rather hot and frustrated by this stage. Another man told me I would have to go to Bukhara. I was pointed back. Around again. Down there. Down here. Then a man stopped his car and waved me over to him. I told him I was just looking for a hotel. He took out a pen and paper. 'Good,' I thought, 'he's going to draw me a map.'

But instead he started to write: 'B... U... K... H...'

"Forget it, I'll go to Bukhara!"

I felt like giving up on the idea of a hotel as I left the town and then battled on through the rest of the afternoon, but with the wind being so strong there was no hope of pitching my tent in the exposed land-scape either, and I did not know where I would sleep. My salvation finally came in the early evening when I made one last plea for a hotel to a man at the roadside, and out of sympathy he took me home with him.

The man, dressed in tracksuit trousers and a Dolce & Gabbana sweater that I was pretty sure he hadn't bought new, introduced me to his wife and two young boys in their simple concrete home. His wife wore clothes quite typical of the women I'd seen in Central Asia, with a long, blue dress replete with floral patterns, and a pink bandana-style headscarf tied in a knot at the back. Their house was essentially just one room that was completely unfurnished except for a cheap television and two huge piles of colourful blankets. These were thick and rigid, almost like rugs, and had colourful floral designs all over them. Some of them were quickly laid out in a square on the floor for us to sit around. This was the dinner table. Later these would be taken away and replaced with thicker ones to turn the room into sleeping quarters. It certainly seemed like a creative use of space to me, and made me think about just how superfluous real furniture actually was.

Dinner was brought out, and consisted of chewy flat bread, fried eggs, a pot of tea, and a bowl of individually wrapped little chocolates. These chocolates, the kind that might be saved for Christmas and special occasions back home, were to be found everywhere in Uzbekistan, quite a treat.

Unfortunately, I was extremely tired, and the last thing I needed was for the whole neighbourhood to pop in to see me, but of course that is what happened. It was always an amazing experience to stay with local families, but could also be very hard work at times, and particularly so now, coming a mere twenty-four hours after the culmination of The Desert Dash. As a result, I'm ashamed to say that I responded to all of this fantastic hospitality by falling asleep at the dinner table. My only defence is that it did very closely resemble the bedroom. Seeing my condition, the crowds left, and the family ate in silence, before putting me to bed, with all of us sleeping in the same room but nobody making a sound all night. It was wonderful.

I finally made it to Bukhara the following afternoon, and I was enormously pleased with what I found. As a classic Silk Road trading point, it was full of historical significance and breathtaking architectural wonders. Blue domes and giant tiled facades adorned a labyrinth of yellow-brick walls and buildings and archways. I found it absolutely amazing, but I would be lying if I said that what I really loved the most about Bukhara was anything other than the air-conditioned hotel room with the comfortable bed that I checked into for a few nights.

And I was not the only one. When I arrived at the hotel I noticed a familiar, shiny, white bicycle already there. It belonged to Andreas, and we were reunited once more. It was good to see him, and to be able to thank him for helping me so much that final morning in Turkmenistan, but I wasn't sure if his presence at the hotel was really a good or a bad thing for my recovery. He did some nice things, such as taking me out to dinner, but he also did some weird things, such as the time I noticed him wandering around the courtyard.

"Andreas. Seriously? Are you naked?"

Looking up, the nude Austrian walked over towards the open door of my room.

"Stop! Do not come any closer."

He came closer.

"What the hell are you doing?"

He was very definitely naked.

"What?" he responded. "I walk around naked all the time in Austria."

"Well, you're not in Austria now. This is a public hotel. In a Muslim country."

He put some shorts on.

I closed and double-locked my door, lay down on the bed, and relaxed while listening to some music videos on the television. It felt good to close the door on the hectic outside world for a while and lose myself in my own thoughts. A song that I knew well came on, 'Wake Me Up' by Avicii. It had been playing all the time when I'd been stopped in Munich six months earlier waiting for my passport, but I hadn't heard it since. Listening to it again took me back to that time. It reminded me of how I'd been feeling back then, impatient and eager to push on east as I researched and planned the route ahead. The Desert Dash had been something I'd been thinking about often, looking forward to, but from Germany it had seemed so far away. Now it was over already, I had actually done it, and I was recovering in Bukhara, Uzbekistan. The thought struck me like a lightning bolt and left me buzzing with excitement. I wasn't researching Asia any more. I was actually in Asia. Right in the thick of it.

"..I hope I get the chance to travel the world, but I don't have any plans..."

One of my favourite lines in the song. It made me think of all the many people that dreamed of travelling but somehow lacked the will or the good fortune to be able to make it happen. More than that, it reminded me that I had been just such a person once, making excuses not to go, unable to find a way to get out there and do it. I felt a guilty pleasure in hearing that line now, knowing that it wasn't me any more. I was really here. I was living out my dreams.

I knew that, in this way of life, I had found something that made me happy as a person. There was unquestionably a feeling of genuine contentment deep down inside me. The only problem was that this underlying satisfaction with my life was sometimes in complete contradiction to the daily difficulties that I faced because of it. This was something I became acutely aware of as I left Bukhara and continued cycling through a very hot Uzbekistan, into areas of densely populated agriculture where large numbers of locals wanted to talk with me. Everywhere I went there were men calling out to me. "Atkuda? Atkuda?" they would inevitably shout, a simple Russian phrase asking me where I was from. "Anglia," I would reply. This was a nice, simple interaction. It was quite alright the first ten or twelve times, but after sixty or seventy identical such conversations every day it really got to be quite annoying. On top of that I would get constantly beeped at by cars. That had been happening almost everywhere since Turkey, and I knew it was meant in a friendly, supportive manner, but the novelty had long since worn off. At least half the time the sudden, loud blast of the horn would scare me witless, and in Uzbekistan it was happening more than ever. It was unbearably hot, the wind continued to blow directly against me, and I felt extremely stressed out by all of the constant attention. There was no doubt that Uzbekistan was the hardest country that I had cycled in since... well... Turkmenistan. But apart from Turkmenistan it was probably the hardest ever.

Then late one day I stopped to take a break on a big rock beside a field in which I could see women working. It was a common sight in Uzbekistan. The huge field was dotted with women, covered from head to toe as protection against the sun and the wind, bent over, sowing the land by hand. Throughout the country I had seen this, women doing all the work, ploughing by hand, sowing by hand, everything by hand. And it was always women, the men seemingly doing very little, besides standing at the roadside annoying cyclists. I saw women out in the fields when I set out first thing in the morning, and I saw them as I rode my last kilometres at sunset. All day they toiled, yet whenever I saw them, or had any interaction with them, they had nothing but smiles. Compared with the hardships I saw in their lives, what was my own, entirely self-inflicted, 'suffering'? Who was I, a white, middle-class European man on the adventure of a lifetime, to complain in the face of this genuine struggle. I looked at those women and I felt humbled. A man walked over to me. "Atkuda?" he shouted.

"Anglia," I said, "and I'm very pleased to be here."

Reaching the fabled Silk Road city of Samarkand felt like a major milestone on my journey, a further confirmation of just how far I'd come. The incredible architecture was similar in style to Bukhara, with blue-domed mosques and yellow-brick walls, but here it was taken to a whole new level. Most spectacular of all was the Registan, where a large public square was flanked on three sides by madrasahs, huge buildings of giant archways adorned with ornamental tiles and Arabic script. I sat on some steps that overlooked what was one of the most amazing man-made sights I'd ever been lucky enough to lay eyes on, and tried my best to take in the magnitude of it and what it all meant. As I was doing so I was approached by two young Ukbek men, who introduced themselves, in good English, as Doston and Ashurov. They asked if they could sit with me, as they wanted to improve their English and, seeing as I had no friends, I was more than happy to indulge them. After a while they invited me to join them looking inside the Registan complex, and even offered to pay for me, although this offer was hastily retracted when they realised that the price for foreigners was sixteen times more than for locals.

Inside, the Registan was as impressive as it promised, particularly one dome which was entirely gold-plated. But being in such a special place was made even more enjoyable by having the company of Doston and Ashurov to share it with, and with their English skills I had the chance to hear a little more about life in Uzbekistan. They were both studying Chinese, not because they ever wanted to go to China, but because being a Chinese translator in what was a very popular town for tourists was a good job. Like almost everyone else that I met, they insisted that Uzbekistan was a great country, with a good government that looked after the people, and where they could live happy and peaceful lives.

The two young students then invited me for dinner in a restaurant, and to avoid paying tourist prices we walked for about twenty minutes to a place where local people ate. I told Doston that I was a vegetarian, and he didn't seem to think it would be a problem. The menu arrived and of course I couldn't read any of it. Not that I was given a chance to anyway, as Doston quickly ordered for all of us.

"Wait, what have you ordered? Is it vegetarian?"

"Yes, don't worry," he said. "I have ordered vegetarian, don't worry."

"What is it?"

"Don't worry, it is vegetarian."

A quarter of an hour later and three bowls of noodles arrived, swimming in a broth of animal fat, with great chunks of meat floating in it.

"Erm... what is this?" I asked.

"It's vegetarian. Don't worry."

I used the internet while I was in Samarkand to arrange a host in Dushanbe, Tajikistan, who promised I could look after her apartment over the weekend if I could make it there by Friday. The thought of having a comfortable house to myself to relax in spurred me on to cycle the 480 kilometres from Samarkand to Dushanbe in four and a half days, but in many ways that was a mistake. Adding a pressing schedule to the stresses of the country didn't do anything to make me feel better as I left behind the flat land I'd been cycling on for weeks to struggle up a high pass.

After the pass I reached a police checkpoint, a frequent occurrence in this part of the world, where my name and passport details were recorded in a big book of names that no one would ever look at again. Then beyond it the road split in two. Turn left and I would be heading for Tajikistan, right and it would be Afghanistan. Afghanistan, now that did sound like an adventure. Could I? Should I? Would I dare? Yes, I would do it, why not? I would forget all about Dushanbe, and go off an a whim to Afghanistan. I told my talking bicycle about our new plans.

"Hey bike, turn right. I've made a crazy and rash decision. We're going to Afghanistan."

"No, we're not," replied the inanimate frame.

"Why not? You're not scared are you?"

"Not really. I'm made of steel. But you might want to ask your talking passport."

"What?"

"Hello. I'm your talking passport! We're not going to Afghanistan I'm afraid."

"Why not, you're not scared are you?"

"Yes, actually. But also, I don't have an Afghanistan visa in here, only Tajikistan, so we'll have to go there."

"Oh. Good point. Okay then."

"One more thing."

"Yes, talking passport?"

"Get some more sleep, okay?"

22

Dushanbe, Tajikistan
23rd May 2014

John didn't really strike me as a world cyclist, cigarette dangling from his lips as he greeted me with a grin on Rudaki Avenue, the long, tree-lined boulevard running through the heart of Dushanbe. A tall, slim man of about forty with cropped hair and glasses, he and his partner Gayle were staying with the same host as me, and he'd been sent out to find me. John and Gayle were on their own long cycle tour east across Eurasia, but he explained that they were now being held up by trouble on the Pamir Highway, the famous mountain road that lay ahead for all of us. It was the first I'd heard of such problems. Shootings. Warlords. Angry mobs. Police stations being burnt down. It all sounded terribly exciting, but as I tried to piece together John's words it became apparent what the consequences might be for me. "You do realise what I'm saying?" John said. "The Pamir Highway is closed to foreigners. We can't get through." My onward route was blocked, the continuity of my journey in potential peril once again.

That didn't seem like such an awful thing once John had shown me to the home of our host, Véronique, a French European Union worker based in Dushanbe, where she lived with her eight-year-old adopted son, Gabriel. It was a large house in a walled compound protected by guards, with a big garden, powerful shower, comfortable beds, washing machine, good wifi connection, table-tennis table, two tortoises, and a parrot. After my recent trials it was a little haven of paradise, and Véronique told me I was welcome to stay as long as I wanted. Leaving seemed like it might be difficult, whether the road was open or not.

With the Pamir Highway being a spectacular and increasingly popular cycling route, not to mention pretty much the only way to cross Tajikistan, almost all of the long-distance cyclists crossing Asia were funnelled onto it. And with Véronique being one of the most wonderful people in the world, offering to let cyclists stay with her through warmshowers (an online hospitality network very similar to couchsurfing, but reserved only for cyclists), a great many ended up at her place. Presently there was Gayle and John, and also a Hungarian man, Gábor, who had such a relaxed attitude that most of the time he appeared to be asleep. He was a very tall man of around thirty, with a beard as thick as his accent, and he had been cycling with Gayle and John across much of Turkmenistan and Uzbekistan. It wasn't clear how consensual this arrangement was though, with John revealing to me that they had told Gábor several times that they'd prefer to cycle alone. This request had not been heeded, however, and they still seemed to come as a three.

Lazy days passed. It had always been in my mind to spend a week or so in Dushanbe, a chance to relax and recharge my batteries. After ten months of almost non-stop cycling it was a welcome half-time break before I would have to move on towards the fresh challenges of Siberia, Mongolia, and China that lay ahead in the second period. And the pleasant company made my stop in Dushanbe even more enjoyable. I liked everyone, especially John, who made me laugh, although not so much with his jokes, which were uniformly terrible, but with some of the things that he did. My favourite example being when he went to a party, held for foreign workers in the city, in his pyjamas. The party was good fun, but the day after I had a terrible hangover, compounded by Gabriel, the energetic child that Véronique had adopted some years earlier while living in Rwanda. Gabriel had quickly picked me out as his number one playmate, no doubt due to my immaturity and simple, child-like mind. He was a wonderful boy, but with my stinking hangover he was a bit too much. I managed to buy myself some peace by inventing the 'sleeping' game, and when he got bored with that, the 'punching Gábor in the stomach' game.

All of which was taking place to a backdrop of uncertainty and confusion about the situation with the Pamir Highway. News reports revealed that there had been a serious incident in Khorog, the biggest town on the route, in which an angry mob had burnt down the police station. This violent event, the latest in a series of actions by a local population frustrated with their government, carried the risk of escalating into something more serious, and consequently no foreigners were being allowed into the area. Word reached us that several other cyclists who had left from Dushanbe before I'd arrived were being forced to turn back, and after a few days they started to return. Two French guys, a German couple, a solo German cyclist, and an American couple all arrived into the sanctity of Véronique's home with tales of having cycled for days over awful mountain roads only to eventually find the road blocked and be told that they could proceed no further. It was worrying news. To her great credit, Véronique took the growing refugee camp that had set up tents in her garden completely in her stride.

The Pamir Highway, one of the world's great cycle touring roads, was something that I had been looking forward to riding for a very long time, but now I had to accept there was a real possibility that I wasn't going to be able to do so. The trouble was there weren't a whole lot of alternative routes to get from Tajikistan to Kyrgyzstan. In fact there was only one other, and it involved going over a couple of high mountain passes and through a tunnel known, terrifyingly, as the 'Death Tunnel'. As Véronique explained it was, "Five kilometres long, with water on the ground a foot deep, big potholes which you can't see because they are underwater, no ventilation so it fills up with smoke. Oh, and no lights." It was hardly an attractive alternative to one of the world's great cycle touring roads.

I was undecided. On the one hand I had an angry mob and bloody violence, on the other certain death in a dark tunnel. Neither really appealed. Angry mob... death tunnel... angry mob... death tunnel. I changed my mind back and forth a dozen times each day as to which route I should gamble on. This was a really serious decision, if I got it wrong the continuity of my trip could easily end up being lost, not to mention the potential risk to life that each option carried. No matter how much I thought about it, constantly weighing up my options, I just couldn't decide, so I challenged John to another game of table-tennis instead, and we all waited some more.

Finally the day arrived, with me just about to head off for the Death Tunnel, when it was announced that the powers that be were about to recommence issuing GBAO permits, meaning that the Pamir Highway must be open again. It was great news, and I quickly changed my plans back to my original, preferred route. Gayle, John and Gábor would be able to collect their permits (a necessary extra piece of bureaucratic documentation that granted us permission to the Pamir region) the following morning, but I'd already been given mine when I got my visa in Istanbul, and so I headed off alone.

Initially, the break in Dushanbe appeared to have been just what I needed as I powered through the first afternoon. The next morning, however, was very different. I became concerned about the possibility that the road ahead might still be closed, or even if it was open now, another disturbance in Khorog could easily see it shut down again before I could make it through. The point at which all of the others had been turned back was 300 kilometres of extremely tough cycling away, over a huge mountain pass on a terrible road. The thought of doing that and then being forced to retreat all the way back again was a horrific one. But even if I was allowed through I still had to cycle the whole 1,500 kilometres of the remote Pamir Highway alone. After ten days relaxing and enjoying the company of a number of interest-ing and entertaining people, the feeling of being alone again, this sud-den return to the solitary life, was proving hard to take. Then, if I made it through the Pamir Highway, I would have to cycle fast across Kazakhstan because of only having a thirty-day visa, then fast across Russia for the same reason, and then the same again across Mongolia. And if I somehow made it through all of that, I would then have the exceedingly difficult challenge of cycling across China. Alone. The prospect of all those long and lonely miles ahead of me looked suddenly so daunting, scary and unappealing. This just wasn't fun any more. I stopped my bike, unable to go on, my mood matched by dark clouds that were rolling over the hills in front of me. I took a seat on a rock and said aloud, "I... don't... want... to... do... this... any... more."

Such moments of self-doubt had been rare during my trip, and this was definitely one of the toughest that I'd faced. I didn't want to carry on, but I also knew that I really, really didn't want to quit. I couldn't go on alone like this, though, so I came up with a solution that I hoped might pick me back up again. I knew that Gayle, John, Gábor, and an Englishman named Rob were all supposed to have collected their permits in Dushanbe by now and would be cycling towards the Pamir Highway on this same road. I decided to turn around and cycle back until I found them, and then we could all cycle the Pamir Highway together, with their company hopefully carrying me through to a better headspace.

I knew I'd made the right choice as soon as I came across them. They all looked quite surprised to see me, especially as I was cycling the wrong way, but once I explained it was just because I'd had a mental breakdown everyone was happy. I turned around again, with such a feeling of relief to be back in the company of these new friends of mine. Everything now seemed much less intimidating and a whole lot more fun as the sun came out and the five of us marched on together towards the challenge of the Pamir Highway.

For the next few days we rode on as a happy convoy, along a decent paved road that climbed gradually up through lush, green hills beneath sunny skies. Tajikistan was not a heavily populated country, but we passed through occasional villages, and the Tajiks seemed a friendly lot, often offering us a wave or a smile. We did have one nasty incident, however. I was cycling alongside John when we noticed Gayle, who was in front of us, pull a U-turn and head back towards a group of kids who were loitering beside the road.

"Get him John," she said, pointing at one of the boys. "That one there. He threw a rock at me."

We were both quite shocked to hear such a thing, particularly John, who pulled over close to the offender to confront him. Up until this moment, I had not really noticed John, who hailed from Manchester, as having much of an accent, but now he spoke with an overwhelmingly strong Mancunian tone as he addressed the boy with, "You wanna f*ck off mate." It was such a strong Mancunian accent, in fact, that from the moment it left his lips I knew that John was going to have to be played in the movie by Liam Gallagher. He looks absolutely nothing like Liam Gallagher, but I just don't know of anybody else in the world who could pull off such a perfectly offensive Mancunian threat. Except maybe Noel Gallagher. To be honest, I don't know which is which. It doesn't matter. The point is John was very angry. So was Gayle. For my part I stopped and bravely stood a safe distance away on the other side of the road. There were seven or eight of them and only three of us. Two if you don't count me, and you shouldn't. If it had all kicked off I would probably have done my best to help by cycling off to look for Rob and Gábor, wherever they were. Strength in numbers and all that. But luckily the young hoodlum understood Mancunian surprisingly well, and just ran away.

Putting that incident behind us, we climbed slowly and steadily up a beautiful valley, the mountainsides growing ever steeper as we progressed, until we started to spot snowy peaks up ahead. We knew this was going to be a long and demanding route, however, and we took our time, cycling no more than fifty kilometres per day and taking long siestas to avoid the midday heat. During one of these we stopped beneath the shade of a mulberry tree and, as the others all snoozed, I came up with a quite brilliant idea for a game. The dismal failure of my earlier creation, Pine Cone Wars, during my time cycling with Dr Dave made me realise that it would be a mistake to suggest playing that now. There were also no pine cones. But there were mulberries, great piles of them, and so, in a moment of inspiration, Mulberry Wars was born. I was so excited I woke everyone up to explain the rules to them, briefly summarised as, "We throw mulberries at each other." I received a mixed reaction, with some of my companions unenthusiastic, others indifferent. Nobody wanted to play. Disappointed but not deterred, I played Mulberry Massacre by myself, and just threw mulberries at the boring old fogies. I was sure it would bring us all closer together as a group.

However, my efforts appeared not have been enough, as a few tensions did begin to develop between us. On our fourth morning Gayle and John found a clever solution to this, by cycling off as fast as they could in the morning to get away from the rest of us. It was fairly obvious that they had grown tired of riding in such a big group and preferred to experience the Pamir Highway by themselves, which I thought fair enough. Rob, Gábor and myself consulted, and decided that we would stick together as a three, and let the other two go off and do their own thing.

We pressed on together on a road that was by now rough gravel, twisting and turning around dusty cliff faces as we climbed still higher. Occasionally we came to a stream cascading down the cliffs and, with bridges being somewhat scarce here, we had to cycle right through the water. The stream bed would be made up of large rocks, and it usually took a great deal of skill, confidence, and luck to make it through in one go. Needless to say, I almost always ended up with wet feet.

Around lunchtime the three of us came across Gayle and John, sitting at the side of the road playing scrabble with alphabet biscuits. "We think it will be best if we split into two groups now," Rob said. "We'll go on as a three, and leave you two to do your own thing."

"Good," Gayle said, "I think it's the best idea."

And it was all settled amicably with a smile.

Rob and I rode on together, leaving Gayle and John to their game, but after a few kilometres we realised that Gábor was not behind us. We were a team now, the three of us, and so we stopped to wait for him to catch up. We waited and waited. Enough time passed that we were concerned that something might have happened to him, but just as we were about to go back and check, a cyclist finally appeared. It was John, closely followed by Gayle, closely followed by Gábor. I'm not sure he really understood the teams.

So we ended up pretty much cycling all together as a five again for the rest of the afternoon, until we arrived in a remote little town. This was our last opportunity to stock up on supplies before the very high and very difficult mountain pass that loomed ahead. I knew I was going to need to fuel my body with top quality nutritional products for this challenge, and indeed it was as I was buying my kilogram of biscuits that I bumped into a friendly local. This man, Muhammad, told me that he had left school early, but had taught himself English so well that he now worked as the language teacher in the town. He was a lovely guy, approximately mid-thirties and well-dressed in a dark suit, his gold teeth sparkling as he spoke. We chatted for a while, and the topic of conversation moved around to family. "How did you meet your wife?" I asked.

"She was my student," he said with pride, raising his hand to give me a high five, as if this was a tremendous achievement. I greeted his hand with mine, slapped him on the back, and told him, "In England, you'd get arrested for that."

As I went out of the shop to put my biscuits on my bike I saw that the sky had turned black like smoke, and a huge thunderstorm suddenly swept in. Rain and wind lashed down in an apocalyptic display, and the prospect of cycling anywhere became rather unappealing. Muhammad quickly stepped in, inviting the whole lot of us to stay at the house of the grinning shopkeeper, who happened to be his uncle.

The opportunity to spend the evening with a real Tajik family was wonderful, especially as Muhammad's English skills meant that we could learn a lot about the country as we sipped our sweet tea and ate bread and sweets, sitting cross-legged on the floor of his uncle's living room. He told us a lot about the problems of the country, the widespread corruption at all levels, and the general dislike most of the country had for their dictator. The large number of different ethnic groups made Tajikistan a divided country, especially as the president generally favoured only his own people. Muhammad made me nervous telling us that this area was a major focal point for the civil war of the nineties, and that he thought it was only a matter of time before the people would rise up again. The recent troubles in Khorog were a sign of this growing discontent, and listening to Muhammad made me feel like maybe we were being a bit naive to be cycling into this region now.

I got more nervous when Muhammad told us that his uncle had just been contacted by the police, and it had nothing to do with teachers marrying their students. They wanted to know what we were doing in the house, what we were talking about, why we were there at all. It seemed they wanted us to leave, but we had no place else to go. We never actually saw the police, all of these goings-on were only conveyed to us by Muhammad, on the phone to his uncle, who himself didn't arrive home until later. By the time he did get back, things seemed to have been sorted out and we were permitted to stay, no doubt with a bottle of vodka or a few dollars sent the way of the corrupt cops to smooth things over. Convinced this had been the case I later tried to give Muhammad some money to cover the cost of the bribe, but he proudly refused my offer, as I knew he would.

Muhammad's uncle and his wife made us feel so very welcome into their home, and a third family member also came over to see us. He was wearing a black bomber jacket and burst into the room with such force that for a moment I thought the police were conducting a raid. Thankfully, he was not the police, but in fact a humorous character who would be continually referred to simply as 'the relation'.

Conversation swung back towards the topic of families, and us five travellers all confessed that we were not married, nor had any children. Heads were shook in disbelief at this. For the majority of people in this part of the world it seemed that family, and having children, was the very main point of life. Not having children by a matter of choice was a concept that they found very hard to understand. Fortunately, however, 'the relation' made up for our collective reproductive shortcomings by revealing that he had three wives and twelve children.

'Twelve children,' I thought. *'Wow, we could have such a great game of Mulberry Wars!'*

The rain had made the road very wet and muddy, and the going was clearly set to be very tough as we headed off the next morning. Gayle and John pushed on ahead again and it seemed like we were back to our smaller teams. Splitting up hadn't exactly worked the day before, we'd ended up sleeping all five packed in one room like sardines, but Gayle and John seemed to think it was worth another shot.

Gábor, Rob and I soon came to a section of road that was flooded. And I really do mean flooded, the road had literally turned into a river. Up ahead, we could see Gayle and John bumping their bikes off-road across a field of rocks to get around it, and Gábor, presumably in a desperate attempt to catch them up, tried to take the shorter route by pushing on directly through the water. I wasn't silly enough to do that, so I joined Rob in crossing the boulder field. This terrain wasn't ideal for loaded bicycles, and a particularly nasty bump caused a clip on one of my rear panniers to snap, sending the bag falling off to the ground. I was in trouble now, and consequently not too best pleased when I saw Rob and Gábor reunite back at the road on the far side of their respective obstacles, then cycle off together, leaving me behind.

'So much for being a team,' I thought, as I dug out some cable ties and strapped my pannier onto my rack. I didn't appreciate them abandoning me like that, especially as it was an hour and a half before I caught them up, and when I finally did they had put a mighty river between us.

I'd reached a point that we'd been warned about back in Dushanbe – a big river where a bridge had recently disappeared. Great torrents of water the colour of milky coffee gushed with frightening force before me. All four of my fellow cyclists stood safely on the far bank. It had no doubt been a difficult crossing for them, but the water level was rising by the minute, and I needed to get across quickly or it would be too late for me. Gábor waded over to help, but I was so annoyed at having been left behind that I told him I didn't want any assistance, and instead detached my front panniers to take my things across in stages. Most of my first crossing carrying these bags went okay, but the last section of the river had a really strong current, and I was almost knocked clean off my feet. I somehow kept my balance and arrived at the far side, where John stood. I told him I was annoyed and didn't want any help now. "Chris, you can't do this alone," he shouted over the roar of the river. "You need to let Gábor help you. Don't be too proud."

Well, if there is one thing that I can say for sure, it is that I am not too proud. I had to admit that John was right, sometimes I needed the help of others, no doubt about that. "Gábor," I shouted, after almost being washed away on my return journey to him and my bike, "I'm going to need your help after all. Can you push the back please, and I'll push the front?"

We manoeuvred the bike out into the fast-flowing river. Immediately I realised that taking the front panniers off was a mistake, for it made the bike very back-heavy, and I struggled to hold onto the front as I fought against the relentless current. The water was so strong that rocks were being carried downstream and I heard these clanging against the spokes of my front wheel, battering it, forcing the bike to turn against my wishes until it was almost pointing downriver. Oh, was I ever glad that I had a tall Hungarian man with a firm grip on the back now? What chance would I have stood alone? Even with his help I struggled to pull the bike back on course towards the far bank, with the river continuing to try and rip it from our grasp. And as we inched forward into the strongest part of the river it seemed that the worst was going to happen. The current took control and my bike almost escaped us, was almost carried away, taking all my dreams with it. John was on the far bank waiting for us, and I made a desperate cry to him for help as I began to lose my footing, with the constant barrage of rocks pounding my ankles almost too much to handle. The previous evening Spiderman had been playing on the television for Muhammad's nephews, and now visions of the superhero came back to me in the way that John leapt from the bank into the water, with no fear for his personal safety, to rescue me. It might be just my poor memory of course, but I seem to recall him wrapping a Spidey web around the handlebars and hauling us all to the safety of shore, tall Hungarian, bike and all.

23

Tajik mountains
7th June 2014

Beyond the river we came to a checkpoint, where a corrupt official took possession of our passports with the intention of holding up our progress and extracting a bribe. He made the mistake of letting us into his portacabin first, however, and the pouring rain outside meant we were in no rush to leave. After an hour or so he decided that none of us were going to give him any money, not while it was still raining anyway, and he returned our passports and told us to go.

From there the climb up the pass really began, and we were not aided by the weather, which had turned the dirt road into a sticky, wet mess. I was once again trailing behind the others when I had another problem. This time my rear derailleur, which had been giving me trouble for some time, became all bent out of shape as I tried to force a gear change. Unable to go on and figuring I had once again been left to fend for myself, I went through my tool pannier to see if there was anything that could help get me moving. I dug out my wrench. It looked like the right tool for the job, although I didn't use it to wrench the derailleur straight again. No, no, I bashed it back into shape. Quite the mechanic I am. As I was doing this I was surprised to see Rob cycling back towards me. I'd had a bit of a go at him for leaving me behind before, and he'd obviously felt bad about having done so, for now he had come back to find me. I liked that a lot.

With my bike 'fixed' Rob and I cycled on together, forming a good partnership as the road deteriorated. The rain finally let up, but there were still patches of mud so sticky that it was impossible to ride through, and we had to get off and push at times. At another strong river crossing we took it in turns to help one another propel our bikes across and there was a nice feeling of camaraderie growing. Rob was different from me in many ways, being a forty-something-year-old business analyst on a relatively short cycling holiday around Central Asia. But he was also similar to me in other ways, as a single guy riding a bicycle on a crappy road through a very unpopulated mountain region, and no doubt happy for some company. He also ate a lot of biscuits.

We overtook Gábor when he stopped to clean his bike with a toothbrush. He was hunched over next to a puddle, using water from that to scrub furiously at his frame. To be fair to him, he had just cycled through a lot of mud. On the other hand, he was also about to cycle through a lot more mud, so it seemed not only a weird, but also completely pointless thing to be doing.

It proved to be the longest, toughest climb of my life, and the weather returned to test us further as a sudden storm began to pummel us with hailstones. My rain-jacket had gone missing in Iran, but I'd fished out an ugly green poncho from the lost and found at Véronique's house, and, as ridiculous as this billowing cloak made me look, I was grateful for it now as it protected me from the worst of the weather.

The storm passed and blue skies returned as we neared the summit, the landscape now consisting of grassy hillocks drizzled with snow, a bit like white sauce on mint chocolate chip ice cream. Rob, who until now had been faster than me, began to falter and this time it was up to me to slow and help him, force-feeding him biscuits to keep his energy levels high for the final push. "I thought you were mad when I saw how many biscuits you were bringing with you," he said. "Now I understand."

Finally the summit appeared, the highest point of my trip so far at 3,200 metres above sea level, and home to the most unlikely bus shelter in the world. Arriving in very slow triumph we found Gayle and John sitting within it taking a well-earned rest. Gábor soon followed us up, and the five of us were reunited in celebration.

A gloriously long descent through the mountains brought us to Kalaikhum. Anywhere else and this settlement would be regarded as little more than the village it was, but after where we had been it felt to us like a metropolis. It was strange to be back in civilization again, picking up tins of beans on the shelves of a (very small) supermarket, and fighting through crowds of people to locate the market (which in this case turned out to be one man with a few sacks of rather odd-looking root vegetables). There were even rumours of a bike shop, but when I asked around I was only pointed to a closed kiosk with pictures of CDs and hammers above it. I just had to hope that my troublesome derailleur would continue to hold.

Rob was so impressed by Kalaikhum, or perhaps so worn out from the pass, that he decided to stop and take a rest day. So, as I continued up a steep hill on the other side of town, I did so as part of a group of four. This new arrangement lasted only as far as the top of the climb, however, because at that point Gayle turned to me and Gábor and blurted out, "We don't want to ride with you any more."

I decided not to take this too personally, as it seemed to be directed mostly at Gábor, but nevertheless I took the 'hint' and let them go on ahead. With Gábor waiting only a matter of seconds before giving pursuit, I was all alone to sit and admire the far bank of the river that the hill overlooked. And it was certainly an interesting thing to look at, for on the far side of the river was, believe it or believe it not, the country of Afghanistan. I looked across and saw men in long robes and women in burkas, and very little traffic save for the occasional motorbike or donkey. From Paris to the Afghan border, I'd come a long way. Whether or not I would be going much further was soon the question, however, as not long after I resumed cycling I heard a 'ping' from beneath me and felt my chain stop moving, bringing me to a grinding halt.

One of the jockey wheels of my derailleur had gone flying off, and the rest of it had become completely mangled. This was a really bad thing, as I couldn't ride my bike without a rear derailleur, I had no spare, and I was in the middle of nowhere, a grenade's throw from Afghanistan.

I fumbled in the dirt for the jockey wheel, found it, then tried to put the derailleur back together again. This turned out to be somewhat akin to trying to put an orange back together having already peeled it and separated all the segments, and having made a smoothie out of it, and drunk it. I bashed, I bent, I stretched, I swore, but all to no avail. My derailleur was a write-off, and I was in a tight spot. There was no way for me to pedal now. I could not ride my bicycle. This was a serious problem for a man trying to cycle around the world.

The road had got a little busier since Kalaikhum, and any normal touring cyclist would surely have been comforted by the idea of sticking out a thumb and hitching a ride out of this predicament, but I was no normal touring cyclist. Instead I found comfort in the fact that I had progressed only seven kilometres from Kalaikhum, and it wouldn't be too far to walk back. That kiosk with the CDs and hammers above it was still fresh in my mind, a beacon of hope in a desperate situation. *'Maybe... just maybe...'* I thought, as I set off walking the way I'd come in the shadow of Afghan mountains, pushing my shameful bike with me. The cries of "Hello, hello" from the small children in their tattered second-hand clothes came as something of a morale boost, and my bike was still functioning well enough to allow me to freewheel down the final hill back into Kalaikhum. Of course I arrived to see that the kiosk was still closed.

I asked around. Promising noises were made. A bearded man in a skull cap appeared. He unbolted the door, ducked inside, and lifted the shutters to reveal a cornucopia of products, including, I believe, both CDs and hammers. I was encouraged to see that the rumours were true, there was a bicycle parts section. Sadly, it only covered about five inches of one shelf. I showed my broken derailleur to the man, more in hope than expectation. He nodded and reached his arm behind a cassette and a pair of brake pads. Back and back went his arm, seeming to reach out into another dimension filled with bicycle parts, before returning to this one with a brand spanking new rear derailleur. I squealed with delight, then cautiously asked how much it cost. He knew that I needed it, he could pretty much name his price. I decided that I'd happily pay anything up to fifty dollars, although I'd probably grudgingly stretch to a hundred. There wasn't a bike shop for hundreds of kilometres and I needed this thing really bad. "Twenty somoni," he said. It seemed like a fair price. If you're not up on your Tajik currency conversions, that'd be about four dollars, or two pounds fifty.

I didn't really expect it to work, it was just a piece of Chinese-made crap, but I had to try, didn't I? I found a good spot and fitted it to my bike, and to my astonishment not only did it work, it worked perfectly. It was a miracle, an absolute miracle. Of course I still had to cycle hundreds of kilometres on a remote gravel road relying on a piece of metal and plastic that cost four bucks, but my bike could move again, and that was all that mattered as I cycled onwards with a big grin on my face. "Hello! Hello!" came the cries from the children. "Hello! Hello!" I replied, with all of us showing impressive enthusiasm, considering it was the third time we'd done it that day.

Ahead of me lay the checkpoint where all of the earlier cyclists had been turned back. This was the moment of truth. Would the long and arduous journey here be all in vain? Would the only thing awaiting me be a long and arduous journey back the way I'd come? Or would I be allowed through to Khorog and the rest of the Pamir Highway? So many cyclists had been rejected here that I was anticipating a mighty garrison of troops and guards, a fortified blockade, barbed wire fences, Alsations, maybe a tank or two, helicopters circling overhead, that sort of thing. Instead I found two men sitting by the dusty road at a picnic table, looking for all the world like they were selling raffle tickets. One of them called me over to add my name to yet another big book of names, and that was it, I was free to pedal on towards the scene of the bloody violence. Hurrah!

There was a charming sense of inevitability about the way Gayle,

John, Gábor, Rob and I managed to find one another again. It was as if a magnetic force were drawing us all together and eventually no one was strong enough to resist it any longer. After all reuniting we cycled as something of a team again, and finally arrived in Khorog as the same group of five that had pretty much left Dushanbe together. And of course it was the angry mob burning down the police station in Khorog that had delayed and aligned our journeys in the first place. I wondered what horrors we might find now as we finally arrived, particularly as it was, against all statistical probability, Friday the 13th once again. But so far on this date I'd already survived an encounter with an alien in Russia and a serial killer in Slovakia, so what was there to fear from an angry mob in Tajikistan? I mean, really?

On the face of it there didn't seem to be any reason to worry. Khorog looked like a regular town, with a few extra posters of the president around just to remind everyone who was boss, and a few burnt-out shells of buildings. It seemed as if the situation had calmed down here now, but I wasn't planning on sticking around. My visa was expiring much sooner than my companions', and as they all settled in for a long stay at the Pamir Lodge, the comfortable accommodation hotspot for all passing cyclists, it was time for me to press on alone towards Kyrgyzstan. It had been a fantastic experience to ride with them. They were all great people, and it had been a first opportunity for me to cycle together in a group, with all the ups and downs that it brought. Best of all, though, the support of these four people had lifted me so much from the negative place I had been in mentally as I left Dushanbe, to a point where I was once again relishing the adventure and looking forward with excitement, not apprehension. For that, they had my eternal gratitude.

For two whole days I cycled uphill from Khorog, at an altitude of 2,000 metres, to the Pamir plateau, which, at 4,000 metres above sea level, was the highest I had ever been. This climb took me up through Gunt Valley, the rocky mountains and grassy meadows of which were much more picturesque than the name implied. It was a long and steady ascent, yet I struggled to adapt to the altitude, and suffered severe headaches and barely slept on my first night on the plateau. The road flattened out at this height and I needed to remain above 4,000 metres for many days, so it was a relief when my body began to acclimatise and the headaches stopped, although the lack of oxygen in the air (barely half that at sea level) made everything noticeably harder.

This was one of the most incredible landscapes I had ever seen, with craggy mountain tops dusted with snow rising from the broad plateau. The road ran smooth and flat as I pedalled beneath big, blue skies dotted with picture-book fluffy white clouds. The only brief intrusions on this silent world were occasional Chinese trucks that would roar past and then disappear over the horizon, quickly leaving me once again to my own world. The scenery was amazing, but it was the remoteness that I really loved. At times half a day went by without me seeing anyone, and the feeling of being so far from civilization on this vast open plain was wonderful.

I'd really enjoyed my time cycling with a big group of other cyclists, and I now also felt happy to be on my own again, yet I couldn't help but daydream of an alternative that would be even better. It had been a long time since I'd said goodbye to Hanna for the last time back in Turkey, and as much as I was loving this adventure, I was also starting to really miss female company. My ideal scenario, my number one dream, was to find a girl who wanted to come with me, an adventurous soul with a passion for both cycling and travelling the world. A girl who wouldn't mind sleeping outside in the cold, or cycling over massive mountain ranges, or telling Uzbek men where she came from. As I cycled alone through the breathtaking landscape I fantasised about meeting a solo female cyclist and having someone to share this journey with. Out of all the cycle tourists I'd met on this journey so far, none had been lone females, and I knew it was likely to remain just a fantasy. But, like so many aspects of this whole project, maintaining a positive outlook was key, and the hope of someday finding my dream girl, finding 'the one', was an extra motivation to keep on pedalling.

Such positivity was certainly necessary on the final pass that separated Tajikistan and Kyrgyzstan. I rose up from the plateau on a terrible corrugated road with the weather getting worse and worse the higher I went. Before long I was engulfed by a full-on blizzard, but I had no alternative other than to continue cycling, for there was nowhere to hide on the exposed mountain ridge. The washboard surface was so bad that I rode on the edge where it was a bit smoother, risking being blown over steep precipices as I did so. With the weather, the lack of oxygen, the road surface, and the incredibly steep gradient, it was one of the toughest climbs of my life. It just went on and on, up and up, higher and higher, but eventually I moved through the blizzard and arrived at the Tajik border post, which consisted of a few nondescript buildings with clouds drifting past them at the summit of the pass.

The descent was no better. The road was basically just mud, and I had to hold my brakes down continuously to remain in control of my bike. My hands were numb from the cold, even before I was hit by another blizzard. When it came I was forced to a stop, as the icy sleet hit me almost horizontally and stung my eyes like they were being jabbed at by pins. Eventually I'd had enough, and pitched my tent to wait for better weather.

The next morning I awoke to see that the sun had returned, and I was free to cycle on. I'd actually spent the night in no-man's land again, and, with Kyrgyzstan not being silly enough to put their border control building in the clouds, I soon reached it at the foot of the descent. I was welcomed by a friendly guard, who enthusiastically called me an "Extreme tourist." It was a title I felt very justified in accepting after the blizzard and the muddy road, yet considering a fairly steady stream of cyclists rode this way all summer, I probably wasn't the first or the last to receive such a compliment from him.

The road next crossed a broad, lush-green valley dotted with occasional yurts. These white dome tents formed the living quarters of nomadic families, and the fields were rife with the animals from which these people made their livelihoods. Two boys came to investigate me, riding over on a donkey to peer at me in curiosity through narrow eyes that sat above plump, rosy cheeks. With a chain of snow-topped mountain peaks as a backdrop it was an incredible welcoming party to introduce me to Kyrgyzstan.

I soon came to Sary Tash, a small village where an old man that stank of cigarettes called me to a halt in the middle of the road. He spoke to me in Russian, and I'd picked up enough of the language by now to understand that he was telling me that the road ahead was closed, and that I should stop here and stay in his hotel. I passed this off as a ruse to get some money out of me, and carried on regardless, up yet another long, steep pass.

It was again a brutal climb, but when I finally did reach the summit I was rewarded with a spectacular view as the road snaked down the mountains on the far side in a series of switchbacks. As I looked down at what was below me, I noticed a tailback of cars not moving anywhere. The words of the old man came back to me. It looked like he was right, the road was closed. But after the effort of the climb there was no way I was going all the way back to Sary Tash, not for love nor money.

I went down to where the cars were waiting, where I was informed that there had been a massive landslide that would take two days to clear. A number of quarrying trucks were busy carrying rocks from the landslide and were, in what seemed to be a very poorly thought out strategy, dumping them back higher up the mountain. A trio of foreign motorcyclists were also there, trying to work out how to get down. One of them, a thickset British biker named Wilko, had spotted a trail going down the mountainside that zig-zagged back and forth before rejoining the road below the landslide. It looked very steep, too much for their big bikes, but Wilko was a very friendly sort of man and he offered to help me get my bicycle down.

We made our way carefully onto what was little more than a goat track. It was very steep, but Wilko was big and strong, and he gripped onto the back of my bike as I held the brakes down full, and in this fashion we edged gradually down the mountainside in the rain.

Back on the tarmac I shook Wilko's hand in gratitude and resumed my ride, feeling pleased that I'd been able to progress past an obstacle that motor vehicles could not. Continuing down beyond the last of the switchbacks I entered another valley, where grassy patches beside a river provided the home for several more yurts, and children shouted and waved to me happily as I passed. But I was getting wet, so I stopped just before a village to put my poncho on. It had been abandoned at Véronique's by another cyclist, and it wasn't hard to understand why, given how ridiculous it looked. But keeping dry seemed more important than looking good for the kids, so I put it on all the same, and it flapped around like a cape as I continued on.

Halfway through the village I noticed the distinctive panniers of a touring bike leaning up against a wall next to a small shop. Naturally I was curious, and stopped to investigate, just as the owner of the bike stepped out of the shop. My heart skipped a beat. It was a girl. An attractive girl. A solo, female, cycle tourist, girl. She looked up at me and smiled from beneath the hood of her red North Face jacket. This was it. I'd found her. After all these years, I'd finally found her.

'Oh God, I wish I wasn't wearing this stupid poncho.'

24

Akbosaga, Kyrgyzstan
21st June 2014

The girl spoke in a French accent to tell me that her name was Anaelle, but after laughing at my attempts to pronounce Anaelle, she told me that I'd better just call her Ana. She had wavy blonde hair and the cutest little upturned nose, and she will be played by Reese Witherspoon in the movie. We stood there for a while, talking outside of the shop and getting along very well. It was great. She was so lovely, and it all felt natural. I always knew that if I only cycled for long enough, and far enough, then eventually I would find exactly this – a good looking girl, also cycling alone, that I instantly clicked with. And I suppose, if I'm honest, deep, deep down inside, I always knew that she'd be going the other sodding way.

"I started cycling from Cambodia six months ago," she said. "Now I'm going to Tajikistan, Uzbekistan, Turkmenistan, Iran, Turkey, then home to France." Or to put it another way, exactly the way I had just come. I felt like crying at this cruel joke that Fate was playing upon me. Still, it was early evening, and I was sensible enough to suggest that we camp together. I told her about the grassy area with the yurts, and we cycled back up through the village to set up our tents there.

Ordinarily, camping so close to local people would result in them coming to investigate, but for some reason we were left in peace to sit outside and chat all evening, with my emergency poncho finding its true calling in life as a picnic blanket. As we talked it became clear that we had a lot in common. Ana told me about cycling in China, about how the drivers there would constantly beep their horns. "When they see you, they toot. When they pass you, they toot. If they see a cow, they toot. If they get in their car, they toot. Its so annoying, and so painful. It makes me so angry, so mad, always tooting."

As I looked at her whinging, complaining face, I thought, *'Wow, this girl is perfect for me.'*

We laid there and chatted until the stars came out. Ana told me about the time when, having just backpacked through Africa, she was pushing her bag in a trolley through a South African mall and was mistaken for a homeless person. This was about the moment when I started to believe we really were meant to be together. I moved closer to her, sensing a mutual attraction, born from the months we'd each spent alone on the road, from the long, lonely miles that had led us here to this moment. A shooting star fizzed across the sky above. I squeezed Ana's hand in mine, and I made a wish. I won't tell you what I wished for, but I'll tell you one thing; I was soon a firm believer in the power of wishing on shooting stars.

Not wanting to say goodbye, the next morning I offered to go back up the mountain with Ana in order to help get her bike around the landslide. She smiled her approval, then ran off to get me a glass of kumis from a small, timid woman in a nearby yurt. Ana explained that kumis, the national drink of Kyrgyzstan, was fermented horse milk. I took a sip. It wasn't quite to my taste. Luckily, Ana had told me that if I didn't like it she would drink the rest, an offer that I held her to. I passed it to her and she slowly downed the glass, inserting the occasional "Mmm" and "Ahh" for the benefit of the watching woman. Ana had been in the country for more than a month, and she was a real pro at the 'pretending to like fermented horse milk' game.

We cycled together back up towards the landslide, chatting away happily on the quiet road, until yet another touring cyclist came towards us. This was a Frenchman named Jacques who had spent three years travelling the world. Upon hearing that I was going back to help Ana he also offered to backtrack and provide additional assistance. *'Dude, you are totally cramping my style,'* I thought.

Ana considered his offer but finally declined it, after looking me up and down and deciding that I was all the help she needed. It was shortly after the two of us said goodbye to Jacques that she told me that she was short-sighted and had poor vision. "Ah yes, of course," I said. "That explains a lot."

We arrived at the point where the road was closed and headed for the track that I had descended on the previous day. I'd rather optimistically thought we'd be able to push the loaded bikes up between us, but the way was rather steeper than I remembered, and there was no big motorcyclist to help. It actually took our combined efforts to push the unloaded bikes up, with the bags being carried up separately in stages. With a total of five switchbacks it took us more than an hour before we were both safely above the landslide.

We cycled the remainder of the pass and then headed all the way down to Sary Tash, where I supposed I had to find an old man smelling of cigarettes to apologise to. But it was another familiar face that caught my eye as we rode towards the village. A motorcyclist zoomed past, then turned and came back to see us. Of course it was Wilko. Lifting his visor he explained that he and his buddies were camping near Sary Tash until the road was reopened. As for what I was doing back on the wrong side of the landslide, that took a bit of explaining. Basically, I pointed at Ana and said "Girl." Wilko grinned and gave me an approving nod.

Ana and I camped that night next to a stream running through the broad green valley, with Tajikistan's familiar snowy mountains stretching across the horizon again. It was an implausible setting, unrealistically picturesque. I felt like I was suspended in a dream. My own journey had been temporarily forgotten as I got lost in Ana's. Neither of us wanted this brief moment to pass. We both wanted to cling on to the temporary escape from reality that this little romance provided, but we had no say in the matter. Her time in Kyrgyzstan was at an end, she had to press on to Tajikistan to keep her visa dates. My own Tajikistan visa had expired, and I could follow her no further. Our fate was sealed by the stamps in our passports. The next morning I watched her disappear off to be welcomed as an 'extreme tourist' and turned back to face my own lonely existence.

"Hey bike," I said. "Why do you always take me away from girls like this?"

"Whoa! I am not having this conversation with you again! YOU are the one pedalling. YOU are the one steering. Did you ever stop to think about me in any of this?"

"What?"

"Ana's bike. Didn't you see? She was orange. Have you ever seen such a sexy piece of steel? One more day and I was in there, I'm telling you."

"Sorry, I didn't think."

"No Chris, you never do think about me."

"I'm really sorry."

"No, forget it, I'm not talking to you any more."

"Erm... yeah okay. Probably for the best."

I cycled on in silence back across the valley, through Sary Tash, and then up the big mountain pass for a third time. This was a task made much easier as a) I knew what to expect now, b) I was still buzzing from having met Ana, and c) I bought a lot of Snickers in Sary Tash. The downhill was also much easier as the landslide had finally been cleared and the road reopened. I freewheeled down the switchbacks, past the yurts, and through the village where I'd met with Ana, then on with the rest of my life.

For a while Kyrgyzstan proved quite difficult. It became uncomfortably hot again as I reached lower altitudes, and the road got a lot busier, which wouldn't have been so bad if anyone knew how to drive. As if having to dodge cars being driven erratically wasn't enough, I also had to avoid stones being thrown at me by kids. The first such incident occurred when I noticed a chubby little boy pick up a stone and prepare to launch it at me. I stopped and looked at him menacingly. It was a hot day, I was sweating, and I was frustrated, so I must have looked really quite menacing. He dropped the stone and ran away. But not more than a few minutes of cycling later I heard a small rock clang into my back spokes. I looked around and saw another land nearby. I stopped, and noticed two young boys hiding behind some long grass. They also turned and fled across the fields at the sight of my menacing glare. I appealed to an old man who happened to be walking along the road, pointing to the troublesome youths and explaining via sign language what they had done. I suppose I was hoping that he might know who they were and be able to reprimand them in some way. He nodded to show that he had understood, then shook his fist at them as they ran away. *'Well, I suppose that counts as a form of reprimanding.'* The man then invited me to have a drink with him, but as he smelt like he'd just been involved in an explosion at a vodka factory, I declined.

The drunk locals, bad driving, intense heat, and stone-throwing children soon had me thinking it would be a good idea to head for the mountains again. I'd heard from Ana about a route through them on gravel roads that she said would be very challenging and very rewarding, and it turned out to be great advice. I was soon leaving behind the chaos of the heavily populated lowland and climbing up through lush green hillsides where cows, sheep and horses grazed in their hundreds. This was the territory of the nomadic yurt-dwellers, and being away from permanent habitation the road was blissfully quiet. The landscape was criss-crossed by streams where I could collect water for drinking as well as washing. I would often use natural water sources such as lakes and rivers for washing myself and my clothes. Many a time during my travels I would hang my freshly laundered clothes upon a barbed wire fence and then jump in for a swim and to merrily scrub myself clean. It was invigorating and with these methods I believed I was able to maintain a certain standard of hygiene. I may not have been doing as well as I might have hoped, however, if an experience I had at a rare village shop was anything to go by. I'd stopped to ask directions of a man who quite miraculously could speak English. As we fell into conversation he revealed that he was a cinematographer who worked in the capital, Bishkek, and he'd got married only two days earlier. I found that interesting, because Ana had told me that it was a tradition in Kyrgyzstan for a man's mother to kidnap whichever woman he had decided that he wanted as a wife. I asked this fellow if this was something that really still happened. "Traditionally, yes," he said. "But these days if it happens the woman's family will usually go to the police." Which seemed fair enough to me. Politeness stopped me from asking if his bride's family needed to do that.

At the shop the man insisted on buying me water and ice cream, which I very much appreciated as it was still hideously hot. Then the owner of the shop, a friendly man with an Islamic skullcap and long black beard, gave me bread, apples, and more water as a further gift. It was yet another example of the generosity I'd experienced so much of all across Asia, and I was very grateful as I crammed the items onto my already overloaded bike. Then the shop owner went too far, and came out with a huge watermelon for me. *'Now where in hell does he think I'm going to put that?'* I thought, although "Thank you very much" was what I said. The only thing to do was to immediately eat as much of it as possible, so I asked after a knife, then shared the watermelon out.

We sat there chatting as we ate, but the shop owner, whose name was Alik, couldn't speak English, so the first man translated for him. "Alik would like to give you some money to go to the local banya where you can take a shower, and to the barber for a haircut and a shave."

Now a more sensitive man than myself might have been offended at this point, but I was too busy laughing at the insinuation that I needed to shave, coming as it did from a man with a long flowing beard. "No, I'm okay. Thank you Alik. I quite like being sweaty and smelly and hairy." Alik sighed, threw his hands up, then disappeared back into his shop.

A few minutes later he returned carrying a bag filled with even more presents for me. I took it from him and looked inside to see some soap, two disposable razors, toilet paper, and a big box of cotton buds. "Have you been looking in my ears too?" I chuckled. Upon seeing my smile Alik snatched back the bag and ran into his shop, returning it to me a moment later with the addition of a toothbrush and some whitening toothpaste. "Oh come on, Alik, really? My teeth aren't that bad!"

Before long Kyrgyzstan became a true adventure, as I found myself riding on rough gravel roads up and over yet more high mountain passes. It was extremely hard work due to the steep gradients and poor roads. Even the descents were slow and painful as I had to constantly hold down my brakes to avoid skidding on the gravel and flying over steep cliffs. It was so tough that I was only able to cycle thirty or forty kilometres per day, compared to my usual average of around eighty or ninety. But for once I had time on my side, and my slow progress gave me the chance to really appreciate my surroundings. The great waves of mountains were so remarkably green they appeared to be covered in felt. The air was fresh and pure. High up I found plateaus where animals grazed and the only people I saw were living such simple lives in yurts. These big white dome tents had been a common feature throughout Kyrgyzstan, and I was curious to see what they looked like inside. Ana had told me that she had received constant invitations into them, but that had not happened for me, something I could only assume was because of my teeth. But then one evening all that seemed about to change when I came across some smiling children. One of these, a girl of no more than ten who had a purple woollen hat half covering her dirty face, was astride a donkey. Another girl, dressed in red, was slightly older and more confident despite not having a donkey to sit on, and asked if I would like to come with them and drink tea. Before I could respond a big black horse came galloping around the corner. At first I thought it completely out of control as it careered towards us, but then I saw that there was a young boy riding it, at which point I was absolutely certain that it was out of control. Fortunately, I think more by luck than anything else, the horse skidded to a halt just before us, allowing the boy to join in with the chorus of "Chai? Chai? Kumis? Kumis?"

I was really excited about my first yurt experience, so I eagerly followed the children around a small hill to where they were living. Imagine my disappointment then, when I saw where they were living, and it was not a yurt, but a rusty, grey trailer. Here I was introduced to the adults of the family, who greeted me kindly, albeit with a slight air of 'I can't believe those kids have brought another bloody cyclist home.' They showed me into the little old trailer, where I woke up Grandad and took a seat at the dinner table/bedroom/floor. A tall glass of fermented horse milk was handed to me, and I politely took a sip. Urgh! No. Who in the world came up with such a concept? The boy, who had perhaps been thrown from his horse, was now sitting on the floor opposite and watched me through keen eyes. "Kumis, in England?" he asked.

"Oh no, I don't know about that. Maybe you can find some in Holland & Barrett."

Then the grandma suggested I put some sugar in my kumis.

'Oh God, yeah. That's a good idea!'

Before long I noticed that the trailer had been almost entirely vacated and, curious to know where everyone had gone, I got up and took a walk outside. It was almost sunset and it seemed that meant it was time to round up all of the animals. A surprising amount of this was done by the little girl in the purple hat on her donkey. She managed to herd 296 goats into their pen all by herself. A more difficult task was provided by the young cows, who had to go in another small pen. This was tricky because a) they did not want to go into the small pen, b) their mothers did not want them to go into the small pen, c) there was a big angry bull that did not want them to go into the small pen, d) the big angry bull was only being kept back by a small girl with a stick, and e) the small girl with the stick was too busy posing for my photographs to do her job properly. Somehow, all of the calves were eventually cajoled, slapped, and manhandled to where they belonged and I turned back to my bike, which was lying on the grass, to discover that a two-year-old was the only thing stopping it being attacked by a cow. The toddler was doing a tremendous job warding the animal off with a stick. The children seemed to be doing an awful lot of the work. And the women too. As ever the men sat around doing almost nothing, although one of them did just about rouse himself to get up and chase away a cow at one point.

The rough roads eventually brought me up to a high altitude lake called Song Köl. This destination had been a target of mine for a while and it didn't disappoint. In fact, it was one of the best places that I had been to on the whole journey. The giant lake was a brilliant blue and sat silently amidst a vast area of unspoilt pasture land surrounded by grassy peaks. Unsurprisingly, this verdant wonderland was home to a great many animals. This meant yet more yurts, and as I set off pedalling around the lake I made it my goal to finally see inside one.

Soon two young boys on a horse spotted me and rode over in my direction, giving me hope that they might invite me to their yurt. They cut across my path and stopped, blocking the way in a style reminiscent of a highway robbery. I came to a halt and said hello, but they did not reply and just looked at me and giggled. They were only about ten years old. One of them had a skull and crossbones on his woolly hat. I heard the other whisper the word "Money" to him. So it was a highway robbery! How exciting! But just as I was preparing to reach for my wallet they galloped off. As they rode away one of them leant back and screamed "Money! Money! Money!" at me, his cries growing fainter as they disappeared across the plains. *'That's not quite the way you do it boys.'*

Time went on and I still hadn't come close to a yurt invitation, but I was trying to stay positive, and another potential opportunity arrived when a young boy on a donkey came over the fields to me.

"Hello," I said, but it garnered no response.

"Hello," I said in Russian. Again nothing.

"Hello," I said in every other language that I could say it in (which was by now quite a few). Still no reaction at all from the boy, who seemed, how can I put this, a little slow. I seized my opportunity. "Take me to your yurt, kiddo."

I followed the child and his donkey across the field to a trio of yurts, where an older boy greeted us. He had the unlikely name of Merlin, was fifteen years old, and by some miraculous twist of fate could speak some English. He told me that the younger boy was his brother, Johnny, and he also introduced me to his older sister, Diana, who was busy hanging washing on a line strung between two of the tents. There were a lot of younger kids about too. Merlin told me that in all he had twelve brothers and sisters, which seemed an awful lot of mouths to feed, especially as the family also owned one hundred sheep, thirty cows, twenty horses, five goats, two dogs and a donkey. Lucky there was so much grass.

Merlin showed me into the yurt. Finally! And it turned out to have been worth the wait, for ducking inside through the rolled-up doorway brought me one of those real 'wow' moments. I came face-to-face with a cosy homestead, the floor and walls all decorated with brightly patterned rugs. The rugs, like the felt of the white yurts themselves, were woven from sheep's wool, but were dyed mostly red, giving me the slightly unnerving impression that I had entered into a giant sheep. Thin wooden struts gave the yurt its dome shape and crossed at a circular hole at the top of the canvas, an opening which made it surprisingly light inside. I was invited to sit down on the floor next to a table, where kumis and tea were served to me by Diana. Why they would always serve two drinks I did not know, for it seemed like far too much liquid. In any case by this stage I had decided that the fermented horse milk was nothing more than a practical joke they liked to play on tourists. National drink my foot, I never saw any of them drinking it.

I was shown to the other yurts. In one of them Merlin's mother was hard at work churning butter with a machine, where she had to constantly crank away at a lever. Sweat poured from her brow. It looked like real backbreaking labour for the poor woman. Then we went outside and met Merlin's father, who was sitting on a stool with a pair of binoculars.

"What's he doing?" I asked Merlin.

"He's watching the sheep."

Merlin then tried to get me to ride on a horse, an offer I declined on account of it not being a bicycle or a boat. Instead Merlin got on the horse and rode beside me and my bike across the grass and back to the dirt track I'd been following. It had been a wonderful experience, to see inside a real yurt, get a little feel for how these people lived, and drink some more kumis.

"Thank you Merlin, I had a magical time."

"Yes," he replied, then after a pause he tentatively asked "I take fifty money?"

"Ah, yes. Okay. For the kumis? Here you go."

I thought I'd better pay up. I had kind of invited myself, and I didn't want anyone to cast a spell on me.

25

Bishkek, Kyrgyzstan
15th July 2014

I enjoyed a welcome week off the bike in Kyrgyzstan's capital, Bishkek, as I waited to be approved for a Chinese visa. I applied for the visa through a travel agency that did all of the paperwork for me, and all I had to do was to provide two passport photos. After the Photoshop disaster in Iran I stressed to the man in the store that I did not want any editing done to my images. But as he snapped away with the camera he shook his head and seemed quite annoyed by the grubby yellow T-shirt I was wearing. I was quite happy with my grubby yellow T-shirt, so you can imagine my surprise when I went back an hour later to collect the photos to see that I had, in actual fact, been wearing a suit. As I had also shaved (the first time in a year that I had been clean shaven) because I'd heard of people being refused Chinese visas for having a beard, my passport photos had me with rather a clean-cut, businessman-like appearance. A little glimpse into how my life might have been, perhaps.

I was able to rest well in Bishkek at the At House guest house, a quaint little refuge run by a soft-spoken Canadian man named Nathan and his Bulgarian partner, Angie. As touring cyclists themselves they had decided to open this place up for weary bike travellers after Angie had found work in Bishkek. Being in a perfect location for those cycling through Central Asia it was very popular, and there were around a dozen riders lazing around, tinkering with bicycles, updating blogs, and otherwise doing very little. Perhaps the most interesting among them was a young Belgian called Tom. He had long dreadlocks tied in a scruffy ponytail and a guitar that he would occasionally strum on, and his most notable trait was that he would frequently and unapologetically let fly with loud farts. One afternoon he asked to borrow my computer as he did not have one. I lent it to him, thinking that he needed it to reply to e-mails or maybe to update a blog. Instead he sat there and watched episode after episode of South Park, long into the night.

Nathan had offered to help me to fix up my bike, a necessary undertaking given the battering it had taken of late and, with the prospect of four months of tough cycling ahead of me, I needed to get it ship-shape. Nathan was an enormous help, and was able to talk me through rebuilding my front wheel with a new rim, and even provided me with a replacement bottom bracket, as mine had broken again. With so much work to do I decided that I might as well strip the bike down completely and take the chance to repaint my rusting frame while I was at it. Some of the less-experienced cyclists of the group stared slack-jawed at the pile of disassembled parts and said they couldn't believe I would ever ride it again. When I'd first bought this bike the mechanic in the shop in London had asked me if I knew anything about bicycle mechanics and I had said that I did not. "You'll learn," he told me. Frankly speaking, I doubted that I would, and yet he was right. I'd picked it up as I went along, often out of necessity when something broke in the middle of nowhere and I needed to look at it, figure out how it was supposed to work, and fix it (usually with a combination of cable ties and duct tape). Now here I was, a few years later, and I was able to completely reassemble my own bicycle in a few hours.

The time off in Bishkek also gave me a chance to talk with Ana, or at least a grainy image of Ana coming to me from an Uzbek internet café. It was nice to chat with her again, of course, but as I caught bits of her speaking excitedly of The Desert Dash challenge that lay just ahead of her it became clear that our lives were literally heading in opposite directions. I had felt a comforting illusion throughout my ride across Kyrgyzstan that she had still been with me somehow, but now it became obvious that we were likely never going to see each other again. For now that was just the way it had to be. It was exactly one year since I'd cycled away from the Eiffel Tower, and my journey was still coming first.

Perhaps thanks to my photoshopped suit I was deemed acceptable to the Chinese consulate, and the final piece of my visa puzzle was in place. I was now free to leave Bishkek, and I headed north to country number thirty-five, Kazakhstan. The mountains were now behind me, and in front lay the great Kazakh steppe that made up the majority of this large nation. I wasn't too sure what 'steppe' was, but from first impressions it looked to be something of a cross between desert and prairie. Grassy sand, or sandy grass, if you will. I was a little apprehensive, concerned that this empty landscape might get a little bit repetitive over the next 1,500 kilometres. On a more positive note, there was plenty of space for my tent. Speaking of which, I'd got a new tent in Bishkek, as the zips on the one I'd started with had broken beyond repair. I'd slept in my new one in the garden at Nathan's guest house, but during my first attempt at actually putting it up in the field (or steppe, to be precise) one of the poles snapped. On my brand new tent. Did I mention it was brand new? After trying hopelessly to splint the pole with tyre levers for a while I gave up and just slept on top of the canvas under the stars.

The next day I made an early start to ensure I got to Almaty, where I had pre-booked a hostel. Around mid-morning, having cycled forty kilometres, I saw another touring cyclist in my mirror and I stopped to wait for her. Yes, yes, I said her! It was *another* solo female cyclist. I couldn't believe it. These lone females on bikes are like buses aren't they? You cycle around for years looking for one, and then two come along at once. Well, not both exactly at once, that would have been oxymoronic. I meant two had come along within a few weeks of each other. Come to think of it, they're nothing like buses are they? Anyway, this one was called Hera, and she rather brilliantly came with her own hapless sidekick, Remco (I was quite jealous).

Hera and I chatted away as we cycled on together towards Almaty, with Remco trailing along behind us, as all good sidekicks should. They were from the Netherlands, and Hera had started her journey from there, in April.

"In April?" I said, surprised. "You started three months ago?"

"Three and a half, yeah."

I was in shock. It had taken me a year to get this far. "How many kilometres have you cycled?"

"5,500. Plus 1,500 by train across Kazakhstan, because the steppe is really not interesting for me."

Even adding these two numbers together it was only 7,000 kilometres. I'd cycled 22,000 by this point. Blimey, I'd done 15,000 kilometres more than I needed to. Fantastic! Hera had taken a straight line approach, crossing Europe to Ukraine, then on through Russia and Kazakhstan. The short, skinny Remco was a friend from home who had only just flown into Bishkek to join her for a couple of months in Central Asia. After Almaty they were planning to loop back down to Kyrgyzstan and Tajikistan. Of course, she was an attractive solo female cyclist who I was getting on well with, you didn't think she'd be going the same way as me, did you?

So we just had to make do with cycling together for the rest of the day, me occasionally stopping to pick up bits of trash at the side of the road that I thought might help fix my tent pole. Remco had never cycle toured before, and seemed like he'd already decided not to cycle tour ever again. In contrast Hera looked a strong and confident cyclist. Her clean Lycra, pristine bike, radiant, tanned face and silky, brown hair made a mockery of my own belief that long bicycle rides must inevitably lead one to resemble a bedraggled castaway. She was also a singer, and offered one or two angelic melodies as we rode. I responded with a very out of tune, "I need a Hera, I'm holding on for a Hera to the end of the night, she's gotta be fast, and she's gotta be strong, and she's gotta be riding a bike."

Arriving in Almaty we found a developed city with modern buildings on wide boulevards, a consequence of Kazakhstan's oil wealth, and more reminiscent of Europe than the Asia I had grown used to.

One main street even had a segregated bicycle lane running alongside it, the first I'd seen in months, which I guessed must have made my new Dutch friends quite homesick. We all took the next day off from cycling, primarily because a silly piece of post-Soviet bureaucracy meant that we had to register our presence in the country at a police station. This pointless exercise involved filling in a form and then waiting half the morning to get a piece of paper in exchange. The rest of the day we spent together, exploring a little of Almaty, visiting bike shops, and hanging out on the bunk beds of our hostel dormitory. Hera and I were getting on well together, but it was destined to be yet another case of what might have been as we said our goodbyes the next morning and I cycled off alone once more.

I reflected on what I had ahead of me with great trepidation as I rode out of the city and back out into the steppe. Riding with Hera and Remco had been a final interaction with the cycle touring scene of Central Asia, and I knew it would be my last. Lots of people cycled the Pamir Highway. Nobody cycled the Kazakh steppe. It was too boring. Too empty. Too full of nothing. I knew, therefore, that it was going to be a stern test of my resolve to cycle every last kilometre. Because of having relatively short visas with fixed dates, and because there were few borders that I knew I could cycle across, I also now had to cycle 4,200 kilometres in the next forty days across Kazakhstan and Siberia. It was a bit like having to do the Desert Dash all over again, only eight times as long. And as if eight Desert Dash challenges wasn't enough, I then immediately had to cycle across Mongolia in thirty days, where I'd heard the roads would range from terrible to non-existent. I had no idea if that was even possible. But if I did manage it, I would then need to cycle across China in no more than sixty days without having time to draw breath in between. And have you seen the size of China, by the way?

I did my best not to think too much about the size of the visa-enforced challenge that lay ahead, and just took things one day at a time. This was tricky, as the days merged into one another, with the reason why nobody else cycled this way quickly becoming clear. The Kazakh steppe was just a whole load of nothing. A vast, empty space.

The landscape all around me was flat, a bit yellow, with nothing in it but a thin band of tarmac stretching forever to the horizon. And it was like that for over a thousand kilometres.

But for me the fact that it was such a whole load of nothing was precisely the appeal. The only way to really know and understand a place like that was to stand in the middle of it, to cross it by bike, to be there, to feel it for all its nothingness. Before starting my trip Kazakhstan had been a place I had looked forward to. I wanted to know what it felt like to be somewhere so remote, a world away from the densely populated England I had grown up in. Now, at long last I was living my dream. Admittedly, the reality was that it was a bit on the boring side. The kind of dream that might put you to sleep. If that was possible. The kind of dream so boring it might put you more deeply asleep. Maybe put you in a coma.

But undoubtedly the monotonous landscape gave me plenty of time to think, and I liked that a lot. The flat, paved road allowed my mind to relax and drift and I would float along in an almost meditative state. Random memories from the journey would come to me. I had little control over what would enter my head. It could be anything. Maybe a shop in Latvia, a street in Iran, a friendly stranger I'd met somewhere. I loved thinking back over everything that had happened, reliving those experiences in my mind. And then I'd project it forward, and imagine how amazing it was going to be to see those wild and remote places in Siberia and Mongolia. Beyond that, how great it would feel to reach Southeast Asia, to finally be free of visa pressures in an area of the world that I was very excited to cycle through. And then Australia. I pictured myself at the Sydney Opera House and tried to imagine how it would feel to arrive there. It still seemed like such a ridiculously long way, especially as I was presently spending my days cycling in the wrong direction, north to Siberia, but I still wanted to see all that I could along the way. Australia would wait, and I was sure it would be all the sweeter for it when I did finally look up at that gleaming white roof.

I was cycling 120 kilometres per day in order to make my schedule, and my daydreams could only keep my mind occupied for so long, so

I came up with other distractions. Inevitably it wasn't too long before I turned to poetry. Yes, poetry. I made up a beautiful poem as I cycled, and shouted it out to the wind. Here are the first few verses.

> *Here I am in Kazakhstan,*
> *Across the steppe I ride,*
> *I'm on my way to Russia,*
> *Across the plains so wide.*
> *The steppe is vast and empty,*
> *Dry yellow grass abounds,*
> *And apart from swirling winds,*
> *Silence here surrounds.*
> *There isn't much to see,*
> *There's a road and there's some grass,*
> *Writing poems as I go,*
> *Does help the time to pass.*
> *My poem is going to be long,*
> *Perhaps a hundred verses,*
> *If life doesn't get more interesting,*
> *It may well contain some curses.*

I won't go on any further. I think by the end there really were a hundred verses, on such diverse subjects as knitting, carrots, and Jeremy Clarkson. I won't bore you with the details though.

As for the people of Kazakhstan, I did meet a few. This mostly happened when a car would pull over and the occupants would get out to ask me what in the hell I was doing out in the middle of nowhere on a bicycle. They had big smiles on their round faces, but I felt a little like they were viewing me as something out of a freak show, as they insisted on having a photo taken with me before getting back in their cars and speeding off again.

Small towns appeared every few hundred kilometres, allowing me to stock up with food and water. The only map I had with me was a large scale print-out out from Google Maps, and so I did not know the exact distance between each town, something which did almost get me into trouble. I'd estimated the town of Aygöz to be about 150 kilometres away, and after cycling that much and being almost out of supplies I was expecting it to be just around the next corner. A couple of European motorcyclists passed me at that point and stopped to say hello. I asked them if they knew how much further it was to Aygöz and they checked on their GPS. I was right, it was just around the next corner. Only problem was, the next corner was 136 kilometres away.

The motorcyclists sped off and I was all alone again, contemplating how I was going to make it another 136 kilometres with almost no food or water. I didn't panic though. By now I had been travelling long enough to have faith that a solution would surely appear. I knew I would get through somehow. I'd find a way. So I continued riding, carefully rationing what I had to make it last as long as I could. After a while another car stopped and a man got out to ask excitedly if he could have his photo taken with me. I shrugged. "Why not?" Then his mother, his baby, and his pregnant wife all got out of the car to have *their* photo taken with me. I thought they were all going to get back in the car and drive off having a good laugh at the crazy idiot cyclist, but then they gave me a half-drunk bottle of iced tea as a gift, and I was humbled by their kindness.

With the extra fluid I was able to battle on into the wind until, some hours later, something finally appeared on the horizon. It was a little farm and strangely the word 'shop' was scrawled on a rickety wooden building near the road. I must admit I didn't hold out too much hope, but I leaned my bike up and walked towards the door anyway, my stomach rumbling with hunger.

Inside I found a very small and very old man crouching at a desk, who looked as delighted as he was surprised that somebody had finally entered his shop. The shelves behind him were predictably bare, but he stood up, mumbled something, and then walked over to a fridge in the corner of the room. He pulled open the door to reveal a blinding white light and, was it my imagination, or were there a dozen angels floating around it singing 'Aaahhh!' There was food in the fridge. Bread. Biscuits. Some seed-and-nut bar that would prove to be delicious. A five-litre bottle of mineral water. One of the angels burst into an inspiring solo rendition of 'Hallelujah'. I was saved.

I grabbed things joyously and put them on the desk. The old man found a piece of cardboard and a pen, and with each item I placed down he wrote the price and added it to the total. He wrote slowly, in large letters, reminiscent of a seven-year-old doing their maths homework. He was adorable. He came up with a total of 1300 tenge for everything, which wasn't as much as it might sound. I looked for the change, didn't have it, and so gave him a 2000 tenge note. He took it from me, turned back to the cardboard and wrote a big 2000. Underneath this he wrote 1300, then he drew a line and methodically did the subtraction, before giving me my change (it was 700). If there had only been a calculator for sale in that shop, I swear I would have bought it for the dear old fellow.

I eventually reached the end of the Kazakh steppe at the city of Semey. On first impressions it did not appear to have been worth the long and boring ride. The run-down tower blocks marked it out immediately as the city that Kazakhstan forgot, for there was no sign of the investment that had made Almaty into such a developed place. This was no surprise at all, for Semey is famous only for being close to the location where the Soviets conducted their nuclear testing. A good reason for Kazakhstan to try and sweep it under the rug, and for me not to hang around too long.

I did have a little business to attend to while I was in town though, and, after much asking around, I eventually found a café in the centre that had free wifi. The café was brightly lit and filled with people. Through the window I could see girls outside cutting by in skimpy shorts, above me a TV was playing pop music videos, and at my fingertips I had the whole entire internet. After a week of nothingness my senses were seriously overwhelmed. I mean, I had a piece of cake in front of me, for the love of God.

But I had to pull myself together, for there was an important decision for me to make. I was about to cross into Russia once more, and I realised that I still had two possible options for my route through it to Mongolia. The plan had always been for me to cycle

3,000 kilometres across Siberia to Lake Baikal and then head south into Mongolia close to the capital of Ulaanbaatar. This was an ambitious and unappealing prospect with only a thirty-day visa, and as I looked at my laptop I began to seriously consider trying the alternative option. There was a road through the Altai mountains that would reach a Mongolian border crossing within 1,000 kilometres. It would completely take the pressure off in terms of the amount of distance I'd have to cycle. The problem was that the only information I could find about this border crossing was that it was for cars only. Walking or cycling the twenty kilometres of no-man's land between Russia and Mongolia was forbidden. If I had to take a motor vehicle it would ruin everything, of course, but maybe there was a chance I'd be allowed to cycle through the border. I was confident Russian border guards could be persuaded if I had enough roubles to bribe them with.

I mulled over my options for a while as I munched on my cake. It wasn't an easy decision, but in the end I decided that it was just too risky to go for the nearer border. Being forced into a motor vehicle for a silly, bureaucratic reason was one of my worst nightmares. And I'd received e-mails from two other cyclists who'd been allowed to cycle over the other border, the one 3,000 kilometres away, the previous summer, so I was certain that was the safest option in terms of preserving the continuity of the journey. It was decided. I would go the long way.

It was a decision that would change the trip, and my whole life, forever.

26

Russian border
2ⁿᵈ August 2014

As I approached the Russian border I found myself thinking
back to the first time I'd entered the country, from Finland
almost a year earlier. Such a lot had happened since then that
I struggled even to imagine myself as the same person. Certainly I
didn't have the same nerves about going to Russia. Quite the opposite. I was looking forward to it.

The border process was surprisingly easy. Nobody checked any
bags or asked any questions, except for one young official at customs.
He asked me if I had any drugs or guns, to which I replied that I did
not, while wondering if anybody had ever said yes. Then, almost as
an afterthought, he asked me where I was going on my bike.

"Australia."

"Okay," he said, smiling and waving me on. "Go. You crazy British
idiot."

And as I rode through into my first little Siberian town my optimism about returning to Russian soil appeared justified. There were
little colourful homes all along the street and a path running separate
from the road that I cycled on. In fact, that quite a few people cycled
on. There were plenty of people about, and they waved at me, or
stopped to say hello. I had expected them to look more similar to
Central Asians than the Russians I'd seen in the west of the country,
but I was wrong. All the people I saw were white skinned, many with

light hair and blue eyes. They looked European. Everything looked European (Eastern European, but you can't have everything). The last time I'd entered Russia I felt like I was leaving Europe, this time I felt like I'd returned there. It felt good. In a way it was just what I needed. I was suddenly back in a country with proper roads, with proper supermarkets, and my mouth salivated to see rows of fresh fruit and vegetables on the shelves. The sudden change had been remarkable. I'd crossed one man-made line on a map, and I'd entered a different world.

After a couple of days riding past green fields I reached the city of Barnaul. The main street was a wide boulevard named Leninsky, where I passed a statue of Lenin. Then across the street I noticed a large Soviet mural on a building with Lenin in the middle of it all. It was red of course. It seemed like this place was really having trouble moving on.

I needed to find help in Barnaul as I'd recently broken my flange. Now I know what you're thinking, but no, the flange is just the part of the wheel where the hub connects to the spokes, which meant I was in need of a whole new rear hub. But I didn't know where I could find a bike shop, and so first of all I needed to find some wifi and ask the internet. A café called Traveller's Coffee looked like it would be up to the task. It was a real wannabe Starbucks, a true symbol of capitalism just across the street from Mr Lenin. I went inside, discovered that they did indeed have wifi, and ordered an orange juice. I flicked open my laptop, checked my e-mails, located a bike shop, downed the orange juice, and asked for the bill. It was three pounds. Three pounds for a glass of orange juice. Unbelievable. Well, that's where capitalism has brought us. Three pounds. I tell you. Lenin must have been turning in his grave.

I cycled across town to the bike shop where several young employees were very friendly and helpful. They had the hub that I wanted, but my request for a mechanic to rebuild the wheel was met with a negative response. This was a problem, as I really needed a professional for this task. Yes, I'd reconstructed my own front wheel in Bishkek, but Nathan had got me started and done all the hard bits, and that was just changing the rim, which meant moving the spokes over one by one. To change the hub meant dismantling the wheel and basically building it up again completely from scratch. There was no way that I could be trusted to do it. But then I had one of those funny moments when I temporarily forgot about my own incompetence, and declared that I was just going to build the wheel myself.

I set myself up in the street outside the shop and started to dismantle the old wheel, which took a while as I had to unscrew and remove each spoke in turn. The guys from the shop brought me out a stool to sit on and watched me keenly, as if they might learn something. To be fair, I was looking like I knew what I was doing at this point, but then taking the wheel apart was the easy bit. I had no real plan as to how I was going to put it back together again. I just kind of assumed it would come to me when the moment arrived.

As I was halfway through removing the spokes there appeared next to me a tall man who I thought to be a fellow cyclist, at least if the tight Lycra was anything to go by. He introduced himself as Vladimir, told me he'd once ridden from Barnaul to Mongolia, and became very, very keen to try and help me. He couldn't speak English though, nor did he know how to build wheels, and his attempts to help soon began to annoy. First he brought me an old wheel from somewhere and tried to give it to me as a gift. It was a thoughtful gesture, but the rim was crap, the hub was crap, and one of the spokes was broken. Still, Vladimir was quite insistent that I should stop trying to build a wheel with a good rim and good hub, and just take this one instead. He even tried to take one of the spokes I'd removed and use it to replace the broken one. "Leave my spokes alone," I said. "I need those." So Vladimir went and got a spoke from the bike shop instead. But then he had nothing to screw it into, and he reached over to my pile of possessions again. "No Vladimir," I protested. "Do not pinch my nipples. You really go too far."

A half an hour later I finally had all of the spokes removed and was ready to start rebuilding with the new hub. I could have got to this point faster, but Vladimir kept handing me his phone with an English-speaking translator on the other end. "Vladimir wants to give you this wheel as a present. Vladimir wants to show you the way to Mongolia. Vladimir is not going to leave you alone. Vladimir likes to poke his nose in." And so on and so forth. It was clear that the pair of them were only trying to help, of course, but they weren't helping, and I was growing ever more frustrated.

My growing frustration was largely a consequence of the simple fact that I was sitting on a stool on the footpath of a street in Siberia with a completely disassembled rear wheel and absolutely no idea how to go about putting it together again. I started by putting spokes in randomly. There were thirty-six holes in the hub, thirty-six holes in the rim, and thirty-six spokes to connect them. Surely, I hoped, there was a chance I might get everything in the right place by mere fluke. My first attempt ended in a dismal failure, with Vladimir continuing his pursuit of the title of 'World's most annoyingly unhelpful helpful man' by grabbing spokes and putting them in randomly too. The English-speaker was soon back on the phone, and when he tried to tell me that Vladimir was going to build my wheel for me I reached my boiling point.

"Listen, I really appreciate all of your help, and all of Vladimir's help, but what I really need right now is for you to leave me alone. He clearly doesn't know what he's doing because he's just put a drive-side spoke on the non-drive-side and even I know not to do that. Please just tell him to leave me alone so I can concentrate. Thank you."

The message was relayed to Vladimir and he picked up his old wheel and stormed off. I assumed he left with the opinion that I was an ungrateful twat, but that didn't matter, the important thing was that he left.

The guys from the shop were still watching me, although any resemblance I bore to a man who might know what he was doing had long gone. They had at least been entertained by my interactions with Vladimir, and now they stood waiting to see what I might do next. Then I was suddenly struck by a moment of inspiration. I asked them if the shop had wifi and they told me that it did. I got out my laptop and loaded up a wheel-building tutorial online. Oh, how much easier this made things. It turned out you weren't supposed to just put the spokes in at random, they all had a specific place. I followed the instructions, step-by-step, and against all odds a wheel began to take shape. Before I knew it I had built the thing. I trued it using my brake pads and got it fairly straight. I'd done it. I put the tyre on, attached the wheel, and loaded all my bags back onto my bike, ready to go. The guys from the shop were looking at me in awe now. I think they almost broke into a round of applause. I'd built my own wheel, all by myself, in the street, in Siberia. I felt on top of the world. Then I noticed my rim tape lying on the floor and had to take everything apart again.

Just as I was preparing to leave, my old friend Vladimir reappeared. He had with him a bag of nuts and a box of teabags which he gave to me as a present. He was a lovely man really. Then he went too far and offered me a pair of Lycra cycling shorts. I never wore such things myself, my legs being too skinny. I was happier in a pair of board shorts. Some people look good in Lycra and some do not. I'm in the second category. As a matter of fact most people are. Including Vladimir. Looking at his own tight-fitting outfit I wondered whether he was offering me a new pair or an old pair of his own. As if noticing my unease, he flicked the shorts over to the inside to show me the comfortable padding. Definitely not new. And in case you aren't aware, most people don't wear anything under cycling shorts. What Vladimir was essentially gifting to me then, at least from a hygiene perspective, was a pair of his old underwear. I thought it rude to refuse another present though, and after he'd put them safely back in a plastic bag for me, I took them. Then Vladimir wanted me to go and put them on in the bike shop changing room.

'Thank you Vladimir, but no. I could put them on now, but what I'll probably do instead is throw them away later.'

With my bike back to full strength I set off on the long road to Irkutsk, although just how long the road was took a little while for the sign makers of Siberia to figure out. I first passed a sign declaring Irkutsk to be 3,000 kilometres away, then a short while later came across one saying 'Irkutsk – 1,000 km'. Before long it was back up to

1,800. I started to think it would have been best if they just put up a sign saying 'Irkutsk – we don't know how far it is, but it's a bloody long way.'

But actually the third sign proved fairly accurate, for shortly after it there began a series of kilometre marker posts at the side of the road with numbers stamped on them counting down from 1,885. With this guide the sign-makers of Siberia grew more confident, and they started putting up signs with tremendous frequency. 'Irkutsk – 1,856 km', 'Irkutsk – 1,854 km', 'Irkutsk – 1,850km', 'Irkutsk – 1,857 km'. Hundreds of these signs, each one with an arrow pointing straight ahead. That'll be the only road, then. All of these signs seemed a little more than was necessary, yet when the road went into a town and hit an intersection or a roundabout with multiple exits the signs were conspicuously absent, and left me to figure it out for myself. So I asked the people, who in Siberia seemed much more friendly and open than they had in the west of Russia. The only trouble was I could not pronounce Irkutsk in a way that anybody could understand, so I had to ask for Vladivostok, which was the only other city I knew in the same direction. Being on the Pacific Ocean, Vladivostok was such a long way that it was a bit like trying to find my way out of Paris by asking for the road to Saudi Arabia. But it was a tactic that worked in Siberia because there was only one road across it, and everyone knew the way.

The distance felt daunting, but I was riding through a wonderful forested landscape. It reminded me of Canada or Scandinavia, perhaps not surprising given the latitude. It was uplifting being out in the wilderness. On both sides of the road there was thick forest of fir, pine, spruce and cedar, part of the incredible band of boreal green that stretches almost the whole way around the world. I looked at that forest and thought about how remarkable it was that it stretched in an almost unbroken chain westwards to Norway and eastwards to Alaska and Canada. It was an inspiring and humbling thought.

It was August and temperatures were regularly above thirty degrees Celsius, leaving me sweating on the steady climbs I faced, and relishing every stream I could splash my face in. Stopping was hazardous, however, for the mosquitoes and sandflies were the worst I'd ever come across. They mostly left me alone so long as I was moving, but stop for too long and I was in trouble. Each evening and morning I'd have to put on baggy clothes and gloves, lift my hood and cover my face with a piece of mesh fabric. This interesting outfit had me resembling a bee keeper that had fallen on hard times, yet it was the only way to survive the process of putting up my tent and taking it down again without suffering life-threatening blood loss.

Another potential threat to life was the traffic. The road was nothing more than a two-lane highway with plenty of trucks on it, and tailgating and dangerous overtaking was par for the course. Speeding cars would pull out to pass trucks, see an oncoming vehicle but go for it anyway. The oncoming vehicle would see the overtaking car coming straight for them, but not brake, just keep on going as well. The overtaking car might just make it in time and pull in with a fraction of a second to spare, or the oncoming vehicle might veer to the side and make an extra half an inch so they could all three squeeze past each other at the same time. This was the first place I'd been to where seeing the aftermath of accidents was a daily occurrence. More than once I saw cars pulled up on opposite sides of the road with their wing mirrors broken and scratches all down their sides where there obviously hadn't been that extra half an inch of room. It was absolute madness. Luckily for me there was a gravel shoulder I could cycle on, so I could keep out of the way and just watch the insanity.

Just after passing through a small village one evening, I came across a woman selling a variety of knick-knacks from a roadside stall. I stopped, as she had one item that had really caught my eye. Draped across a wooden stand was the full skin of a big brown bear, its sharp teeth sticking out from a gaping mouth. That certainly gave me pause for thought, and I asked the woman if there were any more bears in the forest for me to watch out for, or if the hunters had shot them all now. "Oh no, they haven't all been shot. Some of them dance in the circus," she said. No, she didn't. I'm just kidding. She didn't understand English. So I asked her again in sign language if there were bears here, and she nodded and said "Da, da." Seemed like it might be time for me to start taking bear precautions.

As I was taking a photo of the bear skin the woman went over to her stall and, knowing just exactly what a tired cycle tourist might need to buy just before a night in the woods with the bears, she came back with a stuffed weasel.

"No thank you. I don't really need a stuffed weasel."

She frowned, lowered her expectations, and next tried to sell me a mirror.

"No thanks, I already have a mirror."

Undeterred, she made one last effort, thrusting a keyring at me.

"No thank you. It's very nice, but I'm afraid I don't have any keys."

The next morning, as always, I woke up automatically with the first hint of daylight on my tent. With each passing day it was getting more and more difficult to motivate myself to make an early start, though my visa schedule demanded it. Until now I had been keeping a packet of biscuits by my side to eat an energising breakfast in bed, but suddenly fearful of bears, all my food had been left outside. As I lay there still half asleep it was as if I had an angel above one shoulder and a devil above the other. The angel said, "Come on! Get up! You have to cycle 130 kilometres, so get your beekeeping outfit on, get the tent down, and let's get moving."

But then the devil countered with, "Naah! That's terrible hard work. You should lie here in the tent for a couple more hours. It's ever so comfortable in here."

They continued with this back-and-forth for some time, with the devil looking sure to win. But then the angel called to the stand her final witness, which was my aching body, and she asked my aching body why it ached so much. My aching body replied that the previous evening I had failed to find a good spot for the tent and had ended up camping on some bumpy and uneven ground, meaning I'd got no good sleep at all. Then in a rousing closing statement the angel declared that the devil's argument that it was 'ever so comfortable in here' was completely without merit, and the jury was convinced, so I got up.

Before I go on, it's worth noting that, because of the similarities between this brilliant summing up and the final court scene of the film *A Time to Kill*, the angel will be played in my movie by a young Matthew McConaughey.

Although I did manage to get on the bike and start cycling I was not at all happy about it. Each day it had been getting harder and harder to find any enthusiasm for what I was doing. Every day was pretty much the same now. I'd get up, take down the tent, cycle 130 kilometres, put up the tent, and then sleep. And all I could see ahead of me was weeks and weeks of the same. I began to feel down. I needed something to happen.

Then it did. A car pulled over and a man that looked a bit like Ryan Giggs greeted me with a big smile and gave me a tomato. Then he drove off again. If that had been all that happened I wouldn't have been all that inspired. To be honest, I probably wouldn't have even mentioned it. I don't even like tomatoes. But a hundred yards up the road he stopped again, and this time he invited me to stay with him that night in his hometown of Krasnoyarsk, a mere eighty kilometres away. If I accepted I would be falling short of my daily target, but I wasn't about to look a gift horse in the mouth. I'd been hoping for something like this to lift my mood, so I accepted the offer.

With something to look forward to the day passed quickly until the surprisingly large town of Krasnoyarsk appeared out of the forest. I made my way to the address that the man, Sasha, had given me. He showed me inside and let me take a shower and do my laundry for the first time in weeks. He couldn't speak English but we sat down and had a nice chat using an internet translation service. Sasha was such a good guy, into cold water swimming and spearfishing and mountaineering and all sorts of interesting outdoor activities. It was just so nice to be able to relax and have some company for the evening. He even tried to give me a big pot of honey to take with me as a present. "Oh, no," I said, "I've seen enough bear-based cartoons to know not to go camping in the woods with a big pot of honey." Sasha looked confused. I typed and translated my concerns. Sasha laughed and started to type himself. 'Bears might attack people.'

"Thanks Sasha, not exactly selling me on the honey."

But then I saw he hadn't finished.

'Bears might attack people, but only in the early spring or late autumn when they are hungry.'

Hurrah! The biscuits were moving back in with me.

Sasha insisted on giving me his bed in the big main room and sleeping on a mattress in the kitchen himself. It was typical of the man, such a kind thing to do, but it didn't work out quite so well for me. And that was because Sasha had a cat. Naturally, as soon as the lights went out the cat came into the big main room and started to jump around on everything. And by 'everything' I mean 'me'. It was very annoying, and there wasn't much to do about it because I couldn't throw it out and shut the door as Sasha had said not to close any doors as the cat would just scratch them. So I tried to just ignore the frustrating feline and sleep, but it was impossible because I was just lying there waiting for it to jump on me again. Then I noticed that there was also a loud ticking clock in the room. I didn't know why anyone would put a loud ticking clock in the same room as a bed. I didn't know why loud ticking clocks even existed any more, but to have one in a place of sleep seemed like the very definition of madness. It was the most frustrating thing, to try and get to sleep in that room with that ticking clock and that restless cat. Eventually my patience ran out and I dragged myself into a third room which was being renovated. It was empty and so I rolled out my camping mat on the cold, hard floor to try and sleep there. Almost immediately the cat appeared and leapt on me. I threw it out. It leapt back again.

The devil reappeared above my shoulder. "Throw the cat out of the window," he told me.

I looked to the angel on the other side. "I'm with him on this one," she said.

27

Siberia, Russia
21ˢᵗ August 2014

It had been a month since I'd left Almaty, and I calculated that I'd
cycled 3,500 kilometres in that time. I felt quite proud. It was a
real achievement, certainly a lot more than I'd ever done in a
month before. 3,500 kilometres in thirty days – almost 120 kilometres
per day – and I was still going. Exhausted, yes, but nearing the end of
the long road to Irkutsk.

It was as I reflected on this, taking a short break in a bus shelter,
that I was suddenly surprised by the sight of another touring cyclist
racing along. He hadn't seen me, hidden as I was inside the shelter, so
I called out to him, almost choking on my jam sandwich in the process. The rider stopped and came over to me, shaking my hand and
introducing himself as Petr, from the Czech Republic. Though he
would later tell me he was fifty-four, I initially took him for a much
younger man. He was lean and dressed in a black tracksuit, the skin of
his face either tanned or dirty, I couldn't tell, and half hidden behind
orange sunglasses. A mop of greasy hair splayed out from beneath his
helmet.

Petr revealed that he was also attempting to cycle around the
world, and with similar challenges to myself. But for him the primary
goal was to make a circumnavigation without using any motors. I
wasn't too fussed if the boats I used were motorised or not, they were
merely a way for me to cross areas of water to get to the next place

where my bike wouldn't sink, but Petr wanted to use only sailing boats. He told me he'd started his trip from Prague and had cycled 8,000 kilometres in just three months, taking a direct route across Poland, Ukraine, Russia and Kazakhstan. I was impressed.

"Wow, that is really fast," I said.

"But I also took three weeks off because my woman friend came to visit me."

"So you did 8,000 kilometres in only two and a bit months? That's incredible."

"No," Petr shrugged, as if it was nothing. "It is only 3,500 kilo-metres per month. 120 or so per day. It's easy enough."

Way to piss on my campfire, Petr.

We cycled on together, me concerned about my new companion's dark clothing and apparent disregard for the crazy Russian motorists as he weaved erratically between the shoulder and the road. I told him I thought it better to wear bright clothes and have a mirror to see what was going on, but he palmed off my suggestions and said he pre-ferred to look at the nature rather than the traffic. Then he asked me if I'd had many accidents.

"No, none," I replied. "Why? Have you?"

"Oh yes, lots."

Petr's 'woman friend' that he referred to had visited him earlier in Russia and tried to cycle with him, but it hadn't worked out. As he explained, "The first day she cycled, the second day she took a lift in a truck, the third day she was too sick to continue."

I wasn't surprised. The poor woman had never done a bike trip before, and the way he was cycling 120 kilometres per day she didn't stand much of a chance. I thought it terribly unfair of him to treat her like that, and certainly not something I would ever do. To make a girl ride a bike so much that she got sick and had to stop and go home? How awful, what a mean thing to do, I could never do that to... oh, no, wait, Hanna.

For the next few days I rode bits and pieces with Petr, though he had some strange habits that made it difficult to align our journeys.

For one thing he refused to take breaks anywhere other than in cafés, and in Siberia that meant he'd sometimes cycle seventy kilometres or more non-stop, something I really wasn't prepared to do. Neither was he willing to stop and eat jam sandwiches in bus shelters. So we sometimes cycled together and sometimes went our separate ways, and it worked fine. One evening, having finally made it through Irkutsk, we were together to camp next to Lake Baikal. The world's oldest and deepest freshwater lake made for a breathtaking sight, and it had been a fantastic day's cycling on a winding up-and-down road along its southern shore. Petr insisted on always finding water to camp by as he needed to wash each evening before bed, and a driftwood covered beach made for an ideal spot. I was amazed by how clear the lake was as I knelt in the shallow water and allowed waves to roll in and hit me full in the face. It was cold and refreshing and a glorious moment. I hopped around, screaming from the cold. Petr was still busy with his tent and paid me no attention. Later I saw him splashing water on himself in the surf like a madman. The sky turned purple as the sun set. It really was such a beautiful lake. Back in Tajikistan, Gayle, who was on her way to it with John, had told me excitedly that it was so pure you could safely drink the water straight out of the lake, although I wouldn't recommend that any more, not after Petr and I had a wash in it.

On the last stretch from the Russian town of Ulan Ude to the Mongolian border I said goodbye to Petr and he disappeared ahead quickly. He'd found someone to stay with for a while in Ulan Ude, so he was going to do the cycle to the border, then take a bus 200 kilometres back to Ulan Ude. When he was ready to continue he'd bus it back to the border and pick up from where he left off. I found it a bit strange that Petr was happy to jump back and forth like this, given that his goal was to circumnavigate the planet 'without motor.' It seemed to me like he was using plenty of motor, even if he did always continue from where he'd left off.

That was one thing I was proud of that continued to make my own journey unique. To ride a bike around the world occasionally doing side trips by bus or car, then starting again where you left off, was one thing. But to go the whole way around without ever using any motorised vehicles on land was something special. As far as I was aware it would be a world first, I could be the first person ever to do this (Incidentally, if you do happen to know of anyone else who has done this before me, do please be good enough to keep it to yourself, won't you?). But it was a massive logistical challenge. I'd just about made it through Siberia now to the border I could cycle over, but in Mongolia I'd have a similar challenge. Amazingly there were only two points on the whole of the Mongolia-China border that foreigners could cross, and I knew that the one in the east had a twenty kilometre section of no-man's land that was only for cars. That meant a massive trek back west was awaiting me to get to the other border into China that I could cycle over. As for Petr, when he made it to Mongolia he planned to go east. "If they make me get in a car for twenty kilometres, I'll just cycle around in a circle for forty kilometres to make up for it." Everyone does things differently, but for me that would ruin the whole trip. I wanted it to be one continuous journey, all the way round, only using my bicycle and boats. Little did I know it, but this was an ambition that was about to be under serious threat.

It was the 30th of August 2014 and the last day of my Russian visa. I arrived at the border early, keen to begin the next exciting challenge of crossing Mongolia. After hearing from the cyclists that had passed this border the previous year I arrived confident there would be no problems, but as I rode up past a line of queueing cars several local men, mostly money changers, surrounded me. Worryingly they were telling me that I couldn't cross the border by bike and I'd have to take a lift in one of the cars. They were not officials, however, and I was very used to unofficial people giving me wrong information at borders. My research told me that it was not permitted to walk across this border, but that the cyclists had gone through without difficulty, so I didn't panic. I also thought that in the worst case scenario I'd just have to bribe an official or two, and I'd be allowed to cycle.

The border gates opened and I followed a van through, cycling up confidently to a young man in a silly hat and handing him my passport. "Niet velociped," he said, shaking his head. He said some other things too, but I didn't understand them. He clearly wasn't going to let me through on my bike though, which was a problem, a very big problem. In a sudden state of panic I reached into my pocket and thrust the last of my roubles at him. It wasn't very subtle. Ryan Gosling would do a much better job of it. The young guard looked at it like it was a stick of dynamite, waved it away, and told me that I must go back and get in a car. Oh, this was bad, this was very, very bad.

I walked back to the other side of the gates and took a seat, where I was immediately surrounded by the men again, who all resumed telling me that I needed to get in a car. "Niet machin," I said. "England to here, no cars. Only bicycle. No cars" Then they told me I needed to get in a car. So I told them, "Niet machin. England to here, no cars. Only bicycle. No cars." Then they told me that I needed to get in a car. It was a very repetitive conversation.

Every so often the gates would be opened and two or three vehicles let through. I watched the two guards. As well as the young man in the silly hat there was a stern-faced young woman dressed all in black who looked like she would be of no use to me whatsoever. I could see beyond them that not one hundred metres along the road the vehicles stopped and the occupants got out to walk into the customs building. There was clearly no logical reason why I should need to get into a motor vehicle to be driven a hundred metres just to get out again. After a while I approached the young official again, and tried to be nice to him. I asked him his name, complimented his hat, and told him all about my trip. I'd come all this way by bicycle, surely they could make an exception for me. I also waved a hundred dollars around a bit, just to tempt him. He shook his head.

"This is criminal," he said.

'Jeez... when did Russian officials become so straight-laced?' I wondered.

"Look, why can't I just go through on my bike?"

"It is law."

"Well, it's a silly law."

"Yes. It is Russian Federation law."

Although this wasn't getting me anywhere I wasn't about to get in a car just yet. It was still morning and the border was open for another ten hours, so I took up my position just outside the gate and waited. I couldn't believe that after all the effort of getting this far, a whole month riding all day, every day, to get to this border, my hopes and dreams were in danger of being ruined right here. After a while an important-looking woman strode in through the gate and I saw the young official speak to her and point at me. It seemed he was asking her if I could cycle through, good man that he was. Her response appeared to be a very swift, "Niet, he can get in a car," and she walked off purposefully towards the customs building (oh, she was allowed to walk) to get on with more important things. My hopes died a little more.

A few other officials came out of the gates and I tried to talk with them, hoping to find someone with both sympathy and influence. I did manage to find an older, balder official who was friendly, but he insisted that there was no way around it, I had to take a motor vehicle. Desperate for ideas, I asked whether putting an engine on my bike would be enough for it to be allowed through, and he said if it had a licence plate too then it would. I considered going back to the nearest town and trying to find a mechanic to fit some sort of mock engine and register me with licence plates, but the idea was pure fantasy, and I thought it better to wait by the gates in case something should happen.

But the day slipped by and nothing much more did happen. I just sat there feeling sorry for myself. How stupid it was that my goal of circumnavigating the planet by bicycle and boat was going to end, not because of it being too hard, not because of sickness, or injury, not even because of an attractive girl, but because of ridiculous bureaucracy. I thought about how I could have not even come here. I could have just gone straight from Kazakhstan to China. But then I'd found out about those guys cycling this border the previous summer. I'd even e-mailed them to check. "Yeah, you can cycle across that border, no problem," had been their response, and the adventure of

Siberia and Mongolia had drawn me in. Now I was here, and I couldn't cycle across this border, no problem. My visa was about to expire. I had no plan B. Hope was fading fast.

The hours ticked by and at four in the afternoon things weren't looking good. Another official came out, spoke to the guard on the gate, and strode toward me. This was it. This was the moment. He was obviously here to deal with me, one way or another. He was either going to help me, or all hope was gone. We shook hands and I knew I had to get this right. He spoke no English though, and the conversation went nowhere until he passed me a phone with an English-speaking woman on the other end of the line. I knew what she said next was crucial. It was going to decide everything. "Hello. The officer would like to tell you that you must get in a car to cross the border. You cannot cross the border by bicycle."

My heart sank at this brutal introduction, as I noticed two other men arrive and shake hands with the officer, though they wore plain clothes and looked unimportant. Although the conversation hadn't started well I pleaded with the woman, telling her all about my trip, how far I'd cycled, how important this was to me. She seemed to soften, and asked to speak again with the officer. I handed him the phone, they spoke for a moment, and then the phone came back to me. "I'm sorry, but he says you must get in a car," she said, "it is the law."

I was desperate now, and decided to try the bribe thing again. "Please, can you ask the officer to escort me personally across the border. I can pay him one hundred dollars for this service." The phone went back to the officer, and he spoke longer with the woman this time. He seemed to be perking up. This was it. I'd got him. Just like in the movies. I'd been saved at the final hour by some swift back-hander to a corrupt Russian. Brilliant. What a scene. Then the phone came back. "The officer says you must not try to bribe people. It is a criminal offence."

The phone left me again and it wasn't coming back. The conversation was over. Then one of the unimportant-looking men asked me in perfect English, "What do you want?"

"I just want to go to Mongolia by bicycle."

"You cannot. You must use a car to cross this border."

"Yes, I heard about that," I sighed.

"And if you try to bribe one of my officers again, I shall have you arrested."

Whoa, you're more important than you look, aren't you?'

Suddenly I realised that this was probably the man that I needed to convince, and he spoke English. What a shame I'd made such an appalling first impression.

"Erm... it wasn't really a bribe. Just a fee for escorting me across the border."

"Call it what you will. Now, you will not cross this border by bicycle."

"But why not?"

"It is the law."

"Surely you can make an exception. I have come all the way from England by bicycle. I haven't taken any cars in 27,000 kilometres. If I take one now it will ruin everything."

"We won't tell anyone."

"No. I can't do it. Please help me."

"We can help you to cross this border in a car."

"That doesn't help me. Is there another border I can cross by bicycle?"

"Yes."

"Where is it?"

"900 kilometres away." He gave me directions. "There you can walk across the border."

"Are foreigners allowed to use that border?"

"No, it is for Russian nationals only."

In actual fact the closest border that I could cross out of Russia was over 3,000 kilometres away into Kazakhstan, but on the plus side I did know that I could cycle over it, because I'd already done so once. I only had an hour of my visa left though, and cycling 3,000 kilometres was a bit of a push. Mind you, I would cross three time zones, so it'd be more like four hours. Still a little out of reach. If I'd had more time on my visa I swear I would have cycled all the way back though, I swear I would. I wondered what the fine would be if I overstayed on my visa by a month in order to do so. For some reason I thought it a good idea to ask the unimportant-looking important man.

"What happens if I overstay on my visa? Just out of curiosity, like?"

"You will be arrested, driven to the city, go to court, pay a lot of money, arrange new papers. It will cost you a lot of time and money, and you will spend a lot of time in cars."

"That doesn't sound all that good."

"Can I see your passport please?"

"Erm... yes."

"Your visa expires today."

"Yes I believe it does."

"So you must leave today."

"Yes."

"By this border."

"More than likely."

"So, what are you going to do?"

"Doesn't look like I have much choice, does it?"

"No, you don't."

The gig was up. It was all over. There was no way out. I'd been boxed into a corner. I'd done all that I could, but I really did have no choice now. Nowhere else to go. The officials insisted I find a lift immediately and there was no point waiting any longer. There were several pick-up trucks lined up at the gate that could easily accommodate my bike. Behind the wheel of one was a relatively attractive but ever so moody-looking Mongolian woman, who I tried asking first. She had no interest whatsoever in helping me so I moved on. Behind her was another pick-up, this one crammed with people. There was no space for me, but a young, friendly man, sympathetic to my plight, spoke to the woman in the first pick-up and then told me I could go with her. So I threw my bags and bike in the back of her trailer, then went to get in the passenger side door. There was no handle. The woman indicated that I should get in the back seat, so I did.

It was the first time I had sat in a personal motor vehicle in over three years. In fact I hadn't been moved at all by any motorised transport on land since May 2012 (the Barcelona Metro, if you're interested). I'd had a good run. Paris to the Mongolian border by bicycle and boat. How stupid for it to end like this. The end of my goal to cycle around the world. Everything was ruined. I sat in the back of the pick-up and an incredibly sad song came on the radio. I thought about Paris, cycling away from the Eiffel Tower with such hopes. So much had happened since then. The ride around Europe, crossing Turkey and Iran, nearly killing myself to complete the Desert Dash, the difficulty of the Pamir Highway, and the long sprint through Kazakhstan and Siberia. It was all for nothing. All of it. I'd made it such a long way, yet it just meant nothing now. Through the window of the cab I saw two old women sitting on a step, a line of Soviet tower blocks behind them. What a bleak place, what a pathetic way for it all to end. The gate opened. The woman turned the ignition. The truck rolled forward. And the tears streamed down my face.

28

Altanbulag, Mongolia
30th August 2014

I was left standing at the side of the road, my bags in a muddled heap, my bike leaning against a fence. I'd only just had time to get everything out of the truck before the relatively attractive but ever so moody woman sped off, covering me in a cloud of dust. She'd paid me no attention during the whole border process, and I'd winced from the back seat as she managed to almost hit one bystander despite driving less than a kilometre. But one way or another I was in Mongolia, and now I had to find a way to pick up the pieces of what had just happened.

By chance there was a car beside me with a British number plate. The beat-up old car was covered in dust and logos that gave it away as a participant in the Mongol Rally, an event in which teams drive from London to Mongolia. A cheerful young Englishman got out of the car to greet me. He was a chubby young guy and seemed ever so happy as he asked me what I was up to.

"Well, I was cycling around the world, but I'm not any more. They wouldn't let me cycle across this border, so my trip is over. I'm not sure what I'm going to do now, actually."

That brought his cheerfulness down a notch. Only one notch, mind you.

"Oh, come on," he said. "It's only a few hundred metres. Just don't tell anyone mate."

I didn't know why everyone kept saying that. As if what other people think we have done is somehow more important than what we have actually done.

I put my panniers back on my bike and rode off, through a small border village where all the houses had brightly-coloured roofs and young children chased horses down the otherwise empty main highway. In complete contrast to the thick forest on the Russian side, I was soon out on a wide open, grassy plain, amazed again by the abruptness of the change. I was in no mood for cycling, however, and there seemed little point now, so I soon stopped to make camp. I had a nice location at least, a sandy spot sheltered by one of the few trees around. I sat outside of my tent and stared, deep in thought, watching the sun as it gradually curved towards the horizon and then dropped below it, setting the sky alight with a bright orange that faded to a deep purple, then eventually a black peppered with pinpricks of light. During all this time I reflected back upon what had just happened and tried to work out what to do next. If only I'd had Petr's rules, I could just cycle around in a circle for two kilometres and continue (I did try this actually, but it didn't make me feel any better). According to the challenges I'd set for myself right at the start, my attempt to circumnavigate the world using only my bicycle and boats was over, clearly. There was no getting around that. I knew most people wouldn't care about a few hundred metres, but for me it was all or nothing, and it was over, simple as that. I came to terms with that surprisingly quickly. But what was I going to do next?

The difficult challenge of cycling across Mongolia had lost all of its appeal now, and my first thought was to ride only to the capital, Ulaanbaatar, and catch a flight out of there. I already had my working holiday visa for Australia, and I considered flying straight there. That might sound like I was quitting, but I didn't see it that way. I still wanted to cycle around the world, I just felt like I was going to have to start all over again somewhere new, at some time in the future.

The next morning I cycled into the small town of Sükhbaatar and found a hotel and restaurant with wifi. The girls working in the restaurant had little interest in me, and appeared to have little interest in life in general. It was that kind of place. Nobody seemed to care much for anything, with the exception of the man who pushed in front of me to buy his bottle of vodka. He had some zeal about him, at least. But the wifi in the restaurant was much better than I could have hoped, and I started looking at my options.

It now struck me that I really shouldn't fly anywhere. I mean, I had been forced into using other transport at the border, but doing so through my own choice would actually be much worse. By chance I had this insightful revelation at approximately the same time that I saw the price of flights out of Mongolia. Purely coincidence, you understand.

I sat for a long time, contemplating what I was going to do, and then, just as I was about to wrap things up and leave, I was struck by another moment of inspiration. I was staring at the list of challenges that I'd set myself when it suddenly came to me. In an instant I understood just exactly what I was going to do, precisely how I could make everything alright again. It was perfect... simple... brilliant. It was such a fantastic idea that I wondered how it could have taken me fifteen hours to think of it (and not, as one would expect, much longer). My idea, simply put, was this: I would just keep going.

I'll just allow a short pause here for you to take in the magnitude of my inspirational idea.

Yes, I would just keep going. Obviously my attempt to complete a continuous circumnavigation without motor vehicles had ended, but why should I end everything? There was no need for the challenges to be inextricably linked to one another. All I had to do was to reset the second challenge – the circumnavigation by bike and boats – and keep right on going with everything else. Oh yes, I would just carry on with the trip, exactly as planned. Then if I made it all the way around and back to Europe, instead of stopping there I could keep right on going until I arrived at a point, most likely in China, that was reached after the fateful events of 30th August 2014.

Essentially then, I still had to cycle all the way around the world. But, as my recent meetings with Hera and Petr had shown me, with a direct approach I could probably do the extra bit from Europe to China in three months. What was another three months going to be on a journey that was always going to be counted in years? As for the other challenges, there was no need to restart on those. They were still a part of the whole journey. I'd still done them. I hadn't suddenly not done them because of one kilometre in a vehicle. Mongolia was coun- try number thirty-six, I'd cycled 27,000 kilometres, the circumnaviga- tion aspect had been reset, this book can go on, the movie deal remained possible, and I was suddenly back on top of the world.

29

Outer Mongolia
1ˢᵗ September 2014

Early impressions of Mongolia were mixed. The tree under which I'd spent my first introspective evening turned out to be the last I saw for a while, as the scenery turned to grassy, treeless hills dotted with yurts and animals, reminiscent of Kyrgyzstan. There were not many cars on the road, but those there were would often slow down, either to offer me a lift, shout something unintelligible at me, or simply to stare. The slowing down just to stare at me was something I soon grew to hate, but I had positive experiences too. One time as I sat taking a break beside a small stream two men approached. Conversation was slow, as I quickly discovered Mongolian to be an incredibly difficult language (with the exception of the commonly-used greeting of "Hi" which I'd quickly mastered). The men offered me some of the meat they had with them, pointing to a horse grazing nearby to explain its source. As a vegetarian I declined, of course, though I was already wondering how I was going to get on in this country with my unusual dietary preferences. But the men were very nice about it, and left me with a bottle of coke as a gift instead.

A short while later I met another local, this one a man who bounded down the hillside towards me as I pedalled. He was coming from a van that was parked up on the grass, and he was dressed in a khaki outfit that made him look exactly like a grown-up boy scout. I stopped and was surprised when he spoke to me in good English to explain that he was also a cyclist. He immediately got out his camera to prove it, and he showed me all of his photos as we stood there at the side of the road. As well as ones of him and his wife with their bikes, we trawled through dozens of him fishing, hiking and camping.

"Here's one of me with a big fish. I am champion! With this fish I am champion! Oh, here is one of my son."

"How old is your son?" I asked.

"Eight! Eight o'clock!"

"I think you mean eight years old."

"YES!" he screamed.

The photos went on and on until eventually a message appeared on screen saying 'battery exhausted' and I had a reprieve. Now we could just talk.

"I speak English and Russian. I translate Russian," he spoke quickly.

"Oh, is that your job?"

"NO!" he absolutely screamed. "My job is fishing. And drinking vodka. And f*cking! I f*ck every girl! Every girl!"

There was a pause in the conversation at this point, I think for us both to take in the gravity of this lie. Although he was in much better shape than most Mongolian men I'd seen of his age, who had generally either been strutting around with massive beer-guts spilling out of ill-fitting clothes, or else lying unconscious next to empty vodka bottles, I just couldn't believe that *every* girl would want to sleep with him. I mean, there were too many girls, and not enough hours in the day, and he was wearing socks with sandals.

Deciding to break the silence, I asked if I could take a photo of him before I left, and he proudly agreed. He wasn't happy with my first effort, however, and insisted I take another of him, full-length to show off all of his green things.

"My green socks, my green sandals, my green shorts, green shirt, green everything."

"Why is everything green?" I asked.

"Because I am president of the Green Party. Political party. The Green Party."

"Oh..." I was a little surprised, and keen to find out more. I wanted to ask about their policies, how popular they were in Mongolia, but before I could, he went on.

"It's good. I can drink vodka. Lots of vodka! All day, vodka, vodka! Very nice life!"

The road was paved but it rose and fell steeply, and a headwind slowed me even more. As a result I wasn't even able to make a hundred kilometres per day. This was a concern, as I had a long way to go and I knew the pavement would end soon and I'd have to continue on sandy tracks. If I couldn't manage much distance on the tarmac, how was I going to do it off-road? In truth, I wasn't sure if it was even going to be possible to cycle across this country, and during my research I had failed to find a single cyclist who had done so without resorting to other transport. Ahead of me was a tremendously exciting challenge.

One thing I had gathered from my research was that in order to navigate in Mongolia I would need a very good map and a GPS. Naturally enough I had neither of these things. But a chance encounter with a Frenchman did at least give me some vital information. We met at the top of a peak, him walking up from the opposite direction pushing a bicycle. His name was Cedric. In his thirties, he had a scruffy long goatee beard and a ponytail protruding from his baseball cap. Dressed in dusty blue shorts and T-shirt, his lean body seemed tired. And no wonder. He told me he'd left France three years previously, and *walked* to China, where he had wandered hungry and picking up random bottles of water from ditches for nine days before realising that China was too big to walk across. Then he'd bought this bike, new, for fifty euros (which probably explained why it couldn't go uphill), and had used it to cross Mongolia.

Cedric had entered Mongolia from China at the border crossing I planned to leave by, so I knew I had to get as much information from his as I could. He fished out his very detailed map to show me his route, although he couldn't do so exactly because the road he took wasn't on the map.

"I thought I was on this road," he said, "but actually I was on a new road that went around here and down here."

I took out a pen and some paper, jotted down some notes, and drew a crude map from what he was telling me. Then I asked him about the area I'd have to cross that was entirely unpaved.

"How was the road to Altay?"

"Bad, very bad."

"But it's possible?"

"Mmm."

"Well, this doesn't look so bad," I said, and it really didn't. It appeared I only had 600 kilometres of unpaved 'road' to get through, and I basically only had to make two turns in the whole country.

"I don't know." Cedric looked concerned. "Mongolia is the hardest country to navigate in. I got lost several times." This was a man with a very good map and a GPS, who'd *walked* to China, but I now had a map drawn with my own fair hands, and I couldn't see how I could go wrong. Especially now I'd met someone who'd crossed Mongolia by bike. Now I knew it was possible, at least.

"Actually I hitched lifts with cars for half of it. It really was too difficult."

"Oh."

I decided to bypass just around Ulaanbaatar, Mongolia's capital. It had been described to me as 'one of the world's worst cities', and nobody seemed to have anything good to say about the place. In a way that almost tempted me to go, just so that I would be able to boast about having seen one of the world's worst cities. But as luck would have it I used to live in Coventry, and I considered the box already ticked, so I didn't go to Ulaanbaatar.

I did look down on it though, from a hill as I passed by. Well, bits of it. Skyscrapers poking through a layer of smog mostly. It's also one of the world's most polluted cities, and I reflected on the sad irony that the sky in Mongolia seemed to be a much brighter sort of blue than anywhere else, yet the majority of the country's population couldn't see it through their own exhaust fumes.

I continued on up the hill, leaving Mongolia's only city behind and heading back to the vast empty spaces of the least densely populated country in the world. It wasn't completely unpopulated though, and I was soon called over by a small group sitting on the ground in the shade of a fence. As well as a few older men there were a couple of younger women and a baby, so I thought it perfectly safe. Nothing wrong with a family picnic. As soon as I arrived beside them a big glass was filled with vodka and handed to me. Of course, this was a Mongolian picnic. I took a sip and tried to hand it back, but I was encouraged to drink it all. The wind was blowing the same way I wanted to cycle, and I was feeling quite strong, so I thought a little tipple wouldn't hurt, and downed the glass. The man who had given me the vodka then gave me a glass of water to drink as a chaser, presumably because nothing gets rid of a foul taste in your mouth quite like water. Next he took an interest in my hair. Mongolians don't have much in the way of body hair, so he was fascinated as he touched my beard, then pulled at the hair on my arms that was turned white from the sun. I didn't really mind the attention, not even when he started stroking the hair on my legs, but when he made a grab for my balls I decided to put a stop to things. Then I noticed a goat that was lying nearby, legs tied together and evidently not long for this world. As it was nearly lunchtime I thought it time for me to move along, lest I have to witness the poor animal's demise first hand.

Well I can't say for sure that the vodka was a good idea, but the rest of the day did seem to fly by in a bit of a happy blur. As the day drew towards a close I was whizzing along with the wind at my back, the road still paved, the scenery lovely, and the sun, which was descending to the low hills on the horizon almost directly in front of me, casting a mesmerising array of colours across the sky. At that precise moment I felt like life really couldn't get any better. But I think that maybe life might have noticed me thinking that because it then decided that it was going to raise the stakes. I'm not exactly sure if it was the vodka, but I thought I might have heard life say, "You don't think I can get better? Just watch this!" and then three motorcycles suddenly appeared. Heading the same way as me, they pulled alongside to say hi. The first had two Frenchmen on it, the second a cheerful British guy, and on the third, with tremendous credit to life, was the most beautiful girl in the world.

"Hello. My name is Dea," she said. "I'm from Denmark."

Even beneath her bright red helmet I could see how beautiful she was. In that brief split second I felt a rush as the thought struck me that this could be her. This could be 'the one'. I wondered if this was what love at first sight felt like. Or maybe it was still just the vodka.

I was brought instantly back to reality as Matt, the Brit, spoke. He explained that all four of them were backpacking and had just met in an Ulaanbaatar hostel and decided to rent these motorcycles together for a short tour of Mongolia. The type of bike they were on, a lightweight and not very powerful one, almost more of a scooter really, was to be seen everywhere in Mongolia. It was almost a twenty-first century Mongolian horse, perfect for the off-road conditions, and I'd seen locals using them to do everything from rounding up animals to transporting ambitious loads (including on one memorable occasion a live goat). None of the travellers had ever been on a motorcycle before, but they all looked like they were enjoying themselves. They all seemed very nice too, and one of them was the most beautiful girl in the world, so I suggested we find a place to camp together.

There was nowhere to camp along the road, so we went off up a track that led us towards a yurt. Alerted by the noise of the motorcycles a man appeared at the entrance and, showing the hospitality I'd grown used to all over Asia, he called us over to invite us all inside. The yurt was simply furnished with a couple of beds, a table, and a central stove. It was the home of the man and his wife, their grown-up children having apparently moved away.

With tea being handed out all round I got talking with Matt, who rather annoyingly had positioned himself sitting between me and Dea. Having removed her helmet I could now see her properly, and my original assessment of her as the real, genuine, actual most beautiful girl in the world was confirmed. She was tall with long, blonde hair, shaved short on one side in a stylish way, and she had the most incredible blue eyes and innocent smile. She had really cool shoes on too, and I desperately wanted to get to know her better. What a shame Matt was in the way. I talked to him anyway. He was a twenty-five-year-old short little bearded chap on an overland journey to Australia, travelling by any means he could find without flying. It was an interesting trip, but I thought even more interesting was one that he'd done before.

"I once rode a unicycle from Calais to Gibraltar," he said, smiling.

"Wow. That's impressive. How was it?"

"Yeah good. Erm... the hills were a bit hard."

By now our host woman was passing around a tray of pieces of hard cheese for us to eat. I took one and, while it certainly didn't taste good, forced myself to eat it. Matt didn't like his either, and slipped it discreetly into his pocket so as not to offend. Later on, when we were back outside, he fished it out and one of the French guys snatched it off him and gobbled it up. They do like their cheese, don't they?

Our host man was a lot of fun, and put on a CD to keep us all entertained. I was expecting some traditional Mongolian songs, but instead we opened up with 'Hey Macarena' and he did a dance for us. His moves weren't ones that I would have ever associated with the tune before, but it was certainly very entertaining.

Dea was clearly way out of my league, but at least I felt I was one up on the competition. The two French guys sat there and hardly said a word, and Matt, despite being a genuinely great guy, was delightfully short. Then a friend of the two French guys showed up. He'd already been riding around on his motorcycle for a few days and had been directed here to meet up with everyone. In through the door of the yurt he ducked, then he straightened up and nearly bumped his head on the roof.

'Oh good, just what this party needs,' I thought, *'a tall, handsome man.'*

Unfortunately, the lazy woman in the yurt hadn't prepared dinner for eight, so we travellers all moved outside to put up our tents and make something to eat. I wasn't going to miss my opportunity and I put my tent up in record time so that, being a consummate gentle-man, I could offer to help Dea with hers before anyone else. I then clambered around getting in her way trying all the while to look like I knew what I was doing. I was sure she was impressed. When all of the tents were eventually up we all sat down to a dinner of cold sand-wiches together, before everyone said goodnight and retired to their sleeping quarters.

I walked away across the barren ground to take a pee before going to bed. The air was cool. The night sky filled with stars. I wandered back towards the tents and noticed an outline beside one of them. It was Dea, sitting cross-legged, gazing at the horizon where the moon was just beginning to emerge. Everyone else had vanished.

"Would you mind if I sit with you?" I asked, hoping the desperate loneliness of my own existence hadn't been conveyed in the tone.

"Of course not, sit."

So I did. And for the first time we were alone, and we talked. Dea was on a four-month trip, taking in Mongolia, China and the Philip-pines. She'd been travelling alone, until meeting the others in Ulaan-baatar and making the spontaneous decision to go on the motorcycle ride. She told me about her life back in Denmark, where she studied Danish and music. She also explained how she loved to travel, and as she did so it occurred to me that she really was the sort of adventur-ous girl I'd always been looking for. But she struggled to grasp the concept of my own adventure. "I never heard of anyone cycling the world before," she said. "It sounds incredible, but I really don't think you'd ever be able to persuade me to travel on a bicycle." The way she said it, it sounded like a challenge.

We stared at the moon as we talked and talked. It was almost full, a brilliant orange, and breathtaking in its simple charm. Its beauty was mirrored in the girl next to me. It was just a perfect evening. I'd found someone intelligent, someone intriguing, someone it just felt right to be with.

With the moonlight outlining her face I moved slowly towards her, nervous excitement tingling through my body.

And we kissed.

30

Outer Mongolia
4th September 2014

I woke up happy. It felt so good to have found this girl. This beautiful, amazing, wonderful girl. And she was going the same way as me. Just a shame she was doing so on a sodding motorcycle, wasn't it? We'd stayed up almost the whole night talking, instantly feeling connected to one another. But our moment together, as special as it was, could not be prolonged, and it seemed like another case of what might have been, as I waved Dea goodbye and watched her ride away alongside a tall, handsome Frenchman.

"Well, there goes another one. Hey bike, why aren't you a motorcycle? We could keep up with her then."

"I don't know mate, why aren't you a tall, handsome Frenchman?"

"Ah, touch, talking bicycle, touch."

"I think the word you're looking for is touché."

"Oh, piss off."

I continued cycling west alone, determined not to feel sorry for myself. Meeting Dea had been fantastic, and I wished I'd had the chance to get to know her better, but she was gone, and once again I had to force myself to focus on what I was doing. The challenge to ride my bicycle around the world was exactly that, a challenge, and it was taking me to the most extraordinary of places.

Moving away from Ulaanbaatar the road, though still paved, had almost no traffic on it. Gentle dry, yellow hills encircled me, resembling waves on an ocean, with occasional yurts the only sign of habitation, like little lifeboats bobbing about. And most incredible of all was the sky. It seemed impossibly big, somehow filling more space than it ever had before, and it was a blue more brilliant than I'd ever imagined it could be. White fluffy clouds would sometimes hang out close to the horizon, neither willing nor able to fill this vast expanse of sky. The sense of space was overwhelming.

For several days I had no real contact with people, unless you count the cars that slowed down to stare at me, or the occasional man who would shriek loudly at me while passing by motorcycle. I found this loud shrieking weird, and not particularly pleasant, but I thought it might be a form of greeting, and took to responding with a wave. Aside from that I had some very nice conversations with cows, sheep, goats, horses, and, one time, a pig.

So you can imagine my surprise when I came across another touring cyclist as I approached the end of the paved road at the town of Bayankhongor. This was a young Korean man with floppy black hair and the easy-to-remember name of Bak Hyung Yeol. He explained that he was cycling a big loop, from Korea, across China, then back via Mongolia and Siberia, which meant he had just come from exactly the direction I was heading. What was more, he'd apparently cycled the whole way, so I was keen to find out everything that I could.

He started by asking me if I had a GPS, and looking very concerned for me when I said that I did not. At least I now had a map, recently donated to me by a passing Mongol Rally team. According to this map, the road ahead passed through a couple of small villages between Bayankhongor and the next town of Altay, 400 kilometres away. But Bak Hyung Yeol told me that the road didn't go through any villages. On my map it clearly did. But Bak Hyung Yeol was insistent, and said that the road passed fifty kilometres south of those villages. Then he told me that there was no road, just desert, and I started to think maybe Bak Hyung Yeol had been cycling in the wrong place.

I'd heard one or two worrying stories about Mongolia, and I

thought it prudent to ask Bak Hyung Yeol if he'd had any trouble along the way. I was thinking along the lines of potentially being robbed, or running into trouble with drunk men, but instead he told me that he'd seen wolves on the road. Then I noticed that, in what was the most extraordinary luxury item I'd ever seen a touring cyclist possess, he had a hammer strapped to the back of his bike. "Is that for the wolves?" I asked.

"No," he said, "for the tent."

Well, I guess you can't always find a rock, can you?

I thanked Bak Hyung Yeol and wished him well, then rode on into Bayankhongor. With 20,000 inhabitants it was a large town by Mongolian standards, and I wanted to find a welder. A part of my front rack had snapped and I needed to get it fixed before I headed off-road. I stopped at the first place that I found that looked like it might contain a mechanic and by great fortune bumped into a man that could speak English. He told me there was a guy around the corner who could do the weld, but I thought I'd better take advantage of his language skills to ask about the route ahead to Altay first. After looking very concerned when I said I had no GPS, he gave me one of the greatest pieces of advice anyone had ever given me. "Just follow the electric pylons," he said. Just follow the electric pylons. It was brilliant. Then he told me not to cycle at night, which I wasn't planning on doing. "Seriously, don't cycle at night," he repeated, "there are wolves."

I found the welder and had to act as his assistant, holding the rack while he went to work. He put on his big welder's mask and I, who was just as close to the action, held my hand over my face. Soon the job was done with my arm only slightly singed, and I asked him how much he wanted. I was a bit concerned he might try and rip me off, but he only asked for 1,000 tugriks (about 30 pence). I gave him 2,000. I can be amazingly generous like that.

Bike fixed, I went to the supermarket to buy supplies which, because of the limited vegetarian fare available in Mongolia, consisted almost entirely of stale bread and chocolate-coated peanuts. I hadn't seen any fresh fruit in almost two weeks. Bak Hyung Yeol had told me that for the next 400 kilometres there would be nowhere to buy food or water, and not even any yurts to ask things from. Estimating that it was going to take me five or six days to reach Altay I crammed fifteen litres of water and as much food as I could onto my bike. It made it ridiculously heavy, and I wobbled and struggled to keep my balance on my way through town.

When the edge of town appeared the road abruptly stopped. In front of me was a big range of hills. All over them a series of rutted tracks split and crossed one another and went here, there, and everywhere. There were a lot going off to the left, a lot going off to the right, and a few more in the middle for good measure. Remembering the wise words I'd just heard I looked for the electric pylons. There they were, a steady row of them leading up alongside the tracks to the left. Great. Then I looked again at the tracks to the right and saw another row of electric pylons beside them. Oh dear. What to do? Maybe this was going to be harder than I thought. I wasn't even out of town yet and I was lost already.

I retreated to a gas station that I'd just passed and asked the attendant for the way to Altay. He pointed to the tracks to the left. It looked from the few clouds of dust on the hillside like that was the way that most of the traffic was going, so I was happy, and set off in that direction. It was immediately difficult. I had six or seven tracks to choose from, all going in roughly the same direction, but all as bad as each other. They were simply carved out of the rough ground by the weight of previous passing vehicles and were bumpy and rutted. To make matters worse it was a long climb up the hill, a good twenty kilometres, into a stiff headwind. With the amount of weight I had on the bike it was really tough going. I consoled myself with the thought that at least I didn't have a hammer.

There wasn't much traffic going up the hill, but most of what there was came to see me, the drivers often switching tracks just to hunt me down. In most cases I was offered a lift, including once by an ambitious motorcyclist. I had to laugh. "I know you can fit a lot on those motorcycles, but you're not getting me, my bicycle, and fifteen litres of water on there, and that's a sure fact."

A short while later I pulled up to an oil tanker that was mysteriously parked up. I needed to reorganise the load on the back of my bike which kept slipping off, and there was nowhere else to lean it in this treeless world. The driver, a middle-aged pregnant man, came over and told me it was fine to rest my bike against his truck. His T-shirt was pulled up almost to his nipples and he rubbed his huge exposed belly as we conversed in sign language. He asked if I wanted a lift, writing '400km!' in dust on the side of his cab as a warning as to how far it would be to the next town. I nodded, thanking him, but insisting it was not a problem. The man, his chubby face showing great concern for my foolishness, then put his finger back on the truck, and drew a surprisingly good picture of a wolf.

I was frankly getting a little worried by how often I was being warned about wolves, and that evening I felt nervous cooking my dinner outside my tent. I was really all alone out in the middle of nowhere, and the appearance of a full moon did nothing at all to ease my fears. I decided to take some precautions, and put my heavy chain lock together with my frying pan. If any wolves came I would bang the two together and it would make an awful noise. And if this wasn't enough to scare the wolves away I'd seen enough cartoons to know that a frying pan made a fine object with which to hit animals over the head with. It seemed like a good plan, and I slept easy, at least until I remembered that my frying pan didn't have a handle.

The next day I woke up relieved to be alive, and enjoyed a blissful morning. Cycling on the tracks was actually quite fun, and it felt like a real adventure to be somewhere so completely empty. I only saw one car all morning. All was well, right up until the moment it dawned on me that I was probably lost. I was still following the electric pylons, but the fact that all the traffic had gone off somewhere in a different direction had me suddenly doubting the electric pylon strategy. I continued on, growing more anxious, until finally I saw what I thought was a second car of the day. As I got closer to it, however, I noticed it was actually the same one that had passed me earlier, now broken down with its bonnet open. A family was sitting on the ground beside it and I stopped to ask if they were alright. They said that they were, and there wasn't much I could do for them. I enquired as to whether the tracks we were on led to Bombogor, the first village marked on my map. They insisted that they did, which was encouraging, although given the fact that there had been no other vehicles other than me and them for the last six hours I had to consider the possibility that perhaps they too were simply lost.

But I carried on, trusting them and the electric pylons primarily because I had few other options. And around twenty-four hours of rough riding later I did eventually stumble, with great relief, upon Bombogor. It was just a small collection of houses a hundred kilometres from anywhere, and as I entered this village I think I must have looked like an alien from another world. Children swarmed around me, saying "Hello, hello" and laughing and giggling at me. Looking at their smiling faces I wondered what it must be like to grow up out here, a million miles from the hectic world I'd left behind.

Beyond Bombogor I followed the electric pylons back out into the wilderness. Contrary to what Bak Hyung Yeol had told me, there were one or two yurts along the way, and it wasn't long before two young boys on a motorcycle invited me to visit theirs. I followed them, laid down my bike, and ducked inside. An older son greeted me, wearing a traditional thick robe that was the outfit of choice for about half the men I'd seen so far in Mongolia (the other half wearing Western clothes, usually well-worn). He'd matched the bright blue robe with leather cowboy boots, and he looked like he could have been from another time, at least until he pulled out his iPhone. The advance of technology had reached even this far-flung corner of the globe, with solar panels and satellite dishes outside most of the yurts.

This yurt was more brightly decorated than others that I'd seen in Mongolia, with colourful floral designs on the walls and even a similarly patterned carpet on the floor. It struck me that it was not exactly a bad place to live. A little cramped, perhaps, but I thought it must be lovely and cosy during the cold winter months to all huddle up together, and throw another cow pat on the fire.

We were soon joined by the mother and the father of the family, who served me warm horse milk, curiously unfermented, and a big brick of rock hard cheese that I couldn't even bite into. The mother soon brought me another type of cheese, which was softer, but still not quite to my taste.

I put the cheeses to one side and got out my map. Everyone crowded around and even the elder son put down his phone long enough to come and look. He pointed out the big river that was coming up. I'd heard much about this already, and I was worried I might find it difficult to cross, but it was just another obstacle for me to overcome. I finished my horse milk, thanked everyone, and went to leave. The cheeses I'd tried to discreetly leave behind were scooped up and handed to me as a parting gift. Such kindness.

The tracks were terrible now, a rough washboard surface that limited my speed to seven kilometres per hour even on the downhills. But I persevered until finally I got down towards the river. The Mongol Rally team had told me they hadn't known how to ford it, and had needed to follow a truck through, describing their crossing as 'quite scary'. Bak Hyung Yeol had told me he'd managed to wade across, but had got very wet. I didn't fancy getting wet too much as it was a cold day. But as the track swung down around a corner and the river came into view I couldn't believe what I saw. There was a bridge across it. A great big bridge. Whatever route those muppets with their GPS units were following, it wasn't half as good as mine.

By now I'd worked out that there were probably two roads (and by roads I mean collection of tracks). The one I was on, which went up through the hills and the villages, and another further south that went straight across the flat desert. Presumably that was where Bak Hyung Yeol and most of the traffic was, which explained why I had hardly seen anyone.

I needed to keep my daily distances high in order to make it to the border before my visa expired, and that was difficult to do as I was frequently faced with either thick sand or hard washboard. My bike would often come to a complete halt in a patch of loose sand and I'd have to jump off and push it out again. The washboard was no better – a hard, corrugated surface where I'd bump up and down, my whole body being jolted miserably. Progress was dismal, but I stuck at it, staying on the bike from eight in the morning until eight in the evening, and managing about sixty kilometres for my efforts. To put that in perspective, had I been taking part in the London Marathon, at that speed I would have finished in last place, just behind the fat man in the deep sea diving costume.

My perseverance was finally rewarded when I came down out of the hills I'd been struggling through and could see, far away to my left, the dust clouds of a couple of vehicles. My theory that there was another route to the south was confirmed, and it seemed I would soon be reunited with it on the final stretch into Altay. Then a car came towards me. It was another team taking part in the Mongol Rally, two Australian men with big beards, who stopped to ask me the way. I told them about the two routes, that the one to the south was probably flatter and easier, but that this one had better scenery and passed through the villages.

This caused a division between the two men. The driver, who was cheerful and friendly, wanted to keep going on this scenic, adventurous route, but the guy in the passenger seat, who I'll refer to as Old Grumpy Guts, wanted to switch to the southern route.

"It doesn't make that much difference really," I said, trying to placate the argument. "Either way you'll be in Bayankhongor by the end of the day."

"It might not make much difference to you," Old Grumpy Guts said to me, perhaps failing to appreciate I'd been toiling away on a bicycle for several days, "but it does to us."

I felt terribly sorry for the nice guy. "It's been like this for 20,000 kilometres," he said.

In a way it made me realise just how lucky I was, as we said goodbye and I saw them immediately pull over to argue about it some more. First of all, that I wasn't trapped in a hot car. Second of all, that I was travelling alone. Oh, of course a lot of the time I longed for company, yet I had to admit that being on my own meant I had complete freedom. I didn't have to consult anyone else about which route to take. I could get up when I wanted, stop and camp when I wanted.

There was no need to compromise. My life and my journey belonged to me. If Daniel had come with me I never would have been able to go to all these places. I was sure he wouldn't have been as bad as Old Grumpy Guts, but would he have been up for the long sprint across Kazakhstan and Siberia? Would he have wanted to ride across Mongolia? That's not to say that it wouldn't have been good with Daniel, it probably would have been, but it certainly would have been different. And I was really very happy with what it was without him. My freedom was something I valued highly, it was perhaps the thing I treasured the most about my lifestyle.

In any case, I'd heard Daniel had found his own happiness, now in love and engaged to a girl from his home province in Canada. He never would have met her if he'd been off gallivanting around the world. Which made me think. What if I got all the way around the world, and then found out that 'the one' had been living in Newport Pagnell all along?

Six days of sweat and toil after leaving Bayankhongor I finally made it to Altay, a town of about 15,000 people that felt like the biggest city in the world to me. I lost most of the day trying to find somewhere to use wifi in order to inform the outside world that I was still alive, thanks to being given terrible directions by drunk men back and forth around town. The vodka alcoholism in Mongolia was undoubtedly the saddest thing about the country. Every shop I went to had as much vodka for sale as it did food, and consuming it was obviously a national obsession.

Leaving Altay, I still had a few hundred kilometres to do on the off-road tracks. Again it was very difficult as I was now crossing a section of the Gobi desert and, though it was flat, there was a lot more sand. At times I had to get off and push my bike because the sand was just too thick to gain traction. When I was lucky the sand would thin out and I'd have more washboard to bump slowly over. It was tough, traversing this harsh terrain, but it was also a magnificent experience. Apart from the occasional passing vehicle, maybe twenty per day, I was alone. During my breaks I would sit eating my chocolate-coated peanuts and look around and take in the silence. I was physically exhausted, but the empty vistas in every direction, the 360 degree panorama of nothingness, was strangely comforting.

After several more days of digging my way through sand I followed Cedric's directions to turn left at a salt lake and head up into the mountains. After riding up a dry river bed I found my way to the Chinese mine he had told me about and I knew that I had made it. A band of tarmac sparkled in the sunshine. Built to service the mine, I knew that this paved road stretched the final 400 kilometres to the Chinese border. My trials with Mongolia's off-road tracks was at an end, and I felt a sense of joy and relief to have succeeded. With my plans to restart the circumnavigation aspect of my journey after I crossed into China, I might have been tempted to skip the difficult ride through Mongolia, to just accept a lift in a truck. But I was glad that I had not. The whole point of this journey was to challenge myself, to ride my bike in the wild places, to see, to experience, and to conquer the world by bicycle. And once again it felt good to prove that anything a car could do, so could a bicycle. Besides, I probably wouldn't have felt comfortable getting into a car in Mongolia, given the likelihood that the driver could have been drinking. I still hated cars, I hated how dangerous they were. People would sometimes ask me if I wasn't scared of the dangers of travelling around the world, of being mugged, or killed in my tent, or getting sick, or being attacked by wild animals. But I always knew that by far the biggest danger to me was posed by motor vehicles. Spending so much time on the world's roads as a vulnerable road user I appreciated how dangerous cars could be, and I still failed to understand how the human race had come to rely on a mode of transport that caused so much death and misery on a daily basis.

Little did I know it, but as I whooped with delight to feel my wheels turn freely on smooth tarmac again, I was just a few short hours away from fully experiencing the terrifying consequences of a motor vehicle accident first hand.

31

Gobi desert, Mongolia
21ˢᵗ September 2014

As I freewheeled down from the mountains I was impressed by the sight of a huge salt lake glistening in the broad valley below me. Beyond the lake more peaks distorted the horizon, and somewhere beyond them, I knew, was China. The land around me remained barren, but a few very hardy shrubs offered signs of life. I once again felt lucky to be in such an incredible place, so far from civilisation.

Reaching the bottom of the valley I passed by the lake and closed in on the village of Tsetseg. Knowing that this would be my only chance of food and water for the next 250 kilometres it was a welcome sight, but unfortunately the paved road didn't share my desire to go to Tsetseg, and for some reason curved around it. That left me with five kilometres of desert between the road and Tsetseg to cross. It seemed my off-road experience in Mongolia wasn't quite over yet after all. But I noticed a few buildings on the road a little further ahead, and decided to put off going to Tsetseg until I'd seen what they were. Maybe somebody had had the initiative to put a shop on the road to save people like me from a ten kilometre detour. No such luck. As I rode closer, I could see that they were just some sort of garages, with quite a few men standing outside, but alas no shop. It looked like I was going to have to go to Tsetseg.

Then suddenly I looked up. I'm not sure why. There might have been a horn. There could have been a screech of brakes. I can't remember. Maybe I just looked up at that moment by chance. What I saw was hard to believe. About 500 metres ahead of me, maybe a little more, a Land Rover type vehicle was leaving the road. For some stupid reason the road was raised a couple of metres above the desert, and the vehicle headed straight down the steep-sloped embankment. Then suddenly it flipped and started to roll. It rolled over and over and over again in a billowing cloud of dust. All of this seemed to be happening in slow motion, and with each roll the terrifying situation in front of me became more and more serious.

I was right opposite the building, so I called out to the men standing outside the garages and pointed at the accident scene. Their looks of shock confirmed that they knew what had happened, and I imagined they would all jump in a vehicle and drive down as quick as they could. I was relieved that I wasn't going to have to deal with this on my own, but I started pedalling quickly to the scene to see if there was anything that I could do.

I'd sometimes thought about what I would do in this situation. I think most people have. I always envisaged myself running fearlessly in like David Hasselhoff to administer first aid and CPR, apply bandages and tourniquets and get everyone on their feet by the time the emergency services arrived. At the very least I would run fearlessly in. But let me tell you, it's not like that at all. Not at all. Oh, I had every intention to run fearlessly in as I laid my bicycle down, I really did. But then I looked up and saw the scene in front of me and I froze. My head span and my legs went to jelly and I didn't know what to think or where to look or what to do with myself. The vehicle was right-side up again, but it was a complete wreck; it looked like it had been through a crusher. Spread out on the ground to the right of it, evidently thrown from the vehicle as it rolled, were the bodies of four men. And they were bodies. They were all dead for sure. They were covered in dust and horribly contorted, their limbs sticking out at funny angles. I could not believe what I was looking at. This was something from a movie, a video game, this wasn't real. I turned away, covered my mouth, held my head in disbelief. I was in shock.

There was a blue pick-up parked up next to me that had been

involved in the accident somehow. One man, dressed in yellow, was sitting in it. Another man, who must have been in the pick-up too, was running around among the bodies. He was grabbing at rocks, tearing at his own hair, and throwing himself around like a man in severe shock.

A white car came along the road towards us and I flagged it to a stop. I told the people in it that we needed to call for help, which seemed like a pretty obvious thing to do. I'm not sure they did anything, however, other than stare slack-jawed at the horror movie in front of them. None of them were going to do anything, the men back at the garage were nowhere to be seen, and no one else was coming. The distraught man from the pick-up began to shake the bodies wildly as if trying to wake them up. There was a sudden moment of clarity, as I realised that nobody else was going to do anything, and that I really was going to have to pull myself together and do something. If any of those men were still alive the very least I needed to do was stop that idiot from shaking them to death.

I ran down the slope into the carnage screaming "STOP SHAKING THEM" at the man. He was a short man, thirties, with wild, unkempt hair. He was all over the place. I couldn't tell if he was drunk or in shock or both, but at my shouting he went back to leaving the bodies alone and merely flailing about the place. It was horrific, the whole scene. No longer was I looking at it from afar. I was in amongst it now. I was a part of the horror. Trembling, I crouched beside the first of the stricken men and, with some astonishment, realised he was alive and conscious. From some basic first aid course I'd done almost a decade earlier I remembered ABC, Airways-Breathing-Circulation, needed to be checked. His airways seemed clear. He was breathing okay. He had a strong pulse. He was doing remarkably well on all three counts, and was beginning to writhe about, moaning and groaning a little. When checking his vitals I'd noticed a strong smell of vodka on his breath and, had I not known better, I could easily have mistaken him for someone who'd just had a few too many. He'd even managed to land almost exactly in the recovery position, and I moved quickly on to the next guy.

He was much worse off, lying on his back with his legs bent out sideways at funny angles. His eyes were closed and his face pale and covered in dust. He looked very, very dead. I opened his mouth to check his airways and saw some chewing gum floating around at the back. I reached my finger in to try and scoop it out, aware as I did so that I could not afford to let it slip off and fall to the back of his throat. With some relief I got it out first time and threw it to the ground. The man was breathing. I couldn't believe it. He was breathing. Whenever I let go of his mouth, however, his jaw clamped shut and his breathing became much worse. The only way to keep him breathing well was to hold his mouth open. But he was breathing, and I needed to check the others.

I ran over to the third man, who was lying with his back to me. As I got closer I saw a pool of blood next to him, blood on his clothes, blood where his head should be. From the angle I was approaching from it appeared that he had been at least partially decapitated. He was dead, there was no doubt about that. I recoiled in horror, and couldn't bring myself to go any closer. Instead I turned and ran to the fourth man who was lying further away. He was a good fifteen metres from the vehicle. He'd been thrown such a long way that I couldn't believe it when I found that he too was alive, breathing and semi-conscious. We had three people alive and breathing, and what we needed now was an ambulance.

I looked up to see that the white vehicle had driven off, but a motorcycle had stopped, and the rider came down to us. Like the other guy he seemed either to be drunk or in shock, running around in despair and to my utter disbelief he too started to shake the men. "STOP SHAKING THEM! NO!" I screamed at him, making it very clear that this was not a good thing for him to be doing. "Ambulance! Doctor! Phone ambulance!" I said, making telephone gestures with my hand. He started trying to make phone calls. Other cars came along the road and I ran up to try and get them to stop, but they just drove past. What was wrong with these people? Why did they not help? I had no idea where the nearest hospital was. Maybe back in Altay, some four or five hours drive. But Tsetseg was so close. Just five kilometres or so away. "Is there anyone there who can help? A doctor?" I implored, pointing at the small village across the desert. But nobody understood anything that I was saying.

The first guy who'd been running around madly got back in the pick-up and drove off with the guy in yellow, who'd done nothing at all to help. They had been involved in the accident, might even have caused it, and now they were fleeing the scene. Now it was just me and the motorcyclist left to look after the victims. I was spending a lot of time with the unconscious man, holding his mouth open so that he could breathe. He was a thin man with a gaunt face and a high forehead. He looked so much like death. His dusty, lifeless face would be the one that would haunt me.

I turned to find the motorcyclist rolling one of the others out of the recovery position. "Stop it! You have got to keep them still! Is there an ambulance coming? Has anybody called an ambulance?!" It was useless. I really appreciated the fact that he was the only one who'd stuck around to try and help, but unfortunately the guy was an idiot. I tried to get him to hold the unconscious man's mouth open so that I could do other things, but he couldn't understand what I wanted. It was such a simple task. Instead he tried to start giving mouth-to-mouth. "NO! Stop it! He's breathing! You don't need to do that!"

I knew that I had to suck it up and go and check on the bleeding man. I approached with caution, expecting to find a corpse, but to my complete astonishment he too was still breathing. He wasn't as bad as I'd first thought; the angle must have made it look worse than it was. He did have a head-wound, and a lot of blood around his ear, but he wasn't bleeding heavily. His breathing was rasping and he clearly had blood in his throat. I wanted to clear his airways so I tilted his head gently so that blood flowed out of his mouth. I was no longer in shock, not scared or disgusted. I was just working on instinct, trying my best to keep these men alive.

It was just me and the motorcyclist for a long time. I don't know how long. Maybe fifteen minutes, maybe an hour. Cars did come along and I'd run up to the road to stop them. I remember one clearly, a Chinese family. "Please help! Please call an ambulance, call for help!" The man rolled up his window and drove on as if nothing had happened. This same thing happened two or three times, my faith in humanity dwindling with each passive dismissal of these men's fight for life.

But there were still four breathing men and if it was going to take four or five hours for an ambulance to arrive then so be it, I was just going to do what I could to keep them alive until then. I ran over to my bike and grabbed some clothes, with the idea to check for wounds and stem blood losses. I went over each men in turn and amazingly couldn't find any serious external wounds. I was sure they all had massive internal injuries, especially the man with blood in his throat, but there wasn't anything I could do about that, and the clothes were used to prop heads and try to keep people still in the recovery position.

Finally, after what felt like an eternity, a convoy of vehicles came along the road. I prayed that they were coming to help, and I felt an enormous surge of relief to see three women with stethoscopes around their necks leap out and come running over. I pointed to the bleeding man and said, "He's the worst," and they ran over to him. They checked his heartbeat and injected him with drugs and set him up on a drip. Suddenly it seemed like there were people everywhere. I noticed the man from the blue pick-up, the one who had been running around crazily, and I realised that he hadn't fled the scene, but had gone to Tsetseg to get help.

Before long an ambulance arrived. I would later find out it had come from the mine. A male doctor jumped out and started treating another of the men. I stepped back and felt a sense of relief. With four medics now on the scene, the pressure was off me. But with that came the first feelings of emptiness, the first sense of 'did this really just happen?' as I stared blankly, feeling suddenly unable to move.

I noticed that there was a police detective wandering around, smoking a cigarette, not doing anything to help. He was pretty old, surely the only policeman in Tsetseg, and rather seemed like he'd seen this too many times before. I went over to him to try and tell him what I'd seen of the accident, but he was completely uninterested. Then I was greeted by the Safety Officer from the mine, a friendly man who could speak English. As two of the accident victims were lifted onto stretchers and carried to the ambulance this man translated what I told him to the detective. I pointed out the guy from the pick-up truck, said that he'd been involved in the accident. The detective showed no interest at all in what I was saying and I never even saw him try to speak to the guy. I think he just wanted to get home for his tea. I really thought the detective should at least speak to the man who had been involved in the accident, and I added to the Safety Officer, "I think he might be drunk."

"A lot of people are drunk," he replied matter-of-factly. It was really true. A bottle of vodka had been lying on the ground between the stricken men throughout, very likely thrown from the vehicle at the same time as they were.

There was only room for two in the ambulance, and the other two had to be taken in other vehicles. The first man, who'd appeared to be in the best condition, was moved carefully by a dozen hands into the back of a van. But I watched in absolute horror as the man from the pick-up and the motorcyclist, the two fools who had been running around shaking people, and who both seemed drunk themselves, picked up the unconscious man and carried him, dangling limply between them, over to a car where he was hurled onto the back seat. This actually happened. With four 'doctors' and a police 'detective' on the scene, this actually happened. A man who had been lying motionless and unconscious on his back having been thrown from a vehicle, a man who could have untold spinal damage, was moved with such carelessness and was now going to be transported in a crumpled heap on the back seat of a car.

The ambulance and all of the other makeshift emergency vehicles took off in the direction of Tsetseg across the desert tracks, the crowds dispersed, and the detective went home for his tea. And then there was just me left there, alone to stare blankly at the wrecked vehicle and the bottle of vodka that lay as it had landed, motionless in the sand.

32

Tsetseg, Mongolia
21st September 2014

I felt numb. Completely and utterly empty. Not knowing what else to do, I started cycling across one of the off-road tracks towards Tsetseg. I was only vaguely aware of being on my bicycle. It felt like I was just floating over the sand and gravel, my thoughts a mess. A little tractor-trailer thing drove past that was filled with young children. Oblivious to what had happened they waved at me with big, happy grins on their faces. I forced a smile and a wave back, realising in that moment with astonishing clarity just how precious and fragile a gift life really was.

Rolling events back in my mind I began to wish that I'd asked the Safety Officer from the mine for an e-mail address or something so that I could find out what had happened to the injured men, and I got annoyed with myself for not doing so. I decided I'd go straight to the hospital in Tsetseg to find him. But as I arrived onto the dusty streets of Tsetseg I knew for sure that there was no hospital. It was just a village, maybe a couple of thousand inhabitants at the most. At best it would have a little clinic. The men were all seriously injured. They needed operating theatres and intensive care units. What were they going to get here? A place to lie down and be given drugs to ease the pain until they died?

I cycled up and down streets of run-down buildings, searching without success for wherever it was the men had been taken.

Everything was eerily calm, there was no hint of any drama. I found myself beside a row of shops, where a handful of people were going about their normal business. I still needed to buy supplies of course, but going into a shop and buying three days' worth of food wasn't an easy thing to do. I felt sick. I felt guilty. I felt like I had abandoned the men now that I was no longer helping them. Eating was the last thing on my mind. I did eventually manage to buy some food, but I spent a lot more time just standing in the street, staring blankly ahead of me, trying to process the afternoon's events and just not being able to. Then a blue pick-up came along and parked opposite me, and I recognised it as the one that had been involved in the accident. The man in the yellow, the one who had done nothing at all to help the victims, got out and walked over towards me. I lifted my head in a nod of acknowledgement, and for a brief moment it felt like we were in this together, and he was going to stop and tell me where I could find the men, and how they were doing. But instead he looked straight through me like I wasn't there and walked into the shop behind me. I didn't know what it was that he was buying, but I could take a good guess.

Knowing there was nothing more for me to do I cycled out of Tsetseg on some sandy tracks that looked like they would cut across to join the paved road in the direction that I wanted to go. I was completely lost inside. I really needed someone to talk to, but it was impossible. Instead I had to cycle a 250 kilometre road along which there would be precisely nothing other than empty desert. I knew it would be days before I would have the chance to even speak to anyone about the accident. I'd needed to be mentally strong before to overcome obstacles on this journey, but this really was something else.

A motorcycle came along the track behind me and I moved out of the way to let it pass. I hoped it wouldn't stop. The last thing I wanted was to try and communicate with anyone in Mongolian now. Of course it did stop, and as it pulled off the track it almost lost control and ran into me. Getting hit by a motorcycle really would have topped the day off nicely. The two men sitting on the bike grinned inanely and tried to talk to me. I looked blankly back at them. It all seemed pointless. I felt dead inside. "Yes I am going this way. You can see that I'm going this way. I'm not in the mood for this, sorry." And I cycled off. They overtook me. A short while later I saw them parked up on a little hill, the two of them sitting on a rock and taking big swigs from a bottle of vodka. I was so done with this country.

The sun set without me even noticing. As it grew cold and dark I realised I was still out in the desert and the track I was following had no intention of joining the paved road. So I started to push my bike, trudging through loose sand in the direction of tarmac. There was nowhere good to camp, the landscape being so exposed to the elements, but I realised that it didn't really matter if the wind flapped noisily at my tent all night. It wasn't like I was going to be sleeping anyway.

I put up the tent and lay down, then spent the entire night replaying everything that had happened, over and over in my mind. I beat myself up about things. Things that I could have done. Things that I shouldn't have done. Eventually I realised that it didn't really matter. All of the men were going to die. They were so badly hurt. They needed proper hospitals now, proper surgeons. Where was the nearest hospital? Altay? But even that was only a town of 15,000. Probably the only place these men could be treated was in Ulaanbaatar. It was days away, across those terrible tracks. And no doubt the hospitals there were overrun with drunks that had crashed in the city. I couldn't see how the men were going to get the emergency care that they needed. I would not have been surprised if none of them survived the night.

The world suddenly seemed such an awful place. I hated the idea that everyone involved in the accident was drunk, and I hated the way so many people didn't care to help. From the cowards at the garages who did nothing, to the cowards that drove past without stopping, all the way through to the detective who could not have cared less about investigating what had happened. What was wrong with these people? Where was the humanity? Up until this day my journey had repeatedly highlighted to me the fundamental goodness in people.

Suddenly my faith in humanity had taken a big hit.

The next morning I was almost surprised to see that the sun still rose. The sky was once again a perfect blue, and life would go on. But I felt terribly alone. I needed someone to give me a big hug and tell me everything was going to be okay, but I had no one. I was going to have to find a way through this by myself.

I felt suddenly, absolutely aware of death. I passed a dead rodent on the road, then the skull of a goat, a cow's carcass, then the burnt-out shell of another car wreck. It was as if the world was trying to tell me something. Approaching the end of my third decade on earth my own mortality, and the suddenness with which this amazing gift of life may be ripped away, was being brutally demonstrated to me.

For two days I just cycled. The road was long and straight and almost empty, which was alright with me. It started to look more and more like the Kazakh steppe, which shouldn't have been too much of a surprise, seeing as I was close to being back there having spent the last two months almost going full circle. There were very few cars, but those that did come along would often stop to try and talk with me. I did my best to explain that I wasn't interested in talking. I was sick of Mongolia and tired of Mongolians. Every time I saw an empty bottle of vodka at the side of the road it made me angry. And that happened a lot. I decided to count the bottles for a while, and found that there were on average twelve per kilometre. So in one day I must have passed around 1,200 empty vodka bottles, all of them thrown away from moving vehicles. Considering that there were maybe thirty or forty vehicles driving along this road per day, the Mongolian alcohol problem was clearly absurd.

Eventually I reached Bulgan, one final little Mongolian town. It was a much more lively place than others I'd seen, with dozens of children running around playing in the streets. For a moment I felt better about Mongolia, but then a Land Rover type vehicle sped down the road far too fast, uncaring and risking the lives of the children. As it flew by I caught sight of its occupants – four men laughing and joking and no doubt passing a bottle of vodka around. They looked like they were off for a carefree joyride. I almost broke down. It was time for me to leave this country.

As I arrived finally at the border I resolved to try and leave all the negatives behind. All I needed to take from Mongolia was the reminder that life is precious, and that I should not take it for granted, but strive to live it to the full.

China, I hoped, was going to be a new start. And as soon as I crossed the border it was once again immediately apparent that I was in a different country. First of all there were trees, which I noticed were turning a pretty yellow. They reminded me that it was autumn, a season that I loved to cycle in and that I had almost missed. The river in the valley that I was following had also been used to irrigate things, and I was taken aback by the simple sight of fields of grass and farmhouses.

There was a town not far across the border, about twenty kilometres. Don't ask me what it was called. Even if I could read Chinese this town wasn't on any maps, as it was still in the process of being built. My introduction to the great Chinese construction project had not taken long as I rode down streets surrounded by men laying paving slabs, with half-built buildings and cranes looming over them.

My primary goal was to find a hotel and it wasn't too difficult, as it was a big, garish pink building. It cost only about ten pounds per night, but it was modern and well-furnished, with wifi and a hot shower. It felt so good to be in such a civilised place after Mongolia. I took my first shower for a month. Although I'd already cleaned off the blood I'd got on me from the accident victims it felt like I was still washing it off as I scrubbed and scrubbed. It wasn't until after my second shower that I started to feel clean. I lay down on the bed and flicked on the widescreen TV. Just to be able to watch news channels and pop videos and silly Chinese game shows was a great relief. I felt like I was in a completely different world from that which I'd left behind at the border.

I treated myself to a second night in the hotel, partly because the next day was my thirtieth birthday, and partly because I really needed a day off. It was my first rest day in more than two months.

I had just finished reading 'The Great Gatsby' and there had been a quote in it that really struck a chord with me: 'I was thirty. Before me stretched the portentous, menacing road of a new decade.' It could hardly have been any more appropriate for me under the circumstances. After what I'd been through I was suddenly so very aware of my own mortality, and there really wasn't much else for me to do but to spend my birthday feeling thoroughly sad. The Great Chinese Firewall had blocked me off from communicating directly with anyone, and there was no chance of finding any English speakers among the construction workers that formed the majority of the new town's population. I was back in civilization, but I felt more alone than ever.

But just when I was giving up on the day I managed to find a way to access my e-mails, and I saw that I had one that offered a glimmer of hope in the darkness.

Hey Chris

Are you about to enter China? Or are you stuck in the Mongolian wild west?

Now I'm in Beijing. How about we keep in contact with each other? It would be great to meet you again, though I'm pretty doubtful about if you will convince me to join you on the bike. But you can try :-)

I hope you're doing good!

Xx Dea

Progress Report
Mori, October 2014

1. Circumnavigate the planet

The Eiffel Tower: 2.3° E. Mori: 90.3° E.
88° out of 360° around the planet.
(24.4% of the way around.)

2. Do so using only my bicycle and boats

Ah yes, bit of a problem there. Starting again on this one.

3. Pass through antipodal points

Not yet, not yet.

4. Visit all of the inhabited continents

Two out of six now.

5. Cycle at least 100,000 kilometres

29,570 kilometres completed. Just the 70,430 to go.

6. Cycle in 100 countries

Cycled in thirty-seven, need sixty-three more.

7. Return with more money than I start with

About £4,000 down after fourteen months, but with a
working holiday visa for Australia in my pocket.

PART THREE

MORI TO SINGAPORE

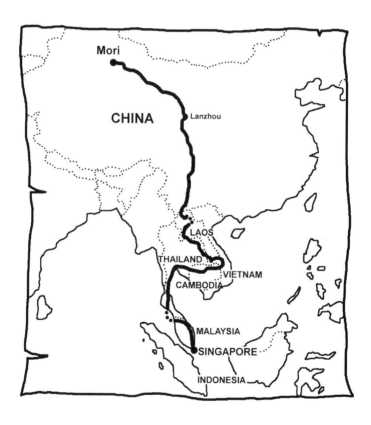

33

Mori, China
1ˢᵗ October 2014

S adly, there was no Eiffel Tower in Mori, but I decided that a funny-looking sculpture in a town square would suffice. Its base was a large silver ball, with two tall, jagged spikes pointing skywards out of it, and something like wings hanging off the side of those. I'd asked a cheerful young girl named Sunny who worked at my hotel to come and take a photograph of me posing in front of it, to commemorate the start of my world tour. There was a big board partly blocking the sculpture though.

"What's this doing in the way?" I asked.

"It is because today is China's national day," Sunny replied.

"What an extraordinary coincidence. It was France's national day the last time I started." It got me to thinking. Maybe I should stick around for my leaving do. "Will there be a big party tonight then? Fireworks, that sort of thing?"

"No."

"Oh. Paris had fireworks."

But what exactly was I doing starting a world tour by bicycle halfway through a world tour by bicycle? Well, after I'd been forced to take that motor vehicle across the Russia-Mongolia border I'd spent a month going the wrong way, and nothing was going to get me to go back to Mongolia. That left Mori, China as the most logical place to restart my circumnavigation attempt. If I resumed heading east and eventually made it all the way back around to Europe, then continued across Asia again to re-enter China from Kazakhstan, well Mori would be the place I would hit first. Of course, after all that had happened to me recently the very notion of doing all that seemed completely absurd, but I couldn't think of anything better to do, so I declared this to be the start line for a new attempt to circumnavigate the planet using only my bicycle and boats. I declared it to myself, because Sunny had no idea what was going on, but she took a very fine picture.

I thanked her and said goodbye.

"We'll see you again?" she asked. Maybe she had been paying attention after all.

"Yes, Sunny. I hope so."

And then I was off on my grand world tour. Ironically at a time when I was already 29,000 kilometres into my grand world tour. It was ironic because 29,000 kilometres is the distance you are required to have cycled in order to qualify for the 'having cycled around the world in the fastest time' world record, as made famous by Mark Beaumont. It seemed that I'd cycled 29,000 kilometres just to get to the start line. But how exciting it was to be at the beginning of such a journey. The whole world still lay ahead of me. Just think of it. The whole world. Apart from Mongolia, I wasn't going back there.

Unfortunately, the first few days of my new world tour failed to live up to the billing. I was once again crossing desert, essentially the same one I'd spent the previous two weeks crossing a little further north in Mongolia. Going west-to-east instead of east-to-west made little difference in terms of scenery, but in China I could cycle on the wide shoulder of a modern motorway instead of bumping along on rough tracks. This greatly improved my rate of progress, but was mind-numbingly boring. For days I rode along on the shoulder of this road, the grey highway cutting through the grey scenery as it played on a continuous loop. I felt so alone it was unbelievable, and all I could see ahead of me was thousands of kilometres of the same.

Consumed by my own boredom and loneliness, and still suffering from the trauma of the accident, for me these were the darkest days of the trip so far.

I reached the town of Hami and, although it was only the middle of the day, I decided to check into a hotel. I needed to find a way to motivate myself for the rest of the desert. I couldn't just keep going like this. I was in a sorry state of mind, not wanting to go on, but absolutely not wanting to give up either. This was the hardest of times for me, but even so it never seriously occurred to me to quit. The truth was that this journey had become my life. It was what gave me purpose. It was everything to me, and to give it up was almost too scary to consider. It was my identity. I had no idea what else I would do.

But how was I going to find the motivation I needed to continue? I tried to use the wifi in the hotel to search for couchsurfing hosts along my planned route, to give me some English-speakers to look forward to meeting up with. But the stupid website wouldn't work. I checked warmshowers. No hosts available. It looked like I wasn't going to be getting any motivation that way.

There was at least a very nice man on reception in the hotel who could speak a few words of English. In the morning he and his wife took me to the local market after I'd asked where I could find some fruits and vegetables (until this point I had been surviving on cheap packaged food from motorway service stations). Now this market was really something special. *'Here, at last, is the real China,'* I thought, as we walked among throngs of people, some of them wearing surgical masks against the pollution, shouting and haggling amongst rows of apples, grapes, potatoes, carrots, onions, everything. I noticed chickens in tiny cages, others running free in the dust between people's feet. As I sat with my new friends eating a delicious noodle breakfast I had the idea, for the first time in as long as I could remember, that maybe the bicycle wasn't the best way to travel. While I was being bored to tears on the expressway, all of this was going on – real, interesting, exciting life – and I was missing it.

The market experience lifted my spirits, but didn't make me feel any better about the prospect of returning to the desert. I went back to my hotel room and checked over my e-mails one more time. And there it was. A simple e-mail, and all the motivation I needed. I started cycling like a madman.

I only left the hotel at two in the afternoon, but I made it eighty kilometres in five hours, going all out, as fast as I could, a lung-busting, thigh-burning effort to make distance. No doubt you'll be wondering what could have brought about such a sudden change in attitude. Well, I'll tell you. An e-mail from the most beautiful girl in the world.

It was Dea, writing again to tell me that she could be in the city of Lanzhou on the 17th if I could. If I could? Could I ever! Like an actor accepting a role that requires a skill he can't do, I enthusiastically first replied, "YES! I can! I'll see you there!" and then tried to work out how to make it happen.

Looking it up, Lanzhou appeared to be more than 1,350 kilometres away, and I only had twelve days to make it. In theory possible, but the only two things that I really wanted to see in China (apart from the most beautiful girl in the world) were both between Hami and Lanzhou. Making detours to visit the Great Wall and the Rainbow Mountains would increase the distance and decrease the time available for cycling. To do it all I would need to average 120 kilometres per day. With shortening days and the prevailing winds against me it seemed close to impossible. But it wasn't impossible. There was a thin slice of possible there. I accepted the challenge. The race was on, and there was absolutely no time for feeling sorry for myself any more. I'd felt something special that one night with Dea in Mongolia, and now I had the chance to see if it could be something more. A second date with an amazing, interesting, beautiful girl was on the cards here. What kind of obstacle was 1,400 kilometres of desert with that kind of incentive?

Well, the next morning 1,400 kilometres started to feel like a bit more of an obstacle when a strong headwind pegged back my progress. It really did feel impossible, pedalling along at less than ten kilometres per hour. But opportunities to go on dates with gorgeous, blonde, Danish girls do not come along very often while riding a bicycle across China. If I didn't make this one it seemed highly unlikely I'd get another chance. Consequently, my brain promised my tired legs that the wind would get better in the afternoon if they only kept pressing on. My legs didn't believe my brain, but due to the way my nervous system functions they had to do what it says, and they kept going. And oddly enough the wind actually did move around in the afternoon and I made almost 120 kilometres in the end, and my legs had to apologise to my brain a little bit for doubting its future-predicting abilities.

After a 150 kilometre day that raised hopes, the wind returned again with a vengeance. It was a terrible wind. A nightmare wind. A soul-destroying wind. A kick-you-in-the-nuts-and-poke-you-in-the-eye wind. And nothing to block it. Only the flat, featureless desert. But I battled hard against it. I knew that if this wind kept up for a few days then I wouldn't make it to Lanzhou on time, but I just kept on fighting, hoping things would get better. My brain made the same promises to my legs that the wind would die down in the afternoon, but this time it was wrong. My legs were pretty mad about this, but there really was nothing they could do, they were literally at the mercy of my brain. So I cycled the whole day, from sunrise to sunset, and had seventy kilometres to show for it. It was a long way off my daily target, but enough to keep me just the right side of possible.

That evening as I sat cooking eggs outside of my tent, feeling utterly exhausted, I saw something quite incredible. By chance I happened to look up towards the moon and I did a double-take. I knew it should be about time for another full moon, yet there was almost nothing there, just a thin sliver of light. There were no clouds and nothing else to obscure it. The only logical explanation, which my tired brain did surprisingly well to quickly figure out, was that I was witnessing a lunar eclipse. I'd never seen a lunar eclipse before, much less seen one by mere fluke, having happened to look up at the right moment. I watched in silent awe for the next twenty minutes or so as the shadow of the Earth moved slowly across the surface of the moon. It was a humbling moment, as I thought about how what I was seeing there was the shadow of the very rock that I was hurtling about through space on. Gradually the moon was restored to fullness, and my own spirits were equally replenished. It had been an amazing moment, reminding me that even on the toughest of days magical things could still happen.

The big moon would soon prove a considerable help to me. I'd decided that I needed to make up time, and the way to do that was to get up and start cycling at two in the morning. By now there was a secondary road running alongside the expressway that was safe to cycle on, and there was almost no traffic on it for me to worry about. I loved it. There's a peaceful tranquillity to riding by moonlight, and a childish sense of joy at being out adventuring while the rest of the world sleeps. A highlight was sneaking in the back door of a service station and seeing the surprised look of the staff. Westerners weren't a common sight here, much less one coming in at four in the morning to stuff his face with Red Bull and crisps.

Daybreak came and by midday I was arriving at the city of Jiayugan, with a hundred kilometres already in the bag. That meant I had earned myself a little bit of free time to spend, advantageous considering Jiayugan marked the western end of the Great Wall of China. I was very excited to be here, to have reached such an iconic landmark. But far from the romantic visions I'd had of seeing the Great Wall rise from the desert, my approach to Jiayugan brought smoke stacks and cooling towers, and some of the most polluted air I'd ever had the misfortune to breath.

Turning off into the city I found a wide boulevard with an extra road on each side filled with bikes. For a little while it felt more like the Netherlands than China, with bikes going everywhere. A lot of them were electric, or motorised, but at least a few were pedal powered. And there was a lot of green too, with trees and shrubbery providing a segregation from the main traffic that, at least at first, gave the impression of a safe and enjoyable place to ride a bike. Sadly, all of that broke down as I got further into the city, when crossroads and roundabouts started appearing. Chaos reigned. Utter chaos. It seemed like cars turning right from the main street had priority over bikes going straight on, but only sometimes. And bikes were going in both directions up each side road, and would just turn across one another. People were walking in the side road, cars were parked there. I went amidst all the madness and just did my best to survive. And as for the roundabouts, well I went right across town twice and did at least six roundabouts and to this day I have not the faintest idea whether I was supposed to give way left or right.

Eventually I'd navigated enough of this traffic to find myself at a fort that I thought marked one end of the mighty Great Wall of China. I couldn't be entirely sure, because although the information boards at the fort had been translated into English, they had been done so by someone who could not actually speak English:

'It was built in Ming dynasty, for the reason of building on the west, people named it jiayugan which was earlier than shanhai-guan built nine years.'

'Ah, yes. I see.'

'Jiayugan's west is the ancient battlefield.'

'Is it indeed?'

'The nine spring in the east, summer and winter Tigers are very clear, does not stop.'

'No, no, you've lost me now.'

'The city in city and the trench out the city strengthen the city to be unconquerable.'

I gave up on the information boards and just looked around. I'd been under the impression that the Great Wall of China was pretty old, so I was quite surprised to see that this fort was still being built. Scaffolding covered one wall, with workers busily reconstructing. In fact, the whole place had been a little too well restored, the bright yellow walls polished to a fine sheen. That seemed to be the way of things in this country, to take old things and make them look new. Despite this, the Chinese visitors seemed quite impressed; one or two

I noticed appeared to be crying tears of joy as they entered.

But my priority was to see the actual Great Wall itself, and it was surprisingly difficult to find. I had to search all around the fort until I finally discovered it, streaking away from one corner. I'd dreamt of this moment ever since I was a little boy. I had visions of the Great Wall snaking its way up and over mountains, a fearsome and impenetrable turreted structure. Instead what I saw before me looked like, well, just a wall. It wasn't possible to walk on it, there were no turrets, and it looked like anyone with either a rope or a hammer would have no trouble penetrating it.

To say I was disappointed would be an understatement. This wasn't what I'd come to see. What a waste of time. But I looked at a map I'd picked up of Jiayuguan and noticed that there was another tourist sight marked on it called 'The Overhanging Wall.' That sounded like it might be more along the lines of what I'd been hoping to see, but it was eight kilometres away, in the wrong direction. I didn't really have any more time to spare, but I wondered when I would get the chance again. I mean, this was the Great Wall of friggin' China, of course I was going to go. So I left the fort and started cycling as fast as I could to get to it.

I cycled on through the city and out the far side, past more cooling towers, towards a range of mountains. And as I got closer I got happier, for I could see, climbing up into them, something that actually looked like the Great Wall of China.

I was soon realising my childhood ambitions and standing upon the Great Wall. It was all very well restored here too, but at least you could walk on it, and it had turrets. I thought it was brilliant. Unlike at the fort, there were hardly any other visitors here and it was possible to climb up the steps to the ramparts high on the mountainside. I was very happy as I skipped along up the wall; I had fulfilled a dream.

A couple of days later and I found myself fulfilling another. I hadn't dreamt of visiting the Rainbow Mountains for quite as long as I had the Great Wall, but ever since I'd seen photos of them a year or two earlier I'd longed to see them for myself. Now I could. They stretched out in front of me, covering a vast area overlooked from the viewing platform that I shared with a few hundred Chinese tourists. The mountain range was made up of lots of pointy triangles, as if modelled on the spine of a Stegosaurus, but the defining feature was undoubtedly the colour scheme. Streaking in diagonal bands across the rock was an amazing array of colours. Red, orange, yellow, green, blue, maybe even a little indigo and violet. It wasn't hard to work out how the mountains got their name, and while the photos I'd seen must have been enhanced because in real life the colours weren't as vibrant as I'd been led to believe, it still made for an amazing sight.

The scenery was very special, so unique, something I'd never seen before. I wondered what could have caused such incredible geology. There were information boards, and, despite more questionable translations, I picked out all the right words. Sedimentary, tectonic, oxidizamization, but it still just didn't quite make sense to me. I mean, I understood how stripes of different coloured rock could form horizontally, but I just couldn't see how there could be stripes in the vertical plane. It just didn't make any sense. As I looked at the crowds eagerly snapping away on their cameras it occurred to me that, and this is mere speculation, I'm not trying to cause trouble here, but if any country was going to paint a bunch of stripey colours over a mountain range to create a tourist attraction, well, it probably would be China.

Reaching more populated areas, the secondary roads became mayhem. Absolute mayhem. There really was no other word for it. Well, chaos, perhaps. Madness. Insanity. Bedlam. Okay, there are lots of words. But mayhem covers things nicely. It was the morning rush hour, and everyone was going everywhere. There was a wide shoulder, but even that was a dangerous place to be, with bicycles and electric bike and motorcycles and little three-wheel trailers and all sorts of things in it and about half of them going the wrong way. The road itself was busy with cars and trucks and crazy overtaking going on everywhere. All along were side roads that vehicles would turn down without warning, or emerge from suddenly without slowing down or giving way. They would just shoot straight out into the madness and if the road was too busy they'd just go along on the shoulder, the wrong way if necessary, until there was space to get out. This was something I found particularly annoying when they happened to drive straight at me. And then there was the beeping. Just constant horn beeping from all and sundry (apart from me). The motorcycles beeped as they passed the bicycles and the cars beeped as they passed the motorcycles and the trucks beeped all the time. Anyone racing out from a side road beeped to announce their arrival and anything already in the road beeped to greet them. It was a terrifying experience, one that I am still trying to put behind me to this day.

I sneaked back onto the expressway, which was perversely a much safer place to be. It also meant that I could make faster progress as I continued my pursuit of arriving in Lanzhou by the 17th. With my sightseeing detours completed I was free to focus on making it on time for my date. Seeing Dea again had become the ultimate carrot on a stick, driving me on to more 150 kilometre days and more night-time rides. I would catch a few hours of sleep by finding a gap in the fence that lined the highway to pitch my tent in the desert. On one memorable evening I struggled to find a way out. When I eventually did I was confined to a small space beside a ridge, one that I was quite alarmed to discover I would be sharing with none other than a human skull. It was just lying there on the ground, grinning at me. I poked it with a stick. It looked pretty old and had a big piece missing from the back. My best guess was that it had been dug up during the construction of the road and the Chinese workers, superstitious of such things, hadn't wanted to move it. I would have happily moved on myself and found somewhere else to spend the night, but there really wasn't anywhere else for me to go, so I named the skull Ow Mi Nek, and settled in for the night.

It was a bit of a restless one. Every time the wind flapped at my tent my overactive imagination thought it the ghost of Ow Mi Nek coming to kill me. And every time a truck beeped on the highway my overactive imagination thought it the ghost of Ow Mi Nek farting. But the night did eventually pass, without incident, and I was free to press on towards Lanzhou.

The desert finally ended and, at the insistence of an eager police-man, I left the expressway and returned to the secondary road for a climb up into grassy mountains. These were unpopulated, so the road was at least much calmer on the ascent. On the long descent, however, the road just got worse and worse the closer I got to Lan-zhou. Returning to a fertile valley, I was once again in the midst of traffic chaos. Foremost in this were the trucks that roared along giv-ing way to nothing. The trucks were absolutely at the top of the food chain, and good luck to anything that wasn't smart enough to dive out of their way when they came beeping through.

The standard of driving was appalling. Double overtakes were quite common (I even saw a truck overtaking a truck overtaking a truck). Triple overtakes were rarer, but I certainly saw them once or twice. The pollution was also terrible. I had to put my sunglasses on just to be able to see through all the dust. The beeping was unending. It was horrible. Then I got to an area where it had rained, and the dirt shoulder became the wet and muddy shoulder. Because of this, pedes-trians and everything else that had been on the shoulder moved into the road to avoid the mud, and the chaos went up another level as everything swerved to avoid them. Personally, I still preferred to cycle in the shoulder despite the mud and, with no mudguards, I was soon sprayed all over with mud and filth.

On the evening of the 16th there seemed to be nowhere for me to wild camp, but I eventually found some allotments on the outskirts of Lanzhou with some unused plots where I could lay my head for a few hours. Then I was up bright and early for the final mad dash into the city. Lanzhou was a giant place with an overwhelming amount of traffic and it was a nerve-jangling ride. There were one or two narrow bicycle lanes, though these provided little comfort, seeing as many of the locals had misinterpreted them as 'going in the wrong direction on your motorcycle' lanes.

One way or another I made it to the train station, and as I did so I felt a tremendous sense of achievement and relief. I was on time for my big date. 1,400 kilometres of desert, a couple of mountain passes, detours to visit tourist sites, some terrible roads, encounters with the police, a human skull, but after all that, here I was at Lanzhou train station, ready for my date with the most beautiful girl in the world.

I took a seat on a bench, my bike in front of me. It looked a filthy mess. It was absolutely caked in mud. Then I looked down at my trousers. They were similarly covered in mud and dirt. I looked at my hands. They were dark brown. I suddenly remembered that I hadn't had a shower for twelve days. I'd also been wearing the same clothes for just as long, day and night. Clothes that hadn't seen a washing machine for two months. I was completely exhausted from all the night riding. I had chapped lips and burnt skin from the sun and wind. My hair desperately needed cutting. My beard desperately needed trimming. I looked like a tramp. A filthy, dirty, mud-covered tramp. It was almost midday. I had a good feeling about this date.

34

Lanzhou, China
17th October 2014

People were everywhere, scurrying about outside the train station. I sat and watched them as I waited, twisting my hands together with nerves. Clearly my appearance was likely to be to my disadvantage in terms of creating a good first impression, but I told myself that didn't really matter, so long as I was careful to greet Dea with a heartfelt compliment. As long as I remembered to do that, to make sure she knew that I thought she looked good, which she inevitably would, then I hoped she might forgive me for my own appearance.

And then she arrived, but she took me by surprise, coming from the opposite end of the building to that which I had anticipated, which threw me slightly.

'Don't forget the compliment,' my brain reminded me.

"Dea! Hi. You... you're very tall!"

*'You f*cking idiot.'*

"Yes I am," she said.

I'd made a bad start, no doubt about that. And as a consequence there built up rather a long pause, with neither of us quite sure what to say next. I thought I'd better try and apologise. "I'm sorry," I said. "I haven't spoken to anybody in a very, very long time."

To my great relief, Dea seemed willing to forgive me this, and even let me go and get myself cleaned up in a hotel before we went out anywhere. Which was, undoubtedly, a good idea.

I was soon freshened up and ready for our big date, the first date I'd ever been on wearing one of my date's spare T-shirts. I took Dea's hand in mine as we walked through the streets, at least partly because I was scared of the traffic.

"What do you feel like eating?" she asked.

"Hmm... how about Chinese?"

We both giggled. I liked this girl. She laughed at my jokes. And she was looking great in an old green army sweater. She wasn't wearing any make-up. She didn't need any. She just looked good all the time.

"So, I'm the most beautiful girl in the world, am I?"

She'd been reading my blog. Great!

"Yes, yes, you've been reading my-"

"But I'm not the *only* most beautiful girl in the world it seems?"

A little too much of my blog, perhaps.

"Ah yes, well, those other girls were before I met you, of course. I didn't have the frame of reference. Ah look, this place looks alright. Shall we eat here?"

We went inside the small restaurant and tried to order food from the enthusiastic waiter. It was always a tricky task for me, being a vegetarian. There was food going out to another table and so we pointed at the things that looked the most vegetarian, asked for those, took a seat, and hoped for the best.

"So, how was your motorbike trip?" I asked.

"It was great. I never thought about riding a motorbike before. I just overheard the guys in the hostel talking about it, and they invited me to go along. I just thought, why not? The woman in the bike shop could tell I'd never ridden a motorcycle before. She said I could just go on the back of one of the boys' bikes but I was like, NO, I want my own bike!"

"And you had a good time?"

"Oh yeah, it was really amazing fun. But it was very hard work. We went off-road, on the Mongolian trails. It was really an adventure. We were free to go where we wanted. Just able to choose our own route, set up camp by a river. I loved the sense of freedom."

Our food arrived. We each had a bowl of noodles, and then two slightly vegetarian-looking dishes were placed in the middle. Now that we could see them properly it was clear that they both contained meat. They'd also been cooked in animal fat, so even the vegetables tasted like meat. "You're going to have to eat all of this," I said. Then an old woman came over and tried to ruin my noodles by pouring the meat dishes over them. "No!" I screamed, fighting her off. Once she'd been thoroughly deterred I then had to eat my plain noodles with chopsticks. I can't use chopsticks. Things were going well.

"I was really pleased you chose Charlize Theron to play me in your movie," Dea said. "She's my favourite actress."

I'd made a joke on my blog that all the motorcyclists she'd been riding with in Mongolia would be played by Charlie Boorman, but Dea, not being quite as masculine, would be played by Charlize Theron.

"Maybe it was fate that you chose my favourite actress? Ryan Gosling and Charlize Theron, they'd make a good couple, don't you think?"

As a matter of fact I did.

Anxious to keep the date going and unsure of what else there was to do in Lanzhou, after our meal I took Dea to a bridge to watch the traffic. When cycling in such madness it was terribly stressful, but standing on a pedestrian bridge looking down upon it was great fun. "Look at that guy," I cried, "walking across the middle of it all. And what is that car doing? Look, they've made a traffic jam when there were only about six cars trying to move through the junction." I thought it was brilliant to watch, I really did. I'm not sure Dea found it quite so entertaining, but she put her arm through mine. I looked up from the traffic. God, her blue eyes were incredible. She was like a super model. I had no idea how I got this lucky.

"Let's go back to the hotel," she whispered in my ear, "together."

The next day we found ourselves lying in the big hotel bed, our bodies entwined. By now I was pretty sure I must have died and gone to heaven, but I was definitely okay with that, because heaven, it turned out, was mind-blowingly awesome.

"It's really a shame I have to leave tomorrow," Dea said with a sigh.

"Are you sure you wouldn't rather cycle with me?" I asked, more in hope than expectation, and more in desperation than hope.

"No, my flights are all booked. I'm going to the Philippines. I've wanted to go there for a long time. I'm going diving. But you know, I do have some time next month. After the Philippines I have a few weeks before I go home, and I have no plans yet."

"Come and cycle with me in Laos!" I said, getting overexcited. "It'll be amazing, Dea. Laos will be a much better place to cycle than China anyway. It's such a good idea."

I knew Dea was the right kind of person for cycle touring. She was an adventurous, spontaneous girl, a free spirit. I knew she would love it, if she only gave it a try.

"You must come to Laos. Please."

"I don't know if I want to travel on a bike. I think it's incredible what you do Chris, I really do. I just don't know if it's right for me. But… maybe."

Sitting in Lanzhou bus station, tears started to roll down Dea's cheeks. "I don't know why I like you so much, I can't explain it," she said.

"Can't help you there, I'm afraid. It's a bit of a mystery to me too."

Dea's bus pulled up. It was already time for us to go our separate ways again.

"So, I'll see you in Laos?" I asked.

"Yeah," Dea wiped her cheeks and slung her backpack over her shoulder, "Maybe. Let's see."

Then she gave me a big kiss on the lips and climbed aboard the bus.

And I was alone again.

I needed to spend a few more days in Lanzhou in order to extend my visa, so I moved to a cheap hostel for a few days. It was a good one too, surprisingly clean and well furnished, with all Chinese guests apart from me. There was one other chap there who could speak a little English. A friendly man of about forty who was in town on business, he was sleeping in the bunk below mine and we soon became friends. I asked him if he would be able to help me, as I needed to visit a dentist again, and I could use a translator. One of the root canal fillings I'd had done in Iran had cracked and half of the tooth was loose. Unfortunately he was busy working, but "Don't worry," he said, "Uncle Lee and Miss Liu will accompany you tomorrow." I looked at his pointing arm, outstretched towards an old man and a young woman lying on (different) beds across the room.

So, the next morning Uncle Lee, Miss Liu, and I marched off together to a nearby hospital, with me wondering just how much use these two non-English speakers were going to prove as translators. But to their credit they did help me locate the dental department of the hospital, something that I likely would not have achieved alone. Here I was welcomed to take a seat in a dentist chair. I was relieved to see that it did look like a proper dental surgery, and the man who poked around in my mouth even looked like a real dentist. He couldn't speak English, though, so his diagnosis remained unclear until another dentist arrived and sat down beside me. I was pleased when he spoke to me in good English.

"A part of your tooth is broken. It must be removed." He had an American accent.

"Okay. Can you replace it?"

"No, it is too difficult. Most of the tooth is okay. It is strong for now. When will you go back to England?"

"Erm, not that soon."

"When you go back to England they can maybe replace the tooth. Here we cannot do it. But you should have the piece of broken tooth removed now, so that it won't become infected."

"Yes, okay."

I was relieved to finally be talking with this professional English-speaking dentist, and I had great confidence in what he was telling me.

"I am an eye-doctor," he added, before walking off.

A couple of days later, my broken tooth having been successfully treated, I collected my passport with an extended visa. I now had twenty-nine days to get to the Laos border, and I knew that this second half of the 'China Challenge' was going to be much harder than the first. Instead of a flat desert I was now going to face endless hills, and with no prospect of getting another visa extension, any delay due to failure of man or machine could end my hopes of a continuous circumnavigation all over again. Still so tired from Siberia, Mongolia, and the race to Lanzhou, there was no doubt that this was going to be another huge challenge and as I prepared to set off I recalled what other cyclists in Central Asia had told me of China. "It's not possible to cycle across China." "I had to take a train." "There's no way you can do it in two months." The general consensus had been that this was where my luck would run out. But I knew they were wrong. For one thing my luck had run out at the Russia-Mongolia border, of course, but quite aside from that, I wanted to prove them wrong about China. So I thought back on something that Will Smith had said to me once: "People can't do something themselves, they wanna tell you that you can't do it. Don't ever let anybody tell you that you can't do something." And I knew he was right, although, now that I think about it a bit more, he might not have been talking to me when he said that. I think it was in a movie. Anyway, it still spurred me on.

I needed to feel spurred on, because riding my bicycle out of Lanzhou on the crazy streets was horrible, and it was several days before there was any real let up in the traffic. I kept pressing on, and felt rewarded when I made my way up beyond the heavily populated regions. Up and up through mountain ranges I climbed, until I found myself at altitude, crossing over the eastern fringes of the vast Tibetan Plateau. The landscape on the plateau was mostly grassland, though it was frustratingly not as flat as the name might imply, but rather still rising and falling constantly. It was a wonderful place to be though, the only settlements I passed through being Buddhist villages. Colourful prayer flags flew from homes and temples, yaks roamed the fields, and I invented a fantastic new game called 'Spot the Monk' to pass the time. The only problem now was that, though the days were filled with blue skies and sunshine, the nights up high were cold. I longed for my old winter sleeping bag, thrown away in a fit of space-saving passion back in Turkmenistan, but all I had was a cheap summer sleeping bag. Although I must credit the manufacturers for the fact that the cheap sleeping bag had not yet broken, despite having been in the hands of a man who breaks everything for well over a year, it was simply not designed for October nights 3,000 metres above sea level on the Tibetan Plateau.

Five days out from Lanzhou I reached Langmusi, a mountain village that I had heard was worth visiting for its monasteries. I decided to stop and spend a night in a hostel here to avoid sleeping out in the cold, and it proved to be a good decision. Taking the evening off, I explored the historic old village, which was a real cultural melting pot, with Buddhists, Muslims and Han Chinese wandering the streets.

The monasteries were impressive – incredibly colourful and ornate collections of buildings and structures. These examples of the finest works of man were complemented by the finest works of nature, as rocky buttes glowed red in the last of the day's sun beyond them. To the south and west more jagged and raw mountains towered, twinkling with fresh-fallen snow. The village sat in the middle, surrounded by this stunning nature, hidden from the world.

I found a spot high up on a hill where I could just sit and watch the people going about their business on the streets below me. Skullcaps mingled with the red robes of the monks and the dark wrap dresses of the Buddhist women. Rows of prayer wheels were everywhere around town, especially around the monasteries. All of the Buddhists that walked down the hill went via a row of these prayer wheels and set them spinning. It occurred to me what a nice little idea prayer wheels were; so much easier than getting down on your knees.

A herd of cows came trotting along the street below me, and they started to wander off randomly down side streets, diverting this way and that as if out of control. A few of them even went into a garden and disappeared into a dilapidated wooden shed. A man hobbled along behind them all, no doubt the cowherd, who I took to be losing his cows by the dozen. But then it dawned on me what was really happening. The cows were all going home, to just exactly where they were each supposed to be. They all knew what they were doing. It was a nice moment, to take an evening out from my constant cycling to just look and see. I felt good. The Tibetan plateau had been quite wonderful. I began to feel like I was going to do this. As I strolled happily back to the hostel I really felt like I was going to make it through China. And who knew what I had to look forward to when I made it to the Laos border. Did I dare to believe that Dea would really join me there? I got back to my room and opened up my laptop to check my e-mails. I had one from Dea. Was she coming to Laos? I was about to find out.

35

Langmusi, China
29th October 2014

I would really love to try and travel in your way, you've made me pretty curious about what its like – I believe it can be amazing going slowly through a country only by your own physical power, being in the countryside and the nature and camp all the time. If it was just about that I would come and join you for sure.

But its not; I can't come with you Chris, cause I can't get more involved with you. I wish I could just say "YES lets do it", cause that's the good crazy approach to life, but sometimes you also have to be carefull with yours and others hearts and I've had enough hurted feelings and pain myself and around me just recently. I can't go in there again, not yet.

I hope you'll understand. I'm so glad that I met you and that we made life a little more crazy. I really like you and care for you, you're a very great guy and the most handsome man (who's not tall) in the world.

Xx Dea

Not tall? Not tall? Talk about rubbing salt in the wounds. I felt deflated. I sat there in my little room and read the e-mail again and again, trying to process Dea's rejection. I knew that she'd only recently got out of a long-term relationship, and so I could completely understand her reasons. That didn't make it any easier to take, though. Without the prospect of cycling with Dea in Laos to look forward to, my mission to ride through China once again felt daunting. In all likelihood I was never going to see her again. I suddenly felt unbelievably alone in the world.

There was no real benefit in feeling sorry for myself though. I knew I had to bring my focus back towards my main goal of cycling around the world. From the very beginning I had been saying that I should avoid being distracted by members of the opposite sex and it was time for me to prove it. Dea or no Dea, I was going to make it to Laos before my visa expired.

The next morning I set off with both vim and vigour, climbing still further through the grasslands until I was ascending over a high pass almost 4,000 metres above sea level. With no hotels or settlements for a hundred kilometres and snow beginning to fall I wondered how I was going to survive the night at such altitudes. I was finally saved by a family of nomads living in a collection of tents who invited me to spend the night. By morning the whole landscape had turned white under a blanket of snow, the streams of triangular prayer flags between the tents providing the only colour. I waved my saviours goodbye and continued to the summit of the pass. It turned into a beautiful day, the sun shining down from the blue sky on the white peaks as I reached the top and whizzed triumphantly down the other side.

I descended for days beside gushing rivers that carved through steep-sided mountain ranges alive with the colours of autumn. Early one morning I was stopped by a young Chinese man named Anji who was travelling around the country on a bright red motorcycle. He was very friendly and it was a pleasure to meet him, although, not having much time to spare, I ate a packet of biscuits at the same time as our roadside conversation in an extraordinary act of multi-tasking. Anji's English wasn't great, so before long we resorted to communication through his smartphone translator, which was always guaranteed to be good entertainment value. Understanding that I was in a hurry, he passed me the phone and it read, "Would you like a draw?"

"Well, Anji, it's a little early in the morning for that isn't it?"

But then he indicated by pointing at his bike that what he actually meant was whether I'd like to be towed along behind his motorcycle for a bit. I quickly weighed up the pros and cons of this intriguing offer.

Pro – I'd get there quicker and make up time.

Con – Technically it would be cheating and my trip would be ruined.

Pro – It would be the most exciting thing I would ever do.

Con – It would be the last thing I would ever do.

Pro – I couldn't think of any more pros.

Con – We would get beeped at A LOT.

"No thank you, Anji, I'm okay."

But Anji wasn't done with the kind offers, and next invited me to come and have lunch with him in a nearby restaurant. It was nine in the morning and I'd just eaten a whole packet of biscuits, so it seemed like the ideal time for lunch, and I agreed. Of course I didn't really have time, but opportunities to socialise with the Chinese had been frustratingly infrequent, and I didn't want to blow through the *entire* country without spending any time with anyone. And it was well worth it as Anji was such a nice young fellow. He was from Beijing where he worked as a furniture maker and he was having the time of his life riding his bike around for a few months and getting to know his own country. He was very excited that I was from England, and told me that it was his dream to visit someday. I put down my chopsticks, looked at him puzzled, and asked why on earth that was. He typed his response into the phone and handed it to me: "Because I have seen Mel Gibson's Braveheart."

As I got further south the road became increasingly busy. For long sections there was no shoulder and with trucks and buses blasting around blind corners this was definitely some of the most dangerous cycling I'd ever done. The only relief, ironically, came while passing through the towns of Maoxian and Wenchuan, where the road was wider and safer. Both of these towns had been almost completely destroyed by an earthquake in 2008, a tragedy in which a staggering

87,000 people had lost their lives. Riding through a valley hemmed in on both sides by impenetrable mountains I shuddered imagining what it must have been like to be trapped here after the quake when I saw broken bridges and caved-in tunnels. Yet in Maoxian and Wenchuan themselves there were no visible signs of the catastrophe. Everything had been rebuilt with modern tower blocks. Further down the valley I came to Yingxiu. Also destroyed by the earthquake it had likewise been rebuilt, though perhaps for questionable purposes. Groups of Chinese tourists stepped off buses and walked around snapping photos of perfect-looking new buildings, following their chattering guides who carried bright flags above their heads so as not to lose anybody. I followed and looked around at the new buildings, but something wasn't right. There was no laundry flapping from the balconies, no locals in the street. There was absolutely nobody here other than the tourists.

I followed everyone to the school, possibly the only building in the whole area that had been left exactly as it was after the earthquake. Fifty-five people died here, most of them young children. Now tourists posed for photos in front of it. I walked around the outside of the buildings, away from the tourists who didn't stray far from the front where the best photo opportunity was. A leafy park now filled the spaces around the white concrete school buildings. Cracks ran through these buildings like scars. All of the windows were gone. Plants and mosses filled the cracks and threatened to gradually reclaim the buildings. Birds nested in the roofs. The air was still and it was a cold and grey morning. A moment of poignancy. It was terribly sad to think of the nightmare of that day, the tragic loss of life, the horrific aftermath, the never-ending scar for those left behind.

The gift shop opposite could not have been more inappropriate.

I came out of the mountains and enjoyed a few days of flat cycling crossing a broad plain. Being China, the whole area was densely populated and busy, but I was able to find a good road, following a route kindly suggested to me by a reader of my blog. Peter, a Danish man who lived in China, had been following me online for a while and, no doubt fearing the worst, had contacted me to provide me with detailed maps and route advice to guide me through the rest of the country. Peter's help would prove invaluable, and I was already feeling the benefits. This road he'd suggested was a brand new 'Safety Highway' where a big shoulder was given over entirely to slower moving vehicles. And there was quite a collection of weird and wonderful slower-moving vehicles using it, including bicycles, motorcycles, motor scooters, electric scooters, electric bicycles, rickshaws, electric rickshaws, tricycles, and a tiny little red van that looked like it belonged to Postman Pat.

All of us went along together in this lane quite happily, but intersections remained a little tricky. This was because I'd spent my whole life thinking that red lights meant I should stop. However, it turned out that in the bicycle/motorcycle/electric rickshaw lane in China a red light meant just keep straight on going and swerve in and out between any traffic that might be crossing the junction to your left and right. But even knowing that this was the correct way of doing things I didn't much like it, so I usually pulled over and waited for a green light, at which point I could move on. This felt much safer, apart from I'd still have to avoid the bicycles/motorcycles/electric rickshaws that were running the red lights to my left and right of course. On one occasion, however, I came up to a red light where it looked as if the road to the right was completely blocked off by a construction site where yet another new tower block was being built. With no exit on the right there was no real need to stop, and so, following Chinese road etiquette, I proceeded through the lights.

I didn't get far. I was still being cautious and I suddenly saw that there was actually a site entrance to my right and a car was approaching it. I pressed my brakes down firmly to come to a halt safely. There was a squeal from behind and I felt a big shadow approaching at speed, bearing down on me. Before I knew what was happening there was a clattering noise and I sensed I was in trouble. I fell off the bike sideways and landed hard on the ground, smack on my butt. Dazed, I looked up to see what had happened. An electric rickshaw had gone straight into the back of me when I'd stopped. Oh, the irony. So many years cycle touring and this was my first real collision, and it was with an electric rickshaw... on a Safety Highway. Oh, the humanity!

People came around to help. Two of my panniers had broken off, one from the impact of the rickshaw and another from hitting the road. With the help of the passers-by I got myself back on my feet and all of my things to a safe space. I hadn't come off too bad, just a little shocked and with some pain in my lower back. The driver of the rickshaw seemed concerned and to his credit was hanging around, presumably to see if my bike and I were both okay. The bike looked alright but I flipped it over just to make sure. The rear wheel was very, very out of alignment and had a big kink in it, but to be fair that was probably just because I'd built it.

"Everything seems to be okay, don't worry. I'm fine. It was my fault anyway, I shouldn't have stopped at the red light like that. No harm done." I looked up. The rickshaw driver was already gone.

I spent a restless night, tossing and turning to try and get comfortable with the pain I had in my lower back troubling me on the hard ground. Finding places to wild camp in populated China wasn't easy, and usually I had to make do hiding in an unused plot. On one memorable occasion I found myself cycling after dark in a narrow valley that had construction crews working round the clock on building a new expressway through it. The only place I could find to lay my head was a tiny patch of trees, with my feet about a metre from the road. With the lights and noise of trucks giving the illusion that they were constantly about to run me over it was one very long night. But I had to hide in little nooks like this, for asking people to camp on their land invariably brought negative responses from local Chinese peasants, who would look terrified of me and wave me away. It was the only place in the world where I found the majority of people reluctant to help. Even the task of exchanging money for a hotel room was frustratingly difficult in this land. An old rule that barred foreigners from staying in hotels meant that many hotel owners remained cautious of hosting me, and I would often be told there was no room at the inn, even when there were obviously no other guests.

I'd sometimes spend two hours trudging around town to four or five hotels trying to find one that would take me. China was one very complicated and difficult country.

I was struggling to keep up the pace in order to make it to the border on time, and so it was with great relief that the pain in my back subsided over the next few days as I climbed back into the mountains. Far beyond the deserts and the Tibetan grasslands I now began to travel through tropical rainforest, quite a contrast from what had gone before. But China was getting the better of me. Every single day the weather was dull and grey, the skies hidden by a layer of smog. I didn't see the sun for two weeks. My days were completely filled with cycling up steep mountains and through dark and scary tunnels. There was just no time for anything else if I was going to cycle every kilometre. A bad night's sleep, a tough day of cycling, and repeat. Nobody in China could speak English and I had no time to stop and talk anyway. I felt like I was just existing. I was cycling only to get somewhere better. I had become nothing more than a slave to a bigger dream.

My focus became entirely on just getting to the border. I was sure that once I got to Laos everything was going to be different. I would have no more visa deadlines, no need to hurry anywhere, and I'd heard so many good things about Laos. "People are so nice there," and "People speak English," and, most alluring of all, "People don't beep their horns there." Oh yes, Laos was it, Laos was the promised land. I daydreamed all day about it. It was what kept me going. All that occupied my mind. My legs pedalled on, my mind thinking, *'Laos, Laos, Laos.'*

Mojiang was a hectic and crowded town that, if one sign I saw in town was to be believed, marked the Tropic of Cancer, that invisible line across the Earth that meant I was officially in the tropics. It also meant I was nearing the end of my long push south. I mean, somewhere beyond the Tropic of Cancer lay the Equator, and somewhere beyond that lay the Tropic of Capricorn and Australia. I was practically there, really.

As always, I stocked up on silly little packaged food in a small shop and prepared to resume the struggle. But as I was about to hurl my tired leg over the frame once more and ride on towards another day of certain mediocrity, I happened to see a wild and crazy bearded man heading along the road towards me. Such a sight would not always get me excited, but he was on a bicycle, and at this moment in time another European cycle tourist going the same way as me was a vision of such magnificent splendour that I almost fell to my knees and wept.

"Hello!" I cried out with great joy. "Stop! Stop! Are you from Italy?" I asked, looking at his bright blue hooded top emblazoned with that country's name across it.

"No, I am from the Basque country of Spain."

"Well, who cares, you can speak English!" I shook the man's hand eagerly. The sheer joy I felt at having a simple conversation should not be underestimated. I had been living in my own head for too long. Now suddenly I'd found someone also cycling to Laos to share the journey with. I felt like I'd found my saviour. It was a miracle. And by coincidence, he did look quite a bit like Jesus, with his thick beard and tanned skin.

Alex and I compared our stories and bad-mouthed China together as we cycled on, dodging stray chickens as we went. Having somebody else who shared my exasperation at this difficult country made it so much easier to bear. But not all of Alex's experiences in China had been negative.

"Have you noticed how Chinese girls have a thing for Western guys?" he asked.

"Erm... no, I haven't actually."

"Really, they love Western guys. They are always saying hello and flirting."

"No, no. I haven't had any of that. It must just be you."

"No, they love Western guys."

"They don't love me."

"They love Western guys."

"They don't."

"They do."

"Let's talk about something else. Your bags are not waterproof?" I asked.

"No, but it never rains much."

"That's true actually. I can't remember the last time I got rained on."

"I only had a few days of rain on my whole trip."

"And the rainy season here is over."

"Yes it is the dry season. It never rains here this time of year."

"I only had one day of rain in the last six months."

"It never rains."

"No, it really never rains. People think it rains a lot but it doesn't."

"No, it never rains."

Then it started to rain.

But not even the rain could dampen my mood now. Peter's excellent directions had us following a nice, flat road beside a river that allowed us to cover a big distance and put the border firmly within our sights. The only difficulty we had was finding somewhere to camp. We had the river below us to our right and steep mountainsides to the left. Any flat land, including the verges at the side of the road, were cultivated by the locals that lived in little roadside shacks.

Eventually, we found a patch of land that didn't look like it was being used for anything and decided it would be a good spot for our tents. But it was close to a house and we were spotted, so we asked if it would be alright to sleep there for the night. Anywhere else in Asia we would have been greeted with smiles and invited in for tea, but seeing as this was China, we were instead told to clear off.

With darkness starting to close in we were getting worried, but then we came across some more buildings that lay empty. The main house was boarded up, but inspecting the other buildings we found a little brick thing with a sheet of corrugated metal over it that was just about big enough inside for our two tents. The fact that it was almost certainly the former living quarters of a pig or two did not deter us in the least. We put up our tents and settled in for the night, marvelling at the unpredictable nature of this way of travel. When I'd got up that morning I could never have anticipated spending the night in a pig sty with a man that looked a bit like Jesus, but that was just what made life so exciting.

For a couple of days Alex and I rode on together, climbing up and down mountain slopes covered almost entirely by banana plantations. It was a real shame to see that the native rainforests had been replaced, but the exotic shape of the endless banana leaves was enough to make me feel like I was in the tropics. The heat and humidity was another clue, even as the omnipresent smog continued to hold back the sun. But the bunches of bananas that hung from the trees were all hidden by blue plastic sacks.

"I wish all these bananas weren't wrapped up like that. It would be good if we could take some," Alex said.

Now, in my life I've come across a number of people who think it okay to take a little fruit from trees when no one is looking. It is hardly the crime of the century to steal an apple from an orchard, this I know. But I always ask them, "Would you steal fruit from a supermarket?" And of course they always say that they would not. Then, with an annoyingly smug face, I say, "Well, you should, because if you steal from a supermarket it only hurts the supermarket, but if you steal from an orchard, then you hurt the farmer." Usually the defendant will then gaze at me in awe, as if they have been enlightened by my great wisdom.

So I looked at Alex and asked him if he would steal bananas from a supermarket. He tilted his head from side to side and said, "Well, with a supermarket it is more difficult."

More difficult! More difficult! But not wrong! I was shocked by the unusual deviation from the normal course of this conversation.

"There are thousands of bananas man, if I take three or four bananas they aren't going to care, it won't make any difference."

"But it is stealing."

"I don't think it is stealing. If I'm hungry I think it's a good way for me to get food."

"It is stealing. These people are very poor. You come from a developed country, you have every advantage and opportunity in life.

You must understand that your poverty is self-inflicted?"

"Come on man, they aren't going to miss three or four bananas."

"But there are hundreds of people coming along this road each day. What if all of them take three or four bananas?"

"Yeah, okay. I know not everyone can take them. But luckily they don't. Most people are like you, they are not like me. But I am a special one."

Holy cow, maybe he really was Jesus.

I didn't like Alex very much at this moment. I understood that when I cycled with other people we were always going to have our differences, and that I was always going to find things about the other person that I didn't get on with. I'd been annoyed when Rob and Gábor had left me behind in Tajikistan, and in Turkmenistan Andreas's fondness for getting butt naked wasn't quite my cup of tea, but I really did need to draw the line at stealing from poor people. The banana plantations were punctuated by tin-pot shacks, the people living here evidently struggling just to survive.

"I'm sorry Alex, I don't want to ride with you any more."

"Come on," he replied, annoyed. "Don't be child man."

I thought this oxymoron would be the last I heard from Alex as he disappeared up ahead of me on the next hill. On a positive note, the anger and frustration of our argument got me up the steep climb without really noticing it. I was too occupied by my own thoughts. I considered the idea that a lot of the long distance solo cyclists I'd met seemed to be quite self-centred, and I had to include myself in that. Maybe I wasn't stealing from the poor people I passed, but I certainly wasn't doing anything much to help them either. These were lives born to poverty that could never dream of experiencing the world through my own privileged eyes. Alone again, I began to question myself more. What was I doing here? Why was I doing it? What was the point of my own life? I had to concede to myself that this whole cycling around the world lark was a selfish endeavour, no question about that. I was helping nobody but myself. I decided that I had to do more for other people in the future, I just didn't know how. For the time being I was tired and frustrated, and so I resumed my focus on just getting to the Laos border. I could worry more about the deep and meaningfuls later.

Again it was difficult to find anywhere to camp. It was almost dark and I desperately needed to find somewhere as I descended down the mountain. Finally I found a good place, an empty plot of land at the side of the road. Well, it was almost empty. There was already one tent there. "Hello Alex," I called out. We made friends again, both offering apologies and recognising that in a sense we needed each other. Our disagreements were mostly nonsense anyway. They were simply the culmination of all our frustrations, our loneliness, of months spent cycling alone, of missing people back home, of the heat and the hills and the endless beeping, of this most trying country.

The penultimate morning in China brought us to Mengxing, and in this town we stopped at a supermarket. This excited both of us, being the first we had seen in a very long time. After taking it in turns to do some shopping we were sitting on a bench outside when Alex noticed that there was a phone shop next door. He asked the owner if it would be okay to use their wifi for a minute. I didn't really care about using the wifi myself, but seeing as Alex had the password I thought I'd just check my messages and flipped open my laptop to do just that. I had a message on the guestbook of my blog from a name that I didn't recognise. At first the message seemed a little strange, mostly because it was from a bicycle. Yes, yes, I had a talking bicycle myself, but have you ever heard of a bicycle that could type? What an absurd idea. Anyway, I read through it and as I did so it soon dawned on me who the message was really from, and just what it meant.

"Hey there two-wheeled fellow
I hear you're about to enter Laos after racing through China the last couple of month; yes, rumours are running fast around here. I'm a blue, sporty bike from Vientiane. I've been standing outside a shop with a "For sale" sign long enough to be bored and eager to get back on the road again. Today I really tried to look attractive when a young woman came to the shop looking for a bike. You know, bending to the side on the foot stand, let the front

wheel fall to the left side in just the right angle so that the metal catched the sunlight. It worked! The young woman took me for a ride, was very pleased, and bought me. She looked rather strange to me, very tall, white skin and yellowish hair that she for some reason had cut short on one side while the rest was long. She didn't talk to me – yet! I guess it takes some time and some kilometres on the road through mountains, rain, breakedowns, loneliness and heartbreakes before you start doing that – so I'm not sure about what she's up to, but she bought rack and panniers too, so I hope she's planning a longer tour round the country. I heard her talkin to the shop owner about going all the way up north with busses tomorrow and then start cycling. The shop owner found it kind of funny to buy a bike and then put it on a bus, and I agree, but what am I to do about it? Anyway, it might mean that we'll be driving around the same roads in a couple of days and I thought it would be good to meet and go together for a while. I could use some good stories and advice from an old expert like you to get started again (and I think my girl could use some experienced advice from your guy too, seems to be the first time she's going on a long tour on a bike), and after several months racing through northern Asia alone with Chris I suppose you could use the company of a two-wheeled fellow who knows what it's like to be a humble vehicle for a crazy human?

What do you say?
Happy wheelturns!"

Please forgive the spelling mistakes, I imagine it must be very hard for a bicycle to type. But the most important thing was what the bicycle was telling me, and what it was telling me was that Dea, the most beautiful girl in the world, was completely insane. She had changed her mind, and taken a crazy chance, and just flown to Laos and bought a bike and was going to ride with me after all. The promised land just got a whole, whole lot more promising. A massive grin came over my face and I fist-pumped the air in joy. It was as if the weight of the world had just been lifted from my shoulders. All of the stresses of China just melted away in an instant and I felt as light as air. Leaving China the next day wasn't just going to be good, it was going to be amazing.

My legs felt so tired. My whole body felt weak. China had come so close to breaking me. But it hadn't broken me. It was my last morning, the last few kilometres to the border, the last few pedal strokes before something so much better in the promised land. Alex was no longer with me. We'd lost each other somehow on the final mountain pass without a proper goodbye. It didn't matter. Not now. I'd done it. I'd made it through. Without any question this had physically been the hardest few weeks of the whole journey. Forget Siberia, forget Mongolia, forget the Desert Dash, this had been the hardest of all. China was brutal. Partly that was because I insisted on cycling the whole way, of course. Had I slowed down enough to engage with the people and places I might have had a better experience, but that was a sacrifice I chose in order to continue the integrity of my journey.

It would be impossible to summarise China. It's just too big. From the vast desert to the snowy mountain plateau to the tropical rainforests, this huge country had pushed me to my physical and mental limits. There was too much air pollution, too much noise pollution, too much construction and too much chaos. At times the people were great, often they weren't, but you can't generalise about 1.4 billion. When I'd entered the country I didn't know anything about it. It was a complete mystery to me. It confused and intrigued me. And now, two months later and cycling up to the border gates to leave, I felt just exactly the same way. China remained a mystery. I had absolutely no idea what was going on. I was just pleased to have passed through, to have made it to the end, and now I felt no desire to ever return to China. And yet at the same time I had this feeling that at some point in the future I would surely come to miss China on some weird and unexplainable level, and I would just have to go back.

Which was lucky, actually, because Mori's in China, isn't it?

36

Lao border
21st November 2014

I felt such a sense of relief as I sat outside the gold temple-like archway that was Laos' most wonderful arrival building. I was filling in my application for a thirty-day visa, and I was taking my time. It was exactly four months since I'd cycled out of Almaty and began on the quest that had taken me 11,500 kilometres across Kazakhstan, Siberia, Mongolia and China. Discounting my week off in Lanzhou I'd averaged exactly 100 kilometres per day over that period, and this was now the first time in a very long time that I did not need to rush. Filling in that form was an absolute pleasure. I savoured every second of it. The man who'd given me the form was wonderful too – a very jolly fellow, quite well-fed, who asked me about my trip and excitedly explained that Laos was soon opening up an embassy in London which he had high ambitions to be sent to.

"I usually have a very important job in Vientiane," he said, keen to stress that he had only temporarily been sent to dish out the visas at this remote outpost. His friendly manner was in keeping with his colleagues (and in sharp contrast to the Chinese border officials I'd just been dealing with, one of whom had been asleep), and I was made to feel positively welcome into Laos.

But I had a new motivation not to slacken my pace just yet. I didn't know where Dea was, as all I had to go on was that slightly cryptic message from her bike indicating that she was taking a bus north. It looked to me like the biggest town that she'd be able to reach by bus was Namor, a further forty-five kilometres south of where I was. But if that was where she was, then so be it. I wanted to get there and see her, and I still had the afternoon to make it to Namor. Or to put it another way, I was going to begin my life after rushing, by rushing.

I received my visa from the nice man and wished him good luck in London. I then needed to pass under the golden arch and have my passport checked one last time. As the man there thumbed through it, I glanced ahead into Laos and saw a blue bicycle parked up on the grass. Because I was very tired and have a tendency to be somewhat stupid, my first thought was that it was Alex's bike, and that he had got to the border first and was waiting for me. But as I looked more closely I saw that it wasn't his bike. Continuing to act like a fool, I next thought it must belong to one of the local men gathered nearby. Then at last, finally coming to my senses, I noticed the beautiful, blonde girl sitting on the kerb next to the bike. I broke into a huge smile. It was over. I didn't have to rush anywhere. Dea was here.

My passport was returned to me and I hurried over to see Dea just as if it were a movie scene. Wait a minute, there was a movie going to be made about this journey wasn't there? I'd almost forgotten about that. So, yeah, okay:

Ryan Gosling rushes over to Charlize Theron and, carefully remembering his mistake from Lanzhou, doesn't tell her she's very tall.

"Dea, you look beautiful," I said, with a sense of pride in my new-found compliment-giving abilities.

"Thank you," she said. Then she looked me up and down. I looked down at myself.

"I'm sorry I look like a tramp," I said. "I didn't have a chance to..."

"That's okay," she laughed, "you always do."

And then she kissed me.

Unfortunately, the border town of Boten looked suspiciously like China. The shops were all Chinese, the big buildings looked Chinese, even the street signs were in the confusing Chinese letters. We stopped to get something to eat, where we were shown the price in Chinese yuan. It was a disaster. I'd finally cycled out of China, only to arrive in China. Thank goodness Dea was with me to calm my nerves.

It would be very nice if I could say that we then cycled on together out of Boten into the Lao countryside. What actually happened was that Dea cycled very quickly out of Boten into the Lao countryside, while I laboured slowly far behind her. Now that I no longer needed to be cycling anywhere, my whole body objected to the concept with quite some ferocity, and my brain could offer little in the way of convincing reasons to keep pedalling. The best that it had to offer was, *'We need to catch up with the beautiful girl who came all this way to cycle with us,'* but my aching body countered that with, *'Nah, let's just collapse in the bushes, she'll come back and find us.'* As it happened my brain won, but when I did catch up to my energetic and excited new cycling companion as she stopped to wait for me, I was quick to suggest that my tired body would really appreciate stopping and finding somewhere to sleep as soon as possible.

Fortunately Dea, being such a nice person, was very understanding and agreed. And with even more good fortune we found a suitable guest house just eight kilometres after the border. "Great job. Well done Dea, eight kilometres. It's your first day cycle touring, best not to overdo it. Let's sleep here."

We were out of China now. After Boten, that mysterious Chinese town on the wrong side of the border, the real Laos had thankfully started. Our road had weaved gently downhill through sparse forest dotted with bamboo huts, to the small village where the guest house was. Everything felt immediately more relaxed than in China, and the sun had even reappeared. I knew this was a new beginning. Dea had bought a bike in Laos' capital, Vientiane, and we had three whole weeks to cycle back there together. As darkness descended we sat outside and talked excitedly about the adventures that lay ahead of us. I couldn't believe Dea had changed her mind. "It was too good of an opportunity to turn down," she said. "I had to do it. I was too curious about you, and I was too curious about this way that you live and travel. I wanted to experience it for myself. I realised, even if I might get hurt, it's worth it. I want to live."

Three other guests were sitting around a table at the front of the guest house, and they invited us to join them. They were young and all from Laos, and they introduced themselves as Dow and Fun and Mr Ha. Dow was an extremely excitable girl who gave an enthusiastic thumbs up when she heard we were travelling by bicycle. She handed us all cans of beer and offered us some of the food that they were eating, which mostly consisted of some unknown skewered meat. I politely declined, but Dea, not being a vegetarian, tucked in.

"What is it?" we asked. The English of our new friends wasn't very good, but the answer we got from Mr Ha very definitely sounded like "Puppy."

After that Mr Ha helped us to learn some Lao. I actually had the time now to immerse myself in a country instead of just racing across it, and I intended to do just that. Luckily, Lao appeared to be a very simple language, with most of the words consisting of a single syllable. Mr Ha also taught us some of the beautiful Lao script, which, quite unlike Chinese, consisted of a sensible number of characters not entirely dissimilar to the Roman alphabet and yet quite different, and much more twirly.

Dow and Mr Ha provided us with a great introduction to Laos, its people and its language. As for Fun, well she failed to live up to her name, sitting watching videos on her phone and eating more than her fair share of puppy. But this was a special night, and not even Fun could ruin that. Dea, a talented musician, got out the ukulele that she travelled with and began to play, the sound of her sweet voice penetrating the stillness of the night. Her voice was so beautiful and so real and it made me so happy to hear. Moths flittered around a single bulb above us, as I looked around me and tried to make sense of this scene. Just the previous morning I had woken up in China completely stressed, fighting with Alex, with no idea that I would ever see Dea again. In two days my whole world had changed. The reward for my perseverance was here. I felt like I was seeing the world through new eyes, and everything was so, so good. And it was all ahead of us.

I would have happily stayed another night or two at the guest house, but Dea was itching to get cycling. The irony that this amazing girl had shown up and was so eager to start cycle touring at the exact moment that I wanted a break from it was certainly not lost on me. But her enthusiasm encouraged me, and so we rolled out and down the road. "This looks like a good place to stop for lunch, Dea," I cried out in vain, as she zoomed on ahead.

We did stop for lunch after an hour or so, at a little wooden hut of a restaurant where the previous evening's Lao lesson came to fruition and we were able to successfully order food. A couple of guys working in the restaurant knew a little English, and one stepped forward and spoke slowly to ask us, "Where are you from?"

"England and Denmark."

Then he racked his brains searching for more English, before eventually finding another question. "And what is your nationality?"

The rest of the afternoon was an absolute delight, spent cycling on a relatively peaceful road through small villages of bamboo huts, where scores of young children waved and cried out to us. "Sa-ba-deeeee!" they chorused gleefully, Lao for hello. We waved and sabadeed right back at them. The atmosphere was so friendly, so welcoming; Laos really was turning out to be the paradise that I'd dreamed of.

We camped that night on a flat plot of land that looked like it had been cleared to be used for building a house. It was within sight of the road but in this safe, friendly country we had no concerns. Children walking home along the road squealed with delight and waved to us at our campsite. We had no worries. As darkness fell we were left alone and just laid outside, talking for hours under a clear night sky, where shooting stars and fireflies competed for our wishes.

We set off early the next morning, undeterred by a thick fog that was doing its best to disturb our blissful new existence. This fog was soon set in its place by my optimistic companion. "Doesn't it make everything look mysterious?" Dea said. "I love this!" And before very long the fog gave up and floated away, and left us to our sunny happiness.

Another thing that might have set us back was a long and steep climb that I would have thought a stern test for anyone who'd not done a bicycle tour before. As it turned out, however, the long and steep climb was a stern test for no one but myself. Dea sailed up with a big smile on her face, as if she didn't even realise we were going uphill, while I trailed along behind, as usual, coughing and spluttering my way to the top.

Just before reaching our goal for the day at Oudomxay we noticed a sign at the side of the road indicating that there were some hot springs one kilometre away. Intrigued by this, we turned off in the direction that the sign pointed, anticipating a soothing dip in a warm natural bath. We didn't get far though, because there was no clear road in that direction, just some dirt paths that took us into a village of bamboo huts. Unsure of where to go but keen for an adventure, we went over to some local men and women in the hope that they might offer us some direction. What I was very much hoping that they wouldn't offer us was lunch, because they were kneeling on the ground and in the midst of squeezing out the intestines of an animal that, judging from the decapitated dog's head next to them, may until recently have been the family pet. Doing our best to ignore their culinary undertakings, we asked for the way to the hot springs. Unfortunately, neither Dea nor myself had yet grasped enough of the language to understand their complicated directions, and so two young girls of seven or eight, themselves quite unaffected by Lassie's mutilation, were assigned to act as our personal escorts.

The two girls danced and skipped ahead of us across a field, looking back occasionally to make sure that we were following. Although whatever crop that had been grown here had been harvested, it was still bumpy going, and not easy to push our bikes across. On the far side of the field we reached a house where a few people loitered idly outside. We were encouraged to leave our bikes, and, sensing that our journey was likely to get even more 'off the beaten track', we did just that.

Our assumption proved correct, the next obstacle being a steep slide down a muddy embankment. Once this was cleared we navigated our way around a mean-looking buffalo and then came to our next challenge. A fast flowing and very wide river lay before us, at the sight of which I rather foolishly asked if this was the hot springs. The response of the young girls was to giggle and shake their heads and run off into the river. Dea and I shrugged, took off our shoes, and waded in after them.

The stones on the riverbed were not easy to walk on and the water was cold, but it was not more than a foot deep. The energy of our two little helpers meant that they were soon most of the way across the river before they looked back and saw us struggling across the hard stones. Back they came, splashing water as they merrily danced their way towards us. They then offered to carry our shoes for us, my big old trainers being almost the same size as the girl who took them from me.

After the river crossing we found ourselves in a clearing of green grass and followed the girls still further across this until finally we arrived at our intended destination. Dea and I broke into rueful smiles. After our long and arduous expedition it was all we could do to laugh. Our hot springs were little more than a tepid, muddy puddle. "They made a sign for this?" Dea laughed.

Swimming was impossible but I made the best of it and washed my hands in the muddy water and said it was very good for my skin. Quite aside from anything else, we both had to admit that the journey was more important than the destination, and we agreed that getting away from the road to what was a beautiful location had been well worth the effort. I'd grabbed a couple of bananas from my bike when we'd left it at the house and I gave these to the two young girls now as a thank you. Then I wanted to take a photo of their bright and cheerful faces, but as soon as I got the camera out they ran away, back across the river and far into the distance. "Oh dear," I said, "do you remember the way back, Dea? Right at the buffalo wasn't it?"

In the largish crossroads town of Oudomxay we treated ourselves to two nights in a very grand and fancy hotel, the price of which was a mere five pounds per night each. The receptionist suggested to us that it was a good idea to go to a Buddhist temple up on a hill to watch the sunset. This we did, and it was indeed a nice, relaxing place to take in the view. While we were there a student approached, hoping to talk with us in order to practice his English. I thought that a great idea, not least because the man, Seepong, was very short, and I looked tall next to him.

Seepong was a very nice and thoughtful young man, and he told us a lot about Laos, the people and its culture. To repay him, we invited him to dinner. He took us to a restaurant that had an English menu and a few Western dishes, and we got so excited by it all that we ordered much more food than we could possibly consume. I mean, there were chips, made with potatoes. Do you have any idea how long I'd gone without potatoes? That alone would have made my evening, but the company of these two wonderful human beings, as well as a healthy dose of BeerLao, made everything seem just perfect. Seepong was absolutely the sweetest man on the planet. He was very grateful to us for taking him out and speaking English to him all evening, and he wanted to return the favour when Dea mentioned that she was having trouble registering her SIM card in Laos.

"Can you speak to the company on the phone for me please?" Dea asked.

"Yes I can," he said, "but I will need to lie and tell them that it is my phone."

He took the phone to make the call and, perhaps slightly drunk and certainly very happy, he looked at Dea with his innocent eyes, now quite excited, and said, "I've never lied before."

I heard again from Suzy and Dino, the British couple I'd travelled with back in Iran. They had passed through Oudomxay just before us, then taken a road northeast to Muang Khua, before hopping on a boat down the Nam Ou river to a place called Nong Khiaw. They recommended this route, and both Dea and I felt like it was a good idea to follow their advice. For one thing, it would mean getting off the main highway, which, although more closely resembling a British country lane than a major arterial route, nevertheless had a few trucks on it. And secondly it meant we could take a boat, which, being allowed within the self-imposed parameters of my challenges, sounded like an excellent way to score myself an extra rest day and some free distance.

The road to Muang Khua was peaceful and quiet, and after a few initial climbs settled down and followed a tributary of the Nam Ou, which made for cycling that was as easy as it was scenic. Bright green foliage lined the road and the banks of the river and it felt like we were really getting into the heart of the real Laos. We passed through several small villages that were alive with people. "Sa-ba-dee!" cried the children. Although they were dressed in dirty, torn clothing, their faces were still filled with joy as they waved and held out their hands to high five us as we passed. The adults smiled too, and encouraged the younger children to wave to us, and held toddlers on their knees and moved their arms up and down for them. These looked like some of the poorest people I'd ever seen, yet they were so welcoming and so friendly. There were so many young children it was incredible. It seemed like they were the dominant force in this nation – where the average age was just twenty-one – and the villages sparkled with the energy of this youth.

Reaching Muang Khua, a lively little town built at the apex of two rivers, we looked around for a hostel that had been suggested to us by Suzy and Dino. Not sure where to look, we spotted an older German couple and asked them for directions. Michael and Gisela were their names, and although they weren't much use with directions they were very nice. They had driven their campervan here all the way from Germany. Well, almost all the way here. They had left it in Nong Khiaw and chartered their own boat for two days, which had brought them up river that morning, and on which they planned to return the next day. Seeing as we had just asked them if they knew anything about the public boat, the kind-hearted couple asked if we would like to join them on their boat instead.

The boat was a long, wooden construction, just wide enough for two to sit side-by-side. Our captain sat hunched at the front, motoring us along, the boat sitting low in the water. It was quite an exciting ride too, with several sections of rapids that the captain expertly navigated. We journeyed further through the unknown, with untamed jungle on either side of us creeping down to the water's edge.

Come lunchtime we stopped on a deserted beach and made ourselves at home. Michael had brought his fishing gear and the captain ran off and quickly procured for him the largest worm anyone had ever seen to use as bait. Alas for poor Michael, that worm would remain the catch of the day.

While he busied himself not catching fish, Dea and I went and lounged in the sun. She got out her ukulele and sang Eddie Vedder's song 'Society', as I swam in the refreshing river and listened. The song was one that had always resonated with me. The madness of the work, work, work lifestyle. The pressure to always want more money, just to buy more things, things you don't really need. *'There are people in offices right now,'* I thought, as I lounged by the beach in Laos, watching this amazing girl sat cross-legged on the sand, singing a song that confirmed we were on the same wavelength.

"Society, you're a crazy breed. I hope you're not lonely without me."

Dea finished singing and put away her ukulele, and I challenged her to a sand castle building competition. She then strangely constructed an artistic (and somewhat phallic) sand palace. Nevertheless our judge, the captain, declared hers to be the winner. Fuming, I next challenged Dea to a sand castle battle. There were many rules, but in simple terms it involved throwing wet sand balls at one another's castle until one was destroyed. Suddenly Dea's penis turrets didn't seem so formidable, and the benefits of my short and sturdy structure become apparent. I was the inevitable winner, and after the complete destruction of Dea's palace I moved the bulldozers in and constructed a water slide there instead.

After a few more hours sailing through more spectacular scenery it was almost dark by the time we pulled up in Nong Khiaw. Almost as soon as we left the boat I had a sudden and most welcome reunion with an old friend. Dino came running down the beach and gave me a big hug. I was very pleased to see him again for many reasons, but the primary one was that he was very strong and he quickly scooped up all four of my heavy panniers and carried them up the many steps that led to the village above us. Suzy and Dino had picked out the very best accommodation for us, a guest house with a balcony overlooking the river.

Dinner that night was special. It was the first time Dea had met Suzy and Dino of course, and the first time I'd seen them since I'd tiptoed out of the Tehran apartment we'd all been staying in early one April morning. This was, I must add, not to get away from them, but simply because I had to get going east, whilst they went on a bus tour of southern Iran. Since then they had come within a day of catching me up in Tajikistan before I zoomed on ahead again. But with my lengthy detour through Siberia and Mongolia they had nipped in ahead of me and, after also completing the China Challenge, had been taking things so easy since arriving in Laos that even Dea and I had been able to catch up to them.

"Are you leaving tomorrow?" I asked.

"No, no, we'll stay another day," Suzy said.

They were in no hurry now, and I understood completely.

With Dino and Suzy planning to take another rest day in Nong Khiaw it made perfect sense for Dea and me to do the same. The small town was in an unbelievably picturesque setting on the banks of the river, and seeing as our rooms had the best view in town, not to mention hammocks, I was happy to settle in for a while. The town itself was overrun with white faces – evidently with it being such a stunning location and a jumping off point for boat trips up the river, it had become a popular choice with the Lonely Planet crowd. I couldn't help feeling that the town might have lost some of its charm as a result, but it did mean we could enjoy a little more variety in our diets beyond the standard rice or noodles we had become accustomed to. Pizza, burgers, fresh bread, and fruit shakes were some of the delights on offer to cater to the whims of a Western crowd. We indulged.

Somehow mustering the collective energy to steal ourselves from our hammocks and away from our pineapple shakes, in the afternoon we cycled out to some nearby caves. The caves were huge amphitheatres carved into the limestone cliffs. But it was also humbling to see them, as they had apparently provided a sheltered place for the local people to hide during the Second Indochina War. I'd always known this by its more common name, the Vietnam War, but it's a name that fails to recognise that the war was not confined to Vietnam. The actions of the Americans in Northern Laos actually represented the heaviest bombing campaign in history. 270 million submunitions were dropped on Laos, an estimated thirty per cent of which failed to explode. Forty years on and tragically 300 people were still being killed every year by disturbing these unexploded bombs. That was why we weren't doing much wild camping.

The next morning our quartet of intrepid explorers cycled away from Nong Khiaw in the direction of the former royal capital, Luang Prabang, with a surprising level of enthusiasm. Lazy days would blight our progress no more. No longer were we to be held captive by tourist treats. Now we were out to investigate the real Laos, far away from all that tourist claptrap. Well, at least until we got to Luang Prabang.

There were a great many Buddhist temples along the road, always intricately and imaginatively decorated with gold and other bright colours. Monks wandered among them, with shaved heads and neon orange robes. We passed more villages, more children smiling and waving. Women walked along the road with sacks of wood on their backs. A man knelt weaving bamboo to form the walls of a new home. Other men gathered around cheering as two fighting cocks squawked and clawed at one another.

After witnessing all that, we were all feeling a bit worn out and decided that the thing to do was to stop for a long lunch so that we could regain our strength. As we looked out for a restaurant, we saw a big building that had some beer advertising on it, and, thinking that it might be some sort of food and drink establishment, we stopped to make enquiries. A man outside told us that it was no such thing, but he was so friendly and spoke with such excellent English that when he invited us in, offering us beer and fish, we found it quite impossible to refuse.

We left our bikes outside and ducked into a dimly lit breeze block building that, though sparsely decorated, seemed to be the home of many people. A crowd of men and women sat around a long wooden table, and the four of us were encouraged to take our place at the end of this table. It appeared that everybody had just eaten, but more food was soon prepared for us by a couple of women in the kitchen (the kitchen, in this case, being the dusty floor just next to the dining table). Soon fried eggs appeared, along with a big communal basket of Laos' favourite staple, sticky rice. The man that had invited us, whose name was Nuan, showed us the correct way to eat such food. He grabbed some of the sticky rice and rolled it into a ball in his hands, then dipped it into the egg.

"But remember," he said, "no double-dipping and no finger-licking."

An interesting addition to the food was the alcohol. It started harmlessly enough with BeerLao, the national beer which seemed to have a complete monopoly over the Laos beer market, being poured into glasses of ice for us. Every few minutes a toast would be made, and we would all have to clink our glasses together and take a drink. Nuan and an old, stony-faced man opposite him, referred to as The Chief, were the protagonists of all of these toasts. The Chief soon started to look a little the worse for wear, but that didn't stop him from upping the ante, and calling for us all to finish our drinks every now and then. We would then have to take it in turns to down whatever we had in our glasses. It was all becoming eerily reminiscent of my student days.

In the midst of all this merriment I succeeded in talking with Nuan, a man that used to work in a 600 dollar a night hotel in Luang Prabang (hence his good English skills), where he was paid only 150 dollars per month. He had, however, recently moved home to look after his mother. He didn't seem to be presently doing a very good job of that, though, because he said that this building was not actually his home. As a result I began to wonder just how welcome we really were here, especially as, aside from Nuan and The Chief, we were the only ones drinking. The other end of the table remained quite sober, even when the Lao-Lao appeared. This was a strong home-made rice wine of unknown but considerable alcoholic content. Nuan encouraged us each to take a shot and we obliged.

"Now you have one eye," he told us. "You must drink another shot, so that you have two eyes."

Suzy, Dino, Dea and I consulted as to whether we should stay or go. If we were going to do any more cycling we were going to need to leave soon. The point of no return was fast approaching, but we decided the only thing to do was to stay and see it through.

By the time I had myself two eyes, two legs, and an arm we moved outside, where I think we were all surprised to see it was still broad daylight. There was a big pond behind the house where the family bred fish for eating and selling, and the fish we were promised was soon grilled and served to us. I abstained, and took the opportunity to learn more of the Lao language from Nuan, scribbling everything he told me furiously onto a piece of paper (I would look at this paper the next day and not be able to make head nor tail of it). With The Chief having gone to lie down somewhere, I attempted to build some bridges with the rest of the family, and they seemed to appreciate my (albeit quite slurred) attempts to communicate with them in their own language.

What they may have appreciated less was my interfering with their baby chickens. A dozen or more chicks had been placed beneath an overturned woven basket to keep them all in one place, but one of the chicks had been left outside in the garden by mistake. It looked to me like this little chick was feeling lonely and wanted to return to the companionship of its siblings because it kept running up and down the sides of the basket, looking for a way in. With Nuan's permission I took it upon myself to help this bird by grabbing it, lifting up the basket, and throwing it inside with the others. What my simple, intoxicated mind had failed to anticipate was that when I lifted up the basket some of the other chicks might make a run for it, which of course they did. Suddenly there were three or four little chicks on the loose, scampering away across the garden. I clumsily dashed around after them, eventually scooping them up, at which point I was told that there was a hole in the top of the basket for putting the chicks in. I used this correct chick-returning method, but there was still one bird on the loose. I ran desperately after this guy, as he tried to hide and sneak away from me beneath tables and chairs. Finally I got a hold of him and threw him back into captivity. Then I sat down, momentarily satisfied with myself, until I realised what I'd just done. No animal lover am I.

Although Nuan had earlier suggested to us that we could sleep at this house, that invitation appeared to have been rescinded, possibly at some point during the baby chick debacle. It didn't matter, he told us, for there was a guest house just 500 metres up the road. Well, that guest house turned out to be a bit further away than that, and the 900 metres it took us to actually get there I could only define as some of the most difficult of the whole journey. Unlike the previous 34,000 kilometres, I found during these 900 metres that it was very tricky simply to keep my balance without the bicycle toppling over, and for some reason everything was much more blurry than it had ever been before. But we all made it, and after checking in we followed Nuan to a restaurant for even more food and, yes, alcohol. Having indulged further we were thoroughly satisfied and said goodbye to a departing Nuan, thanking him for his great company and giving him some money to cover the costs of our extravagances. It had been a fun day, for sure, and a long one too. A day in which we had certainly got to know the real Laos, the happy contentment in our souls (and our stomachs) a testament to that. It was dark. It was late. The stars twinkled overhead and we were all ready to go to bed.

"What time is it?" I asked.

"Seven thirty."

37

I was a little on the dazed and confused side when I awoke. My head was in pain and my muscles ached. I realised I must be unwell, or, perhaps more likely, hungover, as I looked up at the bright pink mosquito net above me. I turned my head. Two beautiful blue eyes looked into mine with a mixture of pity and affection. Things with Dea had been going really well, and it seemed that not even my drunken escapades had managed to spoil it. Looking at her angelic face I had two trains of thought. The first was to wonder just how it was possible for anyone to look so good first thing in the morning, the second to ponder what business this beautiful and intelligent girl had with a filthy urchin like myself. But trying to solve a conundrum like that in my state just made my head hurt all the more, so I decided I'd better just appreciate it, and I rolled over and went back to sleep.

It was another nice, sunny day outside and I was eventually persuaded to wake up properly so that we could resume our ride. As my hangover subsided with the exercise and the fresh air I was able to fully appreciate the company that I now kept. Many times during the long and lonely ride across China I had fantasised about this. It had often felt like I would never make it here, yet now I really was free from deadlines and cycling at a pace at which I could fully experience and appreciate things, alongside people whose company I greatly enjoyed. With Dino being the most laid-back person ever and Suzy not so very far behind, out little peloton had a stress-free dynamic as we laughed and chatted our way through the Laos countryside. Life was good.

But we were not the only cyclists enjoying the relaxed pace of this pleasant country. Far from it. On our ride into Luang Prabang we joined forces with an Australian named Adam, and a father and daughter team from the States, Michael and Jocelyn. Southeast Asia was popular cycle touring territory, and there were even more encounters when we reached town. Luang Prabang was once the capital city of Laos, plus the seat of the royal family until all that monarchy business came to an end in 1975 at the climax of the Second Indochina War. It was therefore probably the most important location in the history of the country. Now, however, it was more like the tourist capital of the country, with foreigners flocking to check out the mixture of Buddhist temples and French colonial buildings in the surprisingly small town. Whether or not the rapidly increasing tourist industry in Laos was really for the best was in many ways questionable, however. One morning Dino, Dea and I woke up early to see the alms giving ceremony. Suzy had read the reviews of the alms giving ceremony and was suitably put off not to want anything to do with it. She'd also read them out loud to us, but we were all being quite stupid, and went anyway.

Traditionally, this centuries-old ceremony would involve orange-robed monks walking around town to be handed food by local people, who would kneel on the pavement before them. Monks are not supposed to work, or to have money, and the community therefore would support them in this way. Unfortunately, in Luang Prabang the process had been hijacked by the tourist industry, and we found Suzy's predictions to be correct. In essence what we witnessed was a collection of tourists kneeling on the pavement and offering food to the monks, while other tourists stood in their faces taking photos. Apparently the whole thing had become such a farce that even the monks didn't want to partake in it any more, but the tourist board said they had to, or they'd just get lay people in and dress them up as monks to keep up appearances.

Another sorry example of the tourist influence came during our visit to the most famous of the temples, Wat Xieng Thong. The ornate building, adorned with facades of gold leaf and curved red roofs, was undoubtedly impressive. We ascended a series of white steps, removed our shoes, and stepped inside, where the eye was immediately drawn to a large golden Buddha. Below this was a display of many other smaller Buddhas, as well as candles, lights and other offerings. For a moment the four of us were the only ones there, but as we walked around admiring the intricate drawings on the pillars and walls, a small procession of people entered. There were two monks in traditional orange robes, with one shoulder bare and bald heads shining, but there was also a young boy wearing the same outfit in white. He was walking with a man that appeared to be his father. They were followed by a few other Lao people, and then, behind them, by a group of French tourists and their rather loud tour guide. My French had not improved greatly since those early days in the French countryside, yet I knew just enough of it to comprehend that this was the day that the boy would become a monk. The father was here to give him away to the monastery. Only temporarily, I should add, it being very normal for boys to spend some weeks or months living as monks before returning to their families. Still, he was young, not yet a teen, and this was no doubt a major moment in his life.

The two adult monks took up positions in front of the big Buddha, facing the others. The boy and his father were directly opposite, and behind them the other people, most likely family members. Further back, Dino and I took a seat on the floor to silently observe the ceremony. Dea and Suzy preferred to leave, wanting to be respectful and not intrude. But I felt like Dino and I were being respectful, keeping quiet and tucking our feet under us. We knew it was basic etiquette not to stand higher than the monks or to show our feet. Sadly, not all of the tourists who wanted to see the show quite understood this.

The ceremony was fascinating. One of the monks held up a shield of some sort and chanted mantras for a long time. Prayers were said, gifts were offered, and then the young boy was taken behind a screen where his father emotionally exchanged his white robes for orange ones. All of this was very special to witness. What spoiled it were the foreign idiots that kept entering the temple and, without showing the least courtesy, remained standing, talked loudly, and snapped photos, often with the flash. One particularly obnoxious Frenchman leaned over some of the family with his video camera to get a good close up of the proceedings, while a Chinese woman squawked loudly at the back. It was all rather shameful, and made me reflect a little on our world and question what it was about our silly modern life that made it so unbelievably important to record everything. No doubt most of the people who came in and took photos would go away and publish them online with narcissistic intentions to show everyone how very interesting their lives were. *Look how great I am, look what I saw today.* Yet, how many of them actually saw it? Actually really paid attention? How many realised that this was likely the most important moment of this child's life? How many noticed the apprehension in his eyes when he glanced behind and saw all the cameras and smartphones pointed at him? And I'm ashamed to say that I too wanted to take a photo. I hated that, and wondered why I couldn't just appreciate the moment. But I resisted, and Dino and I slipped out quietly.

On our last night in Luang Prabang we met up with Michael and Jocelyn again, and another touring cyclist that they had picked up somewhere, and we all went out for dinner. The new cyclist was a twenty-two-year-old German kid named Robin, who had cycled most of the way from Europe (although in a sensible move he'd taken a flight across most of China). I happened to be sitting next to Robin during the meal, and I was very glad about that, as he soon proved himself a most interesting character. Having spent a few weeks cycling with a pair of Swedish magicians, he'd picked up a few card tricks which he offered to show me. I agreed, saying I'd show him my one and only card trick in return. Robin then proceeded to blow my mind. His tricks were amazing. I'd never seen anything like it before. I was so impressed that I lost all interest in showing him my trick, feeble as it was by comparison.

The other interesting thing about Robin was that he had just bought a boat. Apparently he'd had enough of cycling and thought he'd rather boat the rest of the way along the Mekong. There weren't any boats taking passengers downstream this year because there wasn't enough water to do it safely, so Robin had just gone out and bought his own boat, and evidently he'd decided that there would be plenty enough water for him because he planned to row it all the way downstream to the Mekong delta in Vietnam.

"I've got one of those long boats you see the locals using, got a good deal," he said proudly.

"But have you ever boated before?"

"No, never."

"Do you know anything about boats."

"Not really."

"Do you know anything about the currents?"

"No."

"The dams?"

"Dams?"

Was he going to die? Yes, probably, but I had to admire his guts. His sense of adventure was an inspiring and refreshing blend of bravery and stupidity. We all wished him the best, and, after he almost cycled straight out in front of a tuk-tuk immediately after saying goodbye to us, I think we all said a little prayer for him too.

Dino, Suzy, Dea and I left the tourists behind and cycled out of Luang Prabang along a dirt track. The decision to take this road-less-travelled was soon vindicated, as we were instantly transported back to the real Laos that we knew and loved. Each time that we passed through a small village of simple wooden homes, we heard "Falang, falang, falang!" – originally the Lao word for its French colonisers, but now extended to encompass all foreign visitors – spread through the village like wildfire. Young faces then sprung up from windows and from behind door frames and from all manner of nooks and crannies and the adorable chorus of, "Sa-ba-dee! Sa-ba-dee!" once again echoed through the humid air.

The dirt road, however, was a challenging one. Although it was vaguely following the Mekong, it was not at all flat. The climbs were short but extremely steep, and in between them there were many river crossings, few of which were bridged. I was impressed once again by how well Dea handled this tough terrain. She just took it all in her stride, looking like she was having the time of her life. She really was a tough cookie.

The same could not really be said for me, and no sooner had we made it back to a paved road than I came down with a terrible ailment. I felt feverish, suffering with a headache, nausea and a poorly stomach. But the guest house we were staying in was a bad one in a small town. Noticing that the much larger town of Sayaboury was just forty kilometres down the road, and as it was likely that there were medical professionals and pharmaceuticals in Sayaboury, I thought I should do my best to get there while my strength held.

So we all continued on, with me lagging behind. The hot sun did nothing at all to alleviate my symptoms and I had to stop often, although I had no appetite to eat anything. Dea waited patiently for me, but I told Suzy and Dino to go on to Sayaboury where they planned to eat lunch before pushing on. Their visas were almost at an end and they needed to hurry along to Thailand, so this was going to be our last morning together. And I use the word 'together' quite wrongly because from then on they were nowhere to be seen as I laboured along painfully. It was a dire struggle for me, those last few kilometres, but finally I made it to the town and found my friends sitting in the shade of a restaurant.

Joining everyone at the table I suddenly came over feeling much worse than before. The restaurant felt incredibly hot and I had a terrible urge to vomit. I felt so bad that I was sure I must be suffering from malaria or dengue fever, but for the moment the only way I could find to make myself feel any better at all was to catapult myself out over the low wall of the restaurant and lie quietly on the grass outside for a while. I remained there until Suzy and Dino finished their meal and then managed to rouse myself to get up and hug them goodbye. It was a shame to part like this. They had become good friends and it was sad to see them go, the transient nature of my friendships once again painfully highlighted.

With Dea's help I was able to crawl to the nearest guest house. Luckily it was a good one, with a fan and wifi and a TV and a sit-down toilet and a big, comfortable bed, which I immediately laid down upon with no intention to move from for a good long while, except perhaps when nature called me to the sit-down toilet.

The wifi was very useful, for it allowed me to self-diagnose myself without having to trouble any medical professionals. After looking up all of my symptoms I quickly surmised that, not only was I indeed a likely victim of both malaria and dengue fever, but that I had also somehow contracted several other diseases, including ebola, smallpox, and the common cold. Realising just how very sick I was I told Dea that we had better stay a few nights at the guest house and she was, as befits the sweetest girl in the world, very sympathetic to my plight, as she stroked my forehead and made promises to look after me.

Now, it's a funny thing, but every time I fell sick when I was alone I tended to be able to do a pretty good job of just getting on with things, but happening to fall sick in the presence of someone else I suddenly had terrible trouble doing anything at all for myself, and I flailed about the bed, protesting that I was too weak to do anything and complaining that I couldn't find the TV remote. Fortunately for me, Dea remained very patient and never lost her cool or her good cheer, and she simply dug out the TV remote that I'd been lying on and gave it back to me and stroked my hair some more.

We ended up staying four nights in Sayaboury and that put us under some pressure to make it to Vientiane on time for Dea's flight home. But our prolonged stay was not without its benefits. For one thing, lounging around on a big double bed with a beautiful girl was something that could be enjoyed despite my awful sickness, and, in actual fact, I think this favourable situation was a major factor in my eventual recovery, something that may be of interest to the medical community. I also felt like our time in Sayaboury brought us closer together, and Dea even made use of the time to write a song. Entitled

'Lovers in Laos' it was the first song that she had ever written, and it was astonishingly good. When she played it to me, strumming the strings of her ukulele and piercing the air with her beautiful voice, the passion and deep feeling that she transmitted with her words made me well up inside. We had something really special here, we really did.

Interestingly enough, a couple of days after I'd recovered and we were able to roll onwards from Sayaboury, Dea herself came down quite unwell. She had all the same symptoms as I'd had, and it was very likely that she'd come down with the same tropical affliction from which I'd suffered, writhing on my death bed for four days straight. No real surprise then, that after a single afternoon of rest she was up at six-thirty the next morning, bright-eyed and bushy-tailed and ready to continue. Her speedy recovery was advantageous, as we needed now to hurry along for the last few days and one rather large obstacle still stood in our way, a huge mountain pass.

But it wasn't just one steady climb, the road went up and down like a roller coaster through the thick Lao jungle. The gradient was unbelievable, twenty or twenty-five percent at times. It was the kind of steep where all we could do was battle as hard as possible for each pedal rotation, bending over the handlebars and putting our backs into it, or standing and using all our body weight to grind the pedals around. Whichever technique we used, neither of us could manage more than fifty or a hundred metres at a time, before being forced to stop to catch our breath.

Whenever the road levelled off and became a normal steep climb of seven or eight percent it actually felt like bliss. "It feels like we're going downhill," Dea said on such a section. Once again she was taking all this in her stride. I hadn't met my match with this girl, I'd met an absolute superstar. Certainly she was no contender for the still vacant position of my hapless sidekick, for I was the hapless one and she the heroine. She spurred me on, even as the downhill sections disappeared and we just climbed and climbed towards the top.

Reaching the summit of long climbs was always rewarding, but it was even more so alongside Dea, to see the joy on her face as she realised we had succeeded. We whizzed down the other side, exhilarated by our velocity on the descent, then whooped with delight to reach flat farmland again, the mountains behind us.

As we set up camp in a field just off the road, we noticed yet two more touring cyclists riding along the road. We called out to them and they came over. Germans Henning and Sebastian had only just started their Southeast Asia tour from Vientiane a few days earlier, but they were already enjoying the experience. Sebastian was travelling with a guitar, so Dea suggested we all have a sing-song. She pulled out her ukulele and we had a lovely evening singing along together. It also attracted the attention of a couple of local men who came and joined in as well, making for quite a party altogether.

Alone in our tent that night Dea was buzzing with happiness about these wonderful chance encounters and the unexpected situations that travelling by bicycle throws your way. Admittedly, it was fortunate that she'd joined me in what was probably the best country I'd ever been to for cycle touring (I doubt she'd have loved it in China quite so much), but she was absolutely taken by this lifestyle.

"I think I'll try and do a bike tour by myself in Europe in the summer," she said. "I just love it. You meet so many people this way. It really shows you the real country. It's just a great way to travel."

I thought back on our first meeting in Mongolia, when she'd said she didn't think she could ever travel by bike. I was so happy that she'd given it a go, because she really did seem to be converted to cycle touring. The only problem was that she had to go back to Denmark and finish her masters degree, which was going to take another year.

"Maybe I can come and find you after that?" she asked. "Where will you be?"

"Still in Australia maybe. Or cycling through the Americas."

"Oh. I would love to cycle with you through the Americas."

"Really? Would you want to do this for a long time then? Months, or years?"

"Yes. I think so. Do you think I could? Would you like me to come with you?"

It was an idea so precious, I almost dared not imagine it.

All that was left now was a fairly straightforward couple of days alongside the Mekong, which we'd found again beyond the mountain pass. On our last evening camping we found a perfect spot – a big, empty beach right on the river. There was absolutely nobody about, except for a couple of cows that eyed us with curiosity, and the location was ideal, with soft sand leading down to the gently-flowing water. We'd stopped early, so there was time to go for a swim before dark. After splashing about happily in the water for a while we stopped and held one another. Dea's face in front of me was lit up by the low sun. It shone like gold, her blue eyes dazzling like precious stones. I'd called it right from the moment I first saw her. She really was the most beautiful girl in the world, no doubt about that. It was such a fantastic moment, to hold her in this amazing place, and yet, how could this moment possibly be more sad? As I hugged her tight I stared over her shoulder at our two pairs of shoes, sitting side-by-side on the beach. Both pairs looked bedraggled from months of travel. Somehow those shoes looked so full of sorrow, the knowledge that in a few days they would be thousands of kilometres apart, almost unbearable.

Our last day cycling together was also our longest distance, but the final ninety kilometres into Vientiane was on a well-surfaced, flat, wide road, and we did it easily. It was such a sad day. The last time we would wake up next to each other in the tent, the last time we'd stop to eat fried rice at a little restaurant, the last time we'd take an ice cream break together. It felt like Dea had only just arrived. How could she possibly be leaving again so soon? It felt like the shortest three weeks I'd ever known.

We reached Vientiane, often referred to as one of the most laid-back of capital cities. The amount of traffic had us questioning that description as we dodged our way through to the centre and found a guest house. The going rate here was several times that of the rural guest houses, but ours at least had a Swedish bakery just opposite it which, unlike most bakeries in Sweden, also served french fries. We got ourselves some of those, and a couple of beers, and sat on the balcony of the guest house to watch the world go by.

Unfortunately, this combination of fried potatoes and alcohol made me feel quite unwell again. We had big plans to explore Vientiane's night market and then go to see some of the other sights before ending up at Laos' famed ten-pin bowling centre, but I felt really rather light-headed by the time we'd walked down the street. We made it as far as the night market, a collection of stalls selling a variety of clothes and knick-knacks on the promenade of the Mekong, but I felt awful again, and had to sit down. We decided that the only thing for it was to go back to the guest house. I felt terrible to have ruined our last evening, but Dea said it didn't matter what we did, just that we were together.

Morning came too quickly, but I was feeling better and we visited the Swedish bakery for a breakfast sandwich. Dea then reluctantly returned her bike to the shop where she'd bought it a few weeks earlier. Time was passing, the clock ticking too fast. Dea had to leave for the airport all too soon.

We returned to the guest house and lay down on the bed, holding each other for the last time. It had been such an incredible three weeks. To think back over everything that happened was a form of torture. Here she was right in front of me, this girl I'd been looking for for so long, and yet she was about to be ripped away from me. She was leaving. She would soon be on the opposite side of the planet. And there was absolutely nothing that I could do about it. The tears soon started to flow. I felt an aching pain through my body, encompassing me. It was such a real, raw emotion. I hated that feeling so much, but I also appreciated it, for reminding me that I was alive. We cried and cried. I wanted to tell her not to go. I wanted to come with her and jump on that plane. I did not want to lose this girl. Not now. Not like this. But we both knew that this was how it had to be.

We carried our bags down the stairs and I loaded up my bike outside the guest house. Dea had only her backpack. No longer was she my cycling companion. It was time for her to return to her life in Denmark. A lump formed in my throat. It was so sad. I felt hollow. I'd found something so, so good here, and now it was slipping through my fingers. Dea's taxi pulled up and we embraced one last time. It was an embrace that we both wished would never end, but that inevitably had to. She slipped away and climbed into the back seat of the cab. A little wave from the window as the taxi pulled away down the street, and that was it, she was gone.

She was gone.

I collapsed onto a bench, and the tears came again.

38

I wanted to find a cheaper guest house where I could sit and feel sorry for myself for a few days, so I got on my bike and cycled around looking for one. It was so hopelessly sad to be riding alone again. There was no pretty girl ahead of me to try and keep up with, no one to stop and consult with for thoughts on directions. Left to the advice of my own solitary brain I simply cycled around in circles for an hour, then gave up on finding a cheap guest house and checked in to a packed hostel instead. I lay on the top bunk in a large dormitory room that was scattered with backpacks and Lonely Planets, and stared at the ceiling, very much achieving my goal of feeling sorry for myself.

After a while I decided that Facebook might be a useful means for cheering me up. Usually a terribly mistaken belief, this time it wasn't. There was a message from Dea. I clicked on it, imagining that it was most likely a message saying that she was at the airport waiting for her flight. But it wasn't. I read it, paused for a moment, read it again, then gathered up my things and ran out of the hostel as fast as I could.

China visa rules f*cked up my plan. I had to change my flight and I'll be leaving tomorrow at noon. Can I sleep one more night and wake up to see your bright blue eyes and wonderful smile? I'll be waiting here at our guest house eating cookies and croissants *until I hear from you.*

I pedalled as fast as I could back to the guest house, and there she was, waiting for me just as she'd promised. It was amazing, not to mention a bit weird, to see her sitting right there on the bench where I'd been sobbing a few hours earlier. It felt like we'd been given a gift. We'd already said our goodbyes, and this extra twenty-four hours we miraculously now had together was just bonus time that could be enjoyed and cherished.

Physically I felt much better, so we agreed that we should make the most of our bonus time and do all of the things we were supposed to have done the evening before. We spent the afternoon walking around Vientiane taking in sights like Wat Si Saket, the Presidential Palace and the Victory Monument. Time slipped by quickly, and it was already getting dark by the time we arrived at the last of these. The Victory Monument was a giant arch that looked a bit like the Arc de Triumph crossed with a Disneyland castle. It was surrounded by fountains and palm trees and made for a nice place to sit.

"It's been so great to have this time together. I felt so sad leaving you. I wish I didn't have to go again," Dea said, as we sat arm in arm on a bench watching the water dance before us.

"I know. Let's not think about that. We should just enjoy this night."

"Yes. You're right."

"So, do you want to go bowling?"

The ten-pin bowling alley in Vientiane proved to be a very interesting and fun place. The other customers were locals, mostly kids out from school. The equipment appeared to be of a retro style, looking like it was straight from the seventies, although on closer inspection we realised that was likely just because that was when it was installed. The good thing about this was that the knackered old machine would sometimes randomly knock down an extra pin when resetting them, so there were plenty of extra points to be had.

It was a very close game, and on my final turn I needed at least a spare in order to win. Perhaps succumbing to the pressure, I could only manage a disappointing three pins with my first go. I turned around in disgust. Dea was starting to look confident. I picked up my last ball from the rack, said some motivational mantras to myself, then turned to face the remaining seven pins. I was pleased to see the machine had kindly knocked one of them down for me, so that it lay horizontally across the lane in front of the others. I saw my chance and with all my might hurled the final ball down the middle of the lane. It clattered into the prone pin and sent it flying, scattering all of the remaining pins left and right. Dea protested. I ignored her. I was the inevitable champion.

But really, it felt like we were both winners.

Although we'd promised each other that there was no need for any repeat of our first theatrical goodbye, the next morning brought a fresh wave of emotional pain and another tearful farewell. It was almost a carbon copy, in fact, as Dea loaded her bag into the back of another taxi and turned to hold me one final time. This time there was to be no reprieve, we knew. This time she was really leaving. I squeezed her tight, not wanting to let go, but I had to. Into the back seat she climbed, as I heard a man nearby giggle inappropriately. He was one of the many tuk-tuk drivers that stood on corners looking for business. I decided I might as well be nice to him, so I leaned one arm on his shoulder as I waved at the back of the departing taxi. I encouraged him to do the same, and the two of us waved farewell to the most beautiful girl in the world. The very considerate man then turned to me and asked, "You want Lao girl now? Falang lady gone. You want Lao lady?"

I didn't really feel that much like sleeping with a prostitute, so I moved my things back to the cheap hostel and resumed my 'feeling sorry for myself' position. I maintained this position pretty solidly for a couple of days, until Facebook supplied me with another interesting piece of information. It came in the form of a post from Robin, that giddy German boy who'd bought a boat in Luang Prabang with crazy intentions to paddle down the Mekong. From what we'd seen of the river as we cycled near to it we had been concerned for Robin's safety. From shore it looked dangerous, rife with rocks and islands, whirlpools and eddies. So it was no surprise to see that Robin's post started with the words "I crashed my boat" and while this predictable calamity was not in itself enough to cheer me up, the fact that he was still alive to write about it was. He was apparently now back on his bike, and bearing down upon Vientiane.

He arrived the next day, yet failed to follow my instructions to come and stay at the same hostel as me, and instead booked into another one because it had a pool table. So we met at a little restaurant down by the Mekong and it was good for me to get out and meet a familiar face. I liked Robin. He reminded me of me, and not just because he had a beard and a bright orange T-shirt, but also because he seemed a little bit, well, I don't know, what's the word... hapless. For example, I met him just as he was finishing up eating at this restaurant in the touristy part of town. Having grown so used to the cheap prices outside of Vientiane, he'd failed to ask what his meal here would cost before ordering, something he seemed to very much regret when the bill appeared.

In order to cheer poor Robin up we walked to his hostel to play some pool. On the way I asked about the boating adventure, and I was very impressed that he'd made it as far as he had without dying, as he reeled off a list of tricky encounters with rapids and whirlpools and dams. In the end he had finally succumbed to a patch of partially submerged rocky ground, which, fortunately for him, allowed him to evacuate to the safety of land. From there he'd cycled the rest of the way, because the boat, of course, was damaged, and would be far too dangerous to risk taking out onto the water again.

"What did you do with it, then?"

"I gave it to a small child."

We got to Robin's hostel, the one which he had chosen specifically because of the the pool table, only to discover that there was no pool table. "I thought there was a pool table," he said. So we left again and walked around looking for somewhere else to play, soon stumbling upon a little den of snooker tables occupied by local youths. We got a table and, after I'd explained the rules, did our very best to play a game of snooker. The trouble was neither of us was very good, with snooker being a much more difficult game than pool. Consequently, it took a very long time to pot all of the reds, about eighty percent of the points we accumulated were in fouls, and the biggest break of the entire match was when somebody potted the black at the end.

We didn't have anything else to do, so we tried another game, but were both worse than we'd been during the first. At one point Robin tried for a long red, needing to use the spider to help him. He was at full stretch and he hadn't chalked the cue, so he completely skewed the shot. The white ball went in the wrong direction and he cursed and jumped up in frustration. As he did so he banged his head on the lights above the table and he cursed some more. I found all of this quite hilarious, of course, and then, in the middle of my laughter I had an epiphany.

This man was completely hapless.

And his name.

His name... was Robin.

I'd found him at last!

Although my relationship with Robin was developing nicely into the long-awaited 'hapless-sidekick-making-me-look-good' scenario, unfortunately my Lao visa expired and I had to leave the country. On the plus side there was another country just across the river, so I did not have to go far to find another location where I could sit and feel sorry for myself while I waited for Robin. He would join me in a few days once his Thai visa began.

It was an easy cycle to the Friendship Bridge that connected the two countries across the Mekong. A simple border process and a quick switch to the left side of the road, and I was in Thailand. It immediately announced itself as a more developed country with the appearance of 7-elevens and Tesco Lotus superstores. These giant supermarkets were just like Tesco back home in Britain, only with a very green colour scheme. They were the first real supermarkets I'd seen since Turkey, and, after a year of buying everything from small shops, my head span with the variety of products that were suddenly on offer.

The Western influences were clear, but the golden temples I passed and the whizzing motorcyclists that passed me confirmed I was still in Asia as I looked around for a guest house. I settled on a place hidden away on a quiet back street, where I was initially welcomed by a round and cheerful man who told me his name was A. A then left me in the hands of his brother, who I was disappointed to discover was not called B. No, he was called Thanarphong Puttichaiyanant, although he very thoughtfully shortened this to Om, for the convenience of everyone.

I was shown to my room, which was of such a peaceful and air-conditioned nature that I ended up staying for ten days. I was, after all, very much in need of a sustained period of rest after all of the exertions of the previous few months. On the first night A took me out to a local bar that belonged to a woman that might have been his sister (I soon found out that Thai people refer to each other as brother and sister, even when they are not remotely related, which made finding out actual family ties difficult). The bar was completely empty, except for a man that might have been A's sister's brother, I wasn't really sure. In order to try and improve my understanding of who people were I asked A if he wouldn't mind teaching me some Thai as we sat sipping our cokes. At first I thought Thai was going to be very easy to pick up, as a lot of the words were similar to Lao. Instead of 'sabadee,' they used 'sawadee.' But then A dropped a bombshell.

"You have to say 'crap' at the end of every sentence," he said.

"Sorry? What?"

"You say crap, to make it polite."

"Really? To make it polite? It has quite the opposite effect in English."

"Sawadee craap!" he screamed.

"And you do this at the end of every sentence?"

"Yes. Thank you is kop-kun craap!"

This peculiar linguistic trait made me sound like I was suffering from an extreme form of Tourette's whenever I tried to speak Thai, but with my immature mind, I was quite alright with that.

Robin arrived in Thailand on Christmas Eve and came to stay at the same guest house as me. It was really good to have a friend to spend Christmas with, to distract me from missing home and missing Dea. We walked around town in the sunshine having exciting conversations, like this one:

"Watch out Robin, we have to turn right at the wat."

"The what?"

"Yes, the wat."

"The what?"

"The wat."

"What do you mean, we turn right at the what?"

"What do you think I mean? We turn right at the wat."

"What? What is a what?"

"What? You don't know what a wat is?"

"No. What is a what?"

"A wat is a Buddhist temple. They have a lot of them around here."

"Really?"

Once we both knew where we going, we went and explored the big market in town, and we were both pleased enough with the pricing structure to buy gifts for one another. As if Christmas couldn't get any better, we then wandered down the promenade beside the Mekong, where we were surprised to see an elephant strolling among the crowds. The men leading the animal around were trying to profit by selling food to tourists so that they could feed it, and they soon came over to us. We had no great desire to feed an elephant, but Robin took it upon himself to whip out his playing cards and show the men his magic tricks. He said it was a great way to break down barriers with people. In the present circumstance it succeeded in breaking down barriers with the elephant, who took a surprisingly keen interest in Robin's skills.

After all this excitement it was time for Christmas dinner. We had heard that an Englishman, one of many expats in the town, owned a bar just down the road and was offering free food to mark the festivities. All we had to do was buy a drink and we could eat all we wanted. This sounded like a mistake on his part, and us two hungry cyclists made our way there, determined to put him out of business.

On our arrival we headed straight for the buffet, which had a surprising lack of Christmas food. Alarmingly, it was also not at all vegetarian friendly, not at all, and all I came out with for my Christmas dinner was a plate of watermelon slices. It wasn't an ideal situation, and when I realised that the Sprite I'd ordered cost two and a half times the normal price I angrily returned to the buffet, where I skimmed the mashed potato off the top of the cottage pie in a desperate attempt to at least break even.

I took a seat with Robin at a table with two old American men. The whole bar was filled with such expats. Since arriving in Thailand I had seen a great many of these men, most of whom had obviously married Thai women and now lived here. Unlike other countries in the region, where relationships between locals and foreigners were generally illegal, here they were encouraged. Having a foreign husband brought great respect to a Thai girl and her family, along with the obvious financial benefits. Presumably the men would also be happy to live with a beautiful wife in a beautiful country, and yet there were surely many downsides. The previous evening we'd encountered a drunk American slob, who shouted across the restaurant about the 'best brothel in Pattaya,' to another expat, 'where the girls do this and the girls do that.' Which seemed a little rude, considering his wife sat diligently beside him.

The two old gentlemen that we sat with now were much less obnoxious, at least. I spoke with one, a seventy-year-old retired lawyer from New York, who described his current situation as a 'marriage of convenience.' It was his third marriage in fact, and he had several children and grandchildren back in the States. He told me that he sometimes thought about going back, but he was settled here now in his marriage of convenience. There was no sign of his third wife this Christmas evening, however. Like almost all of the other expats, he'd come to the bar alone.

On the other side of the table I caught some of the conversation, where Robin, who hadn't quite grasped the situation, was asking an eighty-year-old man how long he'd been travelling.

"I'm not travelling boy! I live here!"

39

Nong Khai, Thailand
29th December 2014

Sadly, Robin did not go on to fulfil his destiny of becoming my full-time hapless sidekick. On the 29th of December he left to take the train to Bangkok, where he planned to see in the new year, before completely abandoning his bicycle and embarking on a backpacking trip around the golden islands of southern Thailand. I really thought he'd have been better off cycling around northern Thailand with me, but the impressionable young man had seen the fun Leonardo DiCaprio had in *The Beach*, and he'd made up his mind.

My own journey resumed a day later as I finally rolled my bike south out of Nong Khai. Aside from the thirty kilometres across the border, I'd done nothing since I'd arrived into Vientiane with Dea two weeks earlier. This quite welcome rest was the longest break I'd had from cycling in a year and a half. But far from feeling revitalised as I pedalled out of town, all I had in me was sadness and loneliness. Cycling presents one with time to think, and suddenly without the distractions of Facebook or a comical young German man, I missed Dea terribly. I missed Robin too, although in a quite different way. In fact I wondered just how any movie could recover from the loss of the primary love interest *and* the hapless sidekick in such a short period of time. Now it was just me cycling on my own again, looking miserable. Who wants to watch that?

At least Thailand did its very best to cheer me up, providing near perfect bicycle touring conditions. The land was completely flat, which meant that my legs could be eased gently back into their task of propelling me around the world, and there were a great many roads to choose from. There seemed to be little roads going off everywhere, all of them in good condition. I hadn't had such a selection of roads to choose from since Europe, and it was a pleasure to be back meandering through the countryside, navigating by the sun once again.

Along the way I passed small villages of homes, the bottom half of which were concrete and the top half wood. In shaded open spaces beneath them people lounged around out of the sun, on benches or in hammocks, crying out greetings to me as I cycled by. I had been wondering how the children might go about this, because I'd learnt that the common Thai greeting of "Sawadee-caap" (the 'r' being usually silent, thankfully) should be accompanied by the brief coming together of the hands in front of the body as if in prayer. This was a difficult thing for me to do while riding my fully loaded bike, and I was concerned as to whether it would be worse to offend the people by not doing it, or to crash. But it turned out to be a non-issue, for the kids just shouted "Hello" in English, and waved, which was a style of greeting I could return without falling off my bike.

It was also easy to find places to camp in amongst the fields, where little wooden shelters were common and provided a nice spot for me to hang out in the evening. I spent New Year's camping in just such a private location. I had no wish of a repeat of the previous year's trouble in Ukraine, so I hid myself away and went to sleep. It was hard to believe that it had only been twelve months since that difficult night in Chernivtsi. So much had happened in 2014. I wondered what on earth 2015 would have in store for me.

The new year got off to an interesting start when I was riding along and saw a white man doing something that looked a bit like jogging. He stopped and asked me what I was up to, and invited me to come to his house and meet his extended family. He was a Swede named Jonas, and I was a little wary at first because of the number of expats I'd seen in Nong Khai that were either rather odd or rather drunk.

But I soon realised that Jonas was none of these things. Not only was he neither odd nor drunk, he wasn't even an expat. He lived in Sweden with his Thai wife, and they were just here, along with their two young children, to spend a holiday with her side of the family.

There were a lot of people milling about the veranda at the front of the house. Jonas did his best to explain who they all were. "This is the grandma, these two are aunts, but my wife was raised by another grandma so her aunts are really more like sisters, I don't know where my wife is, this is Uncle Tui, these are all cousins, this is the family alcoholic, every family has one, this is the husband of the daughter of the first aunt..." and so on, until finally he conceded that he didn't really know who anyone was and gave up.

The day quickly slipped away in an easy and laid back style that seemed so very typical of Thailand. We all sat around talking and occasionally eating and not worrying about doing too much. With no deadline to meet I had no reason to leave, and I was grateful to accept when Jonas suggested I stay the night. The family properties stretched across three houses and I was led to the farthest one where there was a big garden for my tent. Jonas left me to it and I was still in the middle of pitching the tent when a car pulled into the driveway and the man who actually owned this house (Jonas's wife's father, I think) got out. He had no idea who I was, or what I was doing in his garden, yet he greeted me with a huge smile and seemed very pleased to see me for some reason.

Batong was a very nice man and, although we had no common language, his enthusiasm enabled us to understand each other about a few things as he barbecued us up some rice burgers. At one point he seemed to ask me if I had a girlfriend, so I took out my camera and showed him a picture of Dea. But he showed no interest, and started talking about some sort of ploy to speak English. He then started fiddling with his phone, before showing me a message. It was a selfie image, taken at a gym, of a teenage girl, hand on hip, head tilted to one side. Just as I was asking what Batong meant by this, Jonas returned. "Ah, that's Ploy. She's Batong's daughter, but don't worry, she's only twelve, so you won't have to marry her." Then he thought about how long it had been since he'd last been in Thailand and corrected himself. "No, wait, she must be older now. Fourteen or fifteen. Maybe sixteen. Yeah, you might have to marry her."

Common sense told me that Dea would not approve of me marrying a sixteen-year-old girl, so I followed Jonas back to the first house before Ploy could return. Jonas had just remembered that Batong had remarried and there was a dispute between his new wife and the rest of the family that meant they were avoiding each other. Which made it kind of awkward for me to have just put my tent on the other side of the dispute, but heck, I wasn't part of the family, I didn't know where my loyalties should lie. Besides, if I played it right, I was going to get two dinners here. Back at the first house we found a bit of a party had begun, to continue the ongoing new year celebrations. Most of the family now sat on the floor of the verandah in a big circle, where food was eaten and presents exchanged. Jonas and I sat on a table a little away from the main action, however. He told me that he was still treated as something of an outsider. "Thai people are very united as Thai people," he said, "and it is almost impossible to truly become integrated as a foreigner. I've been coming here for years, married into the family, but I'm still known as 'the falang'. That's just how it is here."

We mused on how this kind of attitude would be considered racist in Europe and elsewhere, and had other such interesting discussions on cultural differences. Yet there was no doubt Thai people were extremely friendly and welcoming, and certainly very open to intercultural relationships.

It had been an entertaining evening but I was tired, and before it got too late I headed back to Batong's house. There was no sign of anyone and the car was gone, so I just climbed into my tent and fell into a deep sleep. I think it must have been a really good sleep because when I was woken by a car pulling up and a man shouting "Chis, Chis!" I found it to be extremely irritating. I fear I was rather grumpy about the whole thing, and even the soft, feminine voice that followed couldn't sooth me. "Hello Chris," came a happy chirp of youthful optimism. I unzipped the tent and peered out through bleary eyes to see Batong and his daughter. "It's cold," she said, smiling, "would you like a blanket?"

"No, just let me sleep," I said bluntly, and zipped up the tent.

Well this was a little rude of me, and I felt very bad about it the next morning when I awoke and saw that the car was gone. I wandered back to the first house to find Jonas. He told me that Batong had gone back to work in Bangkok, but that his wife and daughter would be back soon. I decided to hang around until then. I couldn't apologise to Batong, but I could at least to Ploy. There was, after all, a small chance that Batong had never intended to marry off his youngest daughter to a filthy cyclist that he found in his yard one day, and really did just want me to speak to her so that she could practice her English. I felt like fulfilling this wish was the least I could do for the man, so I waited around for her return.

By midday the car was back, so I walked back over to speak with Ploy. She came out of the house to meet me, saying that there was no need for me to apologise. Her English was perfect. She told me that she attended an English school. There was really no need for her to practice it. Maybe her father was after a falang husband for her after all. Well, she was too young for me, of course, and I considered myself taken, but I thought it couldn't hurt to get to know her a bit. Just for future reference, you see, in case Dea ever came to her senses some day.

"What is it that you study?" I asked.

"Chemistry, Physics, and Maths."

"And what do you want to do when you're older? As a job?"

"President," she said, without missing a beat. She was completely serious. In this moment I realised her ambitions in life might extend beyond marrying a tramp. But she wasn't finished.

"Or a Petroleum Engineer."

"Why a Petroleum Engineer?"

"For the money."

Oh, we were definitely on different paths in life, me and this sixteen-year-old Thai girl. She was also avoiding eye contact and definitely didn't want to talk to me half as much as her father had implied, but I was intrigued by her ambitions and pursued the conversation further.

"And why do you want to be the president?"

"Because I like Barack Obama."

"Oh, you want to be president of the United States? You know that you can't? It's impossible." I thought it best to kill this dream early.

"Yes, I know."

"So would you like to be the, oh, what do you have here, a king. Well, you can't be the king either. How about being the Thailand prime minister?"

"Yes. I want to be the prime minister."

"Great. Why?"

"Because I want to change Thailand."

"And what do you want to change about Thailand?"

"I don't know. I just want to change it."

It seemed as it Ploy's policies needed a little work, but she certainly had time on her side, and there was no questioning her ambition. I think she'll be played by Selena Gomez in my movie. Speaking of which, wouldn't Ryan Gosling marrying the future prime minister of Thailand be a great plot twist? It would be so unexpected. The problem, as ever, was that this was just real life, and in real life people don't marry the future prime minister of Thailand. Well, they do, I suppose, but I don't. So I just said goodbye and good luck to Ploy, thank you to Jonas, and then I got back on my bike and I left.

Beneath big blue skies I cycled on through a mixed landscape. There was cultivated farmland, rubber tree plantations, waterlogged paddy fields, and areas of natural woodland. I continued to follow the small roads, where the little traffic there was passed me at a sensible speed without beeping their horns. People everywhere were friendly without being obtrusive. It was perfect cycle touring really. Yet my mood remained sombre. I felt an emptiness inside me. I began to feel that, in continuing to stubbornly pursue my dream, I was losing out on a chance of something special with Dea. It was that old chestnut again. The trip, or the girl? In some moments I considered just getting on a plane and flying to Denmark. But deep down I knew that would be a mistake. Of course it would be fantastic to see Dea again, to hold her in my arms, but beyond the initial euphoria what would happen? What exactly would I do with myself in Denmark? My ambition to travel around the world using only my bicycle and boats would be over. The whole trip, everything I'd worked at for a year and a half, would be ruined. Then Dea, whose mysterious attraction to me I could only really attribute to her having mistaken me for a daring and intrepid adventurer, would have this illusion shattered by me sitting around playing Tetris, mumbling, "I don't know what I want to do with my life any more."

No, no. It was better to keep going. Better to keep the dream alive. She had, after all, said that she might come and join me again in America or somewhere once her studies were over and her thesis was written. It was only a year or two to wait. But it felt like such an infinitely long time.

One afternoon I reached a main road, and, unsure of where to go next, I decided to cycle along it for a bit. Almost immediately I saw a petrol station with a sign advertising that it had free wifi. Perhaps this was Fate stepping in again. I cycled across the forecourt and asked the attendants if I could use the wifi, and the two lovely women pulled me up a chair. Dea was online, so we started to chat and before I knew what was happening it was getting dark. I asked if it would be alright to camp on the grass at the back of the petrol station and without hesitation was told that I could. It was one of the best camping places yet, what with the free wifi and a toilet block just a short walk away. The owners, a youngish couple with a baby daughter, even invited me to sit and eat dinner with them and the attendants. We sat outside under the lights of the building, on the white walls of which geckos darted about gobbling up flies. The table was filled up with a wide variety of food. It all looked and smelt delicious. My lips salivated, and I was invited to help myself. But then I explained that I was a vegetarian and in an instant almost all of the food became off-limits. Instead, a plate of chopped up bread was handed to me, along with a small bowl of mysterious green goo. It's not always easy being a vegetarian.

After dinner everyone else went back to work, and I went back to my conversation with Dea.

"I've just eaten some green goo for dinner, what about you?"

"It's eleven o'clock in the morning."

"Oh."

"Chris, I miss you. It's so hard being apart."

"I know. But this is just the way it has to be. You have to study. You have to write your thesis."

"Yes."

"This *is* the way it has to be, isn't it?"

"Well. Yes. But... maybe there is a chance I could come to Australia to write my thesis."

"What? Really?"

"I'd have to get it checked with my advisor. But, in theory I can write it anywhere."

"Oh my, what a great idea. Come to Australia, Dea. We'll get a place to live together. It'll be amazing. I'm going to stop somewhere to work anyway, and..."

"I can write my thesis at the same time."

"Oh, yes, it's such a great idea."

"Yes, yes, it is. And then, well, then I'll be done studying, and I can just continue cycling with you."

"Really? You really want to do that?"

"Yes, yes. I loved cycling in Laos. I want to live that way. With you."

"Dea. We'll be together in just a few months."

"Yes, I can't believe it."

I looked around at the empty petrol station, the night sky above me, crickets chirping in the bushes. I was tingling with excitement. Maybe, just maybe, I could still have it all.

40

Lao border
12th January 2015

Knowing that I was going to see Dea again in Australia I could now relax and just concentrate on enjoying the rest of my time in Southeast Asia. It was, after all, one of the best regions of the world for cycle touring. And thanks to the way the countries contorted around one another, all fitting together like jigsaw pieces, I was soon crossing once again into Laos. Thailand had been good to me and I was sorry to leave it behind, but that was alright; I'd have to pass through it again before I reached my goal of Singapore.

As I collected my new thirty-day visa and cycled into Laos for the second time I couldn't help but think back on what had happened the first time I'd done so, and I wondered if it was too much to hope that I might see a beautiful blonde girl on a bicycle waiting for me just across the border again. Such miraculous lightning bolts rarely strike twice, it's true, but somebody must have been at least partly listening to my prayers because I did immediately meet such a girl just over the border. Unfortunately, however, the exact terms of my wishes must have got lost in translation because this blonde girl was going the other way, and what was more she was accompanied by a man that appeared to be her partner. And in any case, she was, through no fault of her own, not Dea Jacobsen.

The girl's name was Elena and along with her partner, David, she had been cycling around Southeast Asia for a while. We stopped for a little chat, as is customary in cycle touring etiquette, before continuing our separate ways. They raved about Laos, but at first I was a little disappointed by it. In contrast to when I'd cycled with Dea there were no cheerful waves or shouts of "Sabadee" from the locals along the main road here. I had two theories as to why this might be. Either the people in the south of Laos were much less friendly than they were in the north, or, perhaps more likely, on my earlier visit all of the waves and shouts of "Sabadee" had actually been directed entirely towards Dea.

That all changed, though, when I turned south on a dirt track that Elena and David had suggested to me. It ran alongside the Mekong through little villages of wooden shacks. Chickens and puppies ran around in the dust, and children played everywhere, filling my world once again with smiles and laughter and sabadees. It was a blessed relief to rediscover the real Laos.

But I didn't go far. It was getting late, so as soon as I could I found myself a wild camping place. It was in an area of mixed scrubland, where trees and bushes mingled with patches of flat, dry grass. It was sheltered and hidden – a fine spot – so I put up my tent and called it a night.

I was awoken by the sound of gunshots, a startling thing when you're alone in a tent in the pitch black. In the movie Ryan Gosling will no doubt reach for his 9mm and go out to investigate. In real life I pulled my sleeping bag up a bit tighter. That's something I think Hollywood's leading men don't do enough of – ignore the problem and hope it will go away. As my luck would have it, on this occasion the problem didn't go away, it shone a torch on my tent. Then I heard a great many animated voices approaching. My Lao wasn't quite up to understanding exactly what they were saying, but I imagined they must be talking excitedly about having found a falang prisoner, and were suggesting to me that I go quietly

I unzipped my tent and looked out to see approximately ten men carrying hunting rifles. They were shining their torches in my face and exclaiming loudly, I believe, that yes, they had found a good one here. I suppose I should include words like 'terrifying' and 'petrified' to describe this situation, in the interests of making it a good story, but to be honest with you I just felt a bit miffed about having been woken up. The man who could speak the best English was thrust to the front and he greeted me in a friendly enough manner.

"Hello. My name is Sok."

"Hello sock, what do you want?"

"You cannot sleep here. Danger!"

"Why? Are you going to shoot me?"

"No. Dangerous here. Animals."

"What animals?"

"Snakes!"

Personally I thought it would be difficult for snakes to attack me inside my sealed tent, but Sok was adamant that it was too dangerous to sleep here, and that I should go back to his village with him instead. On the snake front I had to disagree with him, and I rarely do take snake-awareness advise seriously from a man who walks around in the dark in his sandals, but in terms of potentially being shot by one of the hunters, from whom emanated a considerable whiff of alcohol, I had to admit I was not in a strong position. I really did not feel like packing up my tent, but there was something about ten men with hunting rifles that I found oddly persuasive, so I agreed.

I began to pack up my things rather grumpily. I do get quite irritated being woken up in the middle of the night. I checked the time. It was 19:45. Well, I go to bed quite early. I took down the tent, under the watchful eyes of all of the men, loaded up my bike, then marched back to the village with my armed escort. Along the way I began to feel a bit better. Sok had said that there was a house for me to sleep in. Although people in Laos were ever so friendly, I had not yet been invited to actually stay with anyone, so I thought this was perhaps going to turn into a nice opportunity to spend the evening with his family and see inside a traditional Lao home. *Yes, yes, this could be really great,*' I thought. Then we arrived at the village, where I was directed to an empty wooden hut with a raised platform, and told to put my tent up on that. It seemed like I wasn't going to get to see life in a Lao family home, then. Of course I also had an audience for the exciting show that was the reassembling of my tent. Once it was up I indicated that I was going to go back to sleep, and the men nodded and waved goodbye before trundling back off into the night. "Thank you. Good night," I called out after them. "Watch out for snakes."

The next day I continued south along the western bank of the Mekong, following what was nothing more than a narrow, dusty track. To my left I had the wide blue river, to my right an almost continuous line of wooden houses built on stilts. Underneath most of these homes sat whole families who watched me as I passed. More smiles, more waves. The atmosphere was so pleasant that it was impossible to do anything other than fall even more in love with this country. The only problem was where to sleep. There were houses and people just about everywhere, and even if I did find somewhere private there was now the added risk of bands of drunk snake-hunters to consider. But then I remembered that Elena and David had told me that it was sometimes possible to sleep at the Buddhist temples that sporadically appeared along the way. By chance I happened to be thinking this as I passed a temple, and at the exact same moment an old monk called out and beckoned for me to stop. Dressed in his orange robe, he was outside of the gates smoking a cigarette, scratching his bald head, and looking for all the world like someone standing outside on a work break.

"Where are you going?" he asked me.

"Four Thousand Islands."

"Oh, it is too far. You won't make it tonight. You must sleep here, and go there tomorrow."

Son Pot, for that was the monk's name, threw away his cigarette stub and welcomed me into the grounds. I thought I would be camping somewhere on the grass beside the temple, but instead I was shown to a small ornate building next to the accommodation hall. Son Pot lit another cigarette as he welcomed me inside. It was a guest house for visitors, with two beds, an en-suite bathroom, even a TV set. And for one night it was all mine, free of charge.

I moved my bags inside and then went out to find my chain-smoking monk host. He was back at the gates, fresh cigarette in his mouth. About sixty years of age, Son Pot told me he was head of the wat, the other monks being very young. I tried to ask him more about it, but his English wasn't very good. I think he said the youngsters would come for a short time to live as monks before returning to their families. Possibly for two months, although the fact that months sounds like monks left us both confused.

Two men in front of us were busy welding the front gate back on. "We have to keep the buffalo out," explained Son Pot. Then a very loud bell chimed and I asked Son Pot what it was for.

"Because it is time to pray. At six a.m. and six p.m. the bell rings so all the people know that it is the time for us monks to pray."

"Oh. Okay. Are you going to pray now then?" I asked.

"No," he said. "Not in the evenings. I am busy." He pointed at the two men who were doing all the work.

"Oh. So, what about the other monks. Are they going to pray now?"

"No."

I wasn't sure that Son Pot was a very good monk, but he was a very nice one, and that was the most important thing in my book. He didn't seem to like talking as much as he liked smoking though, so I wandered away across the track to stand alone and look out over the Mekong. The air was still and filled with the empty freshness that comes at dusk. There was not a cloud in the sky, and the first stars were beginning to shine through. Behind me in the fading light was the impressive Buddhist temple and in front was the great river. It occurred to me again how very, very far I'd travelled, and how very, very nice this place was. In that moment I felt completely at peace, and in love with my life on the road.

I was woken in the morning by the very loud dinging of a bell. I got up and peered through the blinds. Outside I could see a young boy monk smacking that big bell just as hard as he could. As soon as he stopped, the praying started, and I listened to the melancholic, almost therapeutic sound of the monks all chanting in unison. It lasted for approximately twenty seconds. I guess Son Pot didn't want to overdo it. Then I think all of the monks went out to the village to collect alms, before returning to eat their breakfast in the dining hall. But I'm not sure, I wasn't invited.

A little later I got up and found Son Pot. Seeing that I was preparing to leave he did the traditional monk thing and asked me if I could add him on Facebook. Then he wanted a photo with me, so we posed together. The monk that took our picture was younger than Son Pot, but older than all of the other monks, maybe in his twenties. I took him to be Son Pot's protégé. This assumption was based at least partly on the fact that he too had a cigarette dangling from his lips, and he made an odd sight indeed with his orange robes hanging loosely off one shoulder, holding the camera up with one hand, iPhone in the other. Times were changing. I wondered if he had the meditation app.

On I went along the lovely Mekong track, until I arrived at the area known as Si Phan Don, or Four Thousand Islands. Here the river widened and split, and flowed on around several large islands and countless (although somebody had apparently taken a good guess) small ones. I took little wooden ferries between some of the larger islands, which were inhabited and each covered several square kilometres. These islands were amazing to cycle on. My favourite was called Don Som. There were no roads and no cars, only sandy tracks that weaved between little villages, where the atmosphere was, against all odds, even more relaxed than it had been on the mainland. People smiled, waved, and made me feel welcome in their little corner of paradise. At private beaches I relaxed, and cooled off in the river, swimming amongst the little green islands.

I took another rickety wooden ferry and arrived on the island of Don Det, which was a bit of a culture shock, to say the least. Suddenly I was on a street lined with signs for boat rides and bus tours and happy shakes and kayak rentals and internet cafés and guest houses and white people, horrible, horrible white people were everywhere. I had stumbled upon a backpacker hangout. Hundreds of them were here, and I wondered why. This was not Laos. The few local people didn't say hello to me, they even made me pay for water, and it was clear I was nothing but money to them. I couldn't say that this was really their fault, it was just the way Don Det must have changed to accommodate its sudden tourist industry. I imagined it was once just like Don Som, but the differences now were startling. There was a sandy track circling Don Det, just like Don Som, but this one had a constant line of tourists riding bikes along it. Did they really not know that they could take a two minute ferry ride and then actually cycle in Laos, instead of this strange-fake-tourist-world? I guessed not. Lonely Planet says 'take a boat to Don Det, rent a bicycle and explore the island' and that is just exactly what they must do.

These brief forays into the backpacker world happened every so often throughout Southeast Asia, and I liked them because they reminded me why I loved travelling by bicycle. I wasn't simply going from one tourist location to another, whizzing by the country on a bus or a plane, as most of these backpackers were. I was seeing everything along the way. I travelled so slowly that the journey became so much more than the destination. And the bicycle was such a wonderful means of bringing me into contact with real people in real places. It broke down barriers. Local people everywhere were interested and impressed by what I was doing, and responded in kind by giving me a glimpse into their world. For me this was the only way I could imagine travelling now.

Leaving Four Thousand Islands behind I headed east over the Bolaven Plateau and dipped into what was my fortieth country, Vietnam, for a few days. This was largely with the intention of getting another country ticked off, but I found the roads so dangerous that I didn't want to risk staying any longer than I had to anyway. Ironic, then, that almost nobody in Vietnam used cars. Far from being the peaceful, car-free utopia I'd always dreamed of finding, however, the fact that ninety-eight percent of people were whizzing about on motorcycles, forty-nine percent of them going the wrong way, was truly terrifying. Redeeming features included the people, who were unanimously friendly, and the street food, which was uniformly delicious. There was, in fact, only one moment of real drama during my brief time in Vietnam. It happened when I miraculously found a quieter side road and was free to cycle in peace for a while. Here I passed by three teenagers loitering at the roadside, who seemed to laugh at me as I cycled by. A few minutes later a motorcycle overtook me, the three young hoodlums on it. I was nervous, as there was nobody else about, and became extremely worried when the bike pulled over just ahead of me. The boys all climbed off, looking threatening. One of them approached confidently to block my path. He appeared drunk and was reaching for something in his pocket. I prepared for the worst, and it soon arrived. "Photo?" he asked. "Can we have photo with you?"

After three days I left Vietnam and entered Cambodia. This was one of the poorest countries that I'd been to, and the daily struggle for the people living in the little wooden homes along the way was obvious. One day I stopped and ordered a fruit shake from a restaurant that looked like it was about to fall down, and a young Cambodian asked if he could join me. His name was Monno and he was in his early twenties. He looked smartly dressed in a blue shirt, and he spoke good English, which meant we could talk a little more in depth about his country, but what he had to say was not so pleasing.

He told me about the widespread corruption within the country, about how Vietnam owned everything ("Even Angkor Wat, our national treasure, is owned by a Vietnamese company now") and how regular Cambodians suffered as a result of all this. Monno was one of the lucky ones, lucky to be educated, having received a scholarship through some international program. But in his field of IT there was no money to be made. He told me that in IT he could make only eighty or a hundred dollars (although he did add, "But I'm not that good at IT"). So instead he worked buying and selling furniture, where he could make three or four hundred dollars. These figures, by the way, were not per day or per week, but per month. Hearing that, I was struck by my own considerable good fortune in life, and by how amazing it was that the people of Cambodia, living in a corrupt country under the influence of powerful neighbours, devoid of the financial opportunities we Westerners so often take for granted, maintained such a positive outward appearance. I felt guilty, almost ashamed. Monno smiled, and refused my offer to pay for his juice.

It seemed to me that the people who had the least in the world were also the most friendly, kind-hearted, and generous. And to my eyes there was just as much joy and happiness in the lives of those with a little as there was in those with a lot. Money and possessions, as I'd long suspected, were not the key to happiness. I saw that in the world around me, but I also felt it mirrored in my own existence. I had spent the last few years living on a shoestring budget, sleeping rough, and having very few personal possessions, yet I was as happy as I'd ever been. And finding happiness and strength of spirit in the people of Cambodia, a nation with such a horrific recent history, confirmed that it could be found anywhere. On one occasion, as I was taking a rest overlooking a lake, watching the sunset over its palm-fringed edges, I was approached by an old man. He walked with a limp, his frail body hunched over a walking stick, and I was surprised when he spoke to me in good English. "It's beautiful here, isn't it?" he said, before asking me about my travels. He spoke in a kind, gentle way. Given his age there was no doubt he must have lived through the civil war, perhaps fought in it, and the horrific genocide that followed. He most probably lost loved ones, likely saw suffering and hopelessness on a scale I couldn't imagine. Yet he spoke to me so kindly, with such loving eyes.

As he wished me well and moved on, I was left pondering how it was that such unspeakable evil could happen in a world so overflowing with good people.

41

I visited the magnificent Angkor Wat and marvelled at one of the very great wonders of the world. The staggering array of temples were constructed at the height of the Khmer Empire way back in the twelfth century. As Europe languished in the midst of the Dark Ages, on the other side of the world King Suryavarman II was making use of an excess of slave labour to construct what remains to this day one of the world's most impressive architectural grandeurs, an enduring testament to the size of one man's ego. As I walked through the temples I was almost carried back to the time when it would have been full of people, by the fact that it was indeed full of people. Foreigners were everywhere, snapping photographs and posing for selfies. What a shame all our tourist dollars were going to Vietnam.

I left Cambodia behind and returned once more to Thailand, finding company in the form of another European cycle tourist. This one was a man named Yannis, who hailed from Luxembourg (something the local people we spoke to very much struggled to come to terms with). I initially hoped he might be a good candidate for my hapless sidekick, with his bike being, and I don't say this lightly, even more chaotic in appearance than mine. All manner of items clung erratically to the back of it – a helmet, clothes, various plastic bags, a camera case. Yannis himself was a tall man of about my age, with longish hair tied back under a bandana, and a face hidden behind spectacles and the bushy beard typical of long-distance cyclists. He was great company for a few days, but sadly wasn't as well suited to becoming my hapless sidekick as I'd first hoped. The trouble was he was far too competent a cyclist, and he kept riding on effortlessly ahead of me on the shoulder of the highway. This shouldn't have come as a surprise – I'd yet to meet a cycle tourist as slow as me – and yet in the fairytale world of my imagination I couldn't condone anything other than a hapless sidekick who lagged behind me. It seemed very much to be in the definition of the role.

If I couldn't count Yannis as my hapless sidekick, I could at least soon count him as a friend, as we built up a good natured rapport over the next couple of days. It was a shame then, that our planned routes differed beyond Bangkok, and our ride into that city would be the last of our days cycling together. Having cycled into some of the world's least bicycle-friendly cities, I knew that I needed a plan for entering Bangkok, a sprawling metropolis infamous for its heavy traffic, and, as ever, I had one. When I'd cycled into Mexico City a few years earlier, I'd had detailed maps that allowed me to use small roads, a plan that worked very well. Then in Istanbul, I'd cleverly gone north of the city and followed the Bosphorus in, thus completely avoiding all the traffic. These previous plans had been very successful, which may have led to some slight complacency on my part because this time I'd not really done my homework, and my plan was to... ahem... follow Yannis.

But following Yannis turned out to be a very good plan indeed (even if I do say so myself) because he had an iPhone, and a good map, and he'd been to Bangkok before, and he knew what he was doing. As he directed us heroically through the city streets I began to feel a little like a hapless sidekick myself, which isn't something a leading man should have to put up with, but it did at least save me from having to think. And cycling into Bangkok actually turned out to be quite alright, because we took a busy main road, and for most of the day the traffic was so steadfastly gridlocked that nothing bigger than us was actually moving.

Yannis led us to a very touristy part of Bangkok around Khao San

Road. Weaving through the traffic all day was sufficiently time-con-suming that it was late afternoon by the time we arrived, and almost all of the guest houses were fully booked. This was a little frustrating for two tired and sweaty cyclists, but I made the best of it by volun-teering to watch the bikes, taking a seat and enjoying a mango shake, which gave Yannis the chance to run around and find us a place to spend the night. And it also gave me a first opportunity to study the curious characters around me. All kinds of weird and wonderful people from all over the world were here in tourist town. I may have allowed myself to become a little too distracted, however, as the man who'd sold me the mango shake started laughing and pointing at a stray dog that had its leg cocked over one of Yannis's rear panniers. Before I could react it was too late; the dog had marked its territory, and there was a puddle forming beneath the bag. The mango man laughed heartily. I joined in with him. "It's not my bike!" I guffawed.

Yannis eventually found us a place to stay, and, once showered and spruced up, we regrouped and headed for Khao San Road. This fam-ous tourist street was a world all of its own, with all kinds of restaur-ants and bars with ladyboy servers trying to tempt us in, and hawkers everywhere selling bracelets and hats and fried scorpions. We found a bar and took a seat and watched this kaleidoscope of personalities. There were your typical backpackers, with their colourful baggy trousers and their dreadlocks, then there were your white-haired, old holidaymakers, and then there were the cross-breeds – white-haired, dreadlocked, old, baggy-trouser-wearers. There were muscle-bound lads in gym vests brushing past Sikh men in turbans, and girls in hot pants rubbing shoulders with burka-clad Muslims. Everyone was here. Every kind of everyone. It was as if the whole world had been crowded together on one single street like an extraordinary Where's Wally picture.

Yannis and I were just staring at everything, amazed by what we were seeing, when by chance two nineteen-year-old Norwegian girls came and sat in the chairs next to us. I was not one to let an oppor-tunity like that pass by. And relax, relax, I wasn't hoping to cheat on Dea. I'd just noticed a chance to make up for letting a dog piss on

Yannis's possessions, by chatting to the girl next to me so that he, single and recently clean-shaven, should be free to chat to the other. I'm nice like that.

Well, I won't go into exactly everything that was said in the moments that followed, but I'll tell you one thing for damn sure – if you happen to be a thirty-year-old man and you want to be reminded of how old you're getting, just spend a few minutes talking with a nineteen-year-old girl. I think Yannis and I both quickly came to understand this. The girls were on a three month around the world trip, the kind of thing I would have loved to have done at their age if I'd had the money or the guts to do it. Take nothing away from them, they were clearly having a good time, but they had only arrived in Bangkok a few days earlier, and they were soon leaving, their entire experience of Thailand being based around Khao San Road, which, I think most Thais would agree, was not a fair reflection of their country. Yannis and myself soon exchanged enough eye-rolling glances to agree that these girls were, as we put it later, too 'immature' for us. Or to put things another way, the girls had got matching tattoos the previous night, or more specifically at five o'clock that morning. They laughed as they pointed down at their feet to show them off. On one of each of their big toes was tattooed an animal shape that looked a bit like a pregnant giraffe.

"CAMEL TOE!" they both screamed, giggling hysterically.

Beyond Bangkok I continued alone once more, my sights now firmly set on Singapore and the end of the road, the end of the great Eurasian landmass that I had been traversing for a year and a half. It was tantalisingly close now, and my thoughts were turning to the next great challenge – finding myself a boat to Australia. The first hint that I was getting close came with reaching the open ocean for the first time since Europe. During my struggles in Mongolia and China, about as far from the sea as it's possible to get, I had fantasised about reaching the beaches of Southeast Asia. They had been a beacon of hope in my imagination, a dream I fantasised about often. Now I had finally made it, and the palm-fringed beaches of Thailand proved more beautiful than I'd ever dared believe possible. The fine, white sand was warm between my feet, the sea salty and cool and a welcome break from the heat of the day. Limestone karst cliffs rose out of the water, monkeys leaping from them just for the fun of it. I'd reached paradise. I mean, there were cliff-diving monkeys, for goodness sake. I rode along with a big grin on my face, on cycle paths that ran right alongside the beach. I was on the home stretch.

I took a boat out to the island of Koh Lipe, where I once again crossed the tourist trail. This no doubt once beautiful tropical island was now almost entirely covered with hotels and restaurants, its beaches lined with boats two or three deep for tourist excursions. I'd come this way on the recommendation of Yannis, who'd visited several years earlier, presumably before the tourism had grown quite so overwhelming. But he was right to advise me to come for the snorkelling. I'd never really snorkelled before, and it was a magical experience to swim with all of the myriad tropical fish that called this place home. There were black and yellow stripey fish, and fish that were bright turquoise, fish that were half black and half white, pink fish and purple fish. I also saw a sea snake and lots of starfish. All the while I swam around amazed, saying "Wow, look at you!" which came out very muffled through my snorkel.

Another ferry took me south into Malaysia, where the heat was almost unbearable. I escaped it by immediately heading to an empty beach for a swim. As I bathed another couple arrived for a dip. The man was wearing a pair of board shorts, the woman went in completely covered up by a full length burkini and headdress. Buddhism was out, Islam was back in.

As in every other Muslim country, the people of Malaysia were friendly and kind to me. My interactions with them came mostly when I stopped to eat at little restaurants, where the food, a mixture of Chinese and Indian influences, was cheap and delicious, if a little too spicy for my liking. But I was totally focused on my goal of Singapore now, and Malaysia passed by quickly. My lingering memories would be of the palm oil plantations that I camped in each night, the highway that I followed relentlessly, and the modern shopping malls that I occasionally hid in for the free wifi and the phenomenal air conditioning.

As I put in 100-120 kilometre days, turning the pedals mechanically and drawing ever closer to Singapore, I reflected back on my journey. I felt like I had seen so much, met so many people, it was almost impossible to believe I'd actually done it all. I thought back to when I'd crossed the Bosphorus in Turkey, leaving my home continent behind, with all of Asia ahead of me. It was difficult then to comprehend making it here. I'd had to take it one day at a time, and now that enough days had passed I was approaching my goal feeling like a different person. Asia had tested me in ways I could not have envisaged. I'd turned thirty, come to terms with my own mortality in the face of death, I'd seen poverty and inequality, witnessed the daily struggle of millions, and the joy and courage with which people face the world. I'd met Muslims and Buddhists and Christians and atheists, and all had treated me with the same level of respect and kindness. Whether in yurts or apartments, I'd been invited in to share a tea or a beer, or a glass of fermented horse milk. At times it had also been incredibly difficult, with the challenges of travelling on chaotic streets and overcoming the hardships of being all alone in a foreign land providing constant battles. But I had come through it all. I had survived. I had made it.

Well I had made it to the causeway that tethers the island of Singapore to the Malaysian mainland. There remained the small matter of whether a country renowned for its strict cleanliness would be kind enough to allow the filthy mess I'd become to enter its territory. I was particularly concerned about the appearance of my panniers, which were by now so covered in grime as to be on the verge of sprouting legs and walking off. And then there was also the matter of Singapore's rules and regulations. I was trying to get into a country that dishes out thousand dollar fines for littering, where chewing gum is illegal. What other strict laws might stand in my way? Would my bald tyres be illegal? What about my beard? I was getting myself all worked up by the time I approached the Singapore customs official. '*Oh no!*' I suddenly remembered I had half a pack of chewing gum lying at the bottom of one of my panniers.

The neatly uniformed officer was very, very old. He surveyed my bicycle carefully through his aged eyes, as I pulled up next to him. "I'm getting new bags in Singapore," I blurted out before he had a chance to speak, as if the fact that these ghastly old ones would soon be in the trash somehow justified bringing them into the country. "And I'm getting new tyres too," I added, trying to conjure up an image in the man's mind of me as the clean and respectful member of society I soon intended to become. He smiled and asked me where I'd cycled from, then looked impressed when I told him. Other than that he said nothing, besides suggesting I get some glucosamine for my knees, and, with no suspicion having been raised regarding my inadvertent chewing gum smuggling, I was allowed in.

I'd made it. Singapore, at last. The city-state that marked the very end of Eurasia. The end of the road. Standing at a sign that marked 'The southernmost point of continental Asia' I felt a surge of joy and relief. It wasn't actually the southernmost point of continental Asia, there was clearly a bit of land further south than the sign, but it was close enough for me.

"Well done bicycle, well done."

"Well done yourself."

"We make a good team really, don't we?"

"We do, we do, but I'm afraid to have to tell you that I don't work on water."

"Oh yes, that's right."

It was time for us to find a boat.

Progress Report
Singapore, March 2015

1. Circumnavigate the planet

The Eiffel Tower: 2.3° E. Singapore: 103.8° E.
101.5° out of 360° around the planet.
(28.2% of the way around.)

2. Do so using only my bicycle and boats

Mori: 90.3° E. Singapore: 103.8° E.
13.5° out of 360° around the planet.
(3.75% of the way around. Balls.)

3. Pass through antipodal points

Only moved 3.75% since you last asked. So no, not yet.

4. Visit all of the inhabited continents

Two out of six still.

5. Cycle at least 100,000 kilometres

39,956 kilometres completed. 60,044 to go.

6. Cycle in 100 countries

Cycled in forty-three. Fifty-seven left.

7. Return with more money than I start with

About £500 left of the almost £6,000 I had before.

PART FOUR

SINGAPORE TO SYDNEY

42

Singapore
25th March 2015

Were this adventure truly as romantic as it should be, my quest for a boat to Australia would have taken me immediately down to the marinas and yacht clubs, where I would have busied myself saying, "Ahoy there," to as many people as possible, making acquaintances and connections that would eventually have led me to find a salty old sea dog willing to have me along on his sail boat. But this, of course, is the digital age, and so I put all that on hold for a while, and first busied myself setting up profiles and posting adverts online via websites such as findacrew.net and crew-bay.com, social networks designed to match sailing vessels with crew. As if understanding the importance of this task, my laptop chose this moment to decide that it absolutely would not connect to the internet any more under any circumstances. Fortunately for me, a man named Andy was standing by to lend me the use of his Mac. Andy was a friendly Scotsman who'd taken me in, a touring cyclist himself who had ridden all over the world. He'd settled now in Singapore, and as a reader of my blog was keen not only to host me, but also help me as much as possible to find a boat.

Initially I enjoyed no success online, as there seemed to be no boats at all heading from anywhere in Southeast Asia to Oz looking for crew. Looking at it geographically, I thought my best bet for a lift would be from Bali in Indonesia, to Darwin, Australia, and I did find one captain whose advert said that he was sailing the other way, from Darwin to Bali. I wrote to him on the off-chance that he might have filled in his departure point and destination the wrong way around. Not that I would really trust a captain who got his departure point and destination confused, especially as his username was Captain Grog, but I thought it a good idea to try for a bit of networking. His reply was swift. No, he hadn't got his ports wrong, and he thought I'd struggle to find a lift at this time of year because the trade winds were blowing up from Australia (news that came as something of a knock to my spirits), but he still thought that going to Bali and asking around at the marina down there would be about my best hope.

So I needed to work out how to get myself from Singapore to Bali, and Andy stepped in to tell me about a local man who could help. "His name is SK. He knows everything."

We headed to the Tree In Lodge hostel, which SK was the joint-owner of. He wasn't in, but we found him next door eating lunch at the local hawker centre. These food establishments were popular all over Singapore, and consisted of a canteen-style dining hall surrounded by small food stalls. A great many locals would convene here to eat, perhaps all choosing food from different hawkers and then carrying their trays of food to meet at one of the plastic tables. The food on offer was a combination of the influences that have shaped Singapore, primarily Chinese and Indian. The people, an intriguing racial blend mostly descended from immigrants of those two countries, sat and ate in a fashion more ordered than I had seen for a long time.

As promised, SK was an extraordinary mine of information. He had himself cycled across Asia, from Europe to Singapore, about a decade before me. Now he ran his bicycle-friendly hostel and was keen to try and help me. He showed me an Indonesian ferry timetable, and explained that I could get most of the way to Bali using these boats to hop between the islands to save time. I was slightly concerned about the reputation Indonesian ferries had of being overloaded with people, as well as being noisy, smelly, generally unpleasant, and quite likely to sink. But at least I had a plan now, of sorts – take horrible ferries to Bali, and look for a sailing boat that probably wasn't there.

I first needed to wait for my Indonesian visa to be granted, and so I settled in and spent some more time in Singapore. Andy showed me around, taking me to Chinatown, a place which appeared to have very little in common with the China that I remembered. Little India was a similar story. Far from being the noisy and chaotic places that the names suggested, both were peaceful and orderly. They fitted in very well with the rest of Singapore – a clean, modern, pleasant city that bore little resemblance to the Asia I'd been travelling through for so long.

I liked the architecture. Many of the skyscrapers had modern, bold designs. I was back in the developed world again, and I found something comforting in that. But there was also something rather difficult about it – escalators. Everywhere that we walked there were escalators. The first time that we encountered one was when Andy tried to lead me down to a bakery where we could eat free samples of expensive Japanese bread.

"I'm sorry Andy, but I can't use escalators. Are there some stairs?"

Andy looked understandably confused, and asked me what the hell I was talking about.

"I'm trying to go around the world using only my bicycle and boats. If I take that, then I'll have gone around the world using my bicycle, boats, and that escalator for a few metres."

"What?"

"I'm sorry, I can't"

"There's free bread down there."

But Andy was a good natured man, and took it in his stride, and we went off to look for some stairs. There weren't any, so we took the elevator, which I explained was just about okay because it only moved me vertically, and therefore did not contribute to my progress around the world. This led to some extensive further questions from Andy.

"What about roller coasters? Can you go on them?"

"No."

"What about treadmills."

"As long as I keep running they are probably okay."

"What about roller skates?"

"No, I don't think so."

"Skateboards?"

"No."

"Skis? Oh, you can't go skiing anyway."

"No, I'd have to walk back up the mountain every time."

"What about revolving dance floors?"

"What? No, definitely not."

"What about escalators on boats? Does the fact that you are on a boat counteract the movement of the escalator?"

"They don't have escalators on boats."

After four days of this questioning I decided I'd stayed long enough with Andy, and moved to stay with some new hosts, James and Greta. The day that I moved happened to be the day of Lee Kuan Yew's funeral, and James, Greta, Andy and myself all went together to watch the procession as his coffin was transported across the city. Lee Kuan Yew, by the way, was the founding father of Singapore, the country's first prime minister, a title he held for thirty-one years, and the man responsible for turning a small, marshy, poverty-stricken island into a global economic power.

I had arrived in Singapore a few days after his death, during a week of national mourning. It was a historical moment. His body had been held in state for a week, with people queuing for seven or eight hours to file past and catch a last glimpse of him. Now it was the time for the final procession of his coffin through Singapore's streets.

Perhaps appropriately it poured with rain, and it was a crowd of umbrellas that lined the streets to say farewell to a man that had shaped the entire history of the independent nation of Singapore. From what I understood, people had mixed feelings about Lee Kuan Yew. His leadership had carried Singapore, a tiny island nation with no natural resources, from obscure poverty all the way to the international stage, its people from rags to riches in a few generations. Yet he did so while holding an iron grip on power, imprisoning political opponents, controlling the media, and outlawing free speech.

The procession appeared suddenly and the coffin whizzed past.

Andy guessed it was travelling fast in order to avoid any potential trouble. The government, it seemed, remained paranoid about civil unrest, even with power having already passed to Lee Kuan Yew's son over a decade earlier. But I wondered why the people would rise up against the government, when life here seemed so good. I also wondered how they could. A few days after the death of Singapore's founding father, a video was posted online by a teenage Singaporean, entitled, 'Lee Kuan Yew is finally dead!' In the video the boy, unable, of course, to remember life before Lee Kuan Yew, launched into a foul-mouthed tirade against the deceased leader and his policies. As a result the sixteen-year-old was arrested and put on trial, and was facing a potential prison sentence if convicted.

James and Greta were wonderful hosts to me in their apartment, which also functioned as the base for their production company, Cloudy South. Young and recently married, they were both charismatic personalities, bursting constantly with the energy and enthusiasm that made each of them successful television presenters. They showed me some of their work and I was greatly impressed by a television series they had produced together called *Cook, Eat, China*. To make the show they had spent two years travelling China sampling the cuisine. James was presenting, and I was surprised to learn it was his first time doing so, because he was very good at it.

As well as being a natural in front of the camera, it seemed James was also a dab hand with computers, if the array of production equipment that filled half the apartment was anything to go by. Upon hearing of my own computer woes, he seemed to think that my laptop was not beyond saving, and suggested replacing my outdated Linux system with Windows might get things up and running again. So, on my first evening with my new hosts, James and I sat down and got to work doing just that.

Well, James got to work doing just that. I mostly just sat down. Occasionally phrases like, "Why is that not compatible with a NIFF file?" or "How do we reboot the J-drive?" would float my way, but not knowing my NIFF file from my J-drive I chose to assume these questions were rhetorical in nature. I generally just responded with mumbled grunts that, were they to have been extrapolated into words, would have come out as, "I don't know."

It looked like the process was a tad more difficult than James had first thought, and the hours dragged on. I assured him that he didn't need to trouble himself so much and that he was quite welcome to go to bed, but he responded with a cheerful, "No, I like a project like this. We've got the cycling on. I'm quite happy."

And we did have the cycling on. Eurosport was showing a field of cyclists battling through the windswept Belgian countryside. It was quite an exciting race. That ended, and another cycling race came on, this one in Spain. It wasn't quite as good. After that came a third contest, although by that point I was too tired to note where it was taking place or what was happening. Through all of this James continued his patient task, uploading, downloading, installing, uninstalling. I stayed up, feeling the least I could do was offer moral support. The third cycling race drew to a close, to be replaced by some Ironman Triathlon highlights, that I struggled to watch through drooping eyelids. Then that too concluded, and suddenly we were back to watching a field of cyclists battling through the windswept Belgian countryside. "Ooh, that's a bad sign," laughed James cheerfully. It was four o'clock in the morning. "Nearly there though. We just need to install some drivers now."

His determination was truly admirable, but his use of the word 'we' was quite mistaken. What he should have said was that 'he' needed to install some drivers. What I needed to do now, without any doubt, was sleep.

When I awoke a few hours later I saw that James had finally retired to bed, and I was alone in the living room. I flipped open my laptop to find that Windows had been successfully installed, the wifi was connected, and everything worked perfectly again. It was fantastic, and I decided that I really had to repay James somehow for his extraordinary efforts. Not being particularly talented in any field beyond riding a bicycle very slowly for extended periods of time, it was initially difficult for me to think of a way to do so. But an idea came to me when Greta later returned from a bike ride complaining of a bent rear derailleur that had a habit of getting stuck in the spokes. I stepped in and said I'd fix it up for her, perhaps with an air of confidence that suggested I was more skilled in the art of bike maintenance than I really was. But at least I had the sense to wait until my hosts had left the apartment before I set to work, primarily because I didn't want them to see that my attempt to return the favour for James's all-night-marathon of clever computer reprogramming would mostly involve me smashing Greta's bike very hard with a wrench.

Computer fixed and rear derailleur bent back into shape (sort of), I returned to my own concerns, but there was little in the way of positive news. I was reading things online like, 'So many people down here in Bali looking for a boat. They all give up and fly after a month,' and, 'I was just in East Timor. Lots of people looking for a boat. Didn't meet anyone who found one though.' All of which I found rather deflating. I was beginning to lose faith in the sail boat idea. I had to concede that, even if I was lucky enough to find a craft of some kind down in Bali that was setting sail for Australia, there was still the very strong possibility that they either a) wouldn't be looking for crew, or b) would not particularly want a deckhand with no sailing experience and a rather awkwardly shaped piece of excess luggage. Having said that, I wasn't completely inexperienced; in 2012 I had hitched a lift with a Canadian man upon his small sail boat from Cuba to Jamaica. The only trouble was it could hardly be noted on my resume as *sailing* experience, what with my time during the turbulent twenty-four hour journey being evenly divided between throwing up over the side and lying down below deck wishing I might die.

I suppose it might have been the resurfacing of the memory of that traumatising little escapade that had me refocusing my boat search towards something a little bigger. I also had experience here, for towards the end of my first trip I had returned to Europe from Miami aboard a cruise ship. It had been a few months after my Caribbean mishap, and I must admit that of the two experiences I did prefer the cruise. I mean, there were dancing girls, and a swimming pool, and the only time I felt sick was when I spent too much time at the all-you-can-eat buffet. It had also been surprisingly affordable, and I thought it would now be worth checking to see if there were any cruises heading from Indonesia or Singapore to Australia.

I found a website that listed cruise ship itineraries and went through them one-by-one. It seemed as if my luck was going to be out as there was nothing at all that worked. Then, finally, I stumbled upon something. The twelve day 'Treasure of Asia' from Singapore to Fremantle, departing May 25th. *'Wait a minute,'* I thought, *'Fremantle is in Australia, and I'm in Singapore. This is my boat!'*

I excitedly fired off some e-mails to travel agents that sold tickets for this cruise, asking if I could take my bike onboard, and if it would be possible to book a twin room and then add a second passenger at a later date. It wasn't long before I got a reply into my inbox. I clicked on it expectantly.

'Sorry, but this cruise is sold out.'

'No, no, no, no, no! Why didn't I do all this sooner? Why didn't I book this cruise months ago? Why did I wait until my boat was sold out before realising that it was my boat?'

I was in fits of despair. The cruise idea, which would have worked perfectly if I'd been a bit more organised, was now a dead end. I was going to have to head for Bali and take my chances. It felt like my hopes of making it around the world by bike and boat were once again hanging by a thread, because I knew I wasn't going to find a sail boat in Bali.

But then another e-mail arrived in my inbox. It was from a woman named Sally, another travel agent, but it might as well have been from an angel.

'Hi Chris. Yes we do still have some interior rooms available on this cruise. You can take your bike on board as long as it is boxed. And yes, you can add another person to the room later on. All I need from you is your name and passport number to secure a booking.'

"Yahoo!!!" I had my boat! "Yahoo!!!"

I hastily sent Sally the required information and she requested payment. It was 900 pounds, although that would drop to 450 pounds if I could find someone to share the room with. For passage to Australia

I thought it a very reasonable price to pay, and I had high hopes of recouping most of it at the twelve-day-long, twenty-four-hour, all-you-can-eat buffet. With a bit of luck I thought I might even turn a profit. The only problem was I'd spent almost all of my money by now, and I didn't have 900 pounds. I pulled out my wallet anyway, to see what I could find in there.

"Well hello, Mr Credit Card. How would you like to go on a cruise?"

43

Singapore
5th April 2015

My cruise to Australia was booked, but with it not sailing until the 25th of May I had an empty seven weeks that needed to be filled. I began by trying to find someone to accompany me on the ship, and with the subletting out of half my cabin being worth 450 pounds this was an important undertaking. My first thought was of inviting Dea, but there were two problems with that. The first was that she was busy completing a semester of English studies in Istanbul, which was, despite Turkey appearing an unusual place to go to learn English, nevertheless an important thing to be doing, and didn't allow time for going on cruises on the other side of the world. The second problem was that if I invited her in a romantic sense I would probably not be able to get away with asking for the 450 pounds.

So I thought about who else I might be able to invite, and the only person I imagined would be confident enough of making their money back at the buffet would be a fellow cyclist. Then I remembered Tom, the strange Belgian fellow I'd met in Kyrgyzstan who stayed up all night watching South Park. I recalled him telling me that he too wanted to get to Australia without flying, and after a good rummage through my stuff I managed to turn up a piece of paper with his e-mail address on. I also seemed to remember he'd laughed off the idea of taking a cruise ship at the time, saying that for him it simply had to be a sail boat. As I typed my e-mail to him I thought about explaining that I'd found a sail boat willing to take the both of us. A very large sail boat, with a swimming pool, and twelve restaurants, and for some reason no sails. But I thought better of it, and called a cruise a cruise. His response was fast, surprising, and, well, quite good:

'Yeah yeah yeah, yes man
count me in all the f*cking way
Waaaaw this is amazing news
money is no problem
And yeah count me in
woehoew
alright
cee ya'

I put him down as a maybe.

With it not having taken very long to sort that out I still had seven weeks to fill, so I headed over to Indonesia for a bike ride. I opted against the long ferry rides down to Bali, however, and instead hopped over to the much closer island of Sumatra to explore there for a few weeks.

Indonesia came as a bit of a culture shock. In reaching the developed nation of Singapore I thought I had made it to the end of Asia, I thought I had put all of the chaos behind me. But in going to Indonesia I placed myself right back in the thick of all the wonderful madness once again. The main road was so dangerous, with big trucks blasting their air horns as they passed, and motorcycles whizzing everywhere, that I soon tried my luck on the back roads instead. This was difficult because, although I'd got myself three maps of Sumatra, they struggled to reach a consensus as to which roads existed or where they went. The smaller roads were also pot-holed and sandy and bad, but were still a delight to cycle on. I felt like I was in the wilds of Indonesia, really off the beaten track, exploring places where so few foreigners ever went. Some of the adults cried out happy greetings to me, but the children mostly just stopped and stared at the apparition before them. I wondered if I were perhaps the first white person many of them had ever seen. It was a real adventure. It was fun. At one point I stopped to buy a mango smoothie from a road-side stall, where I spoke for a while with a friendly man named Rico and his two daughters. While I was deep in conversation another man paid for my drink and walked off before I knew what was happening.

I felt so uplifted by all of this that I decided that I wasn't going to hide away and wild camp, but instead try to keep the adventure going. So in the early evening I stopped next to a skullcap-wearing man and asked him if he wouldn't mind me putting my tent up next to his property. He agreed, and as I'd anticipated, my arrival soon caused quite a stir. Within minutes I was surrounded by people, most of them children. Almost all of these children, interestingly and indeed terrifyingly enough, arrived riding their own motorcycles.

As the smiling and laughing crowd around me grew to include the entire neighbourhood, a woman stepped forward who could speak a bit of English. The funny thing about this woman was that she responded to anything I said to her, no matter what it was, with a startled look of abject horror. Still, she managed to translate a few things, and told me that there was a restaurant a hundred metres away where I could get dinner. I thought that the excited mass of people would follow me to it as I walked off in the dark, but strangely no one did.

I sat and ate alone in the little shack of a restaurant and thought about the magnificent day that I'd had. Yet I also felt suddenly a bit sad. The surroundings of both the restaurant and the country itself was all quite reminiscent of Laos, and as I sat eating my rice and eggs I thought about how much nicer it would be if Dea were sitting oppos-ite me. We could share a laugh about all the attention, talk of how nice it was here, how great the people were. I wondered what she was doing at that moment. I missed her.

The next day I was forced to rejoin the main highway at a town called Bagan Batu. It was a sweltering day and I was getting all hot and bothered by the crazy traffic again, so it was a relief when some teenage girls came up to me, squealing with excitement, to invite me to take a seat with them in the shade. It should be noted that the reason that the girls were so keen to meet me almost certainly had more to do with them wanting to practice their English than anything else, and as for me, I was really only in it for the shade. The girl with the best English was a sixteen-year-old called Putri. We sat and had drinks from what I think was her mother's stall. Putri's brother was also there, as well as two other girls who, unlike Putri, had their young Muslim heads covered. One of these girls howled with laughter at everything that was said, unless I addressed her directly, at which point she became terribly shy. The final girl was the funniest. She was called Yesi, and she found particular amusement in pulling my arm hair and saying things like, "Why are you not black, sir? Why are you not black black?" which was one of those jokes where you probably had to be there. But the atmosphere was once again filled with joy and laughter and happiness. The people of Sumatra, I'd by now decided, were simply awesome.

The youngsters invited me to come and visit their English school, so I followed behind their motorcycles, which involved a worrying amount of going the wrong way down a dual carriageway, until we arrived at the Harvard English Course. The school director, Mr Daniel, was not around, but upon hearing of the arrival of a real life native English speaker one of the teachers ushered me before her students for a bit of Q&A. The kids were young but their English was good. They asked me the usual questions, then I was whisked off to the next class, and then the next. Once all of the children in all of the classes knew how many brothers and sisters I had, I was allowed to return to the front of the school, where I found Mr Daniel. He was a very kind, gentle man, with a soft voice. He thanked me for coming with such genuine gratitude that I felt I wanted to do more for him, so I offered to stick around for a week or two in Bagan Batu and volunteer at the school.

It seemed that the Harvard English Course didn't get many foreign visitors, but those that it did get had their photographs pinned to a noticeboard at the front of the school. In fact there were only three photos, that being the number of foreigners to have visited during the school's fifteen year history. One of them was an older man with white hair and a white beard, who stood proudly next to a much younger Mr Daniel in the photo.

"That's Mr George, he is a cyclist too. He was here about seven years ago. Such a nice man. But when he left I tried to call him several times and he didn't answer. I never heard from him again." Mr Daniel looked sad. "I often worry about him. Whether something bad happened. I really do worry. He was from England too. Maybe you can find him for me?"

"Oh, Mr Daniel, I don't know. There are fifty million people in England. Do you know anything else about him?"

"He is a great man."

"Anything else? What about his surname? George must be his first name, do you know his second?"

"I'm not sure. Maybe Smith."

It wasn't much to go on, but I was determined to help this nice man, so I left the school and set about doing some serious detective work. My serious detective work consisted of a three-point plan. First, I posted a copy of George's photo on a cycling forum online, second, I wrote a message along the lines of 'anyone know this man?' and third, I went to bed.

By the time I awoke in the morning the mystery had been solved, and by a quirk of fate it was the man I'd left behind in Singapore who had provided the answer. Andy had seen my message and somehow recognised George's face from another blog he'd read, by someone who had cycled with the man in Thailand back in 2008. From that others had come up with his surname (it wasn't Smith, but it was close), and I put the final piece in the jigsaw by typing the name into Facebook. I wrote him a message and looked through a few of his photos, and there he was, the man Mr Daniel spoke so highly of, middle finger raised to the camera and a snarl on his face. Perhaps, I thought, it would be a good idea for the deeply religious Christian Mr Daniel to not see that. I clicked on to see what else I could find, and came across a profile picture with some writing on: 'I am against all religions because they...' Okay, I guess I had to make sure Mr Daniel didn't see this.

I marched triumphantly back to the school and gave Mr Daniel the good news; the guy that he had worried about for the last seven years was doing just fine after all. I showed him some carefully selected photos I'd saved of George and even set up a short chat between them. All of which made Mr Daniel very happy. "How long was he here for?" I asked.

"He stayed for one night," replied Mr Daniel. "He is such a great man."

This really made me think about the people that I, and others who cycle tour, meet along the way. What for us might seem like a fairly trivial meeting, another stop on the road, a single night in some town somewhere, might be something that the other person remembered forever. Seven years of worrying about a man who stayed for one night; it was crazy, but it was true.

"He is such a great man," Mr Daniel repeated for the tenth time. "And he is a Christian too. He stood in front of us and said a prayer for all of us."

I bit my tongue. *'That cheeky old bugger.'* But Mr Daniel had clearly elevated him to the level of some sort of saint, even after just a night. What was going to happen if I stayed here for a couple of weeks and kept performing these kind of miracles? I watched as Mr Daniel typed another message to send to Mr George: 'Mr Christ is here at the school with us now.'

I thought it might be time for a shave.

I made myself at home in Bagan Batu. I was staying on a mattress in a cheap hotel for three pounds fifty a night. Each morning I'd wake up, go for breakfast at the café next door, then wander the 200 metres to school. There, Mr Daniel would put me in front of a class and say something like, "Mr Chris is going to teach you about past participles today." Then I'd have to admit that I didn't have the foggiest what a past participle was, and I'd have to sit down with the students while Mr Daniel taught us. After school I'd pose for approximately one hundred photographs with children and teachers alike, then wander back to my hotel. The days passed and it started to become a routine. I was building a life.

Another reason I'd decided to stay was to give Tom time to catch up to me. He was somewhere in Malaysia doing a ten day meditation retreat in complete silence. As he was not allowed any contact with the outside world during this period he was proving difficult to keep in touch with, but in our last communication he'd mentioned taking a boat from Malaysia to Indonesia to come cycle with me ahead of the cruise, and I thought it polite to wait for him. I wasn't sure what to expect of Tom. We'd only spent a few days together at the guest house in Bishkek over a year earlier. From what I could remember he had dreadlocks, watched South Park, and farted an awful lot. Actually, I was starting to wonder if he wouldn't be a bit out of place on a cruise.

I'd been in Bagan Batu for almost two weeks when I heard that Tom was done silently meditating and was on his way to join me. It was good news. Life was plodding along and needed something to shake it up a bit, and Tom was certainly about to do that.

It was just a normal afternoon at the Harvard English Course when Tom, or Mr Tom as he was about to become known, arrived. I first caught sight of him across the street and called him over to the front gates of the school. He advanced towards me pushing his bike, a smile on his pale face upon which were two sunken, dark eyes. He wore a filthy grey striped shirt that looked like it was fifty percent cotton and fifty percent sweat, and his dreadlocks flailed out in all directions from beneath a similarly filthy cap. He made for an extraordinary sight, a sort of homeless hippy on a bike, and there was quite a smell wafting along with him too, which could only fairly be described as intoxicating.

Tom squeezed his bike in through the gate. It was absolutely over-flowing with stuff. There was even a guitar strapped to the back of it, in amongst a chaotic, heaving mass of bags and bottles, bananas and baby heads. Yes, I said baby heads. Decapitated dolls, tied to the back of a touring bike. The look on the face of poor Mr Daniel, stepping out of the school proudly in his clean white shirt, was a picture. It was a mixture of shock, apprehension, and, I think, fear, as he stepped forward to nervously shake Tom's hand. Young children milled around, equally unsure of what to make of this bizarre sight.

To be fair to him, Tom did quickly volunteer to go and take a wash, which gave all of us not only a break from the hardy smell, but also a chance to regroup. "He's not exactly my friend, Mr Daniel. I only met him once before, actually," I rushed to clarify, but the glazed look on the headmaster's face indicated that he might be hard to reach for a moment or two.

Fortunately for everyone, Tom emerged from the bathroom a changed man. The smell was gone and he was wearing a clean(ish) shirt. He had even tied his dreadlocks back in a ponytail. I did notice that this tying back of his hair had revealed a skull and crossbones tattoo behind his left ear, but other than that he now looked much less scary to children, which was a plus given our location. Mr Daniel, composure restored, took Tom on a tour of the classrooms for questions from the students.

The next day Tom and I walked to a nearby café for breakfast and on the way I asked him what team the football shirt he was wearing represented.

"I don't know, man," he laughed, and then, looking down at the badge, he read, "Cha-ya-bou-ri. I don't know who they are. I found it at the side of the road. I find all my clothes, man."

I considered this very resourceful of Tom, and decided to chalk it up as a point in his favour as the interview process began over our fried noodle breakfast. The interview, of course, was for the position of my luckless assistant.

"I'm looking for a hapless sidekick, Tom. I think you could be right for the role."

"Yeah, yeah, yeah man! Exactly! I want to be your sidekick. You do all the planning. I don't want to do any of that. I'll just follow. Yeah, hapless sidekick. I like that."

This was the easiest sidekick recruitment yet. He was positively enthusiastic about taking on a subordinate position, and we had weeks of cycling together, followed by a cruise, to look forward to. It seemed like nothing could go wrong now.

"Oh, by the way," he added, in a matter-of-fact manner as he took a long drag on his cigarette, "I'm an alcoholic."

This was, I decided, not something that should be counted against a candidate that had shown such enthusiasm, and could perhaps even be thought of as a positive attribute in the realm of haplessness. Besides, Tom went on to clarify that he wasn't really an alcoholic, but that he just had alcoholic tendencies. He could apparently go weeks or months without drinking, but that once he started, once he had one drink, it tended to lead to a binge that would go on for several days. I made a mental note to keep him away from booze as much as possible.

After breakfast we went into a supermarket for supplies. Tom, showing less resourcefulness now, bought nothing other than a big bag of instant coffee powder. He'd already put away two cups over breakfast. "I drink a lot of coffee, man," he explained, the whites of his eyes glistening. "I used to do a lot of amphetamines, but now I just drink coffee. It's the closest I get to the buzz."

I was getting a little worried now, but decided to concentrate on the positives. For one thing, Tom was very good with the local people. On our way back to the school one of the motorbike-taxi men said hello to us in a way designed to entice us into taking a lift. Had I been on my own I would have said, "No thanks," and hurried on my way, but Tom burst into life, and after an animated greeting involving hand shaking, back slapping, and much laughter all round, the two of them ended up sitting down to eat a second breakfast and share a smoke together.

Once we got back to the school Tom and I sat down at a computer to fill in his cruise details and so that he could transfer the 450 pounds to me. This was it. This was the last chance to back out of the whole arrangement. Once this was done, Tom and I would be locked in together for good. As sidekicks and room-mates go, Tom had said and done a few things that I could put in the 'cause for concern' category, and there were certainly one or two doubts from my perspective. But on balance I reckoned he was a nice, friendly guy, and a very laid-back, easy-going one who, despite tendencies toward alcoholism and farting, would at least guarantee entertainment. We made our arrangements official.

44

Two weeks after first arriving in Bagan Batu it was time for me to move on. Tom and I said goodbye to Mr Daniel, his family, the teachers, and the students, boldly stating that we were off to ride our bikes to Lake Toba, 300 kilometres to the north, and then on a further 200 kilometres to the city of Medan, from where we could take a ferry back to Singapore. It was a long and arduous sounding journey that drew us admiring glances as we waved goodbye. Then after 0.5 kilometres of cycling, most of which had been in the wrong direction, Tom said we really must stop and get something to eat.

After that false start, and with my new companion suitably filled up with fried rice and caffeine, we finally did escape from Bagan Batu, and headed north on the main road. Hopes of having found my hapless sidekick were immediately dented, however, as the much heavier bike of Tom disappeared ahead into the distance. *'Curses. The man volunteers to be my hapless sidekick and I still can't keep up with him.'* I decided that when I did catch him I would explain that I was *letting* him go ahead, as some sort of reconnaissance mission. But when the moment arrived I was too distracted by the amusing sight of him holding up a pair of khaki shorts that he'd found at the side of the road with great glee, until he turned them around and saw a big rip through the back that had him sighing and throwing them down again.

The road was busy and dangerous, so I suggested we turn off and try our luck on the back roads. Tom wasn't as bothered by the traffic as I was and didn't particularly want to, but luckily he remembered his sidekick role and so had to go along with it. And at first it seemed to be the right decision. The traffic melted away and we were left to cycle in peace on a dusty orange road, cutting through a landscape of palm oil which seemed to stretch on indefinitely in all directions. I'd been seeing palm oil plantations all through Thailand and Malaysia, but Indonesia took it to a whole new level. Almost every available space was taken up by the tropical crop. Tom soon warmed to the detour, particularly when we happened upon a group of four or five men sitting in the shade of one of these trees. There was something about them which must have got Tom's sixth sense in action, for he wanted us to go and sit with them for a while. Tom's sixth sense was obviously very strong, for no sooner had we sat down than one of the men pulled out a little bag and began rolling some 'special' cigarettes, which Tom seemed, perhaps not unsurprisingly, quite happy about.

As they passed the joint I saw once again that Tom was very good with the people. They seemed to find him very entertaining and he played on this attention. His bike, with all its freaky add-ons, was also a big draw. All of which I thought quite nice, not least because it meant I could take a break from being the centre of attention everywhere myself.

We continued, and I was quite content on these nice quiet trails, doing my best not to worry about the fact that we were getting really quite lost. Every so often we would reach a fork in the road and have to make a best guess as to which way to turn. There were occasionally a few people around, but they were of very little use to us in the way of directions, so we just blundered onwards the best we could. At one point we passed a rural school yard, where we were spotted by thirty or forty young children who stampeded towards us. Arriving at the edge of their field, they all came to a skidding halt and stared down upon us. Tom took this as an invitation to turn children's entertainer and pulled up in the muddy road next to them to put on a performance of clapping, waving, cheering, and pulling funny faces. Being in such a poor part of the world, I suspected that this was the first time that many of these youngsters had ever seen a clown perform, and it went down very well. So well, in fact, that when we left many of them abandoned the school grounds completely and followed us down the street, cheering us on. It was lovely.

A similarly uplifting event occurred when we reached a small village and stopped outside of a shop to cook and eat some eggs for lunch. This inevitably meant that we were soon surrounded by the entire population of the village. Tom got out his guitar and played some songs for the crowd, which brought a great deal of happiness and joy to everyone, and it was the slightly odd stranger I was riding with who was spreading this joy through the remote backwaters.

From there we continued to muddle our way along, not being entirely sure we were going the right way, until our saviour arrived to help us. He came in the unlikely form of a very short and completely bare-chested man who called out to us as we struggled up a steep climb. Ali explained to us that he was building a house here, and he owned some of the surrounding palm oil trees. He also told us exactly where it was that we needed to go. Then, perhaps sensing how useful he had been in offering these directions, Ali rather boldly asked if there was anything that we could offer him as a gift in return. I thought about it for a moment, then remembered that I had a Playboy T-shirt that had been given to me as a gift in China. I didn't like to give away a present, but truth be told I didn't wear it that much, mostly because it had a picture of the Playboy bunny on it. It also now had some irremovable marks on it, and it wasn't much of a gift to offer really, but it somehow seemed perfect for this guy, who, after all, had no shirt at all. I pulled it out of my bag and handed it to him, pointing out the Playboy bunny with the expectation that he would love it.

"What is this? It's too big for me," he complained. "I can't wear this."

The shirt was returned to me. Meanwhile, Tom had dug into his handlebar bag and pulled out a Leatherman tool. He handed it to Ali, saying, "I never use this. Maybe it will be of some use to you."

"Wow, this is amazing. Thank you!" Ali loved it.

"No problem, man."

"I will remember this for all time," he gushed. I stuffed the Playboy T-shirt back into my pannier.

The condition of the track Ali told us to follow got worse and worse until it became so narrow that nothing bigger than a bike could get through. Dark clouds formed overhead, and I thought it would be a good idea to stop and make camp, but Tom wanted to continue. A few minutes later the heavens burst and we were faced with a torrential downpour that made cycling any further quite impossible. I came to a stop next to Tom.

"I've got a puncture," he cried out.

"Good luck with that, I'm going to put up my tent."

I ran into the palm trees and rushed around as fast as I could in the pounding rain to get my tent up. The rain was so heavy that there was already a big puddle inside by the time I got the flysheet over the top, but I made it and climbed inside to escape more punishment.

"Tom," I shouted out, "just come in my tent until the rain stops."

"Yeah man, in a minute. I'm taking a shower."

Tom stayed outside in the pouring rain for quite a while longer, in fact, before deciding to accept the invitation. He then climbed in next to me completely drenched. I'd pushed the initial puddle into a corner, but now I had another puddle forming very quickly. Worse than that was the smell. Tom certainly was a bit whiffy for a man who'd just taken a shower. It wasn't the most comfortable hour as we sat there waiting for the rain to stop, me doing my best to discreetly hold my T-shirt over my mouth and nose to avoid gagging.

The rain did eventually cease and I was able to escape out into the fresh air, much more appreciative of it than ever before. I emptied the puddle out of my tent, then found a better location for it. Tom put up his own tent and cooked a delicious dinner for the both of us. He was a good cook, and enjoyed making proper meals on his stove in the evenings. I was grateful to be travelling with such an interesting character. He was a lot of fun with the people and was clearly a good guy, and a useful and resourceful one too. I just wished he owned some soap.

Tom patched up his puncture in the morning and we continued along the track, which had become even more difficult thanks to the heavy rain. We muddled along to a river crossing and found, as Ali had promised, a paved road beyond it. Tom whooped and cheered with joy as our tyres rolled smoothly for the first time in days. We had finally escaped the labyrinth of palm oil plantations that had held us captive. But Tom's joy was short-lived, for there was soon a loud bang and he came to a sudden halt. His tyre had suffered a blowout. We pulled off the road to inspect the damage and found a large rip in the side of the inner tube, suggesting he'd pinched it when he'd replaced it that morning. It was a tough one to fix, but in a stroke of remarkable good fortune we'd reached a village, and there was a motorcycle shop just opposite that could do a professional job of patching it for him.

While he went off to do that I was left to entertain a growing crowd of spectators that had come to see what was going on, although when Tom came back and sat down in his chair (yes, he was carrying a chair with him), to replace the mended tube, all of the attention returned to him. Through the crowd came a woman carrying a young baby. "Photo with my child please, sir?" she asked, passing the youth towards Tom. He reached out his arms to take the baby, who then turned its head and saw him for the first time. I can honestly say I have never seen a look of greater distress on any human being than I saw come over the face of that poor child at that moment, and a blood-curdling wail of terror pierced the air. The mother pulled the baby back and carried it away to its nightmares.

"That happens a lot," Tom sighed, returning to his work.

Unfortunately the tyre was still not holding air, because the tube was also broken around the valve. This was a disaster because it was impossible to patch, and Tom didn't have a spare inner tube with him. He had a chair, a Kyrgyz rug, two doll heads, a guitar, a slinky, and a stuffed panda, but no spare inner tube. Even worse, he had twenty-eight inch wheels and I had twenty-six, so even my spare tubes were of no use. Then Tom noticed that the sidewall of his tyre had also been badly damaged in the blowout. Of course he had no spare tyre either, so his chances of riding onwards were effectively over. Looking for a solution, I cycled back through the village to a house where we had a little earlier been invited to pose for a hundred photos after meeting an English teacher who'd told us we were the first foreigners he'd ever seen here. I now had to enquire as to whether there was anyone about with a pick-up who could give Tom and his bike a lift to the nearest town on the main road. This was something I didn't like doing. Even though it was on behalf of someone else, I still hated to ask help from a motor vehicle. It was as if admitting a weakness in my chosen method of transport, even if the situation could have been easily avoided by Tom being better prepared.

A pick-up was found for Tom, and so I was alone again as I cycled the twenty kilometres to Langapayung. Here I was reunited with with my hapless sidekick, who'd managed to find a new inner tube, but not a new tyre. Instead, the man in the bike shop had jimmied a piece of rubber between the busted tyre and the rim, which Tom seemed happy enough with, even though the tyre bulged out in a precarious manner that had me wincing. I would not have wanted to ride on it, but Tom was not fazed, so we cycled onwards, together once more.

We chose to stick to the main road now, fearing that if we disappeared back into the palm plantations we might not make it out again. The road was flat and very busy with motorcycles, cars, and trucks, but if we thought that being on a more populated road would mean a decrease in the attention we would draw then we were soon proved otherwise. People were constantly shouting out to us, from the side of the road, the window of passing vehicles, or the back of motorcycles. "Hello," they would cry, or, "What is your name?" or "How are you?" But by far the most popular thing to shout was, "Hello mister!" This was quite fun for about the first ten minutes of each day, but started to wear a bit thin after the second or third hundredth time, especially with the busy traffic and the hot sun. Indonesia was the most intense of intense countries, but full marks must go to the one woman who provided some light relief by crying out to me as loud as she could, "Hello misses!"

It was a bit of a relief when the road climbed into the hills and there was less habitation, because it meant fewer people and fewer motorcycles. There were still some people, though, and when Tom saw a group of men sitting drinking a strange pink liquid on a bench near the road his sixth sense kicked in again and we had to go and investigate. It turned out it was a homemade alcohol created from the local palm trees, and we were invited to take a seat and try some. Tom certainly didn't need to be asked twice.

I remembered what he'd told me of his alcoholic tendencies as we each took a sip of the fermented drink. It really didn't taste at all nice, but while I scrunched up my nose and shook my head, Tom took the bottle and poured himself a big glass. I noticed that this alcohol was on sale for passing motorists, either in old 500 millilitre water bottles, or in larger bottles that looked like they once contained motor oil. *Who the hell would want to buy alcohol in an old oil bottle?'* I wondered as I sat around with the local drunks. At least hanging around with Tom was introducing me to a side of the country I might not have otherwise seen. He finished off his glass and then poured himself another one. This was soon followed by another. And then another.

Eventually we said goodbye to the men and cycled on, with Tom going on ahead of me as usual. One kilometre up the road I found him stopped. He was next to another man who was selling the same type of pink alcohol at the roadside. He was busy passing Tom a whole old oil container's worth of it. Oh dear.

We climbed up higher into the hills but there was some light rain and we were both hungry, so we decided to stop and have some dinner in the shelter of a little restaurant. There were three waitresses in the restaurant and once again we had to pose for dozens of photographs. Even once the official photo shoot was over, one of the girls kept on taking photos of me across the table.

"How many photos do you have of me now?" I asked.

"Twenty."

"Do you really need twenty photos of me?"

"I love you!" she stammered.

Dinner was good. So good, in fact, that Tom had three. As well as the girls, some young guys turned up to meet us, and there were some older people around too. It was a fun atmosphere as we all laughed and joked and took photos together. That was probably the reason for Tom to suddenly declare, "You know what? I am going to get my guitar and we are going to have some fun with these guys, and then we are going to sleep right there." He pointed at the floor in the adjoining area of the restaurant, a living quarters of sorts which a half dozen people probably already used for sleeping in.

"Well, we can't really just invite ourselves," I said.

"Sometime it happens," Tom shrugged, and walked off to get his guitar.

Until this point we had been very good at talking things through and making decisions together, but it seemed that with a few drinks in him Tom wanted to call the shots. I didn't particularly want to invite myself to sleep in someone else's home, especially when it was the floor of a noisy restaurant, but I also didn't want to be a spoilsport, so I went along with it for a while.

It was when I saw Tom sneaking his oil can of alcohol into the back of the restaurant that I decided to distance myself from him. He was obviously going to be passing it around with some of the young guys. The trouble was, the people here were Muslim, and there was a disapproving hush from the elders when they saw what Tom was carrying. I wanted nothing to do with it, so after a while I left to camp by myself away from the restaurant.

In the morning I returned and found a groggy Tom busy sewing up a hole in his shorts, and I gained some consolation in hearing he'd had a terrible night. The restaurant was an all-night truck stop and had remained noisy all night long, meaning he'd got almost no sleep at all. He also had one rather unbelievable story to share.

"I was lying down there last night," he began, telling his story with far too much glee, "and my balls were hanging out. I didn't realise until I saw one of the guys staring at my balls. Ha ha. I just need to sew up my shorts, man. Won't be long."

"Don't you wear underwear?" I asked.

"No need, man, no need."

There are many ways that cyclists choose to deal with the problems of aggressive and annoying dogs. Some, like me, shout firmly. Others get off and walk. Some just try to ignore the dog, throw pebbles, splash water, or poke it with a stick. I thought I'd seen it all, but that was until I met Tom. His favoured tactic was to cycle directly towards any dog that he saw, regardless of whether the dog was actually being aggressive or not, and himself begin to bark and growl. Tom's dog impression was very convincing, and he never looked more wild or more like a manic lunatic than when he went into this fevered state, dreadlocks waving, head shaking, mouth yapping. And it always, always, always, succeeded in antagonising the dog further.

And there was an increase in the number of dogs as we climbed over more tough, steep hills and then came down into a valley populated by Christians, the more canine-friendly of the two primary religions of Sumatra. There were suddenly churches absolutely everywhere, and the valley was so broad and green, and the sky was so blue, that I momentarily felt like I was cycling in Switzerland in the summertime.

Tom was particularly pleased to find himself back in a Christian part of the country, not because of the dogs, nor any unexpected religious beliefs, but because, as he put it, "It means you can find alcohol." And so we began a new routine where Tom would go on ahead to find some local drunks to sit and chug some mysterious home brew with. I'd catch up and go straight past, but before too long Tom would whizz by me again, going much too fast for a man with no helmet and a tyre that might explode at any moment. A few minutes later I'd pass him again as he stopped to down another drink.

After a whole afternoon of this, I was ahead and stopped to wait for Tom at the top of a hill, where there was a little shop selling nothing but peanuts. I sat and ate some until my tipsy sidekick arrived, very nearly getting himself run over as he veered across the road to where I was. Right on cue, a man came along with a jerry can full of another home made alcohol. Tom made enquiries and the old fellow poured some into a glass for Tom to sample. The liquid came out with several ants floating in it. Tom merely laughed, showed the man, then downed the drink, ants and all.

"Good protein," he chuckled.

45

Lake Toba, Indonesia
5th May 2015

Looking down upon Lake Toba for the first time was a genuinely breathtaking moment. It made all of the effort of cycling in Indonesia feel worthwhile. The huge crater lake stretched out over an area of hundreds of square kilometres far below us, surrounded on all sides by jagged volcanic cliffs. In the centre of the lake lay Samosir, an island the size of Singapore. It was a monumental lake, a staggering sight. And the ride down to its shores was one of the most memorable I'd ever done. We zig-zagged down the mountainside, with every twist and turn providing more sensational views. It was simply a stunning ride.

We hired a local man to transport us across to Samosir on his boat, with the views of the surrounding peaks reflecting in the blue water as we cut through it. And the great day continued when we got to the island, which had a flat road circling it, and where the people were all friendly and cried out to us. I had been thinking that the mood might be different here because of Lake Toba being quite a tourist hotspot, but the people remained very welcoming. And because there was hardly any traffic Tom and I were able to cycle next to each other and talk, and created a game of seeing who could say hello in the most different accents/languages worthy of a response from the locals. It was a fun game. I even managed to have a short conversation with one woman in French. I don't think she knew that she was speaking

French, but she definitely was.

We arrived in the curious little tourist town of Tuk Tuk, which was surprisingly quiet and lacking in tourists. The signs for jet-skiing and pizza and magic mushrooms indicated that we had indeed arrived in backpacker-land, yet the backpackers themselves were nowhere to be seen. This wasn't necessarily a bad thing, and it seemed like arriving in the off-season meant we got the best prices. We found a guest house that was almost too good to be true. There were balconies and hammocks, and we each got our own room right down by the lake, en-suite with comfortable beds, for the almost unbelievable price of two pounds per night each. Arriving here really felt like paradise. We had planned to only stay one night, then press on up to Medan to take the boat back to Singapore on the 12th of May. There was only one ferry per week, and I didn't want to risk taking the one on the 19th, in case we missed it, leaving us stranded and unable to make the cruise. But this place, this place was just too perfect. The most amazing thing about it was the complete silence. "Tom," I said, "I reckon we can take the boat on the 19th. Let's stay here and relax for a week."

Tom didn't need much persuading. He didn't need any persuading, actually. And it was to be a most lovely and relaxing week. With nobody paying us any attention we were able to just chill and not worry about a thing. It was like taking a holiday from Indonesia. I treated myself to lazy mornings, swam in the lake in the afternoon, and sat by it in the evenings, watching the mist hanging over the mountains across the lake. Lone fishermen could be seen reeling in their nets on their small boats, silhouetted against fiery sunsets.

We took to spending time with a young German backpacker named Johannes, who was one of the few other foreigners around. He was bespectacled and proper, and, like a lot of people, found Tom a bit confusing. We hung out as a three for a few days, and one night towards the end of the week we went to the Bamboo Restaurant, which Tom liked to go to, partly because it played a lot of Bob Marley, but mostly because it was right next door.

So the three of us were sitting in the restaurant a bit awkwardly, with Tom occasionally breaking the silence by farting very loudly, raising one arm in the air, and shouting, "Fart liberation front!" when who should walk in but three, yes three, attractive young backpacker girls. Tom had been frequently mentioning to me his desire to find love, or at least sex, and this seemed like a wonderful opportunity. The girls were from the Netherlands, Tom, himself from the Dutch part of Belgium, confirmed. It really did seem like fate and, wanting to help out Tom and Johannes, I managed to angle us an invite to the girls' table. Unfortunately, Tom and Johannes weren't any better at talking to women than they were at talking to each other, and hopes were further dashed by the girls' irritating tendency to mention their boyfriends at every possible opportunity. So nobody went home with any cute backpackers that night. Apart from the cute backpacker girls, who of course went home with each other. But not like that.

Eventually Tom and I had to tear ourselves away from paradise and steel ourselves for a few more days cycling in Indonesia. We headed north towards Medan, once again in the midst of speeding motorcycles and endless cries of "Hello Mister!" We passed by active volcanoes, and stopped one day to hike up one. Thankfully it wasn't fully erupting at the time, but it made for a spectacular location, with steam escaping from sulphur vents near the summit and incredible views over the Sumatran landscape. But Medan was firmly in our sights. The ferry back to Singapore. The cruise to Australia. It all felt so close, but the dangerous roads threatened to ruin everything on the home stretch. To get to Medan we had to do a very long descent on a mountain road. It was a public holiday, and everyone was leaving the city, so there was a constant line of cars coming up the other way. Many of the drivers grew frustrated and overtook the queue, driving on the wrong side of the road, which, unfortunately for us, meant they would often come head-on towards us. I took my time, watching the road carefully. Tom raced off down the mountain at full speed, bulging tyre threatening to burst at any moment.

Somehow we both survived and reached the congested, polluted city of Medan. After much searching we found a hotel near to the Grand Mosque. It was a grotty excuse for a hotel, with no window in my room and a bed that was more spring than mattress, but it served its purpose. The next day we headed for the ferry. It was a really big boat, with many hundreds of people on board for the twenty-four hour journey to Batam. Because it was an overnight voyage we were each assigned a bed. Naturally Tom and I had elected for the cheapest tickets, and found ourselves in the economy section. This was basic-ally just a huge open room with dozens of plastic mattresses lined up in rows next to one another with no dividers in between. Sharing sleeping quarters with hundreds of Indonesians, it was certainly going to be cosy.

We weaved through the crowds and found our way to the beds assigned to us by our ticket numbers. On the mattress next to mine was an obese woman who was so large that many of her more flabby parts spilled over onto my own mattress. For some reason Tom found this hilarious. "Maybe you'll get lucky tonight," he chuckled. The smile was soon wiped off his face, however, when he tried lying on his own mattress and discovered it was covered in bed bugs. And that's before mentioning the cockroaches, which were coming out from under the beds and crawling all over everything.

This was a discouraging start, but once we got under way the boat journey turned out to be a surprisingly good one. There were out-door decks where we spent most of our time, and Tom certainly seemed to be in his element. We were the only two foreigners on board, which naturally made us celebrities, and he captivated some of the other passengers with his guitar skills. I managed to read a fair chunk of a book Tom lent me about how to pick up girls, I was entranced by a beautiful ocean sunset, the boat didn't sink, and we even found a good place to sleep. The communal bed system wasn't popular with everyone, and lots of people took to the floors looking for more restful places in various nooks and crannies. We followed suit, and had one of the best spots, hiding away in the doorway that our bikes were being kept in. I used my bike as a barrier to protect me from the noise of the rest of the boat and slept very well, and if any cockroaches ran across my face during the night I didn't even notice.

Morning came and we reached our destination of Batam, a small Indonesian island just south of Singapore. Then began an extraordinarily chaotic disembarkation process. Quite literally all of the passengers attempted to get off at the same time down a narrow gangway, while porters ran around between them carrying boxes and other items of cargo upon their heads. It sure was a challenge for me and Tom to get off with our loaded bicycles. When we did eventually manage it we found ourselves in a large hangar where, because it was pounding down with rain, all of the people that had been in such a desperate hurry to get off the ship now stood around waiting.

We popped next door to the international terminal and bought our tickets for the final short ferry to Singapore. Tom then went through an emotional goodbye with his doll heads. I'd told him that they probably wouldn't be well received in clean-cut Singapore, and thankfully he conceded it might not be such a bad idea to throw them away. He slam-dunked them into the bin, and we boarded the boat. Indonesia was over.

It was incredible how an hour on a boat could transport us between such different places. There was such an astonishing contrast between the rough-and-ready Indonesia and the comfortable, clean island of Singapore. I wondered how Tom was going to adjust as he stood in the line for customs with nobody paying him any attention beyond giving him a wide berth and discreetly covering their noses. No longer was Tom going to be the centre of attention, at least not the positive attention he'd got in Indonesia.

I'd arranged to stay with a couchsurfing host for a couple of nights. I would have invited Tom to stay too, but something about the obsessive cleanliness of Singaporeans made me think that bringing him into one of their homes might not be a good idea. Instead I cycled him to the Tree In Lodge hostel and dropped him off, apologised to SK, and then left.

My couchsurfing host was a hard-working young man named Jake. He was a really nice guy, but like a lot of Singaporeans he worked long hours, and so I didn't see him much. But there was also another couple staying with Jake at the same time. They were computer scientists from America who were on their own journey around the world. If I thought that would mean we'd have something in common I was soon proved wrong when I asked how long their trip would last.

"Two weeks in total. First we went to Stockholm, a couple of nights in Rome, a stopover in Dubai, after Singapore we'll go to Bangkok for two days, Tokyo for nine hours, and then home."

"Cool."

During the day I walked around nearby Little India and bought some essential supplies, such as an Mp3 player for the long cycle across the Australian desert that was soon ahead of me, and a spray can of black paint. The paint was used on my bike frame and racks during my last two days in Singapore, when I moved back in with Andy. I had heard that Australian customs were very strict, and wouldn't stand for any dirt or muck on the bike at all, and spray painting over the dirt was easier than trying to clean it off.

I also went through all of my possessions and threw away everything that I didn't need, which filled a great big bin liner. I think I threw away more than I kept. Eventually the bike was clean, my gear was organised, and I was ready for Australia. I was ready for my cruise.

The big day arrived and I woke up on the floor of Andy's apartment, very excited. *'I'm going on a cruise! Oh boy, oh boy! I'm going on a cruise!'*

I understand that it might seem a little confusing that I should get so happy that such a luxurious means of transportation was going to carry me the final step to Australia. It was certainly out of keeping with my vagabond existence of the preceding two years, but that was the point. I was going to live the high life for a change. I was going to have a rest. And, most importantly, I was going to eat. A lot!

I gathered my possessions and cycled to the Tree In Lodge, where I was delighted to find that SK had worked his magic on dear Tom. As Andy had told me, SK was known to practically scrub cyclists clean and even Tom had not been beyond his capabilities. As my cruise companion stood before me again I barely recognised him. He had clean clothes on, he'd shaved his beard into a neat(ish) goatee with a twirly moustache, and appeared very much to have taken a shower. Even his bike and bags had been washed to a level that might satisfy Australian customs. Best of all, his new shirt (admittedly fished out of the hostel's second hand drawer) had narrow red and white horizontal stripes across it, which made him look, most appropriately, like a pirate.

We said thank you and goodbye to Andy and SK, and made our way to the port with cardboard boxes strapped onto our racks. As we got close we saw the hulking great Dawn Princess for the first time and cheered. This was really happening. We stopped and took apart our bikes outside the luggage area, putting them in the boxes and handing them to the bemused porters to take aboard the boat. Then we made our way on foot through the airport-style terminal. This involved a considerable amount of queuing, particularly at passport control, but this gave us the chance to try and adjust to the extreme culture shock that had begun in earnest. For both of us it was the first time in eighteen months that we'd been surrounded by white people. And not just white people, but wealthy white people. Even more incredibly they were all speaking in English, or something a bit like it, except that everything they said sounded like a question? Tom was especially taken aback by the variety of body shapes that were on display.

"Why is everyone so fat?" he asked, rather too loudly, perhaps not realising that, also for the first time in a long time, we ourselves could be understood.

"Tom, they can speak English," I reminded him.

"I know. And why are they all so fat?"

Finally we made it through passport control and were able to board the Dawn Princess. It felt more like walking into a fancy hotel than a boat. There were bright lights, lush carpets, spiral staircases, old people bobbing about everywhere. And there we were, two scallywags, who, despite both our best efforts to get clean, surely looked rather out of place here.

But we'd wasted enough time. "Where's the food?" I asked the nearest member of staff.

"Deck 14," he replied, and we were off running up the stairs. A few moments later and we were by the complimentary buffet, a smorgasbord of delicious-looking Western food before us. We began heaping food onto our plates as fast as we could. Pasta and chips and pizza and vegetables and cheese and salad and beans were piled on, and there was not a scrap of fried rice in sight. This buffet was going to be running non-stop for the next twelve days. It was almost too good to be true.

It was a struggle to find anywhere to sit, with everyone else having had the same idea to head straight for the buffet, but we did eventually find a table. After both eating non-stop for about ten minutes we paused just long enough to look up and see a whole room full of Australians shovelling food into their mouths. Tom gazed around, shook his head, and then, as if the answer wasn't self-evident enough, repeated what was fast becoming a catchphrase.

"Why is everyone so fat?"

46

Malacca Straits
26th May 2015

Our first full day at sea passed quite uneventfully and, so far as I can remember, mostly involved the buffet on Deck 14. We did manage to poke our heads outside at some point though, and notice that we were going in completely the opposite direction from that required to reach Australia. We were in fact passing back north through the Malacca Straits, the exact same stretch of water that we'd just sailed south through on our Indonesian ferry, something that would have come as quite a blow to our spirits had it not been fully detailed within the cruise itinerary. Unlike us, most of the Australians aboard were not simply using this ship as a means to get home, but were keen to visit some places, and so we were to spend the next few days stopping so that they could go ashore to do excursions. Our first stop, silly as it may seem, would be all the way up in Phuket, Thailand, before various ports of call in Malaysia as we headed back south.

It was a rainy morning when we arrived in Phuket, and the location failed to impress me, leaving me feeling surprised that this was one of Thailand's top tourist hotspots. The limestone cliffs were not as dramatic as I'd seen on the west coast of the country, the water not as turquoise as in Koh Lipe. Perhaps I didn't give it enough of a chance, though, for as most of the other passengers took to buses and taxis to take them off on excursions, we settled for a café 200 metres from the ship. It had both beer (for Tom) and wifi (for me), and proved quite enough of an excursion for us. I spent the day researching my route across Australia and talking online with Dea. She had finished her semester in Istanbul and had got permission to complete her final thesis in Australia. It was all confirmed. She would be flying in to meet me in Melbourne in just a few weeks. I was so looking forward to see her again. Tom, by contrast, sat opposite me and put away beer after beer, repeatedly chirping, "Chris, we're in F*ck-it!"

We spent the night sailing south again, returning for a third time to the Malacca Straits. It was only later that I found out that this stretch of water was notorious for piracy, something that must have caused one or two of the oldies on board a moment or two of panic when they turned a corner and bumped into Tom for the first time. But by morning we were docked up safely in port on the Malaysian island of Langkawi. It felt weird for me to be back here, having cycled across this island a few months earlier. Having travelled so slowly overland for such a long time it was an odd feeling to be moving so quickly between places and countries.

We were at least on a different part of the island, one that I hadn't been to before, and it was nicer scenery than I'd seen previously. The numerous small forested islands in the bay looked really picturesque as the sun rose on what was to be a beautiful day. Tom and I disembarked the ship and left on an expedition. We once again ignored the buses and taxis and set off on foot, although this time there was no café close by, and we followed the road for several kilometres through the jungle until we came upon a town. Here Tom had ambitions to purchase a bottle of sparkling wine to drink onboard as a celebration of our upcoming crossing of the equator. I settled for the beach.

I lay on the soft sand and watched paragliders as they flew through the air behind speedboats. The beach was almost empty and from where I was I could see north to the mountains that had been my first sight of Malaysia back in March. I thought again how strange it was to be back here. I was itching to get to Australia.

Tom came and found me, bottle swinging in his hand, and we walked back to the boat together. I wasn't sure how much Tom was enjoying the cruise so far. It wasn't really his scene. I thought about this more as we departed Langkawi that evening. There was a special sunset as we sailed away through the small islands and I had on my Mp3 player. As The Verve's 'Lucky Man' played in my ears I looked at the striking scenery around me and reflected on how very lucky I was, and how privileged to be able to travel in this luxurious way, how fortunate to be able to step away from the poverty and struggle I'd witnessed too much of, and to experience a different world aboard this boat. And I thought of Tom, poor confused Tom, and how I could tell for sure that he'd been so much happier on the floor of that cockroach-infested Indonesian ferry.

Once again we sailed southwards overnight and by morning were approaching a Malaysian island. This time it was a port in Penang that we docked up alongside, the tower blocks of Malaysia's second largest city, George Town, gleaming white as the first rays of another sunny day reflected off them.

Tom had already spent two weeks in Penang during his own bicycle travels through Malaysia, having stopped off to look for a sailing boat to Australia. Of course he hadn't found a sailing boat willing to take him to Australia, but his dreams had eventually come true, and today he would be boarding a boat in Penang that would take him down under. Knowing George Town well, he announced that he would show me around and that he really must also visit the hostel that he'd stayed at in order to tell all his friends there that he had finally found his boat.

The inner city of George Town was a UNESCO world heritage site, probably because of all the old colonial buildings. Whether this protection meant that the building of safe footpaths was prohibited I wasn't sure, but I certainly didn't enjoy walking around in the busy Asian roadways any more than I had for the previous eighteen months. So close to the end of Asia, it would have been a tragedy to get run over now. But we walked through Little India – which I'm sure would have looked a bit more like a little version of India had not ninety percent of the people there been white tourists fresh off a cruise ship – and then down a little side street. Ahead of us was the hostel which Tom had stayed at before, and where he needed to return in triumph to reveal he had his boat. As we approached we saw a guest, dreadlocked and scruffy, sitting outside, with at least a passing resemblance to both Tom and a caricature of a backpacker. Beyond him was the hostel manager, who looked up at us. Tom said hello. The manager looked at him vacantly. A few words were exchanged and Tom walked away.

"He didn't recognise you, did he?" I asked.

"No. Let's go."

The next day we awoke to find ourselves once again having made landfall, although this time it appeared we had stopped in the middle of nowhere. Other than the port building and the long pier that extended to it there was nothing of interest to be seen on the flat land that surrounded it. This was because today our port of call was Kuala Lumpur, the capital city of Malaysia, which, unfortunately for the cruise ship, was not really accessible by water. As a consequence, most of the passengers filed onto waiting buses and zoomed off to see the city fifty kilometres away, while Tom and I, intimidated by the idea of walking that far, opted to spend the day on the boat.

We weren't going to waste the day though, and set about on something of a mission. A couple of nights earlier we had taken part in a darts competition that, through terrible misfortune, neither of us had managed to win. The winner was a man named Paul who was incredibly lucky. He made his winning throw by complete fluke, and I know this for a fact, because he didn't even know what he was aiming for before he threw it. "Well done Paul," announced Josh, the Canadian cruise employee who was in charge of such things. "You scored forty-eight, which leaves you on... Oh, incredible, that was just exactly what you needed. You win! What do you want as a prize? Champagne? What's your room number? I'll have a bottle of champagne sent to it."

Now this final sentence caught us by surprise, particularly Tom, who seemed suddenly to wish he'd spent more of his life practising darts. I'd assumed that the prize, if there was one, would have been a pen or a keyring, or some such silly thing. A bottle of champagne was an incredible reward for a man who clearly had only won by accident. And so it was with this still fresh in our minds that on our Kuala Lumpur morning we scoured the Princess Patter, the leaflet that entered our room each evening with a list of the next day's onboard events, for more competitions to enter. "We've got to enter all of these, Tom," I said. It took us a while to get through breakfast, second breakfast, brunch and first lunch, however, and it was the one p.m. soccer shootout that we arrived at first.

I'm not sure why, perhaps because half of the other passengers were fifty kilometres away, or maybe because the passengers that had remained on board were all too geriatric to make it to the sports court on Deck 15 (the only part of the ship not accessible by elevator) but Tom and I were the only participants in the soccer shootout. This was a fantastic state of affairs that seemed to guarantee us a bottle of bubbly, but we still went through with the formalities of the competition. Tom went first, steering his first six shots easily into the small open goal at the other end of the court, before I meanly resorted to distracting him, causing him to lose concentration and finish with a score of eight out of ten. Showing no mercy I then guided all ten of my kicks between the posts and turned to our referee expectantly. "What do I win?" I asked. "A bottle of champagne?"

"No," she laughed. "You can have a pen or a keyring. What's your room number?"

This disappointment would have been enough to crush the spirits of most men, but we had the solace of a second lunch to console us, and we rallied ourselves for the 3:15 p.m. carpet bowls tournament. Being on Deck 5 and involving much less physical effort, this was a much better attended event with about twelve entrants. Tom and I were the only ones under pensionable age, but what we lacked in carpet bowls experience we certainly made up for in enthusiasm. We were sure that the larger field would guarantee that a bottle of champagne would be on offer for the winner, and our youthful determination was in evidence as we each swept aside our first round opponents.

Tom's victory was particularly enjoyable. None of his first three rolls had been any good, all of them wayward or overthrown, and his skilled opponent had managed to get one of hers touching the jack. So with the last throw of the game Tom predictably resorted to hurling the ball down as hard as he could, spectacularly hitting his intended target, smashing the balls away towards his, and stealing an unlikely victory. I whooped with delight and high-fived him as he returned to his chair. He looked almost apologetic towards the elderly folks around us but I told him not to worry. "It's a legitimate tactic, man. Well done. We've got them riled now."

Josh, who was once again running the competition, attempted to stop our unlikely charge through the field by pitting us against one another in the semi-final. His mistake, of course, was that this only guaranteed us a place in the final, and I guaranteed it would be me by insisting Tom have the first turn. With no chance of smashing me out with the last throw of the game I took the win and the chance to go for the champers.

In the final I was up against an old man who clearly knew what he was doing. Not only was his run to the final peppered with near-perfect bowls, but he also stood firm against me before we even began.

"You go first," he told me.

"No, please, you can go first."

"No, no. You go first. Really."

We both knew that going second was a big advantage, but this game was supposed to be good-natured wasn't it, and there was only so long I could stand there arguing with a pensioner. I relented and took the first roll. It wasn't very good. My opponent came in close to the jack. I misfired again. He got even closer. My third roll was worse than the first two. His came in bang on target. This wasn't going at all well. Tom sat by sweating. Our bottle of booze was slipping from our grasp. This was it. I only had one bowl left to rescue the day. Resisting the temptation to go for Tom's smash and grab technique, I instead concentrated all of my efforts on my pitch and length. It felt good as soon as it left my hand, and I watched as it curled around with a perfect trajectory, knocking into the jack and nudging it away from my competitor's balls and into a winning position for me. It had been a flawless shot. I once again let out a little whoop of delight, so proud of myself as Tom beamed from the sidelines.

But my rattled opponent still had one bowl remaining. He stepped up, clearly flustered at seeing his victory slip from his grasp, yet bold enough to hurl his last ball at great speed down the carpet. It smashed straight into my 'winning' ball and stole my glory away from me.

"Oh, that's not fair!" I protested, before marching back to my seat to apologise to Tom. It would surely take days to get over the disappointment of having been so unbelievably close to winning the bottle of champagne. Over my shoulder I heard Josh congratulating the winner.

"Well done, Graham, great bowls. Now, what do you want as a prize? A pen or a keyring?"

We gave up on the competitions after that, and concentrated on third lunch, snack, dinner, tea, supper, and feast-time, before getting dressed up for the party that was taking place on board that evening. I use the term 'dressed up' with a good deal of artistic licence, of course. I don't think either of us actually changed, but Tom put on a Hawaiian necklace, and we were ready. Tom was particularly ready because he had at some point encountered a girl on the ship who he seemed to have taken quite a shine to. "Her name's Briney," he told me. "Briiiney."

I'd been reading more of the book that he'd lent me all about how to pick up girls, and I thought it might be fun to encourage Tom to use the tactics described therein to try and pick up 'Briney' this evening.

The party took place on the open top deck beside the pool and featured music and dancing and such party-like things. It also featured the sea god Neptune, who doused us with a wet towel in a bizarre ritual to celebrate our upcoming equator crossing. Briney, or Briony as I would later discover to be her actual name, or 'the target' as we now described her, was easy to spot. There were only three other young people at the party. Two of them were attractive females – Briony herself, and Monika, a Polish girl I'd met briefly on the first day of the cruise. Unfortunately, the third was an AMOG. For those of you not familiar with the acronyms used within the book I'm referencing, an AMOG is the Alpha Male Of the Group. And this was the ultimate AMOG. A big guy, tattooed arms bulging out from under his vest top, he danced simultaneously with both girls, cautious of any outside interference. "You're going to have to neutralise the AMOG first," I coached Tom as we watched. "After that make sure you get three IOIs, then attempt to move the target to a secluded location, overcome any LMR, and make a kiss close." I think I might have been spending a bit too much time reading this book. "She's a HB though my friend, a real SHB."

What followed was somewhat pitiful. We made our way onto the dance floor and for the next half an hour Tom made repeated half-hearted attempts to get close to Briony, only for his every move to be blocked by the AMOG, who was unerringly good at moving his elbows while dancing in such a way as to prevent any advances being made upon his girls. Tom obviously hadn't paid enough attention to the book, or to me, because he seemed to have entirely forgotten that the key to success with Briony was to first befriend and neutralise the AMOG, and before very long he gave up and went to bed.

The next day was spent entirely at sea as our ship decided to stop pausing at Malaysian ports and at last head south for Australia. After taking part in another soccer shootout, from which I was able to increase my overall winning haul to a pen *and* a keyring, I was walking back alone when by chance I passed Briony, Monika, and the AMOG sunbathing. Briony said hello and invited me to join them as they were about to go for a swim in the pool. Well, if Tom wasn't going to neutralise the AMOG I guessed I might as well do it for him. And not that Tom wasn't enthralling company, but I also thought it might do me good to spend some time with these other people as well.

I introduced myself to the AMOG, who under normal circumstances went by the name of Rob, and made attempts to befriend him as the four of us jumped in the pool. This was very easy because he was actually a nice guy. A twenty-two-year-old chef from Perth, he told me of his plans to soon head to Europe to work for a Michelin chef there, and was in fact so nice that before long I found my allegiance to Tom wavering. I suggested, as I so often did, that we all go and get something to eat at the buffet.

As we sat enjoying our meal we were interrupted by a voice over the loudspeaker system announcing that we were crossing the equator. I strained my neck to look out of the windows for the long red line I was sure stretched across the ocean, but I saw nothing. Still, I decided to trust that the captain knew where we were, and we went back outside to celebrate, my new friends ordering margaritas to sip by the pool as we cruised on into the southern hemisphere.

After a while Tom came and found the four of us, arriving with the bottle of sparkling wine he had bought in Langkawi grasped in one hand. He placed the bottle down on the table in front of us. Briony smiled at him. Here was his moment. I'd laid the groundwork, got us in with the crowd, befriended the AMOG. I'd done all of the hard work. Now all Tom had to do was come in and show his generosity and kindness to Briony by sharing in the celebration.

"Erm..." he said, pointing at the bottle, seemingly aware that courtesy meant he should offer it around. "I was kind of hoping to drink this myself."

With that beautiful introduction Tom skipped off to the bar to get some glasses. He returned with three; one for himself, one for me, and a third which he placed on the table between Briony, Rob and Monika.

"So, do you want any, or what?" he said to them bluntly.

"No, no. It's okay."

He poured himself and me a glass each and we congratulated one another on having crossed the equator. Unfortunately his dramatic entrance appeared to have reminded the others that they all had somewhere else that they needed to be, and it was soon just the two of us again.

We had another sea day to get through and neither Tom nor I had any great motivation to participate in any more competitions. For Tom it was the realisation that Josh must have given away his whole stock of champagne already, while for me it was the realisation that I didn't own any paper nor any keys, and therefore had no great need for the pen or keyring I'd already secured, and certainly had no requirement to win more. Instead we hung out with Briony and Rob, and the four of us, unable to think of anything better to do, sat on the stairway on Deck 7. Tom brought out his guitar and began to play some songs. As a joke I threw my cap upside down on the carpet in front of him, thinking I might try and make back some of his bar bill. Perhaps because of his failure to capture Briony's heart, perhaps just out of sheer boredom, he'd recently decided that five dollars and fifty cents was a reasonable price for a can of beer, and started putting them away with gusto. It was just a shame that his onboard account was linked to my credit card. Thankfully, it wasn't long before a passing old man threw a few coins into the hat, although the eighty-seven cents he donated didn't quite cover it.

The next morning we woke up back in Indonesian waters. The Dawn Princess had docked in a bay next to the island of Lombok, our final stop before Australia, and we were surrounded by volcanic green mountains. We took a smaller tender boat across the shallow water of the bay to reach land, but as we disembarked from this we found not the happy attention we'd had in Sumatra, but dishonest money changers and children begging for money. Something to be expected, perhaps, when stepping off a cruise ship.

Wandering away from the crowds, we found some semi-trust-worthy people who said they could organise a boat to take us to the nearby small island of Gili Nanggu, where my research told me there would be good snorkelling right off the beach. We would also have an English-speaking guide thrown into the bargain, a friendly young guy named Echo, who we befriended as we waited for the boat to arrive. When it did we saw that it was a tiny outrigger; a narrow wooden boat with long wooden logs on either side, held on by long arching supports. There were lots of these funny-looking boats, skimming around the bay like water boatmen.

The boat took a little under an hour to get to the tiny island of Gili Nanguu, where it pulled up at small jetty surrounded by turquoise water. The sandy beach had quite a few people on it, but it was still a beautiful little corner of paradise. We rented masks and snorkels and returned to the beach, where I was surprised to see Briony emerging from the sea, Rob as ever just behind her. They had also rented a little outrigger, which must have had considerably better timekeeping than ours, for they'd already been here a while and had the time for a snorkel.

As promised, the snorkelling was fantastic. There was a lot of coral right off the beach, and just like in Koh Lipe brightly-coloured fish were everywhere. I once again felt privileged by the opportunity to catch a little glimpse into their underwater world.

Back on the beach I sat with Briony and Rob and we tried to look for Tom, but we couldn't see him. Eventually we realised that he'd swum off half a mile away to a neighbouring island. He really did do some strange things, did dear Tom. By the time he returned Briony and Rob had left. Fresh from his swim, he ran up the beach and immediately went up to a girl in a bikini and started talking to her. This was an impressive implementation of the 'three second rule' from the pick up book. This rule essentially states that you must talk to a girl within three seconds of seeing her, to avoid letting negative thoughts enter your head. I guess it must be a useful tool to get talking to more girls, but of course the trouble with the three second rule, as Tom was about to find out to his cost, was that it doesn't leave any time for looking around the vicinity for boyfriends. "Hello mate," came a voice from behind him.

We hurried to take our little boat back as fast as we could. What I found most strange about Tom approaching that particular girl was not that he had the confidence to do it, which I should say I did find considerably strange, but that he did it at all, considering that both the girl and her boyfriend were also travelling on the Dawn Princess, and we'd seen them together every day.

Once back at the port Echo turned less friendly and started asking for more money than we had originally agreed on, which was bad luck for him because we didn't have any more money than that which we'd originally agreed on. Leaving him looking forlorn, we dodged our way back past poor children, forced by some unseen adults to beg us for money, and onto our tender boat. And that was it. The end of Indonesia. The end of Asia. I said as much to Tom as soon as we got on the boat. "That'll be the last time either of us set foot in Asia for a while."

But it wasn't until a little later on that the fact that Asia was over really hit home. I went up to watch the sunset from the top deck of the cruise ship, a little thing that I did every day, with music playing through my Mp3 player. It was a nice thing to do. There were some great views from up on top, and not many people went up there, so I could have it to myself. It was especially useful to be on my own on this day because as a particularly personal song came on and I looked out at the Indonesian mountains across the bay I was suddenly over-whelmed with emotion, and quite unexpectedly, and for reasons I didn't entirely understand, I began to cry uncontrollably. The tears just came and came. I was blubbering like a baby, and yet I felt neither happy nor sad. It was simply an incredible release of emotion at the fact that Asia was over. It had been so incredibly difficult at times, and I remembered some of those times now. I thought back on the accident that I'd witnessed in Mongolia and the terrible sense of loneliness that followed. I thought back on spending my thirtieth birthday alone in that Chinese hotel, feeling so helpless. I thought about how impossible it seemed to overcome that and cycle across that huge country. How did I ever find the strength to believe I could do that? To reach the end of Asia and set sail for an easier life in Aus-tralia. To reach this moment.

But I had reached this moment.

The sky turned pink, the boat sailed away, and Asia was gone.

Next stop, Australia.

47

Fremantle, Australia
6th June 2015

I woke up early in the pitch-black room. I could hear Tom snoring on the bed opposite mine. I felt excited. Not by Tom, I assure you, but by the fact that the boat was no longer rocking. We had arrived, finally, in Australia. I pulled on some clothes and ran out onto the deck to take a look. There it was at last, the land down under. It looked like a port.

Knowing that I had a very long cycle ahead of me I forced down a couple of breakfasts at the buffet, and then it was time for me and the now wide-awake Tom to depart the Dawn Princess and return to the real world of paying for food.

We walked down the gangway and out to meet a friendly man at passport control. "Welcome to Australia," he said, taking only a cursory glance at my passport before waving me through. It was all so informal that I felt I had to ask him whether the working holiday visa I'd applied for had been activated. His response was to say, "I don't know," peer at his screen, then add, "Looks like you've got some kind of e-visa. Don't worry about it, mate."

That was the easy part over with, but I still had some reservations about making it through customs. We collected our bikes and luggage, and wheeled them over on trolleys. "Are you two travelling together?" asked the woman who greeted us there.

"Sort of," I said, an answer that I hoped was sufficiently ambiguous to avoid me having to do any jail-time on Tom's behalf. It wasn't that I thought Tom stupid enough to deliberately try to smuggle drugs into Australia; I just thought he might be stupid enough to *accidentally* smuggle drugs into Australia. I was sure there were corners and pockets of his bags that held things long forgotten, but in any case it didn't matter, for these customs officials were obviously used to dealing with old cruise ship passengers and probably wouldn't have known what a drug smuggler looked like if it stared them in the face. Which was kind of lucky, because it'd probably look like Tom.

As it turned out, everyone was very friendly and they didn't do more than x-ray our bags and then take a quick glance in the boxes to see if the bikes looked clean. Seeing that my tyres had no dirt on them they said everything was fine. I felt a little put out by how little interest they had in examining my bike more thoroughly. I had, after all, spent two full days scrubbing it clean and repainting it for their benefit. They didn't even bother to dig down and find the chainrings that I'd disassembled, individually cleaned, polished to a shiny finish, then reassembled in four different incorrect ways before finally getting back together in the right order. What a waste of an afternoon.

"Do you have anything else? Camping gear? Anything like that?" the official asked.

"Yes, I have a tent."

"Your tent pegs. Have you cleaned them?"

"Yes! Yes! Would you like to see them?"

"No, it's okay."

And with that we were through, and allowed, at long, long last, to set foot on Australian soil. The Australian soil was covered in tarmac, of course, it being a car park that we set foot on, but still, it was an Australian car park. We got straight to work reassembling our bikes, and no sooner had we begun than we were greeted by a man named Rich. Having read my blog online, Rich had written to me and kindly invited me to stay in his home, conveniently located a couple of kilometres from the port in Fremantle. He'd proffered this invitation some time earlier, before Tom had become a part of the bargain, but he'd been good enough to extend the offer to the both of us (against my own advice, as I recall).

The three of us cycled together through the central streets of Fremantle to Rich's home. This was a truly extraordinary experience. It simply did not look real. It looked like a movie set. There were footpaths everywhere, and they were clean, well-maintained, and devoid of any hawker stalls or badly parked cars. There were bicycle lanes, and vehicles moving at sensible speeds, and pedestrian crossings where traffic actually stopped. There were no motorcycles going the wrong way, no motorcycles at all, in fact. And white people walked everywhere, speaking English. I was stunned by how neat and tidy everything looked. I couldn't work it out. Then it dawned on me – I'd travelled so far east, I'd arrived back in the West.

At Rich's nice home in suburbia he found me a map of Western Australia and helped me to plot the first part of my route. He was such a good guy, it was a shame that I wasn't actually able to take up his offer of a place to stay for the night. Dea was flying into Melbourne in a little over a month's time, and, with that being practically on the other side of the country, I was going to have to get moving. In fact I was going to have to average 120 kilometres per day once again if I was going to be on time to meet with her. It was one last rush to make a deadline, and I couldn't really afford to waste a day. Tom was very happy to do so, however. He returned from an ATM and paid me the 150 pounds he'd somehow managed to spend on beer over the previous week, then announced that he'd seen a lot of freaks in Fremantle, and he'd decided to stay.

I gathered my things and prepared to say goodbye to Tom. It was such a shame that it had to end. As hapless sidekicks go, he was the best. I knew I'd never find another quite like him. The three of us were in Rich's kitchen for our farewell, and, in a final thoughtful act, Tom said to me, "Chris, here's one to remember me by," before turning slightly in his chair and unleashing a loud belter of a fart that shook the glasses on the draining board.

A considerably awkward moment of silence followed, finally broken by Rich croaking, "Please don't do that when my wife is at home," and then it was time for a final hug goodbye to Tom, the hapless sidekick to end all hapless sidekicks.

Rich had offered to cycle with me for the day, to show me the way out through Fremantle and the neighbouring city of Perth. As we set off together he turned to me and nervously asked, "I can trust Tom alone in my house, can't I?"

"Yes, of course," I lied, and my ride across Australia was under way.

As promised, Rich showed me the way through the city, a ride we were able to do primarily on bicycle paths. It was an astonishing thing, after so long in Asia, to see such fantastic infrastructure. Both Fremantle and Perth looked modern, interesting, and a little quirky, and I lamented the fact that I couldn't stop and explore, give them the time they deserved. My reason for pressing on as fast as I could was at least a good one. Not only was Dea flying to Melbourne to meet me, but she was planning on building her own touring bike there and cycling with me for the final stretch to Sydney. It had the potential to be the perfect movie-script ending, and I certainly didn't want to miss it.

Having got me east of Perth, Rich turned around to go home and see if his house was still standing, and wished me the very best of luck. Presumably he did this because ahead of me was approximately three thousand kilometres of nothing.

I was amazed by how quickly the bustle of the city faded behind me and the remoteness began. For the first few days I travelled east through an area known as the 'wheat belt' but, while there was farm-land, there was nobody about doing any actual farming. The roads were straight and empty, the fields unoccupied, and the only noise came with the occasional squawk of a parrot overhead. Once a day I'd pass through a town, the streets of which were always deserted. I'd wander into the local public house to ask for water, where I'd find one or two men propping up the bar, who'd point me to the sinks but otherwise show no interest in me. This was almost my only con-tact with people. Then one day I found a man walking down the street of one of these lonely towns who wanted to talk with me. He was a nice old man named Don, who didn't seem to notice that I was in a rush as he talked about the town. He talked about how it had 600 occupants, including two doctors, as there was a hospital, and how they took turns to be on shift at the hospital, and how there were lots of aboriginal people, but how everyone got on fine, about how good the shop in town was, about how mining money was invested in small country towns like this one, about how the community resource centre cost one million dollars, about how the wheat farming was the livelihood, and about how the farmers spent like the Watsons when they had a good harvest. I would have pulled myself away sooner, but at one point he said, "People are in too much of a rush these days," and after that it was difficult for me to say that I was in a rush, and what was more I had to agree with him, and it was so nice to stand there listening to an old-time Australian talk about Australia, and I wished that I didn't have to rush.

After about a week of pretty monotonous cycling I reached Kalgoorlie. This heaving metropolis was another shock to the system, and with its 31,000 residents it was by far the biggest settlement I'd seen since Perth, or would again for the next thousand miles. A gold-rush town, Kalgoorlie was still thriving off the back of the modern-day mining industry, including the so-called 'super-pit' that in aerial photos of the town make it look like it's been hit by a giant meteorite.

I really only had one concern during my brief stop in town, and that was to visit the Woolworths, the cheap supermarket where I could buy groceries at a fraction of the price of the small stores, and at the square root of the price of the Nullarbor roadhouses. The Nullarbor was the long and unbelievably empty stretch of outback that I soon had to cross, and, knowing that the cost of food out there would be extortionate, I wondered whether it would be possible to load my bike up with two weeks' worth of food, then set about trying. I bought myself five loaves of bread, three jars of peanut butter, four jars of jam, ten tins of beans, fifteen bags of biscuits, and a carrot, then loaded up the bike. I realised that I could still carry more, so I went back in and bought a few more bags of biscuits, just to be sure.

I'd dreamt of cycling across the Nullarbor for many years, ever since I'd first read about it in Andy Brown and Tim Garratt's book, 'Discovery Road', one of my earliest cycle touring influences. Reading about it from my bedroom in England, it had sounded like the most distant and remarkable place. Leaving the last small town of Norseman I shuddered with excitement. Ahead of me lay an incredible 1,200 kilometres of long and featureless road before I'd reach another settlement. I'd cycled through some empty landscapes before, but nothing that came close to this. It was truly the outback. Nobody lived out here. It was wonderful.

On my first day on the Nullarbor I'd been making slow progress, and as the evening drew on I decided to just keep on cycling after dark to make my 120 kilometres. It was an amazing experience. There was no traffic at all, and it felt like I was the only person in the world. It was just me and my bike and the white line of the road in my torchlight. Above me a million stars shone, the Milky Way brighter than I'd ever seen it before, arching all the way across the sky like a luminous cloud. And as I looked up at this scene I saw a shooting star and I gasped, for it was not like any shooting star I'd ever witnessed before. It was a massive white ball of fire, absolutely huge, that burned and shot across the sky like a flare. It was so big that I half expected a mushroom cloud to appear across the plains where it landed. I made a wish, and I wished for world peace, and it really didn't seem too much to ask of such an extraordinary shooting star. Except now I've ruined it by telling you what I wished for.

Riding across the Nullarbor was an amazing experience, but it was also monumentally boring, of course. For days on end the landscape never changed – little shrubby trees dotted everywhere in the orange dirt, my band of tarmac slicing through them towards a horizon that I cycled forever at but never reached. There wasn't a lot of traffic, and what there was came in the form of road trains and grey nomads. The former were long trucks with two, three, or sometimes even four trailers, that it was generally a good idea to get the hell out of the way of. The latter were retired old Australians, driving around the country in motorhomes or towing caravans, who offered me a friendly wave as they passed. Most of the time, though, the road was empty, and I was left alone with my thoughts. I could hardly believe that I was really in Australia. I was crossing the Nullarbor, turning the pedals of my bike just the same as I'd done for the last two years, and just ahead of me lay the culmination of all that effort. Dea would be there in Melbourne. The promise of seeing her again pulled me onwards, motivated me on those long days in the outback. We'd ride together to Sydney, to the finish line of this first part of the journey. It was all so tantalisingly close.

If only the wind wasn't so determined to ruin the party. Almost every single Australian I'd met had told me that I should have westerly winds pushing my all the way across the country, yet ever since leaving Fremantle I'd had exactly the opposite. The headwinds drained me both physically and mentally. One day they reached gale force, pegging my progress back to walking speed. I had to keep going though. Staying on schedule was not possible, but I had to do something, I had to make some distance. In any case, my water was low, so I had to make it sixty kilometres to the next roadhouse, come what may.

It was a depressing slog, but after a while saw something that lifted my spirits. As I trudged along I looked up to see a kangaroo about a hundred metres ahead of me, hopping across the road. Two others soon followed, and they all paused for a moment before bounding off together across the desert. Despite being in Australia for two weeks, this was the first time I'd seen kangaroos, and it was an uplifting moment to finally see them. For a few minutes, at least, I had a grin from ear to ear.

What was sadder was the incredible number of dead kangaroos that littered the sides of the highway. There were so very many carcasses in various states of decomposition – victims of the barrelling road trains – all along the road. Some were fresh meat for the scavenging birds that circled overhead, but many were just skeletons, already picked clean.

The day was an exercise in mental torture. I was going at less than ten kilometres per hour and it all felt rather pointless. I knew that I had to keep going, but Melbourne felt like a million miles away, a hopeless and unrealistic goal. Then, when I was ten kilometres from the roadhouse with one hour of daylight and not a drop of water left, having cycled fifty kilometres in eight hours, the wind suddenly dropped. It was like someone had flicked a switch. I exploded like a sprinter out of the blocks. Suppressed for so long by the wind, I now burst forward like a coiled spring. In no time at all I was at the road-house. These roadhouses were little Nullarbor refuges, essentially nothing more than a gas station with some hotel rooms and a rainwa-ter tank, they appeared every hundred kilometres or so and kept me hydrated. Bottles refilled, I was off again into the barrenness. I was determined to turn my fortunes around, and I sprinted on towards the night. In the twilight I spotted three more kangaroos hopping alongside me. It was flat here, with few real trees. There were yet more kangaroos bouncing along over the shrubs. It felt amazing to be racing kangaroos through the outback, but I wasn't done yet.

I resolved to get to 140 kilometres, a realistic target now that the wind was gone and I was able to ride closer to twenty kilometres per hour. Then two kangaroos suddenly leapt across the road in front of me, illuminated by my torch. They couldn't have been more than twenty metres ahead of me. I started to worry about being hit by one of them as they flew about the place. It was so dark, there were so many of them, and the amount of roadkill indicated that they weren't exactly good at avoiding moving vehicles. I got around the problem by making noise. I sang and I shouted, talked to myself, invented characters, warned the kangaroos to stay away.

It was very dark but I remained determined to make it to 140 kilo-metres. I knew that if I could make it to that distance having had to trudge into such an awful wind all day, it could be a turning point, a confirmation that I was going to be able to make this deadline. And the distance disappeared behind me, until with just ten kilometres to go I entered a rare patch of woodland. As I did so two kangaroos hopped out from the trees and across the road just in front of me. A minute later, two more did the same. I slowed down, increased the volume of my shouting. More darted across. Another three, then two more. Suddenly they were everywhere, all going across the same way, left to right, like some giant migration. I was sure that they must be passing behind me too, and I was trapped amidst a herd of kangaroos in the night. I was terrified. I knew if they hit me it was sure going to hurt. I wanted to stop. I wanted out of this. But there was nowhere to go. Even if I ended my day here, short of my target, I'd have to put my tent up in a wood of flying kangaroos. Two more. It was one of the most surreal experiences of my life. I dodged a fresh roadkill. Then another, much more alive one, sprang out just in front of me. "Stay away kangaroos!" I cried out desperately, foolishly. This was crazy. This was too much. But I had no choice other than to keep going, even with more kangaroos leaping out of the darkness all the time.

Finally the trees ended and the kangaroos stopped. I had made it through the madness. I rode on for the final few kilometres, but there was still time for me to hear one last kangaroo. I stopped this time and shone my torch on it. It stood there among the bushes and stared back without moving. It was a beautiful creature, like a cross between a deer and a giant, bouncy bunny rabbit. We held one another's stare for minutes (or at least it felt like it, the kangaroo would have just been staring into the torchlight). Then it too had had enough, and it bounded away into the darkness. I set up my tent, shaking my head in disbelief, and called it a night. And what an extraordinary night it had been.

On the 22nd of June, my sixteenth morning in Australia, I finally woke up to a tailwind. But it was not just any old tailwind. It was a tailwind to write home about. A tailwind that should go down in cycle touring folklore. A tailwind that would carry me to a personal best ever distance and a date with destiny.

I had reached the south coast of the country, and early in the morning I came across two lookout points which offered magnificent views of the ocean crashing into high bluffs. I dared not stop and admire the view for longer than it took to stuff a packet of biscuits in my mouth though, lest the wind should die down while I was distracted. I finally had this wind, this wind that I'd waited so long for, and I was damned if I was going to waste it now. I rode and I rode, and almost didn't stop again, but just enjoyed being carried along. Setting the tone for this record breaking day I cycled one hundred kilometres in what was surely my fastest ever time of four hours and fifty-five minutes.

It was a good record, I thought, but it turned out to be one that only stood for four hours and forty-eight minutes. That second century brought the day to a close, and twilight returned to the Nullarbor. I saw more kangaroos, and noticed how aware they were of me. Sure, they were caught out by the high speed road trains, but I realised how silly it was to think that these nocturnal animals might bump into something as slow moving as me, and decided it would be fine to cycle at night again. I'd already ridden 200 kilometres, but even as the mighty wind began to dwindle I spied another record. My best ever distance for a day was the 227 kilometres I'd ridden back in Lithuania and Poland, and I was going to smash it.

It was a beautiful, clear night. A blanket of stars once again shone overhead and a crescent moon descended gradually behind me as the hours passed. There was almost no traffic. There never was at night. Just the occasional road train, one every ten or fifteen minutes, and I'd hear it from a mile off and get out of the road. It would roar past and off into the distance, then silence would return. It was just me and the empty night, and a goal of reaching 250 kilometres.

The last few kilometres rolled by, and I was so buoyed up I even thought about keeping right on going. But it was late, I was tired, and I would still need to get up in the morning and cycle all over again. So as my cycle computer clicked over to 250 I congratulated myself on a job well done (and said a little thanks to the wind gods too), and decided to call it a night.

I wheeled along slowly, peering into the darkness at the side of the road, trying to look for a place to camp. By now the moon had set and it was completely dark, and I struggled to see the outline of the trees and bushes to work out if there was space to get in and pitch my tent. I was barely moving at all, just creeping along, trying to see in the dark. Then I suddenly heard the noise of a large animal shuffling in the shadows. It was very close, and seemed panicked by my presence. I had visions of those kangaroos flying around again, and I instinctively shouted out, loudly and aggressively, to warn the animal off. Then, before I knew what was happening, I saw the creature leap out of the darkness and straight towards me. It was as if it were actually trying to hit me. There was nothing I could do to avoid it. I braced for impact.

To say that my life flashed before my eyes would be a lie. If anything flashed before my eyes it was a kangaroo with an extremely poor sense of direction. *'I can't believe this is actually going to happen,'* I thought, or at least I would have done if I'd had the time. The kangaroo's kamikaze leap brought it down directly to my left. Then there was that familiar feeling of being about to bump into somebody, and trying to avoid it, but knowing that you can't, except in this case it was with a kangaroo, which made it weird. Then we collided.

At the moment of impact I leant in towards the animal, then fell into it, and actually rolled right over the top of it on my way to the tarmac. By good fortune this action threw me to safety, clear of beast and bike, and somehow my bicycle fell on top of the kangaroo, trapping it beneath it. I was now prone on the cold road, the smell of animal hide in my nostrils, as my assailant struggled wildly, panic-stricken right next to me. I was in shock. Things had just gone from the surreal to the outright ridiculous. There I was, lying on the road in the dark, taken out by a kangaroo that was now trapped by my own bike. I said a rude word, then had the silly thought that I should perhaps do something to help it out. But before I could do anything the kangaroo kicked itself free, and without stopping to exchange insurance details it was away across the road and off into the night. I remained seated on the road. My bike lay horizontal next to me, wheels spinning, lights flashing. Classic hit-and-run.

48

The Nullarbor, Australia
22nd June 2015

After a few moments I gathered my composure and picked myself and my bike up off the road. Amazingly enough there was no apparent damage to either of us. I had been extremely fortunate. I wheeled my bike off the road and pitched my tent, hands trembling. I couldn't really process what the hell had just happened. By the morning I was even wondering if it had really happened, or if I'd just been so tired by the exertion of cycling 250 kilometres that I'd fallen asleep at the handlebars, briefly had a dream about a kangaroo, and then tumbled off. As if to help me clear up the confusion as I was packing up my tent I looked up at the scene of the crime, and I saw a kangaroo hopping across the road. Maybe it was just my imagination, but it appeared to have a bit of a limp. I chased after it, shouting something about the moral and legal issues regarding leaving the scene of an accident, but it was gone again as fast as the night before.

It didn't really matter. My bike and I seemed to have come through the incident unscathed, and I was able to resume my journey. I soon arrived at another roadhouse, where I was disappointed to be told that the tap water wasn't potable, and that massively overpriced bottle water was my only option. But as luck would have it I fell into conversation with a grey nomad couple, who kindly offered to let me fill up my bottles from the large supply of water they were carrying in their camper van.

They were a nice couple, and I was happy to make conversation with them for a while, although I felt so tired from the previous day I could hardly talk. I felt like I should apologise for my fatigued state, and, at the same time, maybe I wanted to boast of my achievements just a little.

"Sorry," I said. "I'm very tired. I cycled 250 kilometres yesterday."

"Oh, is that a long way?" the woman asked, looking unimpressed.

"Yes, I think so," I said, a little disappointed. "I usually cycle about 100 or 120 kilometres."

"Oh, that can't take long. What does it take? Four hours? Five hours?"

"Err, well..." She'd thrown me. "It usually takes me a bit longer than that."

"We went cycling once. Did fifty kilometres in a couple of hours. Didn't we dear? Fifty kilometres, wasn't it? Didn't take long."

I decided not to mention the kangaroo.

The Nullarbor wasn't ready to let me go easily. My extraordinary day had been nothing more than an anomaly, and I was soon battling into the face of the wind again. It only grew more intense the further that I went, but I knew the prize of reaching Ceduna, the first town in 1,200 kilometres, would make it all worthwhile. Ceduna was a proper town, with a supermarket, and I couldn't wait to get there. Yes, my excessive food stores had carried me the whole way from Norseman (with my bike gradually shrinking in size and getting lighter the further that I went), but I'd eaten all the good stuff first, and for the last day and a half I was surviving on handfuls of honey-puffed wheat. Just before Ceduna I came to a fruit fly checkpoint, where all fresh fruits were to be declared and confiscated. I rolled up to the stop line and a man came to ask me if I had any such items on me. I shook my head. "I haven't seen any fresh food for about a week, mate."

I rolled down the main street of Ceduna and found the supermarket, where I ran around like an excited child filling my basket with all sorts of goodies. I'd done it. I'd conquered the mighty Nullarbor, headwind, kangaroos, and all. I'd even come in a bit ahead of schedule, completing the 1,200 kilometres in nine days. It had been a truly memorable experience, particularly the night riding. Cycling all alone in the outback with absolutely nobody around for miles, under all of those stars, that was an experience that I would remember for a very long time. Especially, I think, the bit where I got clobbered by the kangaroo.

If I'd thought that Ceduna would bring about a return to civilization (and I did), then I was wrong. No sooner had I left the town again than I found myself on an even emptier road through land that, although it had a bit of wheat agriculture, was just about as unpopulated as the Nullarbor. For a whole day reaching the next town of Wirrula was the only thing that kept me motivated against the tedium of more boring cycling. For hours I looked forward to reaching it as the day dragged on. Then, as I drew close, I saw signs saying, 'Welcome to Wirrula – the town with a secret', and I got even more excited trying to guess what that secret might be. But then I finally arrived at Wirrula and I found out that the secret was that there was nobody there. It was a tiny hamlet consisting of a few houses, a pub, and a row of wheat grain silos. The only street lay empty. I wandered into the pub. Nobody there. Not a soul in sight. Just a row of empty bar stools. I wandered back out into the empty street. I guessed I'd just have to keep going to the next town of Wudinna. Maybe there'd be somebody there. It was only another 120 kilometres.

One problem of being back amongst the wheat farming was that, while there weren't many people about, there were mice. One night I was awoken by one of them trying to gain access to my tent. It kept scratching against the sides, and I knew that it wouldn't leave me alone once it had a whiff of my biscuits, despite all my best animal impressions. I tried pretending to be a cat, you see, but after a brief retreat the mouse soon returned. Next I tried barking at it like a dog, but this had no effect. My cow impression just seemed to encourage it, and there was nothing else for it but to get up before it could gnaw a hole, and just start cycling at two in the morning. At least there were no kangaroos around in wheat country.

It was looking like being another day to be filed in the 'unremarkable' category, as I made slow and steady progress towards Kimba, the next little town on my route. Kimba prides itself on being halfway across Australia, a neat selling point that some bright spark probably came up with to attract tourists, or at the very least attract tourists to stop briefly and have a coffee. They must have been gambling that no one would look too closely at a map, however, because by my reckoning Kimba was 2,235 kilometres from Perth, and 1,704 kilometres from Sydney. But what was a few hundred kilometres between friends in Australia?

But before I reached Kimba, the town that is fifty-six percent of the way across Australia, something very bad happened. I stopped to oil my chain, and I noticed a scratch on the inside of my left chainstay (if you're not familiar with the names of bike parts, chainstays are the thin sections of the frame that run between the bottom bracket and the rear hub (the bottom bracket being the middle of the bit where the pedals are, and the rear hub being the middle of the circular wheel thing)). It looked like a deep scratch into the paint, but I could think of no reason for there to be such a scratch on the inside, which was not exposed. I was worried it might be something more serious as I continued my ride. Could it be a crack? I seriously hoped not. In the middle of Australia, over a thousand kilometres from Melbourne, that would really be a disaster.

I was soon further delayed by a puncture on my rear tyre. Although it was a pain to have to take all the bags off, turn the bike upside down, and remove the circular wheel thing, all of this did at least give me the chance to examine the damage to the chainstay more closely. I flicked a little of the paint away and recoiled in horror at what I saw. It *was* a crack.

Oh, this was bad. This was very, very bad. My frame was cracked. It was my worst nightmare. The crack ran almost all the way down the inside of the chainstay from top to bottom, and on the outward-facing surface there was a corresponding dent. *What could have done that?'* I wondered, then I realised. *'That damned kangaroo!'* It must have kicked the chainstay when it was battling to free itself.

"Why didn't you tell me about this?" I asked my talking bicycle.

"I thought you weren't talking to me any more?"

"I've been riding all alone in the middle of nowhere for the last three weeks, of course I'm talking to you! Oh, what are we going to do?"

This was a disaster. I'd replaced almost everything on this bike, all of the main moving parts tended to last on average about 20,000 kilometres, yet I'd had the same frame since the very beginning. I couldn't replace the frame, I just couldn't. This was terrible.

I continued on to Kimba, riding as delicately as I could. A great deal of care was taken to avoid potholes and bumps and deceased kangaroos. My removing some of the paint seemed to have encouraged the crack, and it was spreading with such malicious speed that I was reduced to walking and pushing the bike as if it were made of glass by the time I reached Kimba.

It was, of course, a quiet little town of empty streets, but one very good thing about Kimba was that the library had free wifi, and it could be used outside in the street even when the library was not open. I sat there and checked the internet, and learnt with great relief that a cracked chainstay need not mean the end for the whole frame. It seemed it would be fine to repair or replace the problem chainstay, and there was even a specialist frame repair place in Melbourne that could do the work. The only question, of course, was how was I going to cycle the 1,382 kilometres that separated me from Melbourne?

I sat there wondering what to do. I dared not ride my bike in its condition, but I could hardly stay in Kimba forever. Dea was flying into Melbourne in just eleven days. I cursed my luck. It seemed so unfair that this should happen so close to the end. And yet I'd overcome so many obstacles, problems, and difficult situations on this journey, that I knew if I just kept my head and looked for a solution, I could find a way through this one too.

I knew that what I needed to do was to get the crack welded up, but the trouble was finding somebody to do it in this tiny little country town. It was nine-thirty on a Sunday morning, and I had little hope of finding anywhere open, but by some small miracle a woman came walking down the street. I didn't want to miss my chance, and I quickly explained my predicament to her. She was very friendly of course, and wanted to help. After thinking about it for a while, she pointed me down the road to a large farm shed where she thought there might be a man I could ask. Then, as I was just heading off to make enquiries, she added, almost as an afterthought, "Oh, and there's also a man around the corner. That street there. Third door along. He fixes stuff. Oh, but he's a bit... well, he's a bit..."

I already knew that the mysterious man who was a bit [unstated] was the man who was going to fix my bike. I knew it very well, but I still tried the farm shed first. I walked across the big scrap metal strewn yard that the woman had pointed me to and into the giant shed. I called out and a man of about sixty popped his head up. He eyed me suspiciously at first, but warmed to me once my predicament was explained. "No, no, no. Sorry. I don't weld. Sorry about that. Can't help you. Oh, but you could try asking the man who lives over there. That street. Third door down. He's a welder. Oh, but he's a bit... well, a little bit..."

I headed to that street. I went to the third door down. My destination wasn't hard to spot. Amongst the freshly painted porches, double-glazed windows, and manicured lawns of the surrounding homes, this one stuck out like a sore thumb. It was just a clapboard shack, with peeling paint and rusting gutters. Weeds overtook everything. The few windows that weren't boarded up were covered in grime. A large aerial rose from the roof. An old caravan sat in the yard, wheels long ago eroded into the paving. I couldn't even get to the front door through all of the undergrowth. Yes, this was definitely the place.

I knocked on the door at the side of the house, and when this brought no response, tried tapping on the windows. Still nothing. I thought it might still be too early in the morning, so I took a walk around town and returned again, to the same result. Just as I was about to give up, a rusty pick-up came along the road, then turned up the driveway and disappeared around the back of the property.

I followed on foot and saw it park up. An old (and I really do mean old) man peered (and I really do mean peered) out of the driver side window as I approached, with a look on his face that was part "Who the hell are you?" and part "I can't see anything." I said hello and stated my business, telling him that I desperately needed my bike welding, and that I'd heard he might be a welder. He said nothing, and just continued to peer out from a wrinkled face that sat beneath a few determined strands of sparse white hair. For a moment I thought he might have forgotten who I was, but then he suddenly burst into life, swinging open the car door and standing bolt upright, with a loud creak that might have been either the door or something else, I couldn't be sure. "Well, let's take a look at it then," he said.

He was eighty if he was a day, and probably much closer to ninety. He told me that his name was Graham as we shook in greeting. His timeworn hands were trembling, and I wondered if these were really the hands that I was going to entrust my poorly bike to. Yet there seemed no harm at all in letting him take a look and give his opinion. I stripped the bags off the bike and removed the rear wheel, as Graham opened up a sizeable shed in his back garden. I carried the bike frame in, and found a calamitous mess of equipment, tools, and workbenches. In amongst them I was pleased to see at least two welding machines. I flipped the bike over and placed it under a torch which Graham had just about managed to get working. I pointed out the crack and the elderly man peered at it in a way which suggested, worryingly, that he had no idea what was going on.

Graham then suddenly burst into life again. He did so by pulling out an angle grinder and firing it up, moving the rapidly whirring blade towards my bike. I believe I may well have gasped, and was quite likely close to fainting. Thankfully the old fellow turned the blade just in time, parallel to the chainstay, and was only using it to remove the paint from the affected area. Of course. He just wanted to remove the paint, so that he could have a proper look at the damage. I breathed a sigh of relief. That breath was probably quite useful because it was almost certainly the only thing that kept me conscious when in the next instant, and once again with no warning whatsoever, the geriatric man suddenly turned the angle grinder again, and cut a great big chunk out of my chainstay.

He pulled back, then stuck the blade in for another go, sparks flying everywhere. I was now in a state of extreme anguish. My beloved bicycle, my most prized and treasured companion for the last five years, was being mutilated before my eyes. My jaw was on the floor. I couldn't believe what was happening. It was terrifying. Graham then pulled his instrument of torture away from the maimed end of the chainstay, and, shockingly, began moving it towards the other end as if he intended to chop a great chunk out of that too.

Before it was too late I leapt into action and swept my poor bicycle up into my arms, carrying it away from the evil man and back out into the daylight. "Thank you!" I cried. "Thank you, that's enough. I'll be going now." I nursed the poor thing in my arms and surveyed the damage. Suddenly, a cracked frame didn't seem so bad, compared with what I had now, which was a frame with two very large gashes carved into it.

"What are you doing?" It was Graham, emerging behind me.

"What am I doing? What are *you* doing?! You've cut a huge hole in my frame!"

"Well I needed something to weld. I couldn't weld that little crack. It was too thin."

"Look what you've done. My poor bike! You said you were just going to take a look at it!"

"Well you can't ride it like that, it'll collapse on you."

"I know!"

"Bring it back inside. Come on. You wanted me to weld it, and I'm welding it. You think I don't know what I'm doing? I've only been welding for fifty years."

At that moment I didn't very much feel like entrusting my bike back to this man, and yet, unfortunately, I didn't have many options. He was right, I couldn't ride it in its present condition, and there wasn't anybody else around who could repair this mess. Against my better judgement (and my bikes own tremendous protests) I reluctantly carried it back into the operating theatre.

Graham explained that he just needed to remove some paint from the other end of the chainstay in order to attach a clip for earthing the welding machine, and he did this with his angle grinder as I winced. That done, the angle grinder was finally put away, and the octogenarian fired up his welding machine. It fizzed and sparked wildly as Graham jabbed metal in roughly the right place. His hands shook and he clearly couldn't see what he was doing through his grimy welding mask, but somehow a weld began to take shape.

All of this went on for some time. He had, after all, made some considerable indentations with his angle grinder. Eventually he was satisfied and stopped. I looked at his work, and saw that there was still a great big hole in the middle of the weld. Graham scrutinized it himself for some time, then declared, "Little pinhole there," before firing up the machine again for another go. After several more minutes, it was finally done. It was the ugliest weld I had ever seen, but it was a weld. I breathed a sigh of relief. It was over. I could relax. But then my venerable companion suddenly fired up his angle grinder again. He wanted to try and tidy things up a bit. "Stop!" I cried out. "I don't care what it looks like!" But the old fellow could barely hear me even without the noise of his angle grinder, so there was no chance now. He swung the spinning blade wildly around in between the frame, narrowly missing brake cables and gear cables and racks and braze-ons, needlessly risking everything at the last moment. I was practically on my knees weeping, praying to some unknown gods to make this stop. And then, finally, it did.

Graham offered me a coke, and we stood outside and chatted for a bit, mostly about people that he knew that had died. I admired his handiwork. He'd even gone so far as to spray paint it black again, and declared it to be as good as new. I wasn't sure about that, but it was at least in a better state than it had been half an hour earlier.

I thanked Graham and left, Melbourne-bound. For all the trauma he had put me through, I was still extremely grateful to the man. He had got me back on the road. He had kept me in business. Earlier that morning it had felt like my hopes of meeting Dea on time for cycling the last stretch to Sydney had been in great jeopardy. But it had been just one more problem that needed to be solved, one more act of kindness from a stranger, one more obstacle that had been overcome.

I knew it now for sure. There was nothing going to stop me. I was going to make it.

49

Melbourne, Australia
9ᵗʰ July 2014

I pulled my red Drug Enforcement Administration vest on over my head. I'd seen it in a shop in Sumatra and knew that I had to buy it, just for this moment. An airport official eyed me questionably as I did so, although his raised suspicions might have had more to do with the cuddly toy kangaroo that I was gripping nervously under my arm. I was in the still-very-much-under-construction Terminal Four of Melbourne Airport, which essentially consisted of a giant tin shed with a luggage carousel in it. I paced anxiously. I'd waited so long for this moment.

After what felt like an eternity, a door was opened and some passengers began to file in. The first was a young man with dreadlocks who, having thought he'd cleared customs already, looked rather worried by my vest. I waved him on. I wasn't interested in him. I was trying to look over the top of everyone, looking for that one face I'd missed so much. The airport worker was at my side. "Is that your bike over there, sir? You need to stay with your luggage, sir." But his voice was immaterial.

"Yes, yes, I understand," I said dismissively. He was little more than a blur in my peripheral vision because directly ahead, walking excitedly towards me, was a tall, blonde, and incredibly beautiful Danish girl. The most beautiful girl in the world, as a matter of fact.

We embraced and hugged and held one another. It felt so good to feel that embrace again. It had been too long. "I missed you so much." We hugged more, and kissed, and trembled, and hugged, and didn't know what to say to each other we were both so happy. When we let go of each other for long enough I presented my gifts – the cuddly toy kangaroo and the vest, the acronym of which had found a much more appropriate home now.

"Welcome to Australia, Dea."

"Thank you."

"You're very tall."

"Yes I am."

"Are you ready to cycle to Sydney with me?"

"Yes!!!"

But Dea wasn't quite ready to cycle to Sydney with me. She didn't have a bike, for one thing. To solve that, we made our way to Commuter Cycles, the bike shop that had agreed to help put together a new bike for her. At the shop we met with the owner, Huw, an immensely likeable guy with a permanent smile on his face. Dea was so taken with the idea of cycle touring that she wanted to build the bike herself, but she'd organised to get the frame and many of the parts through the shop. She'd already picked out a Saga Soma frame in racing green, and Huw brought it out for us to see. He then helped Dea pick out all of the parts she needed – wheels, bottom bracket, crankset, and so on. This was going to be a really great touring bike, because Dea wasn't just hoping to ride it in Australia with me, but if everything went according to plan, all the way through the Americas and back to Europe with me too.

But Dea's really great touring bike wasn't going to be built just yet. Once Huw had set aside all of the parts for us, we moved on to the next stage of a logistically complicated week in Melbourne, which involved cycling fifty kilometres south. This was because a few weeks earlier I'd suggested we find a warmshowers host to send some bike parts that we'd ordered online to, and then I'd left Dea in charge of finding that host while I was off crossing the Nullarbor. Dea had never used the warmshowers website before, and failed to look at the map, and so she'd accidentally had everything sent fifty kilometres away from where it was needed. Luckily Huw stepped in and offered to lend Dea a bike until hers was built, so we could cycle there together.

This at least gave us a chance to see some of Melbourne on the way through. With its trams, coffee shop culture and Aldi stores, Melbourne was probably the most European city in Australia, and I liked it. There was a good blend of tower blocks, modern art, graffiti, bicycle lanes, and streets bustling with life. We made it through the centre and out onto a bike path that followed the shoreline of the vast Port Phillip Bay for a good twenty kilometres or so. It was lovely. The skyscrapers of the city disappeared behind us and just for a while it was magical to be out cycling with my girl again.

Unfortunately, the day rather got away from us, and it began to get dark at just about the same time that we ran out of bike path. The road going down the coast was extremely busy and we had no choice but to continue by cycling on the footpath. We rode on under the street lights, but I could tell that Dea was tired and no longer enjoying herself.

We finally reached what I thought was the right address. It was the right number, anyway, and it was on the right street, but unfortunately it was an estate agents. I went in anyway, just in case Dea's inability to find us a warmshowers host could have extended to accidentally arranging an appointment with a realtor. The woman behind the desk looked at the address that I had, and said that it was right, but I was in the wrong town. I wanted the same address, but in Seaford, which was another ten kilometres down the road. I went outside to break the news to my weary companion. It didn't go down too well.

But just at that moment, a man walked up to us and announced proudly, "I'm Mick." I looked at him like he was a bit strange, which was fair enough, because he did seem a bit strange. Then he clarified exactly who he was. "You're staying with me ain't ya?" He was our host. "I've got my truck here. Chuck your stuff in if you want."

"Oh, no thank you," I said, and looked around for Dea, but she was already busy throwing her stuff in the back of Mick's pick-up.

I cycled the rest of the way alone and couldn't help but laugh about it. What a start! Our first day cycling together, and as soon as some guy came along with a truck she was off. I made it the last ten kilometres myself and pulled into Mick's driveway. Inside the house I discovered that my first impression of Mick had been correct; the guy was completely insane. He had at least escorted Dea here safely, but he was now running around like a headless chicken, ranting about this and that. He was a middle-aged man with scraggly dark hair, who I'm sure will be perfectly played by Micky Flanagan in my movie. He kept calling us 'kids' and announced that he was going out for the evening. I asked him where and he told me that it was none of my business. "But I'm sure you kids want to have some time alone, don't ya? You don't want a boring old fart like me hanging around."

But before gifting us his house, he sat down and suddenly became very serious as he addressed me. "You're Solo-Man. I know a Solo-Man when I see one. I'm a Solo-Man myself, okay? I know what I'm talking about. You're Solo-Man. But you've got a lady to think about now. You've got to be Not-Solo-Man now, okay? Good boy." And then he went out. I have no idea where.

We stayed in Mick's home for two days. After my long ride across the country I was tired, and grateful for the chance to relax. Mick was busy most of the time, but would occasionally come home and rush around in a whirlwind of loud chatter and manic cleaning. Noticing how tired I was, and after hearing that we were planning to cycle quite fast to Sydney, he berated me. "Look, you've got to slow down, you idiot. Stop and smell the roses, would ya?"

Mick was an odd and sometimes difficult host, but for all his eccentricities his advice stuck with me, and I knew that he was right. The journey wasn't just about me any more, it was about the both of us. I wasn't Solo-Man now. I had to think about Dea, and it was true that the two of us were probably going to have to slow down and smell the roses if this was going to work.

Back in Melbourne, Dea put her new bike together. I stood by to help, but she was determined to do as much as she could herself. "I'm planning to ride this bike for a really long way," she said, "so I want to know every piece of it and how it all works." So I left her to it, and carried my own frame into the specialist repair shop. They looked at Graham's weld with horror, but declared that they could fix things up for me, and they did a good job of it too. The weld was redone, with an extra gusset also welded on to strengthen the whole area.

With two fully functional bikes Dea and I were ready. It was drizzling with rain on the morning of our departure, but it was clear that nothing was going to put Dea off, and she was bursting with excitement as she loaded up her bike for the first time. I was in a similarly good mood. I couldn't believe that she was really here, that she'd come all this way to build a bike and cycle with me. It was almost too much to believe.

The miserable weather didn't last long as we traversed Melbourne on a series of cycle paths and small roads, before leaving the city on a rail trail. As the name suggests, this was an old railway line converted into a trail, and so it was generally flat and had a view of the surrounding countryside with a backdrop of mountains. With no traffic to worry about we were able to ride alongside each other and play games. We soon started one that was inspired by a game that Suzy and Dino had played during their long trip, which involved being the first to spot horses. I knew that Dea loved horses, but what I wasn't aware of was that she was an expert at horse-spotting. I was 20-0 down before I knew what was happening. I suggested it might be a more competitive game if I were allowed to get ten points for each horse that I spotted to Dea's one. This was a good rule, I thought, and within a few days I was winning. Then Dea brought in a further regulation, whereby five points would be subtracted for falsely crying "Horse." I thought this a terribly unfair rule, and my lead soon evaporated to a soundtrack of, "No Chris, that's a cow," and, "No, sorry, that one's a donkey."

It was a nice morning, sunny and not too cold. We were riding on a quiet road, and the only real threat to our peace came from the unlikely source of a few vicious magpies. We had been warned that in the spring nesting season these birds had a habit of swooping down upon cyclists. It wasn't spring yet, but perhaps these magpies were confused by the mild weather because swoop down upon us they most certainly did. *Whoosh!* "What was that?" *Whoosh!* "It's a magpie. Look out!" *Whoosh!* They were mostly aiming for Dea and her bright-yellow helmet. They even made contact with it a couple of times, not that it seemed to bother her. It was a surprisingly exhilarating rush to be attacked by birds, and she had a big smile on her face. "I think I want to go back for another go!" she said, once we were clear of the danger.

Before long we arrived in Paynesville, which was fortunately the literal name of a town, not a figurative expression resulting from a magpie attack. It was a lovely little waterside town with a variety of interesting aquatic birds, including pelicans and black swans, but it was a different kind of wildlife we were looking for. A short ferry ride took us across to a place called Raymond Island. We had heard that this was a good location to see koalas in the wild and, with neither of us having seen them yet in Australia, we were looking forward to our visit.

Once on the island, we locked our bikes up and walked through a patch of gum trees. It didn't take long for Dea to spot our first koala. It was just a little ball of grey fur, curled up and balancing precariously on a tree branch. It looked down at us through sleepy eyes as we jumped up and down with excitement. A real life koala. It was an amazing moment.

But it was far from the only one. We walked on further and spotted another, then another. It was incredible. They were such wonderful animals and it was a pleasure to see them in their natural habitat. They were so casual, so relaxed, just chilling in their trees. Each time that we saw one we both got so excited and happy, and stopped to stare at it with big smiles on our faces for a minute until it was time to look for the next one.

We spotted an adorably cute little guy in a tree that was grabbing eucalyptus leaves and munching on them lazily. As we watched, our necks craned upwards, a man came down the street sitting on a motorised scooter. He was looking very happy too, and manoeuvred his chair over to us. He had a grey beard and was fat and jolly, with a colourful striped hat on his head. We said hello, and after Dea told him she was from Denmark he spoke in a very slow and clear manner, quite unnecessarily. "People think koala stupid. Koala not stupid. Koala smart. I speak koala. Look. I... speak... koala. Look." He then opened up his mouth and made a very loud grunting noise. It seemed like a good effort, although our koala simply turned his head and looked down at the man with a 'not you again' expression, before returning to his supper.

The man, whose name was Coop, then invited us to come and see his house. In his back garden he showed us a variety of different plants that he grew. He had all kinds of things growing there and it was wonderful to see how enthusiastic he was about nature. He also wanted to show us the birds, so he grabbed a handful of seeds from a huge barrel of them and scattered them on the ground. He insisted that there would soon be fifty birds, as he fed them every day. Although only about ten showed up, they were still beautiful. "Look. Crimson. The red one is called crimson. The coloured one is eastern. LOOK! LOOK! That one! Cross. Half-half. Crimson-eastern cross. Very rare. Half-half. Very rare. Very lucky."

Next Coop went and got his guitar and played some songs. He was a bit of a hippy really. He told us that he used to work full-time in an office, but that he was so much happier now, living out here on this island with all the nature. Dea and I understood entirely.

We returned to our bikes and cycled across the island to camp on a beach right next to the water. It was a perfect place to end a perfect day.

"I'm so happy you're here, Dea. Thank you so much for coming."

"I had to. After Laos, this way of life intrigued me too much not to do this. I want to travel, to be here in the nature with you."

I looked out over the calm water of the bay, the sky turning orange, and realised that there was no place I would rather be.

The koalas were not to be the last of the Australian wildlife that would fascinate us. A few days later, at a place called Bombala, we watched platypuses swimming free in the river. They were extraordinary creatures, with their furry bodies and duck-like bills. It's well known that when samples were first sent back to the UK they were dismissed as an elaborate hoax, just too fantastical to be believed. Yet, they were real, for I saw them paddle about in the river just in front of me. As we watched them in fascination from the river bank, Dea stumbled upon a large burrow. She sat outside of this hole for a few minutes, more in hope than expectation, yet her patience was rewarded when a wombat appeared at the burrow's entrance. I joined Dea and we sat there and watched the wombat as it stared back at us, holding our gazes for many minutes. It was another truly incredible moment.

The outback was nothing but a distant memory now, as we climbed up through the forested mountains of Australia's eastern fringes. We continued to ride on rail trails and small gravel roads whenever we could. The main highway would have been quicker, but this was no race. Like Mick had said, it was time to slow down and smell the roses. I'd rushed too much during the past two years, but I was on the home stretch now, and it could hardly have been any better. Everything had come together, it had all just fallen into place. In the movie all of this will probably just be a musical montage, with Ryan Gosling and Charlize Theron smiling like idiots as they freewheel past kangaroos and koalas, platypuses and wombats, on the way to their Hollywood happy ending.

50

We were alone in the forest. It was the middle of another wonderful day of cycling on the quiet gravel roads, and we'd stopped at a rest area to eat our peanut butter and jam sandwiches. Just as I was preparing to leave, Dea looked at me with a cheeky grin on her face. "Chris, have you seen what's on the ground?" I looked around and noticed that the whole area was littered with pine cones. "Do you want to?" she asked, a mischievous glint in her eyes. It was at this moment that I realised that this was almost certainly the girl that I was going to marry.

I couldn't believe it. The ambition I'd held of playing Pine Cone Wars was finally about to be realised, after two long years of waiting. This girl was literally making all of my dreams come true. We excitedly ran around and gathered up ten pine cones each, then concealed them on our bikes and in our pockets. The rules were simple. Ten throws each while cycling, no stopping allowed, five points for a helmet hit, three for a front pannier, two for a back pannier, and one for a body hit. We lined ourselves up and began cycling. Pine Cone Wars was a go!

It began with a great rush of excitement as I went on ahead up a slight hill, cautious of an attack from behind. I burst ahead, then swung around, doubling back towards Dea. It was a poorly thought out strategy, however, as I had no pine cones ready to throw, and all it did was offer my armed opponent an opportunity. A pine cone came flying towards my head. I ducked just in time and it whizzed over my helmet. I swung myself around again, now behind the enemy but still unable to arm myself with a pine cone. Dea, unsure of my intentions, braked suddenly, and before I could react it was too late. I crashed into the back of her, my front wheel colliding with her back left pannier and breaking one of the clips. Thirty seconds into Pine Cone Wars and we'd had our first accident. *'Maybe this is why nobody wanted to play with me before,'* I thought.

Despite that troubled beginning, we decided to continue. It was the ideal location, the road being a decent gravel surface and fairly flat, with a complete lack of vehicular traffic. I next chose to adopt a different approach, and tried coming at Dea from the side, but I missed with my first couple of throws, and she responded with a direct hit on my helmet. A devastating blow, to be sure, but I persevered. More wayward throws followed, until another moment of high drama. Dea, struggling to maintain her balance while simultaneously throwing pine cones, avoiding pine cones, and riding a bicycle, slipped, and her bike skidded out beneath her.

She was alright, but it was her bike that seemed to be getting the worst of Pine Cone Wars. That, and my helmet, which took another direct hit soon after. Desperate not to lose at my own game I came back with a pannier hit and a couple of body blows, but it was too little, too late. My only excuse was Dea's very small head, which meant that I was somewhat disadvantaged, but even I had to concede that she probably deserved her final victory of thirteen points to five. It had been an amazing experience to play Pine Cone Wars, but with two accidents, a broken pannier, and one wounded ego, it seemed to be a game that would be unlikely ever to be repeated.

The road through the forested national park brought us down eventually to a pedestrian ferry. We squeezed our bikes on board and crossed a short stretch of water filled with sailing boats. When we emerged on the other side we were suddenly on the busy streets of a neighbourhood in southern Sydney. Cars jammed the roadways and people hurried along the sidewalks with disposable cups of coffee in their hands. It came as a bit of a shock to the system after the peace and quiet of the national park, but there were at least good cycle paths for us to follow into the city. They carried us past beaches where bronzed bodies relaxed in the sunshine. Teenagers rode skateboards alongside us, and floppy-haired surfers jogged out towards the sea with their boards under their arms. This was undoubtedly Australia's east coast. This was Sydney.

It took us a few hours to ride through the sprawling city, with the anticipation of reaching my goal building with every passing moment. As I rode alongside Dea my mind drifted again. I tried to recall what it had felt like to cycle away from the Eiffel Tower. I wondered how I had ever had the nerve to begin this journey with such a ridiculous, faraway goal in mind. How had I dared to attempt such a thing? Then it dawned on me. I was never cycling from Paris to Sydney. Such a ride was impossible. All I had ever been doing was riding one day at a time. I had just been turning the pedals on my bike, moving myself forward, inch by inch. With every day that passed, every town and village reached, every meeting and experience, I had been moving forward. I had never been cycling to Sydney. I had just been cycling.

Dea and I left our bikes and walked on foot the last short distance to Sydney's famous harbour. As we neared it I insisted we block the view with our hands. We shuffled along through a park, me with my hand blocking out the whole left side of my face, resisting the overwhelming temptation to peek in that direction.

"Okay Dea, I think we've gone far enough," I said. "Now let's close our eyes."

Dea giggled as we moved to the side of the path and felt our way along the harbour wall.

"Are you ready? On the count of three, let's open our eyes. One... two... three!"

And there it was in front of us. The iconic sight of the gleaming white Sydney Opera House, the Harbour Bridge standing defiantly behind it. I gasped. I had made it.

After two years and 46,000 kilometres of cycling, I had made it from the Eiffel Tower to the Sydney Opera House, using nothing except my bicycle, boats, and a pick-up truck driven by a relatively attractive yet ever so moody Mongolian woman. Not *exactly* what I'd set out to do, I'll admit, but pretty damn close.

The best thing of all, of course, was that I was not alone. To reach the Opera House and stand before it was a special moment, but to do so with Dea's hand in mine was really a dream come true. It was hard to believe that I could have got so lucky. I felt lucky anyway, to have been able to even start this journey. I was lucky to have been born in a developed nation. I was lucky to have been well-educated. I was lucky that the pieces of my life came together to make it possible for me to even imagine making a trip like this.

But then to have found such an incredible human being along the way – a smart, brilliant, beautiful girl, who laughed at my jokes and wanted to play games with me. To have found a girl like that, in outer Mongolia of all places, was almost too much to believe. It was nothing short of a miracle. And she wanted to ride a bike with me. She wanted to join my journey and see the rest of the world with me. We were going to have to stop for a while in Australia, so that she could write her thesis, and we could both work pedicabbing to make money, but after that we planned to cycle together. We were going to go to North America, South America, Africa together. This was an end but it was also a beginning. And I was undoubtedly the luckiest man in the world.

We walked around the harbour and as I stood right next to the Opera House, it occurred to me that it really didn't matter if this story ever made it into a movie. Not that it didn't deserve to, of course, what with the happy-love-story-set-up-nicely-for-a-sequel ending. But I didn't care if it did or not, because my journey was not about that. In our world of twenty-four hour internet, of Facebook and Instagram and Netflix, it is easy to forget that the real joy of life is found, not on our screens, but in the real world. I knew that now for sure, because I had seen it. It was there in the smiling faces of Lao children, in the waves of hard-working Uzbek women, in the desire of Indonesian schoolchildren to improve their English, and in the invites to share the living spaces of Lithuanian families and Mongolian herdsman. It was there in every Turkish glass of tea, every Kyrgyz cup of kumis, and every Georgian shot of chacha. It was there in the sunrises and the sunsets, in waking up in the mountains and cycling under the stars. It was there in every chance meeting on the road, in every small act of kindness. It was there in Iranian dentists and Australian welders. It was there in the camels and the kangaroos. Yes, it was even there in the bad things too. In every Chinese horn beep and every crazy Russian driver, in every rainstorm, every headwind. Because in all of this was the real world, for all its faults and all its beauty. These things made life worth living. They made my bicycle ride into an adventure, showed the world to me, and told me that I was alive. And the real world, I had to conclude, was really rather a fantastic place to live.

Yes, I'd made it from the Eiffel Tower to the Sydney Opera House. I had made it, at long, long last, to my destination, but it was the journey that mattered in the end.

Progress Report
Sydney, August 2015

1. Circumnavigate the planet

The Eiffel Tower: 2.3° E. Sydney Opera House: 151.2° E.
148.9° out of 360° around the planet.
(41.3% of the way around.) Still a long way to go!

2. Do so using only my bicycle and boats

Mori: 90.3° E. Sydney Opera House: 151.2° E.
60.9° out of 360° around the planet.
(16.9% of the way around.) Still a long way to go!

3. Pass through antipodal points

Still a long way to go!

4. Visit all of the inhabited continents

Three out of six, still three to go!

5. Cycle at least 100,000 kilometres

46,137 kilometres completed. 53,863 to go!

6. Cycle in 100 countries

Cycled in forty-five. Fifty-five to go!

7. Return with more money than I start with

Time to get to work! Still a long way to go!

The adventure continues:

www.differentpartsofeverywhere.com

ACKNOWLEDGEMENTS

My biggest thanks for helping in the creation of this book must go to the people of the world. I know that's quite a big group to start off by thanking. It's pretty much all-encompassing isn't it? I should just stop there. But no, I'm talking more specifically about all the people who invited me into their homes and shared what they had with me, the people who offered me some food or a drink, the people who offered advice or directions, and the people who kept me going simply with a smile and a wave. There are, of course, far too many of you to name here individually, but I'm so grateful to all of you. The kindness that I experienced from complete strangers was staggering. It is not just that I could not have done it without you, but that it would not really have been worth doing. You made the journey. Thank you.

In terms of the book, big thanks to Paul Curtis and Jeremy Watts for your expert advice with editing. Special thanks go to George Mahood for your encouragement and advice regarding the self-publishing process. Thank you to Julia Wright, Syd Winer, and Craig Skiles for checking through the final book. Also my gratitude goes out to Stephen Blight, Stephen Fabes, Darrell Simonsen, Olly Curtis, Dave Carmichael, Rose and Gary Zinkann, Matt Cundrick, Rich McCulloch, Damian Watson, Hannah Emmett, Gavin England, Milton Miller, Ian MacPherson, and little Matt Downing for reading through some of the early chapters and offering feedback. To all those who offered to read but then never bothered to get back to me with feedback, sorry, you don't get your name in my book. That includes you, Lindsay.

Extra special thanks must go to Lois Holden for the most thorough and encouraging feedback of all.

Thank you to everyone who read my blog during the trip, especially those who offered encouraging words on my guestbook when I needed them most. There are again far too many of you to mention, but I want you to know it really meant a lot and kept me going through the hard times. A special thanks go to Peter Jacobsen, without whom I likely never would have made it out of China.

I'd also like to thank my parents for giving me the very best start in life. Thank you for teaching me how to ride a bike, and for leaving that atlas lying around. Who would have thought it would lead to this, eh? To my sister and her family, my nieces and nephew, Summer, Skye, and Finley. You gave me a reason to return home. Thank you.

Most of all, of course, I have to thank a very special person named Dea Jacobsen. I have to thank her for looking after me so well these last few months as I wrote this book. I have to thank her for encouraging me to keep going with it, even when it felt like I could never make it to the end. I have to thank her for being such a wonderful and loving human being.

But most of all, Dea, I have to thank you for proving to me that dreams really can come true.

Let's dream some more...

25776846R00285

Printed in Great Britain
by Amazon